ABOUT THE AUTHORS

T. Susan Chang and M. M. Meleen are the co-hosts of the *Fortune's Wheelhouse* pod-cast, which explores the symbolism and lore of esoteric tarot. Its initial seventy-eight episodes serve as a primer to learning the visual language of the Rider-Waite-Smith and Thoth decks. Its continuing episodes examine the cards using frameworks borrowed from a variety of occult systems as filters. More information can be found at www.patreon.com/fortuneswheelhouse and www.redbubble.com/people/wheelhouse93/shop/.

T. SUSAN CHANG

T. Susan Chang is the author of *Tarot Correspondences: Ancient Secrets for Every-day Readers* and the co-host and producer of the *Fortune's Wheelhouse* esoteric tarot podcast. She is the creator of the Arcana Case® for tarot decks, which can be found at www.etsy.com/shop/tarotista, along with her line of esoteric perfumes. She reads tarot online, as well as for the Inspirit Crystals shop in Northampton, Massachusetts, and offers an ongoing online tarot course known as "The Living Tarot," which is available at her website, www.tsusanchang.com.

Her interest in tarot is wide-ranging and passionate, and has included: setting up seventy-eight Spotify card playlists; memorizing astrological correspondences for the minor arcana while swimming laps; writing tarot spells; and maintaining a sprawling Card-of-the-Day tracking database (complete with elemental, astrological, and kab-balistical frequency and percentage pie charts). She attempts to learn Hebrew approximately once every fifteen months, occasionally crawls down the stairs headfirst by way of apotropaic magic upon drawing the Tower, and has been known to spontaneously arrange her pancakes into a Tree of Life formation.

When not engaged in tarot-adjacent activity, she teaches writing at Smith College and occasionally reviews cookbooks. She lives in western New England with her family, her feline familiar, and a variable number of chickens.

M. M. MELEEN

M. M. Meleen is a mystic, a magician, and a maker. She is the illustrator, developer, designer, and author of diverse occult-themed creations. She is a co-host and co-creator, along with fellow mage T. Susan Chang, of the *Fortune's Wheelhouse* podcast; together they explore the many wormholes that open up when one delves into esoteric tarot.

Mel is the creator of the *Tabula Mundi Tarot*, the *Rosetta Tarot*, the *Pharos Tarot*, and other works in progress, and the author of *Book M: Liber Mundi*, the *Book of Seshet*, and *Spectrum Fari: The Keys of Pharos*. These works can be found at tarot cart.com, and updates on creative happenings randomly appear on her blog at tabula mundi.com.

In this life, Mel has been often a student, and sometimes a teacher, of ninety-three interests from A to Z: alchemy, art, aromatherapy, astrology, beadwork, beekeeping, bookmaking, brewing, cards, chaos, channeling, colors, Crowley... all the way to zazen, the zeitgeist, and the zodiacal myths. Working with the muse is ever ongoing.

DECODING ESOTERIC
SYMBOLISM
IN MODERN TAROT

Tarot
DECIPHERED

T. Susan Chang

M.M. Meleen

Llewellyn Publications
Woodbury, Minnesota

FIRST EDITION
Fourth Printing, 2025

Cards on cover are from Pre-Raphealite Tarot and Mystical Tarot used with permission from Lo Scarabeo
Cover design by Shannon McKuhen
For interior art credits please see page 625
Tarot Decks Used:
    Ancient Italian Tarot © 2000 by Lo Scarabeo
    Animal Totem Tarot © 2016 by Leeza Robertson and Eugene Smith, Llewellyn Publications
    lustrations from the Rider-Waite Tarot Deck® reproduced by permission of U.S. Games Systems, Inc.,
       Stamford, CT 06902 USA. Copyright © 1971 by U.S. Games Systems, Inc. Further reproduction
       prohibited. The Rider-Waite Tarot Deck® is a registered trademark of U.S. Games Systems, Inc.
    Mystical Tarot © 2017 by Luigi Costa, Lo Scarabeo
    Liber T © 2004 by Lo Scarabeo
    Linestrider Tarot © 2016 by Siolo Thompson
    Pharos Tarot © 2020 by M.M. Meleen
    Pre-Raphaelite Tarot © 2019 by Luigi Costa, Lo Scarabeo
    Rosetta Tarot © 2011 by M.M. Meleen
    Sola Busca Tarot © 2019 by Paola Gnaccolini, Lo Scarabo
    Tabula Mundi © 2014 by M.M. Meleen
    Tarot de Marseille © 2016 by Camoin and Jodorowsky, Lo Scarabeo
    Tarot Egyptiens © 2019 by Etteilla, Julius Laisne, Lorambert, Lo Scarabeo
    Universal Wirth Tarot © 2008 by Lo Scarabeo

Llewellyn is a registered trademark of Llewellyn Worldwide Ltd.

Library of Congress Cataloging-in-Publication Data
Names: Chang, T. Susan, author. | Meleen, M. (Melissa) M., author.
Title: Tarot deciphered : decoding esoteric symbolism in modern tarot / T.
    Susan Chang, M.M. Meleen.
Description: First edition. | Woodbury, Minnesota : Llewellyn Publications,
    2021. | Includes bibliographical references. | Summary: "Decipher the
    symbols and stories of tarot and explore a carefully researched
    synthesis of ideas designed to help you connect with the wisdom of the
    cards"—Provided by publisher.
Identifiers: LCCN 2020050980 (print) | LCCN 2020050981 (ebook) | ISBN
    9780738764474 (paperback) | ISBN 9780738764627 (ebook)
Subjects: LCSH: Tarot.
Classification: LCC BF1879.T2 C5155 2021 (print) | LCC BF1879.T2 (ebook)
    | DDC 133.3/2424—dc23
LC record available at https://lccn.loc.gov/2020050980
LC ebook record available at https://lccn.loc.gov/2020050981

Llewellyn Worldwide Ltd. does not participate in, endorse, or have any authority or responsibility concerning private business transactions between our authors and the public.
    All mail addressed to the author is forwarded, but the publisher cannot, unless specifically instructed by the author, give out an address or phone number.
    Any internet references contained in this work are current at publication time, but the publisher cannot guarantee that a specific location will continue to be maintained. Please refer to the publisher's website for links to authors' websites and other sources.

Llewellyn Publications
A Division of Llewellyn Worldwide Ltd.
2143 Woodale Drive
Woodbury, MN 55125-2989
www.llewellyn.com

Printed in the United States of America

OTHER BOOKS BY T. SUSAN CHANG

A Spoonful of Promises
Tarot Correspondences

OTHER BOOKS BY M. M. MELEEN

Book M: Liber Mundi
The Book of Seshet
Spectrum Fari

DEDICATION

To all the fans, patrons, and listeners
who make *Fortune's Wheelhouse* possible.

CONTENTS

Acknowledgments xv

Foreword xix

Introduction 1

Major Arcana 7

The Fool 15

The Magician/Magus 23

The High Priestess 33

The Empress 41

The Emperor 49

The Hierophant 59

The Lovers 67

The Chariot 75

Strength/Lust 83

The Hermit 93

The Wheel of Fortune 101

Justice/Adjustment   111

The Hanged Man   121

Death   129

Temperance/Art   139

The Devil   149

The Tower   159

The Star   169

The Moon   179

The Sun   189

Judgement/Aeon   199

The World/Universe   209

Minor Arcana   219

Ace of Wands   227

2 of Wands   233

3 of Wands   239

4 of Wands   245

5 of Wands   251

6 of Wands   257

7 of Wands   263

8 of Wands   269

9 of Wands   275

10 of Wands   281

Ace of Cups   287

2 of Cups   293

3 of Cups   299

4 of Cups   305

5 of Cups   311

6 of Cups   317

7 of Cups   323

8 of Cups   329

9 of Cups   335

10 of Cups   341

Ace of Swords   347

2 of Swords   353

3 of Swords   359

4 of Swords   365

5 of Swords   371

6 of Swords   377

7 of Swords   383

8 of Swords   389

9 of Swords   395

10 of Swords   401

Ace of Pentacles or Ace of Disks   407

2 of Pentacles or 2 of Disks   413

3 of Pentacles or 3 of Disks   419

4 of Pentacles or 4 of Disks   425

5 of Pentacles or 5 of Disks   431

6 of Pentacles or 6 of Disks   437

7 of Pentacles or 7 of Disks   443

8 of Pentacles or 8 of Disks   449

9 of Pentacles or 9 of Disks   455

10 of Pentacles or 10 of Disks   461

Court Cards   467

King of Wands or Knight of Wands   477

Queen of Wands   483

Knight of Wands or Prince of Wands   489

Page of Wands or Princess of Wands   495

King of Cups or Knight of Cups   501

Queen of Cups   507

Knight of Cups or Prince of Cups   515

Page of Cups or Princess of Cups   521

King of Swords or Knight of Swords   527

Queen of Swords   533

Knight of Swords or Prince of Swords   539

Page of Swords or Princess of Swords   545

King of Pentacles or Knight of Disks   551

Queen of Pentacles or Queen of Disks   557

Knight of Pentacles or Prince of Disks   565

Page of Pentacles or Princess of Disks   571

Conclusion   577

Tables and Diagrams   581

    Tree of Life Diagram   582

    Table of Decans   583

    Minor Arcana Decan Information   584

    Planetary Dignities   601

    Golden Dawn Color Scales Table   604

    Suggested Reading   *611*

    Bibliography   *619*

    Art Credit List   *625*

ACKNOWLEDGMENTS

Fortune's Wheelhouse is a collaborative effort. It's made possible not only through the work of its two co-hosts, Susie and Mel, but through the support of hundreds of listeners who fund our Patreon site and engage with us in thought-provoking virtual conversations about the most fascinating subject in the world. As we move from the airwaves and internet to the concrete reality of the bookshelf, this book is a tangible record of that community and conversation. Readers, we thank you for inviting us into your minds and hearts. Long may we explore together!

At Llewellyn, we'd especially like to thank Barbara Moore. In addition to her own spectacular body of work as a tarot author and deck creator, Barbara has been a good friend and publishing godparent to any number of creative spirits in the tarot community. We thank her for believing in our work and supporting us as *Fortune's Wheelhouse* takes its next steps into the wider world.

We'd also like to thank Nicole Borneman, production editor, Kat Neff, publicity director, Andy Belmas, lead marketing communications specialist, and Sammy Peterson, production designer, for their tireless and meticulous efforts to bring this complex creation to reality.

SUSIE'S ACKNOWLEDGMENTS

First and foremost, thanks are due to my family, who patiently abide with my many inscrutable forays into the hidden realms. Over the years, Mom's portion of the house has become increasingly overrun with decks, stones, incense, oils, silks and brocades, and books enough to require an office renovation. My workings may be incomprehensible, inconvenient, and at times actually smelly, but I assure you they are meant only to promote domestic bliss!

During the writing of this book, conversations with friends online and off—Erik Arneson, Andrew Watt, Mark Nickels, Sara Eddy—have helped keep my magical headgame in place. Every day, the Fortune's Wheelhouse Academy community on Facebook has been a safe haven for the spell-sharing and intention-setting that get me through each day.

Finally—although it goes without saying—this book would not exist without Mel, artist extraordinaire and my friend and co-host; I'm so grateful our particular brand of crazy brought us together. Our hyperactive angular Mars placements and whackjob Aquarius moons may not be the most obvious formula for a collaboration, but that collaboration is probably best summed up by the ascendant degree for the *Fortune's Wheelhouse* launch: 9° Virgo, whose Sabian symbol is "Two Heads Looking Out and Beyond the Shadows." Let us hope they never stop looking!

MEL'S ACKNOWLEDGMENTS

Infinite gratitude is owed to my best friend and Aquarian husband, who never bats an eyelash at my constant stream of eccentricities—and whose Taurus moon ensures that in the midst of creative output, I remember to stop for meals. He is a rock in the best sense of the word and I probably wouldn't be alive without him.

One of the most surprising and gratifying things that has happened along the course of our podcast adventure was the spontaneous development of the community who found their tribe among us. I've made connections with some wonderful and inspiring people, and for someone who has, for the most part, been reclusive, it has been truly heartwarming to be included in their fellowship.

Posthumous thanks are also due to the co-creators of the Thoth and Rider-Waite-Smith decks, whose innovations made modern tarot what it is today, and to the founders of the Golden Dawn, who created the structure they built upon. The evocative Hermetic tarot titles of *Book T* inspired many of my "astral surfing" meditations and were the catalyst for many of my tarot artworks.

Beyond any doubt, gratitude is owed to my co-creatrix and immensely talented friend Susie. A few years ago, I would have told you I was the last person on Earth to ever do anything as public as a *podcast*. But she has impeccable timing, as she asked if I wanted to co-create the show at a time when I was under a vow to say yes to any fresh developments. The rest, as they say, is history.

FOREWORD

For nearly fifty years tarot has played the role of conflicted protagonist in the dark-comedy-mystery-drama that is my spiritual life. Unlike many tarot enthusiasts, I never (even in my adolescent daydreams) fantasized about becoming a professional fortune-teller or spiritual counselor to rock stars and celebrities. I never yearned for the mysterious power to foresee the future (especially my own), nor ever did I seriously entertain the possibility that there was some vaporous supernatural intelligence (good or evil) behind the oracular voice of tarot.

I wish I could say that my tarot agnosticism sprang from my consummate intellect and mature power of discernment; but alas, I possess neither. No. The simple fact is I am lazy. I am too lazy to dream of any personal power much beyond the ability to arrange comfortable shelter, nutritious food, and the chance to develop the nuances of the odd character I am meant to portray in this life. I lack the ambition necessary to barter with destiny or attempt to strategically scheme to cheat fortune. It's not that I don't hunger for new knowledge and insights and experiences; it's not that I don't constantly seek out new ways to trigger my own awakening to greater realities; it's not that I don't long to know why I exist and what it is I am here to do. Indeed, it is precisely those few *intangible* ambitions that trump the professional and domestic goals that consume the thoughts and hours and lives of most others of my class, culture, and species.

At first, all I was looking for in tarot was a flash card memory aid for studying and organizing the fundamentals of Hermetic Qabalah as an adjunct to my initiatory work as ceremonial magician. Little did I know at the time that tarot would eventually become for me nothing less than the foundation, the framework, the walls, the flying buttresses, even the *ornamentation* of the Temple of my entire evolving magical universe.

Like the authors of this marvelous guide to esoteric tarot, I eventually created my own tarot deck. I think it is safe to say that neither they nor I embarked upon this life-changing odyssey in order to make a lot of money. (Only the childishly naïve believe one can strike it rich creating esoteric products.[1]) Indeed, I never expected my tarot to be marketed at all. For me, these seventy-eight pieces of painted cardstock were the only way I could begin to wrap my meat brain around the complexity of all the moving parts that make up the qabalistic language of ceremonial magick—a spiritual artform to which (in spite of my inherent laziness) I am inexplicably drawn.

Ceremonial magick, at least as it has developed in the last 200 years, is not a singular study. Furthermore, it is a frustrating fact of life that there doesn't seem to be a front door to the temple/university of magick. Every magician I've ever known has confessed that when they started their magical education it felt like breaking into a school building through some unguarded window and then eavesdropping on an incomprehensible master class already in progress. It's true. In order to even approach magick's potential as a self-transformational process, the neophyte must already be armed with a rich vocabulary of a score of diverse subjects, ranging from astrology and alchemy to Hebrew Qabalah, Eastern mysticism, and mythology.

Organized Orders and magickal societies provide the semblance of structure and order to the educational process, and for many of us, these organizations were helpful and gave us a glimpse of the bigger picture of the great edifice of magick. Furthermore, twenty-first century magicians are especially lucky to have the occult wisdom of the ages available to us at our electronic fingertips. This awesome library, coupled with the in-temple dramatic experiences of being involved in an initiatory order, gives the individual a decided advantage over our ancient colleagues.

One of the wisest educational assignments of the great nineteenth-century mystery school, the Hermetic Order of the Golden Dawn, was that the new initiate was required to create their own tarot deck (generically patterned on an archetypal "mother deck"). By taking the time and effort to paint each card, the new magician was in

---

1. Authors' Note: Mel's decks are the *Tabula Mundi Tarot*, the *Rosetta Tarot*, and the *Pharos Tarot*, which are published and available from Mel's website. Although Susie did once create a deck, it's for private use only, and she has no plans to publish it.

effect reprogramming their magickal "software," bringing it into closer approximation to the universal harmonies the cards exemplify. The hours and days and weeks and months the individual spent focusing on every unique symbolic detail of the cards became more than just an exercise in rote memorization; it was a mutation process, a tinkering with one's spiritual DNA, a full upgrade of the operating system of the soul, a magical vaccine injected directly into the quantum dimension of the psyche via the awesome delivery system of *art*. And like art and vaccines, the experience triggers a transformational response that is unique to every organism.

Making your own tarot deck requires you to give yourself a first-class liberal arts education in occultism, but it also does so much more. Almost by accident, you simultaneously absorb the fundamental principles of the Hebrew Qabalah—the alphabet; the numerical and mathematical characteristics. You see laid out before you the seamless associations of elements, planetary spheres, signs of the zodiac, astrological rulerships, exaltations, decan and degree assignments, vibratory color scales, and classic mythological archetypes. Without even realizing what's happening, the novice almost subconsciously metamorphizes into a well-lubricated adept ... a magician.

Perhaps you think I'm exaggerating. Perhaps I am. Even after fifty years of playing various instruments in the tarot symphony orchestra, the only thing I can say with complete honesty is, "It's too soon to tell." But I *am* smugly comfortable with the place tarot holds in my magickal life, and I'm quite happy to share my experiences and (temporary) conclusions about the importance of this marvelous and magickal art. But unlike M. M. Meleen, I'm not much of an *artist* artist. My own tarot deck, while displaying many occult, astrological, and magical correspondences on the cards themselves, is definitely *not* an artistic tour de force. As a matter of fact, my laziness has allowed me to be shamelessly satisfied with simple line drawings I hurriedly created as best I could. My wife, Constance, then colored them in with watercolors according to the strict qabalistic color scales associated with each of the cards.

M. M. Meleen, however is a real, profoundly skilled, and awesomely talented *artist* artist, and her genius renders her eminently qualified to comment authoritatively on the work of other great tarot artists of the past. The transcendent power displayed in her consummately executed works is a testament to the art of magick as a consciousness-elevating tool and talisman. When art at this level is coupled with the archetypal images and qabalistic structure of the tarot, we are blessed with an alchemical marriage whose progeny are miniature monuments of perfection and beauty.

I hope I haven't embarrassed the authors with my praise of this work and the talents of its creators. As you will see as these pages unfold the wonders of tarot's perfect construction, there is more than enough information here for you to embark upon your own tarot odyssey. The book has been organized so as to painlessly reveal the method to the madness. This picture book of tarot is exactly what I was looking for fifty years ago, but more importantly, it comes dangerously close to showing me *why* I was looking for it.

—Lon Milo DuQuette

INTRODUCTION

Every one of us, at the beginning of our tarot journey, has looked at a tarot card and wondered, *What could that symbol possibly mean?* At one level, the answer to that question doesn't matter. You may well be able to read the cards intuitively, even fluently, without having to articulate a definition for the symbol. Nevertheless—for so many of us—a small, mercurial voice in your minds still *wants to know*. Is that an Aquarius sign scratched there in the corner? What are those Hebrew letters inscribed in that square doing there? *Why is that snake biting its tail?!* You feel sure there is an answer, but the card is mute.

Happily, if you've been in a similar situation, you are not alone! In this book you will find answers to these questions and many more.

WHY ESOTERIC TAROT?

Esoteric tarot is more than just a symbol-by-symbol analysis. It is an analysis *and synthesis* that distills and refines the meaning of each card. It provides a structure for the intellect to rest upon, and from the refuge of that space, the mind can rest and recall what is useful as feelings and intuitions arise in the oracular moment. The many myths and symbols tell stories that reflect the infinitely elastic meanings of each card and the multitudes we all contain.

In the main body of the text, we use the examples of the Rider-Waite-Smith and Thoth decks because most are familiar with them. But these esoteric schemas are keys that can unlock any modern deck that descends from them. Both decks share a common root, for their creators were both adepts of the same influential Western occult order that developed much of the esoteric framework tarot is mapped to. Looking at and learning only one of those two pivotal deck systems is like only being able to see an object in one view, while learning the roots they share is like seeing from the front, back, and in profile, as well as from above and below! We show how these keys apply to a wide variety of decks in the other deck illustrations we show and caption.

ASTROLOGY AND ESOTERIC TAROT

We use the astrological tarot correspondences of the Hermetic Golden Dawn. The iconic Rider-Waite-Smith and Thoth tarots are both built on this framework. Knowingly or not, most modern decks are too, when they derive from the framework these sources made popular. Some may be puzzled by a few of their choices at first, but the longer we have worked with the Golden Dawn correspondence system, the more evident its internal eloquence.

In order to make this guide as useful as possible to as many as possible, we focused on those astrological concepts most closely related to esoteric tarot: the elements, the seven classical planets, the twelve signs, and the thirty-six decans; their constellations and mythology. Needless to say, galaxies of further correspondences and vast realms of further inquiry exist, and we hope you will take every opportunity to explore them further on your own.

INTERNAL VARIATIONS OF THE THOTH DECK

There are of course a few differences between Waite's Rider-Waite-Smith deck and Crowley's Thoth deck. While both began with the basic Golden Dawn system of references, Crowley, through discoveries made during his own work as an adept, made a few changes which we make note of in the text. In modern decks, when you see pages referred to as "princesses," or Judgement referred to as "Aeon," or Strength entitled Lust and numbered XI rather than VIII, these are usually good indications that the creator is working within Crowley's framework.

QABALAH AND ESOTERIC TAROT

The Tree of Life, a conceptual diagram depicting the unfolding of creation through ten spheres, or *sephiroth*, has its roots deep in Jewish mysticism. Its branches have extended across the study of traditional Kabbalah for over 1,000 years. One of those branches profoundly influenced the intellectual and magical movement known as Hermeticism, which co-opted the tradition for its own purposes and began to diverge markedly from its precursors with the work of Athanasius Kircher in the seventeenth century. By the early twentieth century, Hermetic Qabalah (the "Q" is widely used to distinguish it from Christian Cabala and Jewish Kabbalah) had developed its own set of conventions, beliefs, and even its own version of the Tree. This version would become a foundational concept across schools of Western occultism, thanks to its core presence in the Golden Dawn's efforts to organize many heterogeneous mystical cosmologies into a single system.

It is Hermetic Qabalah that informs the Golden Dawn's mapping of the Tree of Life to tarot, and therefore when we refer to sephiroth, paths, and Hebrew letter attributions in this book, we are referring to them in a Hermetic Qabalah context. That said, there are times when ideas borrowed (by the Golden Dawn or others) from traditional Kabbalah chime and resonate with their distant Hermetic descendants. We include some of these in a spirit of respect and exploration, and we use the phrase "traditional Kabbalah" to set them apart from the overall Qabalistic framework of this book.

Our spelling choices are those used widely in modern-day Hermetic Qabalah (*Tiphareth* rather than *Tiferet*, *sephira* rather than *sefira*). We recognize that some may view these as a Victorian corruption of Hebrew transliteration as currently practiced, but by observing Hermetic conventions, our intent is to honor the integrity of, and the boundaries between, the separate traditions.

MYTHOLOGY AND ESOTERIC TAROT

In the Mythology section, an eclectic variety of myths are referenced. They include classical Greek and Roman mythologies, Orphic variations, Egyptian myths across many dynasties, Mesopotamian epics, deities of Buddhism and Hinduism, and even a few more modern tales. The criteria for including a story was that it somehow referenced mythological beings with as many of the planetary, zodiacal, and Qabalistic correspondence resonances as possible, while *also* being evocative of the themes expressed in the card. Many were chosen intuitively, based on a feeling similar to the oracular moment. We hope these suggestions offer a starting place for your mythological excavations.

THE *RIDER-WAITE-SMITH TAROT*

The Rider-Waite-Smith (or Waite-Smith) deck is the iconic deck of modern tarot. While not immediately influential on its release in 1910, it blossomed into popular consciousness with its 1971 reissue and has been a global touchstone for tarot ever since. It has provided inspiration for countless modern decks, and a majority of new readers rely on its accessible images (particularly the "scenic" minors) for their first entry into tarot.

The original source text for Waite-Smith is Arthur Edward Waite's *Pictorial Key to the Tarot.* (Unless otherwise noted, all quotations from Waite in the Rider-Waite-Smith sections of the book come from *Pictorial Key*.) Although Waite was a member of the Golden Dawn and well-versed in its esoteric "Book T" interpretations of the cards, he was also clearly drawn to the iconography of what was already a 500-year-old tarot idiom. In the deck we can see influences from fifteenth- and sixteenth-century works like the Sola Busca *tarocchi* and the Tarot de Marseille. And many of Waite's *Pictorial Key* meanings derive directly from the work of Etteilla, the eighteenth-century French occultist.

As the artist, Pamela Colman Smith was famously free to interpret Waite's prompts with as much artistic license as she saw fit—for the minor arcana, Waite's prompts were quite scant to begin with. But she too was a habitué and an initiate of the Golden Dawn circle, and she applied her peculiar genius to the cards in her own way. She did not seem to refer to Waite's esoterics nearly as closely as Lady Frieda Harris later would to Crowley's in the Thoth deck.

So when we speak of astrological myths or Qabalistic symbolism implied in the Waite-Smith images, we are speaking speculatively. We don't attribute any intent on Smith's part to the connections we draw. We are reading *into* the images, not *from* them—as readers have done since cartomancy began.

THE THOTH TAROT

The *Book of Thoth* is the main source text for Crowley's thoughts on the Thoth cards (unless otherwise noted). We sometimes reference other technical *Libers* of his, either because he has specifically mentioned them in his chapter on the card in body or footnote, or because they obviously or wonderfully relate to the card image or message. There are other third-party source books we have found useful in our explorations that are listed in the Suggested Reading section.

The Thoth deck is a masterpiece. Aleister Crowley and Lady Frieda Harris were both mature individuals in their sixties at the time of the deck's creation. Crowley put the entirety of his considerable knowledge—earned over his lifetime of attainments as a spiritual adept—into the symbolism of each card. Each and every card can convey a wealth of profound conceptual esoteric teachings—far more than can be covered in the scope of this book. Yet the Thoth deck owes its evocative beauty to the artist, Lady Frieda Harris. It was Lady Harris who first suggested to Crowley the idea of redesigning the traditional tarot and writing about it—something he at first was highly resistant to. Harris was a co-Mason and student of esotericism and theosophy, but she knew little of ceremonial magic. She offered to pay Crowley a weekly stipend and to paint the cards as book illustrations if he would teach her magic as part of the process and write a comprehensive tarot text. A process that was supposed to take months took five years—and the rest is history, for together they created an enduring magnum opus that continues to broaden minds to this day.

What makes the art of the Thoth deck so compelling is Lady Harris's distinctive art deco style and her ingenious use of projective geometry, which she learned as a student of the disciples of Rudolf Steiner. What made the deck even more esoterically expressive was the incorporation of the color scale system of the Golden Dawn. This system of mapping specific colors to the four Qabalistic worlds of the Tree of Life allowed each card to be an invocation of the essence of the specific path or sephira through the evocative use of color.

The Ordo Templi Orientus (O. T. O.) owns the image rights to the Thoth tarot. Unfortunately, the O. T. O. currently allows publication of the images only in works exclusively dedicated to discussion of the Thoth tarot, without comparative discourse of other decks. While we think that such correlative discussion would only favorably highlight the majesty of Crowley and Harris's brilliant creation, we thus had to forego including these masterful artworks and hope that readers will seek them out in a physical deck or the many widely available online images. It will certainly prove worthwhile to study the images along with our text.

CORRESPONDENCES FOUND—
AND NOT FOUND—IN THIS BOOK

A vast infrastructure of correspondences undergirds the Golden Dawn–based tarot decks we study. In this guide, we chose to focus on correspondences which readers will be able to see fairly easily in any modern deck. (Besides the Rider-Waite-Smith and Thoth decks, we've included images drawn from Mel's decks and several other Llewellyn and Lo Scarabeo decks.)

As a result, you won't be able to look up Yasgedibarodiel, "Angel of the Cadent Decanate of Capricorn" in here. You'll need Aleister Crowley's exhaustive *777* for that; indeed, if you are reading this book, you probably have a copy on your shelf already. You can also use Susie's *Tarot Correspondences*, a general reference for the major historical and magical correspondences relevant to tarot, and how to use them. If you have those texts, a few decks (Rider-Waite-Smith, Thoth, and an M. M. Meleen deck!), and this card-by-card guide, your foray into esoteric tarot is well underway.

MAJOR ARCANA

ABOUT THE GOLDEN DAWN TITLES

The Golden Dawn assigned formal, or "Hermetic," titles to the twenty-two major arcana. These grand and often poetic epithets generally allude to one or more esoteric qualities associated with each card. For example, the High Priestess's Hermetic title is "the Priestess of the Silver Star"; the "silver star" may be the moon, her astrological correspondence. The Empress is "the Daughter of the Mighty Ones": the "mighty ones" may refer to the supernal sephiroth, Kether, Chokmah and Binah, and her path on the Tree of Life forms the base of the triangle they form.

By using these titles to capture esoteric qualities inherent in each archetype, the Golden Dawn joins a tradition of prayer and invocation extending back to the earliest hymns. By uttering the name of the deity and its powers, a supplicant invests her words with additional meaning and ensures her prayers will be heard.

ASTROLOGY OF THE MAJORS

△	▽	⩑	⩗
Fire	Water	Air	Earth

Four elements

The twenty-two major arcana cards can be astrologically divided via esoteric assignment into groups of three, seven, and twelve. The three primary or classical elements that make up all of nature—air, water, and fire—correspond to the cards of the Fool, Hanged Man, and Judgement/Aeon respectively. But what about the element of earth? As the earth element is comprised of a combination of all of the elements in equilibrium, it has been assigned to the World/Universe card, which also is a summation of all that has come before it. Thus the World/Universe card does what we call double duty, for it is also assigned the planetary correspondence of Saturn, who not only rules one of the earth signs, but whose "heavy" qualities are also resonant with the cold weight of Earth. Similarly, the Judgement/Aeon card also does double duty, for in addition to corresponding to the fire element, it is also assigned the mysterious animating fifth element of Spirit: known as *aether,* or sometimes as "void."

Each element has three signs, one of each quadruplicity: the initiator is cardinal, the middle sign listed is fixed, and the last mutable (see the "Astrological Qualities or Quadruplicities" section). The fire signs are Aries (cardinal), Leo (fixed), and Sagittarius (mutable). The water signs are Cancer, Scorpio, and Pisces. The air signs are Libra, Aquarius, and Gemini.

☽	☿	♀	☉	♂	♃	♄
Moon	Mercury	Venus	Sun	Mars	Jupiter	Saturn

The seven traditional planets

The seven "planets" of classical astrology (Mercury, Venus, Mars, Jupiter, Saturn, and our two luminaries, the Sun and Moon) are assigned to the Magician, Empress, Tower, Fortune, World, Sun, and Priestess, respectively. Planets are said to "rule" the signs of their domicile, a place where they are given what is termed dignity, or the freedom of expression that comes with familiar territory. Each planet rules two signs, a diurnal or day sign, and a nocturnal or night sign, while the sun and moon each rule a single sign. The more recently discovered planets (Uranus, Neptune, and Pluto) have also been assigned in modern astrology as dual rulers of the signs Aquarius, Pisces, and Scorpio, respectively.

	☉ Sun—Leo ♌	
	☽ Moon—Cancer ♋	
Gemini ♊ (diurnal)	Mercury ☿	Virgo ♍ (nocturnal)
Libra ♎ (diurnal)	Venus ♀	Taurus ♉ (nocturnal)
Aries ♈ (diurnal)	Mars ♂	Scorpio ♏ (nocturnal)
Sagittarius ♐ (diurnal)	Jupiter ♃	Pisces ♓ (nocturnal)
Aquarius ♒ (diurnal)	Saturn ♄	Capricorn ♑ (nocturnal)

The classical domiciles of the seven planets

The following diagram shows the elegance of the assignment by placing the luminaries and their signs at the top of an astrological wheel. The signs proceed in order around the circumference, with the planets in orbital order along each side, and day and night sign rulerships alternating. It also shows the concepts of how aspects are derived. Each sign has 30° of the circular complete zodiacal band. The opposition shows signs 180° or six signs apart, dividing the circle in half. These are said to be on the same "axis," i.e., Leo and Aquarius. The trine shows signs 120° or four signs apart, dividing the circle into a triangle. The square divides the circle fourfold, with signs 90° or three signs apart. The sextile shows signs 60° or two signs apart, dividing the circle six ways. Adjacent signs or those 30° apart are in semi-sextile aspect. In general, oppositions are polarizing and squares are frictional, but both yield potential growth opportunities. Trines are harmonious but not stimulating, and sextiles and semi-sextiles show possibilities to explore that may yield positive results if effort is applied.

The astrological signs divide the zodiac into twelve 30° segments. Though entire books can be written about the nuances of each sign, each has a short declarative motto that attempts to summarize their nature as concisely as possible.

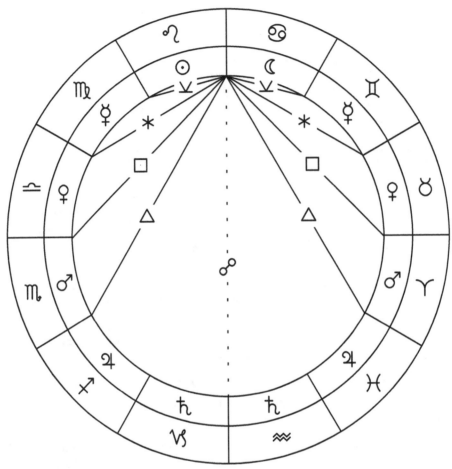

Astrological rulerships diagram

Aries ♈	The Emperor	"I am"
Taurus ♉	The Hierophant	"I have"
Gemini ♊	The Lovers	"I think"
Cancer ♋	The Chariot	"I feel"
Leo ♌	Strength/Lust	"I will"
Virgo ♍	The Hermit	"I analyze"
Libra ♎	Justice/Adjustment	"I balance"

Zodiacal correspondences and the major arcana

Scorpio ♏	Death	"I desire"
Sagittarius ♐	Temperance/Art	"I aim"
Capricorn ♑	The Devil	"I use"
Aquarius ♒	The Star	"I know"
Pisces ♓	The Moon	"I believe"

Zodiacal correspondences and the major arcana

ASTROLOGICAL QUALITIES OR QUADRUPLICITIES

The twelve zodiacal signs can be divided into three modalities or qualities, each into groups of four, one for each element. Cardinal signs begin the seasons, such as 0° Aries being the start of spring (in the Northern Hemisphere). The cardinal signs (Aries, Cancer, Libra, and Capricorn) are active and controlling, tending to initiate. The fixed signs (Leo, Scorpio, Aquarius, and Taurus) are when the season is fully established, and are thus steady, tending to maintain. The mutable signs (Sagittarius, Pisces, Gemini, and Virgo) end the season, and so are flexible, tending toward change. Signs that share a quality or quadruplicity are either in opposition or square to each other. For example, the cardinal sign Aries is on the same axis, or in opposition to, the cardinal sign Libra, while squaring the other two cardinal signs Cancer and Capricorn, who also share an axis.

What does all of this astrology have to do with tarot? While it is by no means necessary to memorize these correspondences and relationships, knowing how elements, signs, and planets interact can add additional depth to your readings by seeing how the related cards may influence and relate to each other when they appear in the same spread.

QABALAH OF THE MAJORS

The Tree of Life is a configuration of ten spheres, or sephiroth, and is the foundation of Kabbalistic—and Qabalistic—thought.[2] Twenty-two paths, each assigned to one

---

2. See the introduction for the differences between these two concepts derived from Jewish mysticism.

letter of the Hebrew alphabet, join the ten sephiroth. The twenty-two major arcana map to these paths with the same three-seven-twelve structure we see in the astrology of the major arcana: three "mother" letters, seven "double" letters, and twelve "simple" letters.

אמש: The three mother letters are *aleph*, *mem*, and *shin*, correlating to the elements of air, water, and fire. From these, according to mystical thought, everything in the cosmos arises—including the fourth element, earth.

בגדכפרת: The seven double letters are *beth*, *gimel*, *daleth*, *kaph*, *peh*, *resh*, and *tav*, and correlate to the seven traditional planets—Mercury, the moon, Venus, Jupiter, Mars, the sun, and Saturn. Like the wandering planets themselves, which draw nearer to and farther from us at different points, these letters vary in their sound: one "hard" pronunciation and one "soft" pronunciation.[3] Their metaphysical significations come in pairs of opposites: e.g., wisdom and folly.

הוזחטילנסעצק: The twelve simple letters are *heh*, *vav*, *zain*, *cheth*, *teth*, *yod*, *lamed*, *nun*, *samekh*, *ayin*, *tzaddi*, and *qoph*. They correlate to the twelve zodiacal signs, in order, from Aries to Pisces. These letters do not vary in their pronunciation, just as the constellations do not vary in their distance from the earth. Metaphysically, they relate to single human attributes, such as mirth or anger.

We use a number of concepts from the Tree of Life to talk about the major arcana.

- The "supernals" or "supernal triad" are the three sephiroth at the top of the Tree: Kether, Chokmah, and Binah. These are considered divine, beyond human comprehension; an abyss (Da'ath) separates them from the other seven.

- The three vertical uprights one can draw through the Tree of Life are the three "pillars": the Pillar of Mercy or Pillar of Force on the right and the Pillar of Severity or Pillar of Form on the left. The central line is the Middle Pillar or Middle Path.

---

3. In modern Hebrew, some of those distinctions in pronunciation no longer exist.

- The "lightning flash" is the zigzag that descends from Kether to Malkuth, touching each of the ten sephiroth in turn. This represents the ongoing act of creation.

- The "Four Worlds" are four stages of manifestation descending down the Tree of Life: the Archetypal World (Atziluth), the World of Creation (Briah), the World of Formation (Yetzirah), and the World of Action (Assiah). There are a number of ways to visualize this. One we use often assigns the three upper (supernal) sephiroth to Atziluth, the next three sephiroth to Briah, the lower three sephiroth to Yetzirah, and the last sephira, Malkuth, to Assiah.

THE FOOL
The Spirit of the Aether

Card Number: 0

Element: ∀, Air

Hebrew Letter: א, *aleph*

Hebrew Letter Meaning: Mother letter: Ox; Value: 1

Path 11: Kether (1, Crown—Primum mobile) to Chokmah (2, Wisdom—Zodiac)

Color Scales in the Four Worlds: Bright pale yellow. Sky blue. Blue emerald green. Emerald, flecked gold

Themes and Keywords: All and nothing. Zero. Beginnings. Emanation. Deity. Creation. Fertility. Air. Breath. Silence. Nascence. Folly and madness vs holy wisdom. Innocence. Ignorance. Going forth.

ASTROLOGY/ELEMENT

The Fool corresponds to the element air, the suit of the mind and reason. Air contains the elements fire and water, yet the Fool's esoteric title is The Spirit of Aether. Aether is somewhat akin to air. The theoretical substance aether, or ether, was once believed to be a universal elastic medium for the transmission of electromagnetic wave forms. Distributed throughout all matter and permeating all space, it was only assumed to be there, as it was invisible, weightless, frictionless, and undetectable. Transmitting light and heat, it was also referred to as luminiferous aether.

The Fool corresponds to elemental air. This image captures a grasshopper
in aerial midflight, while also picking up on the traditional
sun and hobo-bag iconography. (*Animal Totem Tarot*)

Aristotle believed that aethyr extended from the fixed stars down to the moon. The ancient Greeks used the term to refer to the "upper air," the region of space beyond the atmosphere, the blue heavens, and the clear upper air personified. (It's also a term for a highly volatile, flammable, liquid anesthetic.)

In metaphysics the term also sometimes refers to Spirit, or the fifth element, and to the void or vacuum. In Enochian tradition it is the succession of worlds within, surrounding, and extending beyond the material world. All this agrees with the Fool's association with Kether, the sephira of the primum mobile, the outermost moving sphere in the geocentric model of the universe, and with the three veils surrounding the Qabalistic Tree of Life.

Modern astrologers usually assign Uranus, or sometimes Pluto, to the Fool. Because of its association with zero, the Fool also has a resonance with the Aries Point, the point at zero degrees of Aries in the zodiac where the zodiac, and the season of spring, begins.

MYTHOLOGY/ALCHEMY

Both innocent and virile, the Fool is associated with Dionysus or Bacchus, the god of wine and revelry, of fertility, religious ecstasy, and ritual madness. Dionysus is said to be a god of epiphany. An epiphany, or revelation, refers to inspiration received from divinity. His appearance is said to induce a frenzy in his followers akin to divine madness, freeing them from self-conscious cares, fears, and oppressions. His iconography includes pine cones, grapes, figs, ivy, tigers, leopards, and serpents.

Depictions of Dionysus either show him as a mature bearded man, a sensuous and attractive beardless youth, a ridiculously garbed or partially nude androgynous youth, or an effeminate male. Crowley's *777* lists the correct design of the tarot Fool as "a bearded Ancient seen in profile," and though we see him as a bearded jester in some Marseilles decks, modern decks portray him as either a Harlequin, an androgynous youth, or as a sort of "Green Man of the Spring Festival."[4]

The Orphic "first Dionysus," Zagreus the horned, was an underworld god dismembered by the Titans and reborn, paralleling the story of the Egyptian Osiris. The Fool is also associated with Zeus Arrhenothelus, the primordial Lord of Air who embodies the concept that the original god (Tetragrammaton) was both male and female. Though sources list Dionysus as being born after being sewn into Zeus's "thigh"—or testicles—the oracle of Apollo declared Zeus, Hades, and Dionysus "three gods in one godhead" overseeing birth, death, and reincarnation.[5]

The Fool has resonance with Parsifal, the Fisher King, and the Grail Quest. Tales of wandering princes who marry the king's daughter and become king are applicable to the Fool's story.

As the absence of speech and the indrawn breath, the Fool also has associations with Harpocrates, god of silence.

---

4. Crowley, *777*, 34.

5. Julian, *Hymn to King Helios*, 10.

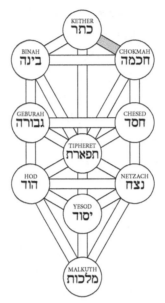

0. The Fool. Tree of Life.

The Fool represents the letter *aleph* (א), one of the three mother letters of the Hebrew alphabet: *aleph* corresponds to the element of air, *mem* (מ) to water, and *shin* (ש) to fire. *Aleph* means "ox" or "bull." Both, like Pan or Bacchus figures, are ancient symbols of fertility and generative power—apt beginnings for the story of creation. *Aleph's* shape depicts a point unfolding in four directions and set in motion—the whirling swastika once revered as a solar symbol before being co-opted in the modern age for darker purposes.

Airy *aleph* also corresponds to the chest, where people take air into their lungs as their first act as living beings. This is the same indrawn breath taken before speech (I—the Magician or Magus). In this silence is contained everything that follows—the beginning and end of all the universe.

The Tree of Life, or all creation, emanates from three "veils of nothingness," known as *Ain* (nothingness or "nothing that is not"), *Ain Soph* (infinity or "nothing without limit"), and *Ain Soph Aur* (limitless light). From these veils then contracts the first sephira, Kether—a dimensionless point of light or "crown." The Fool's path on the Tree of Life runs from Kether to the second sephira, Chokmah (wisdom), from the

Middle Pillar to the Pillar of Force. As the first path on the Tree, it represents "Qabalistic Zero"—the negative space from which all else emanates.

THE FOOL

This Fool is about to step into a wormhole in the fabric of space-time that is in the center of three concentric ouroboros serpents representing the negative veils before Kether: *Ain*, *Ain Soph*, and *Ain Soph Aur*. (*Tabula Mundi Tarot*)

In יהוה, the Tetragrammaton, letter *yod* (י) is said to reside in Chokmah, with its tip in Kether.

RIDER-WAITE-SMITH SYMBOLISM

THE FOOL.

The Fool (*Rider-Waite-Smith Tarot*)

This iconic image of the Fool holds a number of hidden references to the Tree of Life. The white sun at the upper right refers to Kether, the first sephira. Its fourteen rays may refer to 1 (Kether) + 2 (Chokmah) + 11 (path number). The line of the image passes from the sun to the lower left, reflecting the Fool's path from an inside-the-Tree perspective. He could be about to step into the abyss of Da'ath, the void below the supernal sephiroth. Or he might be stepping all the way down to Malkuth, which is symbolized by his white rose. The rose, whose scent he may have just sniffed, is white, as is his shirt and his dog—all conveying purity of intent. Ten eight-spoked wheels adorn his tunic: there are ten wheels for the ten sephiroth and eight spokes for the wheel of Spirit, the compass rose, and the eightfold model of consciousness.

His clifftop altitude, the yellow color of the background, his carefree mien, and the feather in his cap all point to the element of air; the feather's red color symbolizes the life force. We'll see it again in the Death and Sun cards. The Fool's elaborate tunic alludes to both the raiment of court jesters and the rags and tatters of the itinerant madman pictured in earlier versions of the Fool. Finally, his little dog is another holdover from early tarot, though its role—to attack (as in older versions), to warn, or merely to gambol about—is ambiguous.

THOTH SYMBOLISM

The Thoth Fool breaks the mold, an intense, horned, and virile man in green and gold, bursting on to the scene with nothing but air beneath his feet. He's about to be born headfirst through three loops that appear as the wake of a winged caduceus, flying toward his heart. These ovals may represent the three negative veils of existence that the Fool must pass through before entering the path of creation. These circular forms also represent zero, and Nuit fertilized by the winged disk within, conceiving Hoor-Pa-Kraat, also known as Harpocrates, the god of silence.

The card is teeming with symbols representing the beginnings of everything from nothing. The butterfly of air, symbol of the soul entering incarnation, follows in the track behind the winged disk (Hadit), with the caduceus a forerunner of the Fool's evolution to Magus. A dove descends, for Spirit's descent into matter, and the vulture Maut rides the spiral. The Fool holds a flaming pine cone (the thyrsus of Dionysus), and crystal cup of water; combining them creates air and then the Tree of Life. On his head is a diamond of white light (Kether), with the sun (Tiphareth) at the center over his procreative organ, and the crocodile Sebek at his feet standing in for Malkuth: the moon to his sun. The crocodile is also associated with Hoor-Pa-Kraat.

He bears Dionysian grapes and a transparent sack holding blue coins marked with the entire universe: sun surrounded by six planets, encircled by the zodiacal signs. Biting his thigh is a tiger, another Dionysian distraction of lust and passion. Between his legs is a rose, the white of Kether and the rose of Malkuth, with dangling lilies. Crowley calls them the "benediction of three flowers in one," referring to the final *heh*, the daughter of the Tetragrammaton who contains all of the qualities of the father, mother, and son who precede her.[6] Beneath them, the twinned infants (*vav* and final *heh*) embrace, destined to grow into the solar twins, active Ra-Hoor-Khuit and passive Hoor-Pa-Kraat. The background colored the yellow of air is speckled with diamonds in the white brilliance of Kether.

RELATED CARDS

In a sense, you could say that all cards are contained in the Fool as he is the as-yet-unrealized potential of all that will follow. But he is also the representative of elemental air, in the same way that the Hanged Man stands for elemental water, and Judgement/Aeon for elemental fire.

As elemental air, he has a specific connection to the three major arcana of air: Justice/Adjustment (Libra), the Star (Aquarius), and the Lovers (Gemini). Although he begins his journey as a blank slate, he will in time learn to weigh his options, navigate toward goals, and make informed choices. His story is a wayfinding from folly to wisdom; from ignorance to knowledge. Indeed, his mirror image on the Tree, the Magician, is defined by knowledgeability.

The intellectual, airy suit of Swords also reflects this perilous voyage of free will. When the Fool grasps the Ace of Swords for the first time, he becomes literally willful: he has an intention and the will to carry it out. In the 2, 3, and 4 of Swords (*Peace/Sorrow/Truce*), he will encounter his first crossroads, his first crisis, and his first compromise. In the 5, 6, and 7 (*Defeat/Science/Futility*), he will counter risk with goal setting

---

6. Crowley, *Book of Thoth*, 69.

and schemes of varying success. Finally, in the 8, 9, and 10 (*Interference/Cruelty/Ruin*), he faces a paralyzing choice, kills off some options, and thus commits to an outcome. For better or worse, it is the collapse of a quantum state into a certainty.

ADVANCED CONCEPTS FOR FURTHER EXPLORATION

- *Eheieh*—a god name transliterated from the Hebrew אהיה, translated as "I Will Be"

- The relationship between the Fool as first and the Universe as last major arcana

- The descent of Spirit (Kether) into matter (Malkuth) as the "lightning flash" of emanation connecting all the sephiroth of the Tree of Life

- The balancing and cleansing "path of the flaming sword"; another descending process from unity to multiplicity wherein the first swirlings of creation bring all possible energies into balance within the manifest world of everyday experience

- The corresponding ascent of matter (Malkuth) toward deity (Kether) through the "path of the serpent," a redemptive rising of consciousness via a complex connective weaving and balancing of the paths (major arcana) of the Tree of Life

- The fifth and unifying power of the four elemental "powers of the sphinx," the power of Spirit, *Ire*, "to go"—a function of godhead

- Magical Weapon: The Dagger or Fan

- Magical Power: Divination

THE MAGICIAN/MAGUS
The Magus of Power

Card Number: I

Planet and Dignities: ☿ Mercury: rules Gemini and Virgo, exalted Virgo; Day of the week: Wednesday

Hebrew Letter: ב, *beth*

Hebrew Letter Meaning: Double letter: House (Life—Death); Value: 2

Path 12: Kether (1, Crown—Primum Mobile) to Binah (3, Understanding—Saturn)

Color Scales in the Four Worlds: Yellow. Purple. Gray. Indigo, rayed violet

Themes and Keywords: Will. Magic. As above, so below. Words and thoughts with power to bend reality. Words as trickery. Illusion versus change in accordance with will. Knowledge. Skills. Tools. Connection. Transmission. Universal access to all realms. Mind, with all its virtues and flaws. The wand.

ASTROLOGY/ELEMENT

Speedy, tiny Mercury, the closest planet to the sun, has an orbit of only eighty-eight days. It has no moons and flies solo. Because of its proximity to the sun, it rises and sets with it, so it is difficult to see in our night sky. Because its orbit lies inside that of Earth's, it has phases, but we can never see its full phase as it is always behind or in front of the sun. It's never more than twenty-eight degrees from the degree of the sun, being either in the same sign or an adjacent one.

The sun governs force (Spirit), the positive (masculine) polarity, while the moon rules form (body), the negative (feminine) polarity. But Mercury is androgynous, being the mind or messenger between the two. It's one of the most important influences on a chart because it tells much about the mind, which creates reality, and describes the intellect and style of communication. It rules messages transmitted and received, travel, motion, magic, the sciences, and logic.

Mercury's glyph combines the circle of Spirit above the cross of matter and is topped by the crescent of personality (which looks remarkably like a figure wearing a winged cap or transmitting antennae).

Mercury has dual rulership over mutable air sign Gemini as its day sign and mutable earth sign Virgo as its night sign. As Gemini, it expresses its quicksilver nature, curiosity, versatility, and wit. As Virgo, it expresses common sense, attention to detail, deep analysis, and logical thought.

MYTHOLOGY/ALCHEMY

Mercurial gods all bear the creative and compelling power of the logos: the will and word. Hermes (Mercurius) was known as "he of the persuasive tongue." He wears the talaria (winged sandals that give swiftness) and either the petasos (traveler's cap) or winged helmet, and he carries the herald's staff, or caduceus. He is the messenger of the gods, a mischievous trickster, the patron of travelers. Hermes is a friend of those who pursue the occult arts, merchants, thieves, orators, and those in the fields of art and science. In his chthonic form, he takes on the role of psychopomp.

Hermes Trismegistus (Thrice Great) is a form of Hermes combined with the Egyptian god Thoth. Thoth ruled in Hermopolis over the Ogdoad (eightfold), a pantheon of eight primordial gods. He was the measurer of time and the scribe of the gods, and he was credited with the inventions of all branches of knowledge, human and divine: astronomy, writing, science, law, mathematics, medicine, and the measurements that established the heavens and Earth. As a scribe, he appears with the head of an ibis. In the underworld, he appears as an ape. His feminine counterpart was Seshet, "she who scrivens": Mistress of the House of Books, overseer of the royal scribes and library, and dually credited with all of Thoth's inventions.

THE MAGICIAN

The "ape of Thoth" trope on the Thoth deck's Magus is a mercurial reference; here is the ape-as-Magician, complete with the usual wand and analemma. (*Linestrider Tarot*)

Prometheus, who stole fire from heaven and gifted it to man, is also a mercurial figure. Other figures cognate are Loki, Ganesha, and Hanuman.

It's usually the Magician, as the Mercury card, where one thinks to find alchemical mercury. In alchemy, mercury represents the spirit (mind), sulfur represents the soul (consciousness, life), and salt represents the body (matter). Because alchemical mercury is spirit and mind, both the Fool and the Magician share this role just as one evolves from the other.

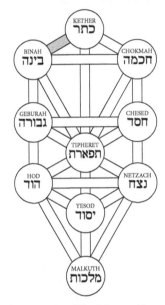

I (1). The Magician/The Magus. Tree of Life.

The Magus or Magician corresponds to the Hebrew letter *beth*, meaning "house." It is the first of seven double letters, each of which will correspond to one of the seven classical planets (ב *beth*/Mercury, ג *gimel*/moon, ד *daleth*/Venus, כ *kaph*/Jupiter, פ *peh*/Mars, ר *resh*/sun, ת *tav*/Saturn). The glyph of Mercury touches every sephira on the Tree except for Kether. As keeper of the House, the Magus creates worlds within worlds and forges connections between above and below, microcosm and macrocosm.

THE MAGUS

The Magus in this card is a cosmic DJ, a mix-master bringing
down the "house" (*beth*, his letter). (*Tabula Mundi Tarot*)

Each double letter marries two opposing powers; in this case, life and death—pointing to his role as interpreter, psychopomp, and traveler between realms. This polarity repeats in the colors of the two sephiroth connected by his path: Kether (white) and Binah (black).

His path travels from Kether to Binah, a mirror image to that of the Fool, extending to the Pillar of Form instead of the Pillar of Force. If the Fool is the intake of breath, the Magician is the outflow, the utterance of the spoken word.

Binah, first sephira on the pillar of form, signals an impulse to enclose and make formed. As the intermediary between Kether and Binah, the Magician turns the ideal into the real. His powers of manifestation draw attention to a core Hermetic principle: that which is above resembles that which is below. Because Mercury corresponds to the eighth sephira, Hod, we also see references to the number eight in both versions.

RIDER-WAITE-SMITH SYMBOLISM

The Magician (*Rider-Waite-Smith Tarot*)

The Waite-Smith Magician, known to all from the yellow box of the classic 1971 *Rider Tarot*, appears here a Western ceremonial magician. Waite says he has "the countenance of divine Apollo, with smile of confidence and shining eyes." His Continental predecessors were tricksters and con men (*Il Bagatto*, *Le Jongleur*, etc.). But now a table once full of hustler's trinkets holds four familiar mystical emblems: a wand, a cup, a sword, and a pentacle. The magic at work here is no illusion, but an act that changes reality.

The magician points up to Kether and down to Binah. "As above, so below" is the Hermetic magician's creed (from the *Emerald Tablet of Hermes Trismesgistus*). Divination and magic depend on this correspondence between the invisible and the mundane. Other binaries are at work: the stark black and white of the Magician's features and robe suggest the sephiroth defining his path: Kether (white, "crown" as headband) and Binah (black). As illustrated throughout the deck wherever roses and lilies appear, red stands for passion, carnality, and the number five; white stands for Spirit, purity of intention, and the number six.

Above his head is the analemma of the sun's orbit, a reference to Mercury's close relationship with the sun.[7] It is also a symbol of infinity, or the Magician's power to

---

7. "The mysterious sign of the Holy Spirit, the sign of life"—Waite, *Pictorial Key*, 72.

manifest everything and anything the heart desires. It is also a figure eight, a reference to the sephira Hod and the number of Mercury.

Finally, the ouroboros or serpent at his waist alludes to the twining snakes of Hermes's caduceus, to secret knowledge, and to the unending cycle of life and death.

THOTH SYMBOLISM

In the Thoth card, the Magus doesn't hold the wand, he *is* the wand, the channel of will. His body is the yellow of his color in the Golden Dawn King Scale, connecting him with both the Fool and the Sun. He is accompanied by the gray cynocephalus ape, who shadows Thoth to mock and deceive.

His gesture is similar to that of the RWS Magician, for similar reasons outlined. His posture also forms the glyph of Mercury, whose tracing encompasses all of the sephiroth of the Tree of Life except Kether.

The top of the wand has the caduceus with winged disk, a symbol for both the phallus and for Hadit. The circular center contains a descending dove, an extension of Spirit (Kether) into form (Binah) and symbolic of the feminine principle within the masculine, since Mercury is an androgynous figure. The wings of the figure appear to extend into pleated shapes reminiscent of the fan, a magical weapon of the Fool (air) from which he evolves. The serpents that entwine the caduceus are crowned: the left with the throne crown of Isis representing Binah (understanding), and the standard crown on the right representing Kether (the crown).

Mercury is always in motion, and here the Magician juggles eight implements, for eight is the number of his sephira Hod. In the air surrounding him revolve his tools and elemental weapons of power:

- Dagger: air and the power "to know"

- Cup: water "to dare"

- Winged Egg: Spirit "to go"

- Scroll: that bears the Word

- Stylus: that writes the Word

- Phoenix Wand: tool of resurrection

- Censer: fire "to will"

- Pentacle: earth "to keep silent"

RELATED CARDS

The Magician, arcanum of Mercury, is the first of seven planetary majors. The two Mercury-ruled zodiacal majors are the Lovers (Gemini) and the Hermit (Virgo). In the Lovers—the "Children of the Voice (Divine)"—we see the Magician's skill with the spoken word and ability to unlock choices. In the Hermit (also called the "Magus of the Voice of Light"), he decodes the written word, performs verbal magic, and acts as psychopomp.

Mercury also rules five of the thirty-six decans: As 5 of Pentacles, or "Lord of Worry" (Taurus I), he rules the anticipation and surmounting of obstacles. As 3 of Cups, or "Lord of Abundance" (Cancer II), he rules ease of communication. As 10 of Pentacles, or "Lord of Wealth" (Virgo III), he is dignified and exalted, and rules mercantile skill and communication with the dead. As 8 of Wands, or "Lord of Swiftness" (Sagittarius I), he is in detriment, yet rules swift, smooth travel and flashes of insight. As 6 of Swords, or "Lord of Science" (Aquarius II), he rules resourceful problem-solving.

In the 8, 9, and 10 of Swords (all Gemini cards), he expresses the mind's curiosity and computational ability; its power to freely make choices and comprehend their consequences. In the 8, 9, and 10 of Pentacles (all Virgo cards), he refines medicines for body and soul and material products to sustain the next generation; he oversees passage between the realms.

One is the number generally ascribed to the Magus. The Sun also enumerates to one (19: 1 + 9 = 10: 1 + 0 = 1). So does the Wheel of Fortune (10: 1 + 0 = 1). The close ties between these three cards speak to questions of individualism and destiny.

ADVANCED CONCEPTS FOR FURTHER EXPLORATION

- The relationship between the Magician and the Fool as progenitor

- The powers of speech and silence as magic, and the tools of the Magician's control over the elements and powers: to create (wand), preserve (cup), destroy (sword), and redeem (pentacle); as described in Crowley's *Liber B vel Magi sub Figura I*, which describes the highest possible manifestation in the physical plane, the grade of Magus

- The tools of the Magician as the ability to manipulate all four elemental "powers of the sphinx": to will (wand), to dare (cup), to know (sword), and to keep silent (pentacle)

- The similarities and differences between alchemical mercury, universal mercury, philosophical mercury, and planetary Mercury

- The emerald tablet of Hermes Trismegistus and the concept of transmutation

- Magical Weapon: The Wand or Cadeuceus

- Magical Power: Miracles of Healing, Gift of Tongues, Knowledge of Sciences

THE HIGH PRIESTESS
The Priestess of the Silver Star

Card Number: II

Planet and Dignities: ☾ Moon: rules Cancer, exalted Taurus; Day of the week: Monday

Hebrew Letter: ג, *gimel*

Hebrew Letter Meaning: Double letter: Camel (Peace—War); Value: 3

Path 13: Kether (1, Crown—Primum Mobile) to Tiphareth (6, Beauty—Sun)

Color Scales in the Four Worlds: Blue. Silver. Cold Pale Blue. Silver, rayed sky blue

Themes and Keywords: Holy secrets. Hidden mysteries. Divinity. Purity. Virginity. Autonomy. Aspiration. Vibration. Astral light. Wisdom. Enchantment. Divination. Silence. Esotericism. Intuition. The anima. Holy Spirit. Unvoiced belief. The cup.

ASTROLOGY/ELEMENT

The Priestess is the planetary trump of our glamorous satellite the moon, glowing with reflected light like a silver mirror. The moon's orbit around Earth is twenty-eight and a half days. A day on the moon is the same since it is tidally locked, forever facing Earth. Ever changing, it shifts through its four main phases of light and darkness: new, waxing, full, and waning. As it changes, humans vibrate and flow with its tides.

The moon affects the tides and the tides within, whether physical, mental, or emotional. Its orbit is the length of the menstrual cycle; it governs all things female. It affects sleep cycles and all the waters on Earth, including those within us. In astrology, the moon is as important as the sun, indicating our emotional capacity, feelings, home life, and bodily functions. It shows our magnetism and appeal to the public. It represents the human soul, our memories, the anima, our nurturing parent, and the many faces of our personality. It's our positive psychism, our intuition, and all that is receptive in human nature. It's our reflective inner light and our subconscious and unconscious feelings and needs.

The moon, associated with the Priestess since the earliest esoteric tarot correspondences, dominates this modern-day reworking of the image. (*Animal Totem Tarot*)

The glyph of the moon is a crescent, showing the reflected light of the sun. Turn it on its side and it looks like the bowl of a cup. This is the cup of the Priestess. The crescent shape when it appears in any of the planetary glyphs represents the cup lofted, the uplifted personality and spiritual aspiration.

The moon has rulership in Cancer and exaltation in Taurus.

MYTHOLOGY/ALCHEMY

The Priestess bears resemblance to the Hellenistic idea of Sophia as the initiatrix and personification of holy wisdom.

The Priestess of the Silver Star is also well represented by Artemis (Diana), whose epithet is Maiden of the Silver Bow. Artemis, with her arrows of silver, is the twin of Apollo with his arrows of gold. Artemis was a maiden goddess of the hunt who guarded her chastity fiercely. Her virtue shouldn't be thought of as asexuality; it signifies her completeness unto herself. Her power is in her autonomy and mastery of self. In spite of her virginity, she was known to help women with childbirth. Her iconography includes the bow and arrow, hunting dogs, and the moon.

Hekate, whose name may be derived from a Greek word meaning "she who works her will" or from one meaning "the far reaching one," is a goddess of magic and sorcery, light, herb lore, witchcraft, necromancy, and the crossroads. Also a virgin goddess, her appearance is often depicted as three-faced, suggesting the new, full, and half moon.

The Egyptian Hathor, with her horned headdress, calls to mind the crescent moon. Isis, sky goddess of magic and wisdom, like the Priestess of the Silver Star, has connections to the cosmos, especially to the star Sirius (the "silver star"). Isis is often depicted as veiled, a personification and allegory of the inscrutability of nature and her secrets. Her temple at Sais was said to bear the inscription "I am all that has been and is and shall be; and no mortal has ever lifted my mantle."

QABALAH—PATH 13

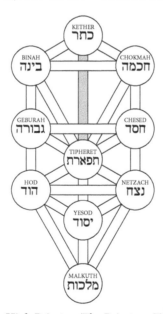

II (2). The High Priestess/The Priestess. Tree of Life.

The High Priestess's path is the longest on the Tree, the first on the Middle Pillar, and the last to exit Kether. It crosses Da'ath, the abyss below the supernal sephiroth, and terminates in Tiphareth. This crucial path connects the divine father (Kether) and son (Tiphareth), the *yod* and *vav* of the Tetragrammaton, the "greater" and "lesser" countenance, the archetypal world of Atziluth and the creative world of Briah, the mind and heart, the primum mobile and the sun. Thus the Priestess connects our sacred origin to our literal source of life. The nature of that connection is known but hidden—inexpressible, esoteric, a mystery hidden in the abyss. The Priestess may correspond to the Shekhinah, the feminine form of God, who dwells here on the earth, striving for reunion with her celestial counterpart.

Her path corresponds to letter ג *gimel*, meaning "camel." The camel is the "ship of the desert," conveying the traveler across long, inhospitable distances. It bears the spirit across Da'ath ("knowledge"), the abyss which destroys the human ego. The camel's unseen reservoir makes survival possible; that reservoir is divine grace, the unknowable intention behind existence. Although we may not be able to express it in words, spiritual belief gives us the sense of meaning we require to live. It is the light that conceals by its brilliance. Thus we see references to the entire Tree of Life in both Priestess versions. Both emphasize the next step on the Middle Pillar—Yesod, the sephira of the moon—where the magic of creation gathers before its final expression in Malkuth.

As a double letter, *gimel*'s attributes are wisdom and folly, for knowledge the rational mind can't express may indeed appear as madness.

RIDER-WAITE-SMITH SYMBOLISM

The High Priestess (*Rider-Waite-Smith Tarot*)

The "queen of the borrowed light" abounds with Tree of Life references: the ten pomegranates depicted (and partly obscured) on the veil, the crown (Kether), the cross (Tiphareth, associated with solar deities and the son), the moon (Yesod), the gray Pillar of Force and the black Pillar of Form.[8] Her hidden "Torah" scroll peeks out from the position of Hod/Mercury.

Yet each of these symbols holds other meanings as well. The crown might be a triple lunar crown evoking Hekate the maiden/mother/crone. It might symbolize the "sun and moon conjoined," or the solar disk/cow horns crown of Hathor. The pomegranates suggest the myth of Persephone and Demeter, reminding us that the High Priestess is a sacred intermediary between realms separated by the veil. The veil itself may separate the unconscious and conscious minds, the living from the dead, the supernal realm from the mundane.

---

8. Waite, *Pictorial Key*, 79.

The Priestess's veil and book, inherited from the early woodcut images, would go
on to appear in all Priestess cards up to the present day. (*Ancient Italian Tarot*)

The letters "B" and "J" refer to Boaz ("in his strength") and Jakin ("he establishes"),
the pillars of Solomon's temple (though they were thought to be made of brass). Their
dynamic, polar form contrasts with the flat gray of the Hierophant's pillars—direct
versus apostolic transmission.

The Priestess's blue robes also evoke the Stella Maris, the Virgin Mary as "Star of
the Sea." As her robe dissolves into water, so water takes on form while remaining
itself—a concept which correlates with virginity or purity.

Taken together, this constellation of lunar symbols conveys secrecy, divine knowledge, faith, divination, and implicit communication between the seen and unseen
parts of a whole.

THOTH SYMBOLISM

Astral warps and wefts swirl, shimmer, and vibrate, veiling her in bluish light and
turning the body of the enthroned Priestess into a radiant cup. Lit by the white brilliance of Kether, the luminous veil conceals by its very brilliance. It separates the conscious from the unconscious: the known from the secret. Crowley calls this veil of
light the "menstruum of manifestation" and the possibility of form that arises from

the third veil of the original nothing behind her.[9] Beneath her, nascent forms are being created in the whorls of nature's seedpods, flowers, and crystals.

As the embodiment of the Middle Pillar, she sits between silver pillars rayed sky blue. Her headdress of disk and crescent and her throne are emblems of Isis. Seven more crescents radiate beneath it, the seven invoking Venus, whose path crosses hers horizontally, for she is both virgin and Eternal Mother. It brings the crescents on her crown to eight, the full division of phases of the moon. On her lap rests a bow that is also the lyre of Artemis. Its three strings recall the threefold goddess and the great mother Binah. The arrow across it, as well as the rainbow light within the cup, connects her to the Temperance/Art card, the continuation beyond her path that leads down to the lunar sephira of Yesod.

Beneath her feet is an inverted crescent. This brings the total crescents in the image to nine, a lunar number. It also mirrors the inverted crescent that shines down upon the moon card. Yet she is firmly above it, signifying her mastery of the unconscious realms.

At the bottom of the card is the camel of *gimel*, showing her nature as a vehicle across the abyss, the place of esoteric knowledge.

RELATED CARDS

The Priestess card, alone among trumps, has had the same astrological correspondence—the moon—across all tarot traditions since esoteric tarot's beginnings in the eighteenth century. The moon rules only one sign, Cancer, corresponding to the Chariot (she is exalted in Taurus/the Hierophant). The Chariot represents the moon's swift orbital speed and heavenly passage: its emotional fluidity; its protective, covert nature; and its role as bearer of news.

The moon rules five of the thirty-six decans. As 6 of Pentacles, or "Lord of Success" (Taurus II), she is exalted and watches over the increase of fortunes and opportunity. As 4 of Cups, or "Lord of Luxury" (Cancer III), she rules the home, tides, and the forming and breaking of habits. As 2 of Swords, or "Lord of Peace" (Libra I), she rules non-ordinary states of consciousness, crossroads, and insights. As 9 of Wands,

---

9. Crowley, *Book of Thoth*, 73.

or "Lord of Strength" (Sagittarius II), she rules natural cycles and memory. As 7 of Swords, or "Lord of Futility" (Aquarius III), she rules illusions, travel, and reckless acts. In the 2, 3, and 4 of Cups (all Cancer cards), the Priestess expresses the hidden bonds of affection between individuals and the mysteries of maternity and sisterhood.

The Priestess corresponds to the number two. Lust (in the Thoth deck) and Justice (in the Waite deck) also enumerate to two (11; 1 + 1 = 2), as does the Judgement/Aeon card (20; 2 + 0 = 2). All portray varying relationships to the Other.

Finally, the Priestess connects with the two other cards of the Middle Path: Temperance/Art and the Universe/World.

ADVANCED CONCEPTS FOR FURTHER EXPLORATION

- The Middle Pillar ritual, an exercise for moving currents of energy through the chakras or psychic centers of the body through a visualization of ascending and descending light

- The relationship between the Priestess, the other Middle Pillar paths, and the paths that form the "bow" of QShTh—קשת

- The "rending of the veil" ritual of ceremonial magic, which lifts the Magician to a higher state of consciousness

- The evolution of Priestess to Empress as she crosses the Empress's path between the supernals

- The seven hermetic principles or truths: mentalism, correspondence, vibration, polarity, rhythm, cause and effect, and gender

- Magical Weapon: Bow and Arrow

- Magical Power: The White Tincture, Clairvoyance, Divination by Dreams

THE EMPRESS
The Daughter of the Mighty Ones

Card Number: III

Planet and Dignities: ♀ Venus: rules Taurus and Libra, exalted Pisces; Day of the week: Friday

Hebrew Letter: ד, *daleth*

Hebrew Letter Meaning: Double letter: Door (wisdom—folly); Value: 4

Path 14: Chokmah (2, Wisdom—Zodiac) to Binah (3, Understanding—Saturn)

Color Scales in the Four Worlds: Emerald green. Sky blue. Spring green. Bright rose, rayed pale green

Themes and Keywords: Fertility. Creativity. Maternity. Love. Sensuality. Beauty and attraction. Wife or mother. Receptiveness. The womb. Life and death. Fructification. Love and war goddesses, also the goddess. Mother Nature.

ASTROLOGY/ELEMENT

Other than the sun and moon, Venus is the brightest object in our sky. Trailing the sunset, she is the evening star (Hesperus); preceding sunrise, the morning star (Lucifer).

Like Inanna of the seven veils, she reveals herself to us in phases. The planet is mysteriously veiled by clouds—and incredibly hot!

Venus signifies female attributes, beauty, and how we attract and go about getting what we desire. Her glyph suggests a figure with welcoming arms, and is comprised of the circle of Spirit over the cross of matter. It looks like the Egyptian ankh, meaning "life." Life emanates from nature. The appetite of life for procreation is born from humankind (the cross) seeking completion (the circle). The glyph is the only one which connects all the sephiroth of the Tree of Life.

The planet Venus symbolizes all we find worthy of desire—usually love and money! Venus loves luxury, pleasure, and relationships of all kinds. She rules two signs: airy Libra by day and earthy Taurus by night. Libra, the seventh sign, represents beauty, harmony, balance, and marriage; Taurus, the second sign, is concerned with the comforts, pleasures, and necessities of life. As the lesser benefic, Venus bestows gifts. Her earthy presents are sensuality, refined taste, and resources: favors that grant prosperity. Her airy presents deal with charm, culture, physical symmetry and beauty, diplomacy, discernment, and popularity. In her fullness she represents all that is creative, whether that involves nurturing children, making music, or the creative arts. Her exaltation in Pisces shows that it is through compassion that she best expresses her ideal of love as sacrifice.

MYTHOLOGY/ALCHEMY

The Empress is the representation of alchemical salt. In alchemy salt is the body and base matter. It is what remains after the process of combustion, the substance that survives death and generates new life. Salt is an enigma; it both preserves and corrodes just as Venus is described by the alchemists as "external splendor and internal corruption." Salt dries things out yet is harvested from the waters of the sea.

Heavenly Aphrodite, born from sea foam, is the "Amorous One," "Mother of Passion and Peace," and the "Giver of Life." Portrayed as an infinitely desirable woman, her domain is that of love, pleasure, and procreation. We must never forget though that her favorite lover was Ares, god of war, and that her predecessor, Astarte, was both a fertility and a war goddess.

Like the Priestess, the Empress is associated with Hathor. She is also associated with Isis, in her role as Queen of Heaven, wife of Osiris, and mother of Horus. Yet Crowley reminds us, "not only Isis, but Nephthys."[10] Nephthys was the sister of Isis, nursemaid of Horus, and bride of warlike Set. She was called "Lady of the Enclosure," representing the gateway much like the Empress is often referred to as the "Gate of Heaven." Where Isis guides the passage of birth, Nephthys guides passage through the gate of death, for one is inherent in the other.

Demeter (Ceres), called "She of the Grain," is a goddess of agriculture and maternal relationships. The name Ceres comes from roots meaning "to feed" and "to grow." The suffix -meter in the name Demeter refers to the word mother. The prefix de- is an old name for a chthonic earth goddess; thus, she is the "Mother Earth." Her most famous tale involves her mourning the abduction of her daughter Persephone, causing the earth to wither in winter. Don't mess with Mother Nature!

THE EMPRESS
THE DOOR

A Demeter figure wears the zodiacal crown (Chokmah) next to a door (*daleth*) opening seven (Venus) visible levels over the sea of Binah. (*Pharos Tarot*)

---

10. Crowley, *Book of Thoth*, 77.

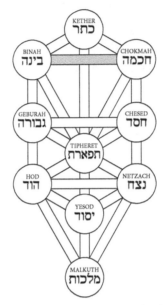

III (3). The Empress. Tree of Life.

The path of the Empress runs between Chokmah on the Pillar of Force and Binah on the Pillar of Form. The first of three horizontal paths, it runs above the abyss of Da'ath and emphasizes the relationship between the three supernals.[11] If Kether is the dimensionless point, Chokmah is a line and Binah a plane. If Kether is consciousness erupting and Chokmah the spark of vision, Binah is the spark received and understood. If Kether is the Self and Chokmah the Other, Binah is the desire to connect the two. Lights, camera, action!

The Empress corresponds to Hebrew letter ד *daleth*, meaning door. As the universal mother, she is the portal through which everything is born. In the concentric model of the universe embraced by classical esotericists, the realm of the stars exists outside the orbit of the outermost "sphere," Saturn. In Qabalah, Chokmah corresponds to the zodiac and Binah to slow, heavy Saturn (who is both Father Time and eternal mother). Thus, the Empress connects the celestial clockwork to our earthly concept of time. She connects the archetypal life force to our natural cycles and seasons.

---

11. Her Hermetic title, "Daughter of the Mighty Ones," refers to her position at the base of the supernals.

This Empress's shield opens like a door (*daleth*), showing a magnified diagram of her heart chambers as a beehive full of honey: the bees of Venus fly out in a golden spiral ratio. (*Tabula Mundi Tarot*)

The opposing attributes of double letter *daleth* are peace and war, reminding us that goddesses of creation are also goddesses of destruction. Shakti, the feminine energy of the cosmos, releases even as it gives form. The door leads to darkness in one direction and light in the other; one cannot enter one room without exiting another.

RIDER-WAITE-SMITH SYMBOLISM

The Empress (*Rider-Waite-Smith Tarot*)

Whilst some planetary correspondences are subtle in this deck, the Empress's could not be more obvious: an unambiguous glyph of Venus, colored in with Venus's green hue, on the heart-shaped stone by her throne. The stone itself recalls older tarot imagery, where the Emperor and Empress were worldly rulers with heraldic shields. But this Empress is the maternal queen of love and life herself; Venus as creatrix rather than consort. Her enthroned figure is curved, possibly pregnant; her setting is lush—a stark contrast to the Emperor's dry mountains. The globe on her scepter is the world itself.

Ripe wheat stalks suggest the Eleusinian mysteries of Demeter (which promised its initiates eternal renewal), as do the pomegranates on her dress, which mingle red and white, passion and purity. By a waterfall, deciduous and evergreen trees rise—possibly arborvitae or cypresses, for Aphrodite's home isle of Cyprus; the goddess is both eternal and cyclical. Perhaps the water's source is Eden itself.

The Empress's pearls recall the birth of Venus from sea foam, off the shore of Paphos in Cyprus. Her diadem of twelve stars refers to the twelve months or zodiacal signs, but it is also marks her as the "woman clothed with the sun, with the moon under her feet, and on her head a crown of twelve stars"—almost a composite of the Priestess and Empress (and the Thoth Lust) figures, and certainly a way of invoking the sacred feminine.[12] Hewn stone, textiles, and natural forms combine, reminding us that humanity's arts are her children too.

THOTH SYMBOLISM

The figure in the Thoth card represents the universal woman, as the "many-throned, many-minded, many-wiled daughter of Zeus."[13] The arch above her refers to her letter *daleth*, meaning "door," and her role as the gate of heaven. Her esoteric title "Daughter of the Mighty Ones" may refer to the supernal parents she connects. She sits between crescents that could be the phases of Venus or the moon. She faces the one waxing (Northern Hemisphere), which signifies growth and increase.

Her posture creates the glyph of salt, suggesting amniotic fluid, and she holds her left arm in the gesture known as *Mater Triumphans* (Isis holding the infant Horus).

---

12. Rev. 12:1 (Authorized King James Version).

13. Crowley, *Book of Thoth*, 75.

In her right hand is the wand of Isis, whose lotus is a metaphor for the Grail, as it sits in water yet opens to the sun. Clothed in emerald green and rose, she sits among twisting blue shapes, symbolic of her birth from water. The dove and sparrow, birds of Aphrodite, correspond to love and promiscuity. Her tunic is embroidered with bees: industrious female workers and honey gatherers. Dominoes on her sleeves symbolize her domestic nature and are surrounded by the spirals of natural growth. She wears the girdle of Venus inscribed with the twelve zodiacal signs.

The tapestry beneath her is embroidered with royal fleur-de-lis and fishes; Crowley says they are adoring the "secret rose" at the base of her throne. Her shield bears the white eagle, a symbol of passive femininity (salt): matter awaiting activation by sulfur. At her side, a pelican feeds her young with the blood of her breast. The great mother gives an inheritance and sacrifice of blood that raises the daughter to her throne.

RELATED CARDS

The Empress corresponds to Venus, presiding over the Hierophant (Taurus) and Justice/Adjustment (Libra). These bookend the growing season in the Northern Hemisphere; the Empress presides over both spring fertility and fall harvest. In the Hierophant, we see her consecrating the union of male and female, earthly and divine, in the service of procreation. In the Justice/Adjustment card, we see her as the great equilibrator, balancing beginnings and endings to maintain the earth's rhythm, creating beauty and equal partnerships.

Venus rules five minor arcana: As 4 of Wands, or "Lord of Completion" (Aries III), she is in detriment, ruling celebrations (especially weddings) and the arts of peace. As 2 of Cups, or "Lord of Love" (Cancer I), she rules attraction, respect, affection, and new relationships. As 9 of Pentacles, or "Lord of Gain" (Virgo II), she rules adornment and gracious living and, as she is in fall, is prone to perfectionism. As the 7 of Cups, or "Lord of Debauch" (Scorpio III), she confers magnetic, visionary artistry, but is prone to addiction and escapism as she is in detriment. As the 5 of Swords, or "Lord of Defeat" (Aquarius I), she rules offbeat sensibilities. In all cases she has the power to cast glamors of varying duration and efficacy. In the 5, 6, and 7 of Pentacles (all Taurus cards), she expresses the miraculous quickening of life and those forces which imperil it. In the 2, 3, and 4 of Swords (all Libra cards), she weighs, judges, and balances the mind to create harmonious relationships.

Three is the Empress's number. Also enumerating to three by reduction are the Hanged Man (12; 1 + 2 = 3) and the World or Universe (21; 2 + 1 = 3).

Venus's exaltation is at 27° Pisces, giving her a special connection with the Moon (Pisces) as well.

ADVANCED CONCEPTS FOR FURTHER EXPLORATION

- The Empress as the gate of heaven or the portal of both birth and death, and her relationship as mother to the daughter of the World/Universe maiden of Malkuth, whose epithets also include various "gates"

- Alchemical salt as the substance of the body, the receptive principle, and the process of dissolution, purification, and recrystalization

- The alchemical concepts of the white queen as the passive or fixed principle and the realm of feelings; the white eagle as "gluten" and vessel of first matter; the lunar white work of purification of the subconscious; and the clarifiying process of *Albedo*

- The relationship between the Empress and the other horizontal paths on the Tree of Life

- Magical Weapon: The Girdle

- Magical Power: Love-Philtres

THE EMPEROR
Son of the Morning, Chief Among the Mighty

Card Number: IV

Sign and Dignities: ♈ Aries, cardinal fire. Ruler Mars, sun exalted; Motto: "I am"

Hebrew Letter: ה, *heh* (RWS); צ, *tzaddi* (Thoth)

Hebrew Letter Meaning: Simple letter *heh*: Window (Sight); Value: 5; Simple letter *tzaddi*: Fish Hook (Imagination); Value: 90

Path 15 (RWS): Chokmah (2, Wisdom—Zodiac) to Tiphareth (6, Beauty—Sun)

Path 28 (Thoth): Netzach (7, Victory—Venus) to Yesod (9, Foundation—Moon)

Color Scales in the Four Worlds: Scarlet. Red. Brilliant flame. Glowing red

Themes and Keywords: Dominion. Rulership/kingship. Structure. Government. Paternity. Selfhood. Sight and vision. Military might. Spring/solar force. The ram. The head. Being first. Competition. Ruthlessness.

ASTROLOGY/ELEMENT

The first of the zodiacal trumps corresponds to the first sign, Aries the ram. Aries is the infant newly born and declaring, "I am." It is a cardinal fire sign, which also emphasizes the idea of beginnings and being first. It's the first sign of spring, starting at the vernal equinox in the Northern Hemisphere. In the body, Aries rules the head and facial features, the brain, and the muscular system. The glyph of Aries looks like the head and horns of a head-butting ram—or the hard nose and drawn eyebrows on a head.

Aries first seeks selfhood. Aries is aware of its individuality and sometimes unaware of the rest of the world. It's the sign of pioneers, leaders, innovators, warriors, and athletes. Aries is the first inrush of life energy manifesting as will. It's the first emanation: the ego consciousness that arises from the collective unconscious of the end of the zodiac (Pisces). It's an adolescent energy, bursting with life force yet inexperienced, like a newly emerged seed striving to grow and eventually finding the structure within form.

Aries is ambitious in the sense that it pursues original yet practical undertakings. It has tremendous willpower and little patience for anything that gets in its way. Aries is ruled by Mars, so all things penetrating, courageous, motivating, domineering, and martial in nature apply. The sun is exalted in Aries, showing the idea of energy combined with authority and a source of vitality, individuality, egocentricity, paternity, and the animating forces of life.

THE EMPEROR

Before a wall of bricks in the Fibonacci sequence, the Emperor contemplates
a bee skep and the structure of the hive, as opposed to the wildness of
the bees and nature seen in the Empress. (*Tabula Mundi Tarot*)

MYTHOLOGY/ALCHEMY

One's first thought for a god of Aries might well be the Greek war god Ares. Yet the nature of ravaging Ares is more suited to the trump of Mars, the Tower. The Emperor is more like the Roman god Mars, who was considered a positive force as a military strategist for the ultimate purpose of peace, a protector of the realm, a guardian of agriculture, and a god of spring.

Athena (Minerva), though female, fits the archetype of Aries well. Goddess of wisdom, she was the daughter of Zeus, springing forth from his head fully matured and armored with helm and spear. She is the goddess of battlefield strategy but had no sympathy with Ares's love of bloodshed—hers was a skill of defense. She is the patron goddess of all heroic quests and endeavors, as well as skilled in crafts like weaving, agricultural planning, and navigation.

Plato identified Athena with Neith, Egyptian goddess of war and hunting, a fierce deity said to make the weapons of warriors and to guard the bodies of the fallen. Neith was also said to be the first and prime creator, fashioning the entire universe and governing its functions. She was said to be both the primeval creator and the re-creator who birthed the sun daily. She is portrayed carrying the *was*-sceptre of rulership and power and the ankh of life. Her crown bore her emblem of a shield with crossed arrows. The Emperor is the alchemical trump associated with the principle of sulfur, the hot and active male principle. Sulfur creates change, and is the actuating principle of life. Sulfur was considered the "first matter," the instigating cause, and that which (like the soul) gave each thing an individual signature.

The number four appears as a square surmounting the throne and in its quadrangular pedestal base. The shield is a holdover from the early Marseille decks, where matching shields typically appear on the Emperor and Empress cards. (*Mystical Tarot*)

QABALAH—PATH 15 OR PATH 28

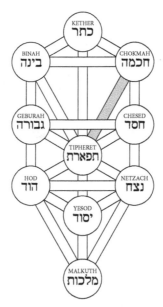

IV (4). The Emperor. Tree of Life. Golden Dawn path attribution.

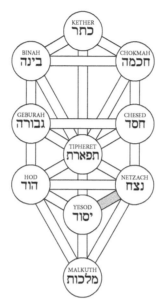

IV (4). The Emperor. Tree of Life. Thoth path attribution.

As a zodiacal sign-based major, the Emperor is associated with one of the single Hebrew letters, but which one it is depends on your tradition. The Golden Dawn originally assigned the letter ה *heh* to the Emperor. *Heh* means window, following the door of ד, *daleth*, and corresponds to sight, the dominant sense of the Emperor's eagle. This placement, path fifteen, positions the masculine Emperor between Chokmah and Tiphareth, the father and the son (or their astrological equivalents, Jupiter and the Sun). It also initiates the orderly descent of the numbered majors and zodiacal signs down the Tree of Life.

As *heh*, or "window," with the attribute of sight, we can think of the Emperor as imposing a structure or frame around his world. The Emperor's vision projects his will onto his surroundings.

In 1904, while writing the *Book of the Law*, Aleister Crowley's spiritual guide, Aiwass, declared that "*Tzaddi* is not the Star." This led Crowley to switch the Hebrew letter attributions of the Emperor and the Star. Thus the Emperor's letter attribution becomes צ *tzaddi*, meaning "fishhook" and corresponding to the attribute of imagination. This balances Crowley's numerical switch of eight and eleven, Strength and Adjustment/Justice. With ה now attributed to the feminine Star, the divine name, יהוה,

now has two feminine (primal and final *heh*) and two masculine parts (*yod*, the Hermit, and *vav*, the Hierophant). It also places the Emperor lower on the Tree, on path twenty-eight between Netzach and Yesod, the sephiroth of Venus and the moon.

As *tzaddi*, or "hook," with the attribute of imagination, we can think of the Emperor as penetrating fertile oceans, inseminating them with his will to produce teeming life.

RIDER-WAITE-SMITH SYMBOLISM

The Emperor (*Rider-Waite-Smith Tarot*)

Pamela Colman Smith's glaring, white-bearded Emperor presents a stark contrast to the relaxed and gracious Empress who precedes him. While she sits in a lush paradise, he oversees a barren mountain world. On his foursquare throne of hewn rock, we see four ram heads, a reference to the rock-climbing, rutting symbol of Aries. (There may be a fifth ram head hidden in the shoulder folds of the Emperor's robe.) Whereas the Empress wears a diadem of stars, the Emperor's crown is manmade, and at its peak a tiny glyph of Aries perches. The ram's head-butting, combative ways echo those of Mars, who rules the head, but they also allude to the kingly Egyptian god Amun-Ra. Waite suggests the Emperor may be described as "will in its embodied form," as well as "the lordship of thought."

The Emperor wears red, the color of Mars, passion, and carnality; beneath his robes he wears a soldier's armor, signifying his rigor and determination. While in the Thoth and Marseille tarots, the Emperor sits with one leg crossed over the other, both of the

Waite-Smith Emperor's feet rest on the ground, ready for him to spring up for action as needed. In one hand he holds the crux ansata (a Christian, stylized version of the ankh), a symbol of life and his dominion over it; in the other he holds a golden orb (the holy hand grenade). Similarly, the figure in the astrologically linked 2 of Wands holds a globe in hand—a resemblance which makes that card a "little Emperor" of sorts.

THOTH SYMBOLISM

A fiery vision in all the colors of flame, the Thoth Emperor sits upon his ram-headed throne, gazing toward the Empress. He wears an imperial crown and regalia, and holds in his hand a ram-headed scepter, a symbol of rulership. His left hand bears a globe topped with a Maltese cross, the orb of his world dominion and establishment of government. His tunic, like that of the Empress, is adorned with the bees of industry. The fleur-de-lis at his feet echoes the idea of monarchy. The royal emblem was postulated to be derived from not only a flower, but also the shape of a bee, and possibly from the angon, called "the sting," a Frankish throwing spear.

His posture, with crossed leg, and triangular arms, forms the glyph of alchemical sulfur, the active and fertilizing counterpart to the Empress's passive salt. His shield with the alchemical red eagle, as the red tincture and gold, is also in complement to hers with the white eagle, symbolizing the white tincture and silver.

The Emperor sits between twinned suns, each with sixteen points. Sixteen calls to mind the Tower—for Mars's rulership of Aries—but is also the sixteen points of a compass rose, showing his global rule in all directions. Sixteen is also the atomic number of sulfur.

By his side are the couchant lamb and flag, which may refer to the Lamb of God: the ego of man crucified. It puts forth the idea of the wild ram supposedly tamed by the structures of good government.

RELATED CARDS

The Emperor, as the card of Aries, is the first of our zodiacal majors. The ruler of Aries is Mars, whose card is the Tower; the other Mars-ruled sign, Scorpio, corresponds to the Death card. In a sense, the Emperor and Death show two sides of the war god: his power and his destructiveness. (With a card number of thirteen, Death also reduces to four, the number of the Emperor.) The Emperor has the authority to channel the Tower's overwhelming force, but he is responsible for its inevitable fallout—Death—as well.

Each zodiacal major corresponds to three decanic minors. In the case of the Emperor, these are the 2 of Wands (*Dominion*—Mars ruling Aries I), the 3 of Wands (*Virtue*—sun ruling Aries II), and the 4 of Wands (*Completion*—Venus ruling Aries III). Here we see the great warrior turned king: bent first on conquest, he next embraces rulership for the common good, and at last celebrates the arts of peace. He is not only a conqueror, but a king and consort as well. Of these three cards, the 2 of Wands is particularly potent, bringing together the Emperor's sign with its ruler, the Tower.

Among the court cards, the Queen of Wands is the principal expression of Aries, as she commands the first two decans (the final decan belongs to the Prince of Disks/ Knight of Pentacles). The most outgoing of the four queens, she embodies some of the Emperor's leadership qualities, his charismatic hold over the hearts of men.

Finally, there's also an oblique argument that the Emperor connects to the Fool, who is in a sense both first and last: his number zero can also be numbered as twenty-two, which reduces to four, the Emperor's number.

ADVANCED CONCEPTS FOR FURTHER EXPLORATION

- Alchemical sulfur, the animating principle, and how it contrasts from and interacts with the alchemical salt of the Empress

- The alchemical concepts of the red king as thought and planning, the active or cardinal principle; the red lion as the fiery kundalini of sexual alchemy; and the process of *Rubedo*, or the solar red work of attaining individuation

- The demiurge as the Great Architect of the Universe as expressed in Freemasonry, Rosicruscianism, and many worldwide theologies

- The symbolism of the cubic stone throne of the Emperor, the fourfold name, and the Cubic Stone of Yesod

- The esoteric title "Son of the Morning" as an epithet of both Lucifer and Jesus, and the concept of the "Sun behind the Sun"

- The connection between the Emperor and the card of the opposite path on the Tree of Life (in RWS, the Lovers; in Thoth, the Sun)

- Magical Weapon: The Horns, Energy, The Burin

- Magical Power: Power of Consecrating Things

THE HIEROPHANT
The Magus of the Eternal

Card Number: V

Sign and Dignities: ♉ Taurus, fixed earth. Ruler Venus, moon exalted; Motto: "I have"

Hebrew Letter: ו, *vav*

Hebrew Letter Meaning: Simple letter *vav*: Nail (Hearing); Value: 6

Path 16: Chokmah (2, Wisdom—Zodiac) to Chesed (4, Mercy—Jupiter)

Color Scales in the Four Worlds: Red orange. Deep indigo. Deep, warm olive. Rich brown

Themes and Keywords: Divine instruction. Initiation. Connecting heaven and Earth. God and man. Teaching. Speaking and listening. Holding the keys. Insides and outsides. Exoteric. Threshold between realms. Bridge-making. Priesthood as mediation. Institutional structures—church and school.

ASTROLOGY/ELEMENT

Behind the initiatory energy of spring comes the planting and the plow, with our second sign Taurus, the bull. The constellation Taurus shows the front end of the bull only and is presumably followed by a plow. As a fixed earth sign, middle of the spring triad, it shows the stable, fertile part of the season. Like all fixed signs, it is connected with a royal watcher star, Aldebaran, which means "the follower (of the Pleiades)." The Pleiades, a star cluster of seven sisters (a reference to Venus, Taurus's ruler) is a star cluster in the bull constellation, associated with reaping when it rises in the east and sowing when it sets in the west. Taurus is also home to the cluster of the Hyades, or seven daughters of Atlas. Aldebaran is the star of the "eye of the bull," and the Royal Watcher of the East, bearer of the power "to keep silence." Royal stars confer glory if their nemesis is overcome. Aldebaran's challenge is to avoid greed and cultivate integrity, especially in business.

The glyph of Taurus looks like the head and horns of a bull. The moon is exalted in Taurus and the glyph shows the circle of the full moon and the crescent of the new moon, showing the sign's fecundity.

The motto of Taurus is "I have" and has an association with resources and materiality, but also sacred bonding with the land. The bull is a symbol of strength and fertility. Bull worship was significant in Egypt, as the prime god Osiris was sometimes depicted with a bull's head, and the priests carefully selected living bulls to represent the god on earth.

MYTHOLOGY/ALCHEMY

The word *hierophant* is defined as an interpreter and priest of arcane and sacred knowledge, especially pertaining to the priest of the Eleusinian mysteries. Taurus is ruled by Venus (Demeter), and the Eleusinian mysteries were initiation rites of worship and sacrifice, the famous secret spring rites of the agrarian cult of Demeter and Persephone in ancient Greece. The rites were in a threefold cycle, which represented Persephone's abduction: the descent, the search, and her ascent and reunion with her mother.

The mysteries involved visions and explorations of the state of the afterlife, and they are postulated to be induced through the use of psychedelic drugs, with the priest handing out the entheogens and interpreting the visions. The priest filled two vessels, pouring one toward the east and one toward the west, as the worshipers looked to sky and earth and shouted, "Rain and conceive!" In the subsequent ritual of the divine child, a child was initiated from the divine hearth fire, and it was proclaimed that *Potnia* ("Mistress"; a Greek term of honor used to address revered females and goddesses) had born a great son. At the high point of the ritual, an ear of grain was cut in silence.

The mysteries were intended to elevate man from the mundane realm to that of godhood by linking him with divinity and conferring immortal status. Some scholars also link the mysteries to a Minoan cult—a reference to the mythical King Minos, of the labyrinth and Minotaur story. In the legend, King Minos's Queen Pasiphaë, a sister of Circe and daughter of Helios who was worshiped as an oracle and diviner and practitioner of the magical arts, was cursed by Poseidon to love a white bull and thus conceived the half-man, half-bull Minotaur.

QABALAH—PATH 16

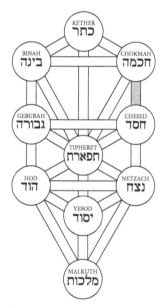

V (5). The Hierophant. Tree of Life.

The Hierophant's path is the first to descend down the masculine Pillar of Force on the Tree of Life. It runs between Chokmah, the supernal father beyond mortal comprehension, and Chesed, the divine father figure addressed in prayer. Chokmah corresponds to the zodiac, Chesed to expansive Jupiter. Thus the Hierophant draws down the influence of the heavens into our known world.[14] Chokmah directs the ceaseless outflow of energy from Kether (the "Macroprosopus"). But Chesed serves as the wellspring of the next six lower sephiroth or "Microprosopus"), making it the "Kether of the lower world."

The Hierophant's Hebrew letter is the phallic ו *vav*, meaning "nail" as well as the conjunction "and." Both join two naturally separate things. The Hierophant is a papal figure, a pontifex ("bridge-maker"), and his role is apostolic: to regulate and embody the connection between the divine and the human, heaven and Earth. Whereas the path of the High Priestess directly connects the two, the Hierophant's provides a mediating structure—organized faith itself. The Chariot, its opposite on the Tree, brings the Grail waters down one pillar; the Hierophant conveys the spark of divinity down the other.

THE HIEROPHANT
THE STANCHION
ו   ♉

This Priest-Prince holds a nail scepter (*vav*) between pillars that have combined with the Kerubic beasts as lamassu sphinxes. (*Pharos Tarot*)

---

14. The Hierophant's Hermetic title is "Magus of the Eternal Gods," as opposed to the Magician's, "Magus of Power."

We sometimes speak of the four letters of tetragrammaton, יהוה, as father-mother-son-daughter. As the third letter, *vav* refers to the son, whose particular place on the Tree of Life lies in Tiphareth, the sixth sephira. Thus we see references to the numbers five and six (human and divine) throughout the Hierophant's imagery. As a single letter, *vav*'s attribute is hearing; this relates to Taurus's rulership of the neck and throat, where the voice dwells.

RIDER-WAITE-SMITH SYMBOLISM

The Hierophant (*Rider-Waite-Smith Tarot*)

The Hierophant teems with church iconography. Gray stone pillars and throne evoke the fixed-earth qualities of Taurus; the name of St. Peter, the original hierophant, means "rock." Contrast these with the dark and light pillars of the Priestess—while she stands for concealed, private insight, he stands for mediated grace, faith rendered accessible. Beneath his feet are the "keys of heaven," emphasizing his role as gate-keeper. His gesture of papal benediction—two fingers up, two down—may indicate "revealed" versus "secret"; as above, so below. (The cover of Éliphas Lévi's *Transcendental Magic: Its Doctrine and Ritual*, a core text influencing tarot, shows a similar hand casting a demonic shadow.) This gesture can also be seen in the 10 of Swords.

THE HIEROPHANT

In this stripped-down Hierophant, the crossed keys and iconic
hand gesture (borrowed from the Waite-Smith deck) subtly
suggest the human-divine conjunction. (*Linestrider Tarot*)

Trinities are everywhere: the triple papal cross, the three-tiered papal tiara (worn by popes until the mid-twentieth century), three crosses on his robe, three human figures. These evoke Father, Son, and Holy Spirit—as well as Chokmah, Chesed, and the path between them. A curious glyph tops the crown's peak: is it three nails (letter *vav*, which both resembles and means "nail")?

The Hierophant's garments echo the Magician's: white alb covered by a red chasuble. His acolytes wear contrasting robes: roses on the left, lilies on the right. As elsewhere, roses and red represent life force and passion (and perhaps Venus, ruler of Taurus); lilies and white represent Spirit and purity of intention. While the Magician's flowers mingle and his robe falls open to reveal his tunic, the Hierophant's remain separate or covered.

THOTH SYMBOLISM

In one of the most enigmatic cards of the deck, a bearded Babylonian priest-prince invokes the magical images of Chokmah—a bearded man—and Chesed—a mighty king crowned and enthroned.

The Hierophant is the initiator who instructs the candidates in the mysteries from the eastern throne. Wearing the red crown of Osiris, he makes a left-handed gesture of benediction. He holds a trefoil scepter, perhaps referring to the Aeons of Isis, Osiris, and Horus—or the three-fold parts of the Eleusinian mysteries.

Two of the Kerubic beasts (angel and eagle) have switched positions, thanks to a vision Crowley received in the twenty-third Enochian Aethyr. The beasts appear as hollow-eyed masks, waiting for the initiated to activate them.

Behind the Hierophant is a rose oriel window for the five-pointed star of Venus's orbit, affixed by nine nails through a serpent, at whose tail is the descending dove of Venus: Spirit brought forth into matter. His throne is an elephant and bull. At his feet a woman—"girt with a sword"—signifies both Ma'at, the "woman satisfied" of the Adjustment trump who is truth personified, and Isis, spouse of Osiris.[15] She also carries a lunar crescent shape for Taurus's exaltation: the scythe for the Eleusinian mysteries when the grain is cut in silence, or the bow of huntress Artemis.[16]

At his heart is the child Horus in a pentagram within an inverted pentagram within a hexagram—the binding of microcosm and macrocosm. On his foot, he wears the ankh sandal strap, for after the Hierophant achieves the fourth power of the sphinx, "to keep silent," he can then access the fifth, "to go," in the way of gods.

RELATED CARDS

The Hierophant, as Taurus, expresses bull- or ox-like qualities: solidity, persistence, generative power. It may at first be difficult to see the influence of Taurus's ruler, Venus, in the Hierophant's liturgical rigor. But the sacramental union of human and divine is code for other things: lock and key, masculine and feminine, lingam and yoni. This sexual metaphor reveals the Hierophant's connection to other cards: the Art/Temperance card, number fourteen, reduces numerically to five and is the consummation of the alchemical marriage seen in the Lovers. Like the Hierophant, it strongly emphasizes the union of opposites.

Venus's card is the Empress; her other sign, Libra, corresponds to Justice/Adjustment. The Empress imagery explicitly denotes fertility (and as Taurus, the Hierophant rules over spring planting in the Northern Hemisphere). Justice/Adjustment's balances imply an awareness of the Other, as well as timing and seasonal equilibrium.

---

15. Ma'at is also the representative of the next Thelemic Aeon, approximately 2,000 years hence.

16. Artemis is another reference to the moon (Priestess), exalted in Taurus.

The Hierophant corresponds to three decanic minors: the 5 of Pentacles (*Worry*—Mercury ruling Taurus I), the 6 of Pentacles (*Success*—the Moon ruling Taurus II), and the 7 of Pentacles (*Failure*—Saturn ruling Taurus III). This sequence pivots on the crucial number six, where life germinates, opportunities arise, and businesses thrive. Before success comes anticipation, belief, and contingency planning; afterwards, evaluation and clear-eyed reassessment. All three speak to spiritual faith and doubt as well as practical matters.

Among court cards, the Prince of Disks/Knight of Pentacles commands the first two decans (the final decan of Taurus belongs to the King/Knight of Swords). His steady, careful stewardship exemplifies the "worry" that leads to "success."

ADVANCED CONCEPTS FOR FURTHER EXPLORATION

- *Vav* as the son connecting the mother of primal *heh* and daughter of final *heh* in the fourfold divine name YHVH

- Union with the Holy Guardian Angel

- The fourth elemental power of the sphinx, "to keep silent," and how it precedes and makes possible the fifth power, where man becomes like deity

- Osiris as *Asar-un-Nefer*, the perfected man who has triumphed over the elements

- Comparison of the Hierophant on the Pillar of Force with the opposite path of the Chariot on the Pillar of Form

- Magical Weapon: The Labor of Preparation

- Magical Power: The Secret of Physical Strength

THE LOVERS
The Children of the Voice,
The Oracle of the Mighty Gods

Card Number: VI

Sign and Dignities: ♊ Gemini, mutable air. Ruler Mercury, Dragon's Head (North Node) exaltation; Motto: "I think"

Hebrew Letter: ז, *zayin*

Hebrew Letter Meaning: Simple letter *zayin*: Sword (Smell); Value: 7

Path 17: Binah (3, Understanding—Saturn) to Tiphareth (6, Beauty—Sun)

Color Scales in the Four Worlds: Orange. Pale mauve. New yellow leather. Reddish gray, inclined to mauve

Themes and Keywords: Analysis. Division and union. Choice. Choosing one's fate. Reception of inspiration. The Emperor and Empress. The Other. Contradiction. Separation creates awareness of other. Binaries. Twins: mortal and immortal. Fruit of knowledge has a mortal price.

ASTROLOGY/ELEMENT

In the air sign of Gemini, what is born after the fertile sign of Taurus now takes its first steps, discovers the other, and is presented with variety. Last in our spring triad comes mutable air sign Gemini, the Twins. Mutable signs morph as the element becomes more ethereal. At the end of the sign, the season will change into summer at solstice as the sign changes to Cancer.[17] Castor and Polydeuces (Pollux), known as the Dioscuri, or "sons of god," are the alpha and beta stars of the constellation Gemini, from antiquity associated with twins. Their heads are positioned between the claws of the crab and the whip of the charioteer (which may explain the difficulties of the 7, 8, and 9 of Swords). In Egypt they represented a pair of sprouting seeds.

Gemini's glyph looks like the Roman numeral two. Two I's, twins, two pillars. When any two "I's" get together, the result is some form of communication. Gemini is ruled by the master communicator, Mercury, the Magus, and the sign takes on his characteristic wit, curiosity, and oration. Skilled applications of speech are a given, and wise operations of the word are the goal. The Lovers are the "Children of the Voice (Divine)" and the "Oracle of the Mighty Gods." At its most sublime, Gemini's goal is to unite in the service of creative union, whether twin souls or just the mind united with itself or with divinity.

Within lunar and solar mirrors that together form the glyph of Gemini,
mythological stories of choice appear: Perseus rescuing Andromeda on the left,
and on the right, either the serpent offering Eve the apple—or Paris,
offering the apple to Aphrodite, choosing her as the fairest. (*Rosetta Tarot*)

---

17. Northern Hemisphere reference.

Gemini rules the nervous system, the sensory function, and the arms, hands, and lungs. Forever seeking the next experience, Gemini reaches out to the world with its senses and makes choices.

Gemini is the sign of explorations of the ever-restless mind. Gemini's motto is "I think." The mind's job is division and analysis, intellectually separating the viewed from the viewer. The mind asks how it can recombine them to greater benefit.

MYTHOLOGY/ALCHEMY

The Hermetic Marriage and the alchemical processes *separatio* and *solve et coagula* are embedded in the symbolism of the Lovers card. Manly P. Hall says of the Hermetic Marriage, "Spirit itself knows no polarity, but manifests as polarity to the accomplishment of the Great Work."[18]

Gemini is the third sign, and the most resonant with the third of the seven alchemical processes: separation, the stage prior to conjunction. (The seven stages are calcination, dissolution, separation, conjunction, fermentation, distillation, and coagulation.) Separation isolates the parts that arose from dissolution and discards those rejected. *Solve et coagula* describes these processes as *solve*, to break down, and *coagula*, to recombine, assumedly in a higher form.

Twin gods and stories of sibling mythology are numerous; we have almost too many choices.[19] The twin and twin gods were often guardians flanking doorways and entrances. To state the saying backwards, when one door opens, another closes. When we make a choice, something is rejected.

Castor and Pollux were born from an egg laid by Queen Leda of Sparta after her union with Zeus disguised as a swan. Usually Castor was described as the son of Leda's husband, and thus mortal, with Pollux as the son of Zeus. When Castor dies, Pollux gives up half of his immortality to his brother. The twins were members of the crew of the Argonaut on its quest for the Golden Fleece. Through Poseidon's blessings, they were made the protectors of sailors.

---

18. Hall, *Hermetic Marriage*, 60.

19. Pun intended! Choices include Castor and Pollux, Geb and Nut, Shu and Tefnut, Apollo and Artemis, Osiris and Isis, Nemo and Tasmit, Hypnos and Thanatos, Eros and Anteros, Phobos and Deimos, Helen and Clymtamesta, Adam and Eve, Cain and Abel, and other sacred twin and sibling stories.

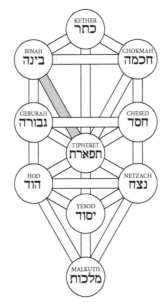

VI (6). The Lovers. Tree of Life.

The Lovers's path extends from Binah to the "heart" sephira, Tiphareth. As the "Children of the Voice," they carry the "voice" of the supernals straight to the heart, through the mercurial art of divination.

The Hebrew single letter of the Lovers is ז, *zayin*, meaning "weapon" or "sword." As the letter *vav* resembles a nail, the letter *zayin* resembles a sword—and indeed, *zayin* is described as a "crowned *vav*." *Vav* brings the light of God to the human world; *zayin* is said to return it. A flaming sword stood between Eden and the exiled Adam and Eve after their fateful act of free will. The abyss (Da'ath, "knowledge") stands between humanity (in Tiphareth) and heaven (Binah). For the soul to return along the path of the Lovers, it must traverse this sword.

The sword concept also plays a role in understanding the Lovers as a card of choice. The Lovers, joined in their alchemical marriage, may be male and female. But they may also be twins (Gemini). Like so many twin stories, theirs involves sacrifice and redemption. To achieve integration, the soul must first differentiate; it must divide by the sword (the *solve* of *solve et coagula*) and see its shadow, then choose to sacrifice the ego to become whole.

As the seventh letter, *zayin* holds numerical mysteries as well—seven represents the astrological house of the Other, the day of the Sabbath (when sex is holy), and the combination of matter (four) and Spirit (three). *Zayin*'s letter attribute is Smell, reminding us that Gemini is an air sign, and that the air element carries both scent and sound (the "voice divine").

RIDER-WAITE-SMITH SYMBOLISM

The Lovers (*Rider-Waite-Smith Tarot*)

In the Rider-Waite-Smith Lovers card, we see a scene that quite clearly shows the myth of Eden: Eve, Adam, two trees, and an angel. Adam stands before the tree of life, its twelve flames evoking the signs of the zodiac; i.e., all life itself. Eve stands before the tree of the knowledge of good and evil; the twining serpent is poised to whisper in her ear. The sun may represent the light of Kether, from which they shall be banished; the mountain may represent Malkuth, the earthly realm where they shall forever dwell. Between them, we have a cloud (Gemini being an air sign) and the "great winged figure." Waite suggests the scene takes place before Eve's fateful bite of the apple, but the sense of heightened tension is palpable.

In fact, Adam and Eve's expulsion scene mentions cherubim and a flaming sword—not an angel with flaming hair! The angel might be Michael of the flaming sword, or Uriel, who stood guard at Eden's gates. But because this is a Golden Dawn–derived deck and the Lovers is a card of Gemini/air, the angel is likely Raphael—healing angel of the east and elemental air, according to the lesser banishing ritual of the pentagram. (The other four archangel correspondences then would be Michael/Temperance, Gabriel/Judgement, Uriel/Devil.) The angel acts as a Christianized symbol of the Eros cherub who once shot his arrows from the zenith of the Lovers card. Still, his role—to preside over the making of fateful choices—remains the same.

This updated Tarot de Marseille imagery adopts the Eros figure as its angel; the lover appears to choose between "respectable" and "common" consorts. (*Universal Wirth Tarot*)

THOTH SYMBOLISM

In the Thoth image is a memento of the Hermetic Marriage, ceremonies courtesy of the Hermit, who marries the Emperor and Empress, as the dark king and white queen, the lion and the eagle, the red and the white, in the rite of the *hieros gamos*. The Hermit is an aspect of Mercury, ruler of Gemini. The hooded figure places his hands (*yod*, Hermit) in the sign of the enterer, "as if projecting the mysterious forces of creation."[20] Around his arms (Gemini) is a scroll (Mercury), on which is writ the Word, which is his essence and his message alike.

Above, Cupid, son of Aphrodite and Hermes (Mercury), is poised to shoot the arrow of will and love. His quiver is inscribed *Thelema* (Will). To Crowley, he repre-

---

20. Crowley, *Book of Thoth*, 82.

sents "the will of the soul to unite itself with all and sundry."[21] His arrow is a symbol of direction and the directed intelligence necessary for alchemy.

In the foreground are the paired red lion and white eagle. In the left hand, the king holds the lance and the queen the grail. Their right hands are clasped. The light child of the dark king grasps the cup in their left and roses in the right, and the dark child of the light queen has hold of the spear and a club. Between them is the winged orphic egg, product of the marriage and essence of all life that results from the union of positive and negative.

Above the scene, swords form the arch, the door for the married couple to pass through. The door is guarded by the pair Eve and Lilith. As a whole the card exemplifies *mutatis mutandi,* the changes needed having been made after respective differences having been considered.

RELATED CARDS

The Lovers, associated with the Mercury-ruled sign of Gemini, answer to the card of Mercury: the Magician or Magus. Alchemically, the Lovers represent the union of matter and Spirit, salt and sulfur. Mercury, the third alchemical element, marries them. Mercury/Hermes, alone among the main gods of the Greek pantheon, partakes of both male and female qualities—apt for the god of twins, choices, ambiguity, trickery, truth and lies. The male and female archetypes brought together in the Lovers may be the Empress (salt) and the Emperor (sulfur); in the Golden Dawn's Tree of Life, in fact, the Magician, Empress, and Emperor occupy a continuous three-part path. The Devil card relates to the Lovers by reduction (15; 1 + 5 = 6); in the Waite-Smith deck, that connection is visually obvious. Finally, the Lovers indirectly link to the Hermit as Virgo, Mercury's other sign.

When it comes to the Gemini minors, The Lovers's presence seems to emphasize the darkest consequences of free will: the 8 of Swords (*Interference*—Jupiter ruling Gemini I), the 9 of Swords (*Cruelty*—Mars ruling Gemini II), and the 10 of Swords (*Ruin*—sun ruling Gemini III). One faces a paralyzing abundance of choice in the 8, an agonizing decision in the 9, and an inevitable consequence in the 10. This illustrates the mind

---

21. Crowley, 84.

turning on itself, but other interpretations are possible: "forsaking all others"; the death of the ego or monkey mind; the austere conclusions of logic.

Among court cards, the King (Waite-Smith) or Knight (Thoth) of Swords commands the first two decans (the final decan of Gemini belongs to the Queen of Cups). All choices come to him for decision in the end.

ADVANCED CONCEPTS FOR FURTHER EXPLORATION

- Compare with the opposite path on the Tree: either the Emperor (RWS) or the Star (Thoth)

- The "alchemical marriage" of the red king (Emperor) and white queen (Empress) as a union of duality, or previously separate polarities

- The stories of the Garden of Eden before the fall, Eve and the serpent, and Cain and Abel

- The Tree of Life and the Tree of the Knowledge of Good and Evil; the Trees as the Pillars of Severity and Mercy

- Adam's choice between Eve and Lilith

- The myth of Perseus and Andromeda, which the Golden Dawn associated with this card

- The Judgement of Paris, as a choice among gifts

- Magical Weapon: The Tripod

- Magical Power: The Power of being in two or more places at one time, and of Prophecy

THE CHARIOT
The Child of the Powers of the Waters, Lord of the Triumph of Light

Card Number: VII

Sign and Dignities: ♋ Cancer, cardinal water. Ruler Moon, Jupiter exalted; Motto: "I feel"

Hebrew Letter: ח, *cheth*

Hebrew Letter Meaning: Simple letter *cheth*: Fence (Speech); Value: 8

Path 18: Binah (3, Understanding—Saturn) to Geburah (5, Severity—Mars)

Color Scales in the Four Worlds: Amber. Maroon. Rich bright russet. Dark greenish-brown

Themes and Keywords: Enclosure. Containment. Maternal protection. Guardianship. Triumph. Might. Grail quest. Self-control. The warrior in service; mission over self. Reason over appetite and will. Soul's journey to meet the ineffable. Vehicles. Indirect motion.

ASTROLOGY/ELEMENT

The Chariot, with armored charioteer and indirect motion, is associated with the sign of Cancer, the Crab. Starting at the June solstice, cardinal water indicates the first and potent inrush of the element. Cancer is about control of the emotional realm. It is considered a maternal sign. At first glance the martial Chariot may not seem like a fit, yet there is nothing fiercer and more protective than a mother.

Cancer is the fertilized womb; it is a nourishing and sustaining sign. It's the protecting principal and represents tenacity. Crabs hold on and don't let go. Cancer's glyph looks like crab claws—or like two nurturing breasts. Crabs carry their hard-shelled house with them so they can return to the enclosure, for inside they are soft. The Chariot is a portable canopied throne or a sort of portable home. Its motion may not always be straightforward, but it is always headed toward a goal.

Cancer is a most subconscious sign. Nothing is clear or direct, and everything is latent or hidden. Cancer lives in the realm of their feelings. Like its ruler the moon, Cancer has a lot to do with mass consciousness because that is mostly based on emotion. Cancer's motto is "I feel"—but be warned: no one is more difficult than a Cancer whose feelings have been injured. They need to come first with those they love and protect.

In this Marseille-based image, we see many precursors later expressed as Cancer tropes: starry canopy, moonlike epaulets, armored warrior. (*Camoin-Jodorowsky Tarot de Marseille*)

As much as they are attached to home, they do love to trek about, for Jupiter which rules distant travels is exalted in the sign. They are very psychic and influenced by their environment. Wherever they may roam, they always need a safe space to return to.

MYTHOLOGY/ALCHEMY

The constellation Cancer lies between Gemini and Leo and north of the head of Hydra. It's inconspicuous, hidden like the crab. Its most interesting feature is the star cluster M44, the Beehive Cluster. In classical times it was known as *Praesepe*, the manger or crib, which highlights the maternal themes. The crab of classical times comes from the story of Hercules and the Hydra, when Juno sent a crab to nip at Hercules's toes. It wasn't always a crab; in ancient Babylonian times it was a tortoise.

At the time of the June solstice, Cancer marks the position of the sun. Mesopotamian cultures saw this point in the sky as a gateway for souls being incarnated. In Egypt, the constellation was Khepra, a form of sun god Ra, symbolizing fertility, life, and rebirth. Khepra, or Khepri, means "he who is coming into being." Khepra "in Thy hiding," at the midnight hour of the sun, is the scarab beetle that rolled the sun across the sky, through the underworld, from the abodes of night, and restored the sun at the dawn.[22] Though a solar god, he is also lunar in the sense of his associations with night. Consider also the two riddles that the sphinx asked Oedipus: one about man's growth, and one about dark and light. Upon hearing his correct answers, she threw herself into the abyss.[23]

The constellation of the charioteer is nearby, sharing a star with Taurus. Charioteers cared for the horses, livestock, and food supplies of their rulers, which seems Cancerian in nature. The story goes that the charioteer, Erichthonius, was a son (of Hephaestus and Hera) who inherited his father's lameness. He invented the chariot in order to roam about with more ease; this pleased Zeus (Jupiter), who placed him in the sky.

---

22. Crowley, *Gems from the Equinox*, 304.

23. Bulfinch, *Bulfinch's Mythology*, 100.

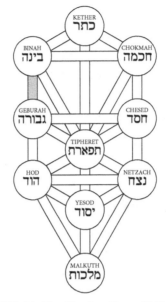

VII (7). The Chariot. Tree of Life.

The path of the Chariot, from Binah to Geburah, is the last to descend from the supernal to the lower realms. Some view the Emperor (Aries/fire), the Hierophant (Taurus/earth), the Lovers (Gemini/air), and the Chariot (Cancer/water) as the four rivers descending from Eden, as they are four mirrored paths from the supernal realm.

Vital to understanding the Chariot card is its connection to the vision of Ezekiel and Merkabah mysticism more generally. In Jewish mysticism, the Merkabah is a vision of God, enthroned in a wheeled enclosure and surrounded by angelic creatures. This journey to glimpse the godhead, related in scripture by the prophet Ezekiel, parallels the journey of the "Great Work," where the spirit ventures up the tree to seek the knowledge and conversation of the Holy Guardian Angel.

The Chariot's single Hebrew letter is ח *cheth*, meaning enclosure or fence.[24] This enclosure metaphor evokes the divine conveyance of Merkabah, but it also suggests the body as container for the spirit, the shell enclosing Cancer the crab, and the "Grail"

---

24. The Hebrew word for life, *chai*, is spelled with ח *cheth* and י *yod*: life is Spirit (*yod*) enclosed (*cheth*).

bearing the alchemically unified soul to its Holy Guardian Angel. To put it in Tree of Life terms, protection is required to cross the abyss of Da'ath.

The enclosing fence of letter *cheth* becomes a wall of cardinal water as the charioteer rides the pipeline in perfect balance. (*Tabula Mundi Tarot*)

In sum, the Chariot's defining quality is the quality shared by all vehicles: it implies motion—whether that is motion forward, the side-to-side motion of the crab, the mystic quest of ascent, journeys within, or the return to the Great Mother, Binah.

RIDER-WAITE-SMITH SYMBOLISM

The Chariot (*Rider-Waite-Smith Tarot*)

Much of the symbol-laden Waite-Smith imagery comes direct from Éliphas Lévi, whose description in *Transcendental Magic: Its Doctrine and Ritual* reads, "a Cubic Chariot, with four pillars and an azure and starry drapery. In the chariot, between the four pillars, a victor…on his shoulder the Urim and Thummim of the sovereign sacrificer, represented by the two crescents of the moon in Gedulah and Geburah."[25] The starry canopy likely refers to Binah, the sea-sky on one end of his path. The crescent moons allude to the moon's rulership of Cancer, though Waite also describes them as "Urim and Thummim," divinatory objects that were probably cast like lots. The charioteer's breastplate and gauntlets call to mind a crab's armor, reinforcing the connection to Cancer.

He stands as if embedded in a solid stone cube—perhaps the "Cube of Matter," which represents our material world. On the cube a winged sun disk, solar symbol of power, surmounts a shield depicting a lingam and yoni because in the Chariot's quest, the ecstatic union of male and female leads to divine knowledge. The black and white sphinxes bear a similar message; they also bring to mind Plato's metaphor of reason, the charioteer who harnesses will and appetite. Waite says he is neither "royalty" nor "priesthood"; while he appears a victorious warrior, he serves a mission given to him by a greater authority.

Behind is a castled city behind a great wall (*cheth*, as previously mentioned, meaning "enclosure") and a river—perhaps a reference to the Chariot as the last of Eden's four rivers.

THOTH SYMBOLISM

According to Crowley, the charioteer's only function is to convey the Holy Grail, shown tipped on its side with revolving rays within: the radiant blood, the spiritual light within the darkness. The Grail symbolizes a womb and the fertilized blood.

The charioteer is said to be enthroned within the Chariot, but there is no need to conduct it because the "whole system of progression is so perfectly balanced."[26] He wears a crab helm and armor colored in amber. Crowley calls the sapphire stars upon it the Ten Stars of Assiah (ten sephira—Malkuth—in the World of Action and Matter)

---

25. Lévi, *Transcendental Magic*, 135.

26. Crowley, *Book of Thoth*, 85.

and refers to them as a celestial inheritance from his mother (Binah). The blue canopy echoes the Binah reference. The connection between mother Binah and daughter Malkuth shows that what begins in form manifests in matter. The canopy is held up by the four pillars: four Tetragrammaton, four sphinxes, and four kerubs of the Universe card corresponding to Saturn (Binah) and Earth (Malkuth). It is embroidered with what Crowley calls "the Word of the Aeon," *Abrahadabra* (though Frieda spelled it as the more traditional Abracadabra). Crowley's swap inserting *cheth* enumerates the word in Gematria as 418, just as the word *cheth* spelled in full. He admits that an entire book could be dedicated to the word *Abrahadabra*. Suffice it to say that it has to do with magic, the Great Work, and the Holy Guardian Angel.

Geburah's magical image is that of a mighty warrior in his chariot. The Chariot bears the fertilized Grail across the abyss, to return to the great ocean of mother Binah, harnessing the martial energy of Geburah to drive the great red wheels.

RELATED CARDS

The Chariot, associated with the sign of Cancer, bears close ties to the card of the Moon: the Priestess or High Priestess. Besides expressing the moon's role as swift traveler and its protective, covert nature, the Chariot reflects the Priestess's journey across the abyss to reach divinity. At the same time, the Chariot's journey partakes of the restrictive, confining nature of the Pillar of Severity—the uncomfortable plane or car ride rather than a bird's free flight.

The Chariot relates astrologically to the three decanic minor arcana of Cancer: the 2 of Cups (*Love*—Venus ruling Cancer I), the 3 of Cups (*Abundance*—Mercury ruling Cancer II), and the 4 of Cups (*Luxury* or *Blended Pleasure*—the moon ruling Cancer III). Of these, the 4 of Cups enjoys particular dignity since the moon rules both the decan and the sign. In these cards, a soul conceived in a place of safety and bliss grows and thrives, eventually outgrowing its confines. As in the story of birth, two parts merge into one to become a complete individual who will eventually be capable of leaving the maternal nest.

Among court cards, the Queen of Cups corresponds to the first two decans of Cancer (the final decan of Cancer belongs to the Knight (RWS) or Prince (Thoth) of

Wands), and particularly reflects the empathic, psychic sensitivities of Cancer's ruler, the moon. She may at times take the protective qualities of the Chariot to an extreme.

ADVANCED CONCEPTS FOR FURTHER EXPLORATION

- The Great Work, or magnum opus, central to Western occult philosophy as a process of uniting and integrating subconscious and conscious psychological processes in order to achieve the philosopher's stone—a metaphor for self-transcendence and enlightenment

- The Chariot as a vehicle for crossing the abyss (the area of the Tree of Life that symbolizes the separation of the supernal triad or deity from mundane reality); a process of ego dissolution through contact with divinity and reintegration of the experience

- Gematria of Crowley's "Word of the Aeon," *Abrahadabra*, a word of creation associated with ideas of the unification of Microcosm (5) and Macrocosm (6), pentagram and hexagram, rose and cross; also, the inclusion of HAD (a name of Hadit) as central to the word

- "Two-In-One, conveyed": a phrase referring to the harnessing of ardor and reason, the balanced marriage of opposing forces which produces a "child" or talisman of creative potential that is the precious object conveyed via the allegory of the Grail (Thoth) or the lingam-yoni and winged orb (RWS)[27]

- Magical Weapon: The Furnace

- Magical Power: Power of Casting Enchantments

---

27. Crowley, *Book of Thoth*, 256.

STRENGTH/LUST
The Daughter of the Flaming Sword

Card Number: VIII (RWS); XI (Thoth)

Sign and Dignities: ♌ Leo, fixed fire. Ruler sun; Motto: "I will"

Hebrew Letter: ט, *teth*

Hebrew Letter Meaning: Simple letter *teth*: Serpent (Taste); Value: 9

Path 19: Chesed (4, Mercy—Jupiter) to Geburah (5, Severity/Strength—Mars)

Color Scales in the Four Worlds: Greenish yellow. Deep purple. Gray. Reddish amber

Themes and Keywords: Passion. Virility. Divine ecstasy. Kundalini. Feminine power. Courageous action. Control and mastery of animal nature. Joy of exercising strength. The beauty and the beast. Apocalyptic goddesses. Sacred prostitution. Pure maiden versus holy whore. Taming versus riding the lion. Moral fortitude.

ASTROLOGY/ELEMENT

The sign of Leo the Lion is arguably the strongest in the zodiac because it is ruled by the sun. Leo is the fixed fire sign, combining the endurance of fixed signs with the element of fire to produce an eternal flame. It is brimming with life force and magnetism: the fire element with the strength of the lion. The glyph looks like a curling lion's mane. It also resembles the main artery and chambers of the heart. In the body, Leo rules the heart and the spine.

Leo's motto, "I will," gives a clue as to the source of the strength. Leo is so strong and vital that it can share the strength with others, giving generously from a large heart. Noble and extravagant, brave or recklessly courageous, Leo shines. Like the sun, though, it is proud. Leo believes in itself as the center of the universe.

The alpha star of Leo, Regulus, means "little king," and it's also called *Cor Leonis*, "Heart of the Lion." It is the Royal Watcher star of the North, with the power "to will." Regulus gives gifts of glory, like all royal stars, if the inner enemy is vanquished. Regulus's nemesis is revenge; it must avoid seeking it even when justified.

Euripides's *Medea* is gruesome, but nonetheless Medea's quote sounds very leonine: "Let no one think of me that I am humble or weak or passive; let them understand I am of a different kind: dangerous to my enemies, loyal to my friends. To such a life glory belongs."[28]

MYTHOLOGY/ALCHEMY

Crowley specifically connects this card to the alchemical process of distillation, "operated by internal ferment, and the influence of the sun and moon."[29] Whether speaking chemically or psychologically, distillation is heating, condensing, and purifying until all dissolves into spirit (distilled) or Spirit (godhood). The process applies heat or agitation with the eventual goal of sublimation. Wine becomes brandy, or impurities of the ego and id are purged. Distillation, like kundalini, raises the light (life force) from the alembic of the lower regions to the height of the third eye.

We can't help but reflect on the alchemical image of the red lion in the card. The red lion of alchemy is the kundalini fire, the force behind semen in sexual alchemy. It is the sheer power of the life force, channeled. Distilled, it transmutes in the proper receptacle.

In myth and legend, goddesses of the lion abound: Chandi, Durga, Ishtar, Astarte, Inanna, Sekmet, Cybele, Babalon. Just chanting their names increases vigor. At the heart

---

28. Flaum and Pandy, *Encyclopedia of Mythology*, 101.

29. Crowley, *Book of Thoth*, 95.

of all the stories is a core of strength and a connection to the act of the *hieros gamos*, the original marriage of the moon illuminated by the sun and united to it; the sacred marriage rather than the formal one of the Lovers. Perhaps the text in the library of Nag Hammadi, *The Thunder, Perfect Mind*, resonates best with the themes of divine feminine strength. It's a treatise rich with meaning for students of both the Qabalah (the Tree of Life) and alchemy (the Tree of Knowledge). It's the divine speech of a goddess of contradictions and power, much as the goddesses of love were also those of war.

Babalon as the Scarlet Woman rides an ecstatic spiral in the form of the lion-serpent (Leo and *teth*) showing Crowley's "joy of strength exercised." (*Pharos Tarot*)

QABALAH—PATH 19

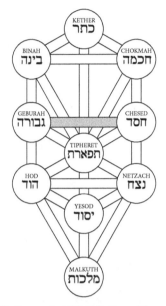

VIII (8). Strength / XI (11). Lust. Tree of Life.

The Strength/Lust card's path travels between Chesed and Geburah, causing the sun (Strength/Lust = Leo, ruled by the sun) and the moon (High Priestess) to cross paths. One of three parallel, horizontal paths on the Tree, Strength/Lust unifies the others— the Empress (Venus) and the Tower (Mars)—into an image of feminine power, life force, or Shakti; a goddess equally formidable in love and war.

One of Strength/Lust's Hermetic titles is "Daughter of the Flaming Sword"—this is a reference to the "Path of the Flaming Sword" or "Lightning Flash," the zigzag path along which the creation is said to emanate on the Tree of Life. Path nineteen, like the other horizontal paths, lies directly along that zigzag, connecting the Pillars of Force and Form and bisecting the Middle Pillar.

The single Hebrew letter associated with Strength/Lust is ט *teth*, meaning "serpent." Lion and serpent form a powerful symbolic pair: as fixed fire (Leo/lion) and fixed water (Scorpio/snake), as alchemical emblems (lion = Sun, snake = Mercury), or as the hybrid lion-serpent gods found across Eurasia. Both represent vitality and life force, but the serpent specifically refers to the kundalini force, the Shakti or divine energy lying coiled at the base of the spine.

As a single letter, *teth*'s attribute is taste. The most primal of senses, it connects humans to the very sustenance of life.

RIDER-WAITE-SMITH SYMBOLISM

Strength (*Rider-Waite-Smith Tarot*)

Strength and the lion have a long iconographic history. Mythic strongman Heracles's first task was the subduing of the Nemean Lion, and he would be depicted wearing its skin ever after; indeed, some early decks depict Heracles rather than the familiar feminine heroine. Waite described his Strength card as "fortitude"—the first of the cardinal virtues (we'll speak of the others in Justice, Temperance, and the World). This accords with the other meaning of "strength"—moral force versus physical vigor.

Ideas of physical and moral force blend in this Soprafino-based design. The elaborate headpiece
foreshadows the infinity sign that would appear in Waite-Smith. (*Ancient Italian Tarot*)

Waite describes the virginal maiden as "*innocentia inviolata*" (we'll see her again
in the Death card). This is not the first time Christian ideas of moral purity have been
equated with strength (consider the Samson myth). In this interpretation, the lion
stands for the passions, the woman for the spiritualized self that rules them rather
than being ruled by them. The chain of flowers "signifies … the sweet yoke and the
light burden of Divine Law, when it has been taken into the heart of hearts."[30]

The lion's remarkable color offers another clue: it may be the red lion of alchemy,
produced when the green lion (or vitriol) consumes the sun (or gold). The red lion
combines sulfur with mercury—the life force brought under perfect control. Thus
Strength's infinity sign may symbolize that sense of unencumbered agency. But it can
also symbolize the solar analemma (the path traced by the sun's yearly passage as
perceived from Earth), or even the figure eight (the number of Mercury). The lion's
outstretched tongue may refer to *teth*, whose attribute is taste.

Finally, her white gown signifies—as elsewhere in the deck, but perhaps even more
so here—purity of intention. Similarly, her garland and crown of red roses become an
emblem of well-ruled passions.

---

30. Waite, *Pictorial Key*, 103.

THOTH SYMBOLISM

Because the new Aeon of Horus occurs on the astrological axis of Leo/Aquarius, the motif of the Lion and the woman (Angel of Aquarius) is particularly potent. Here the theme of maiden and lion transforms into the goddess Babalon, who is drunkenly riding Chaos with reins of passion; Chaos the Great Beast of Revelations. Uniting what was divided in the Lovers, she is the moon to his sun, and together they complete the true marriage.

For Crowley, who loved using supposed blasphemy as metaphor, the apocalyptic "Great Whore" was a symbol sublime, only reviled due to fear. Crowley mentions several instances of divine impregnation as "Old Aeon," and instead, says the father is the serpent—or in this case, the lion-serpent. The Maiden of Strength becomes the Scarlet Woman of Lust. The cup she holds is "the Holy Grail aflame with love and death" in which the sacraments are mingled.[31] The Great Whore is Binah, who accepts all. Those steeped in embedded dogmas and tenets of the old Aeon could not comprehend her. The card shows all we are, dissolving, as an ecstatic process.

The beast's seven heads could correspond to the chakras, reined and united in purpose of kundalini. The beast's tail is the head of the lion and the body of a serpent, with a solar halo of thirteen points. At the top of the card, ten serpents represent the ten horns of the beast "sent forth in every direction to destroy and recreate the world." Ten luminous rayed circles in the background are the nascent sephiroth of the new Aeon.

In the most glorious use of negative space, Lady Frieda works the concept of the blood of the saints (what is joyfully sacrificed) in the praying figures amongst the feet of the beast.

RELATED CARDS

Strength/Lust, the card of Leo, answers to the Sun card. The sun is so central to our worldview that it's hard to conceptualize: vitality, creative force, health, self-worth, identity (or as Crowley puts it: light, life, love, liberty). Perhaps the solar quality most expressed in Strength/Lust is freedom: the liberation of acting in accordance with one's nature. It's not that the Self is no longer rulebound, but that the true will is so integrated

---

31. Crowley, *Book of Thoth*, 94.

within it that all resistance disappears. Perhaps the defining characteristic of health is that the body can do what it wishes—Crowley's "joy of strength exercised."[32]

Strength/Lust relates to three decanic minors: the 5 of Wands (*Strife*—Saturn ruling Leo I), the 6 of Wands (*Victory*—Jupiter ruling Leo II), and the 7 of Wands (*Valor*—Mars ruling Leo III). This sequence shares a narrative form throughout all four suits: the five hungers for what the six effortlessly enjoys and what the seven struggles to hold on to. In the cards of Leo, this comes across as a story of ambition and determination, culminating in a moment of public illumination where one's purpose is fulfilled.

The court card associated with Strength/Lust is the Prince (Thoth) or Knight (RWS) of Wands, to whom belong the first two decans of Leo (the final decan corresponds to the King of Pentacles or Knight of Disks). These show that vital force can light up a room—or be carried away by its own enthusiasm.

ADVANCED CONCEPTS FOR FURTHER EXPLORATION

- Shakti as the Great Divine Mother and supreme goddess of Hinduism, the personification of energy and strength, whose dynamic force has the potential to create, animate, liberate, or destroy the universe

- The "woman clothed in the sun" or "woman of the apocalypse" as described in the Bible's book of Revelation

- Strength/Lust as a combination of love and war (positioned between the Empress and the Tower, the other two horizontal paths on the Tree of Life) and the central part of the Path of the Flaming Sword

- To understand Crowley's card, read chapter 49 of his *Book of Lies* called "Waratah-Blossoms" and *Liber Cheth vel Vallum Abiegni*

- John Dee and Edward Kelly's 1587 scrying and reception of the text called "Daughter of Fortitude" as a predecessor to the Thelemic concept of Babalon

---

32. Crowley, *Book of Thoth*, 92.

- *The Thunder, Perfect Mind*: an ancient Gnostic manuscript speculated to be from second or third century Alexandria comprised of a profound exhoratory poem recited by a feminine divine being

- The precession of the equinoxes and the modern astrological "Age of Aquarius" as a potential inspiration for the "(wo)man and lion" theme as the Aquarius-Angel/Leo-Lion axis, versus the prior Age of Pisces as the Pisces/Virgo axis of "fishes and loaves" or Jesus and Mary

- Alternately, the "woman and lion" as an illustration of the astrological transition from the season of Virgo, the Virgin, to Leo, the Lion

- Magical Weapon: The Discipline (Preliminary)

- Magical Power: Power of Taming Wild Beasts

THE HERMIT
The Prophet of the Eternal,
The Magus of the Voice of Light

Card Number: IX

Sign and Dignities: ♍ Virgo, mutable earth. Ruler Mercury, Mercury exalted; Motto: "I analyze"

Hebrew Letter: י, *yod*

Hebrew Letter Meaning: Simple letter *yod*: Hand (Sexual Love); Value: 10

Path 20: Chesed (4, Mercy—Jupiter) to Tiphareth (6, Beauty—Sun)

Color Scales in the Four Worlds: Yellowish green. Slate gray. Greenish gray. Plum

Themes and Keywords: The holy man, the wanderer. Internal journey. Journeys of ascent and descent. Illumination. Carrying the light within. The psychopomp. Mastery of speech, action, thought. The heights and the depths. Knowledge as medicine. Light in dark corners: detective, reader of clues and symbols, interpreter, diviner.

ASTROLOGY/ELEMENT

When we think of Virgo, the Virgin, we think of the librarian surrounded by books, the nurse serving hospice, or the analyst poring over a spreadsheet. Each in its own way is resourceful and practical, quietly drilling down in service, a solitary seed bringing light.

The constellation is a graceful winged goddess holding a shaft of wheat. The wheat shaft is the alpha star Spica, most fortunate and one of the brightest in the sky, and the entire area is ripe with over 500 nebulas, showing the sign's plenitude and the resources of energy available to the sign.

Virgo is a mutable earth sign; at the end of its period we have the September equinox ushering in the change of season. Virgo is the most feminine and receptive of earth signs; a fully ripened harvest, as yet unspoiled. Capricorn is enterprising and climbs, Taurus is consistent, preferring the stable and field, but Virgo is adaptable and modest, tending to go underground. Virgo is the night sign of Mercury while Gemini is the day sign. As such, Virgo has an affinity with chthonic Mercury, the psychopomp.

Virgo's glyph looks like the letter M with a tail crossing itself, creating a closed loop that represents crossed legs or the untouched female parts. The "virgin" that is fruitful is not such a paradox; it refers to self-sufficiency. The loops of the symbol also refer to the intestines and digestive tract, which Virgo rules. Virgo's motto is "I analyze," and its job, like the intestines with food, is to break information down into smaller and smaller pieces until it can be assimilated.

MYTHOLOGY/ALCHEMY

The constellation of Virgo is said to be the goddess Astraea, the last of the immortals to live with mankind, withdrawing to the sky and abandoning Earth as the Golden Age transitioned to the Iron Age. She was, of course, a virgin goddess, associated with themes of justice, precision, purity, and renewal. It is said that her return to Earth will one day trigger a second Golden Age: "*Iam redit et virgo, redeunt Saturnia Regna*": Astraea returns, returns old Saturn's reign.[33]

---

33. Virgil, *Eclogues*, 28–29.

But the most well-known mythical virgin is probably Persephone (Proserpine), the daughter of Demeter (Ceres) and a goddess of vegetation and growing things. She is most often portrayed as a fair maiden carrying a grain sheaf and a torch, presumably to bring light to her time spent beneath Earth's crust. Persephone was abducted and brought underground by Hades (Pluto), where she ate a single pomegranate seed and was thus doomed to spend half of her time in the underworld. Her mother Demeter withered the earth above with her mourning, causing winter. In time, though, it is told that Persephone came to enjoy her role as Queen of the Underworld.

The Orphic Hymn to Chthonic Hermes states "To you indeed Persephone gave the office, throughout wide Tartaros, to lead the way for the eternal souls of men."[34] Hermes was the only god allowed to visit all three realms: heaven, earth, and the underworld, as his job was not only to be messenger of the gods, but also to lead the souls of the recently deceased to Hades, giving him an all-access pass to wander heights, depths, and everything in between.

The Hermit in this image walks the labyrinth, a journey of introspection and solitude, symbolic of the process of going within. (*Rosetta Tarot*)

---

34. Athanassakis, *Orphic Hymns*, 77.

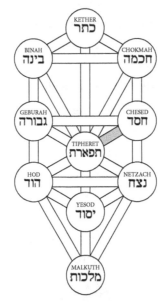

IX (9). The Hermit. Tree of Life.

In one of the many great head-scratching paradoxes of Qabalah, the card of Virgo is perhaps the most profoundly sexual card in the deck. As Crowley put it, "*Yod* = Phallus = Spermatazoon = Hand = Logos = Virgin." To begin to make sense of this baffling formula, we must focus in on the mysteries of the Hebrew Letter י *yod*. Suspended in midair, *yod* is the divine point from which all other letters unfold. It is the first letter of the divine name, יהוה, for the tip of the *yod* is said to reside in Kether, the crown and source of creation. Even the Hebrew spelling of *yod*—יוד—reflects an unfolding reality: point, line, plane.

The meaning of *yod* is "hand"; not the open palm of *kaph*, which we will discuss in the Wheel of Fortune card, but the forceful, pointing divine hand which gives life and directs creation. In Jewish mysticism, the alphabet letters are more than building blocks of language—they are building blocks of the Universe. So when we say the Hermit is the Word or *logos* of God, it is like saying he represents that vast potential power to create. Hence his title, "Magus of the Voice of Light."

THE HERMIT
THE LANTERN

Here the Hermit is shown as the *yod*-shaped flame within the
lantern usually held in the hand of the Hermit. (*Pharos Tarot*)

Yod's number is ten (ten fingers on our hands), and its path in our system goes from Chesed (the "lower" aspect of the father; Kether being the "higher") to Tiphareth (the son). Like the Hermit's lantern, it bears the light or "secret seed" from the unknowable supernal realm to the worlds below. Its single-letter attribute is "sexual love"—not human intercourse, but its self-contained divine counterpart. This is the cardinal virtue "prudence" (not so coincidentally, the name of one of the Hermit's decanic minors).

RIDER-WAITE-SMITH SYMBOLISM

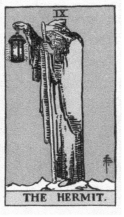

THE HERMIT.

© 1971 U.S. GAMES SYSTEMS, INC.

The Hermit (*Rider-Waite-Smith Tarot*)

What can we make of a card as spare as Pamela Colman Smith's Hermit? Here we have an archetypal wise old man with an eerie, anachronistic resemblance to Gandalf the Grey. Some early versions of the Hermit show him holding an hourglass like Father Time, and indeed Waite says the figure blends the "ancient of days" with the "light of the world."[35] Only time and experience separate the Fool from the Hermit. While the Fool cavorts unheedingly atop his cliff, the Hermit is overwhelmingly aware of his remote perch. His downward gaze suggests the direction of his path from Chesed to Tiphareth, and the peaked hood of his cap perhaps recalls the tip of the letter *yod*.

In his lantern blazes a six-pointed golden star, the emblem of Tiphareth and a symbol for the sun. (Virgo is also the sixth sign of the zodiac.) The Hermit holds it aloft as if to shed its light on the smallest details and illuminate the darkest corners—or, like Diogenes, to seek out an honest man. As the guardian of the sun and the life force it signifies, he holds a golden staff, which emphasizes his mercurial proximity to, dependence on, and responsibility for the sun.

Time plays a subtle but important role in the Hermit's iconography. According to Waite, his message is "Where I am, you also may be"—which is both a call to the quest for truth and a reminder of mortality. In fact, in earlier decks, the Hermit sometimes bore a saturnine hourglass rather than the solar lamp.

THOTH SYMBOLISM

In the Thoth card, the senex appears as ibis-headed Thoth himself, surrounded by green shafts of grain. He contemplates the Orphic egg, from which Phanes the light-bringer was born. A pyramid of light travels with him, for concealed within him is the "light which pervades all parts of the Universe equally."[36]

Thoth too had a role as psychopomp. His companion Cerberus reinforces that symbolism and perhaps hints at the Hermit as an evolved Fool. Cerberus is best known for guarding the gates of Tartarus. In *Liber III vel Jugorum*, Crowley refers to Cerberus, saying, "Nothing shall be said here of Cerberus, the great Beast of Hell that is every one of these and all of these ... For this matter is not of Tiphareth without, but Tiphareth within. The 'every one of these' are the 'beasts wherewith thou must plough

---

35. Waite, *Pictorial Key*, 104.
36. Crowley, *Book of Thoth*, 89.

the Field'...these shalt thou yoke in a triple yoke that is governed by One Whip."[37] He's ultimately referring to the three heads of Cerberus as representing the practice of controlling one's speech, actions, and thoughts.

Central to the card is the hand (*yod*) which bears an eight-sided (Mercury) lantern, within which is the sun (Tiphareth). The sun, as in the Fool card, is placed over the generative organ. The wand at his feet is fashioned to look like a sperm, for the very name hermit not only comes from a word meaning solitary, but also refers to both Hermes and the phallic *herma*. Concealed within is a curled fetus that also resembles a skull. The diamond on its head could refer back to the Fool and Kether or to the four elements that make up life.

RELATED CARDS

The ruler of Virgo (the Hermit) is Mercury (the Magician/Magus), and indeed, the two majors have close ties. The Magician is the "Magus of Power"; the Hermit is the "Magus of the Voice of Light." The Hermit expresses Mercury's role as psychopomp, traveling from mountaintop to chasm, from above to below, bearing the light of truth in his lantern. The Magician is the invisible conductor who directs the Hermit's travels. The Fool and Hermit have a connection too; add wisdom (the Magician) to the Fool and he becomes the Hermit or wise old man.

The Hermit's three related decanic minors are the pentacle or disk cards of Virgo: the 8 (*Prudence*—the sun ruling Virgo I), the 9 (*Gain*—Venus ruling Virgo II), and the 10 (*Wealth*—Mercury ruling Virgo III). In these cards is a late-summer crop nearing its harvest, an achievement perfected: the 8 produces an artifact; the 9 gives its value; in the 10 it is consumed, and its worth is passed on as a legacy—the fruit that drops to the ground becomes the next generation of the tree.

The court card associated with the Hermit is the King of Pentacles (RWS) or Knight of Disks (Thoth). The first two decans of Virgo are his (the final decan belongs to the Queen of Swords). He is the steward of Virgo's bounty, entrusted to collect it at the peak of ripeness and sustain his people through lean times, just as the Hermit bears the light through darkness.

---

37. Crowley, *Gems from the Equinox*, 207.

ADVANCED CONCEPTS FOR FURTHER EXPLORATION

- The Kabbalistic "Ancient of Ancients" and the "Ancient of Days" figures in Judaism and Christianity that archetypally resonate with the Hermit iconography

- The Biblical phrase the "light of the world" and the parables of "salt and light" and "lamp under a bushel" are also relevant to the Hermit card

- Crowley lists "the Vital Triads" in the back of the *Book of Thoth* and includes the Hermit as one of the three Gods I A O (along with the Fool and Magician)—referring to card IX as "the Secret Seed"—a reference to the seed-like form of the letter *yod*, the foundation or seed for all letters, as well as the spermatozoa, the story of Osiris's resurrection and Isis's conception, and the hidden fertility of Virgo and all things below the crust of the earth

- The lyrics of a very old folk ballad, "John Barleycorn Must Die," tell of the personification of the barley crop and the processes of his birth, death, and resurrection as it is sown into the earth, reaped, malted, and transformed by spirits through fermentation

- *Tempus edax rerum*—the saturnine quality of the hermit as "time, which devours all things"

- Note that the Hermit and the opposite path of Justice/Adjustment both have connections with Saturn and time

- Magical Weapon: The Lamp and Wand (Virile Rorce reserved), the Bread

- Magical Power: Invisibility, Parthenogenesis, Initiation

THE WHEEL OF FORTUNE
The Lord of the Forces of Life

Card Number: X

Planets and Dignities: ♃ Jupiter: rules Sagittarius and Pisces, exalted Cancer; Day of the Week: Thursday

Hebrew Letter: כ, *kaph*

Hebrew Letter Meaning: Double letter: Palm (Riches—Poverty); Value: 20

Path 21: Chesed (4, Mercy—Jupiter) to Netzach (7, Victory—Venus)

Color Scales in the Four Worlds: Violet. Blue. Rich purple. Blue, rayed yellow

Themes and Keywords: Being on top—for now. Forces that govern existence. Tendencies. Expansion. Perpetual motion; all things change. Stillness at center. The hand that gives and takes away. The receiving and protective palm. Power of the benefics. Upturn, or change, in fortune. Luck…for the moment. Force multiplier. Fate.

ASTROLOGY/ELEMENT

What better to represent ever-revolving fortune than Jupiter, the largest planet in our solar system, covered by swirling storms and surrounded by moons. Jupiter's moons are named after the Roman god's many lovers. Jupiter is known as the "greater benefic," or greater fortune (Venus being the lesser benefic). It has a generous, benevolent nature and is considered a giver of gifts and good fortune. It inflates and expands that which it comes in contact with, for better or worst—but fortunately, usually for the better.

Jupiter is associated with philanthropy and higher matters of thought: philosophy, ideology, theology, and universal principles. Jupiter is the means through which man communicates with God. Where Mercury rules speedy short-distance travel and commuting, Jupiter rules long-distance travel, mass migrations, and spiritual quests.

Jupiter's glyph looks like the number four, which is the number of its sephira. The glyph is comprised of a crescent attached to the arm of a cross and rising above it. The crescent (like a moon) represents the soul, and the cross, matter. Together they make it a symbol of man's soul triumphing over his worldly experiences, when consciousness is freed from mundane concerns and becomes liberated and impartial as a judge and teacher of divine law on earth.

Jupiter rules Sagittarius as its diurnal sign and Pisces as its nocturnal sign. As Sagittarius, it deals with themes of law, truth, perpetual motion, far travels, and prophecy. Because of its rulership of Pisces classically, it also has some association with themes of faith, transcendence, and self-undoing. Its exaltation in Cancer shows that when it operates from a place of dignity, it is a protective influence.

A spinning wheel spins the blue thread that is woven into life's fabric using a vajra (weapon of Jupiter) as a shuttle. (*Tabula Mundi Tarot*)

MYTHOLOGY/ALCHEMY

Born from the union of primordial gods of sky and earth, Zeus (Jupiter) goes on to couple with—well, pretty much everything that didn't move fast enough. Look closely at any family tree of the gods and you will find it comprised mostly of Zeus's descendants. It's no wonder that the Orphic hymn to Zeus calls him "father of all." The tales abound of his wanton ways. What does this possibly have to do with the Wheel of Fortune? Well, like Zeus, fate has its way with us all, for better or for worse. We can all trace the pivotal moments of our life through seemingly chance occurrences that opened one door and closed another. Some of these unions are fortuitous, others tragic, and some mundane yet pivotal in changing our trajectory.

Because Zeus had saved his siblings from the bowels of their father, he was proclaimed the king of gods and of men. To this day he is associated with fate, law, the sky, weather, protection, and (ironically, considering his philandering) moral conduct.

With Themis, goddess of justice, Zeus sired the three Fates. They are often called "daughters of night" to describe the dark and hidden nature of human destiny. They were also called "daughters of the just heavens" to indicate their hereditary background. As personifications of destiny, they were feared even by the gods, as all were said to be subject to their weavings of the web of circumstance. *Clotho* (Nona) spun the thread of life, *Lachesis* (Decima) measured it to length with her rod, and *Atropos* (Morta) cut it at its determined end.

Alchemically, there is an affinity with circulation, as Hermanubis, Sphinx, and Typhon revolve and represent mercury, sulfur, and salt.

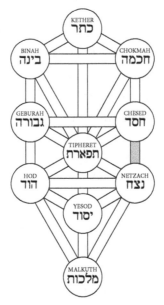

X (10). The Wheel of Fortune/Fortune. Tree of Life.

The Wheel of Fortune's path lies between Chesed and Netzach on the Pillar of Force, whose expansive nature fits well with expansive Jupiter. The sephira Chesed corresponds to Jupiter; the sephira Netzach corresponds to Venus—so it's small wonder that the path between these two classically benefic planets should be strewn with luck and riches. It is also no coincidence that the Wheel is known as the "Lord of the Forces of Life."

Its associated letter כ *kaph* means "hand"—as does the preceding letter, י *yod. Yod* refers to the hand generally and to the hand at work, while *kaph* specifically refers to the palm, outstretched to receive or offer.[38] Both the palm tree and the hand's palm offer shelter from the desert sun; the palm-shaped hamsa amulet offers general protection. These two roles—offering and protection—are also gifts of Jupiter. On the one hand, a fortune is a treasure; a happy abundance of riches. But fortune can also mean fate or destiny, which many believe can be read in the palm of our hands.

---

38. It's also cognate with Canaanite *kappu*, which refers both to the palm of the hand and the protective, shading fronds of the palm tree.

It's worth asking: whose hand turns the wheel of fate? Tarot has answered that question in a variety of ways. Some Western esotericists translate *kaph* as "fist," ascribing to *kaph* an active quality almost reminiscent of *yod*.

As a double letter, *kaph*'s double attribute is wealth/poverty—a reflection on the vicissitudes of fortune. Finally, *kaph* contains the sounds /k/ and /f/ (Greek φ). Crowley, true to form, observed that these were the initial sounds in φαλλος and κτεις, Greek for the male and female generative organs.

RIDER-WAITE-SMITH SYMBOLISM

The Wheel of Fortune (*Rider-Waite-Smith Tarot*)

The Waite-Smith Wheel of Fortune is fourfold in construction, signaling all that is known in the world of matter: directions, elements, Kabbalistic worlds, fixed signs of the zodiac, etc. Spaced around the wheel's rim is the divine name, יהוה, counterchanged with English letters. Most will instantly pick up the word TARO(T)—sometimes called the "book of fate." But you might also see ROTA ("wheel"), ORAT ("speaks"), TORA (the law or "Torah"), and ATOR ("Hathor").

Alchemical glyphs adorn the axes of the circle. At the top, mercury's symbol; at left, the salt symbol; at right, the sulfur symbol. These three are the *tria prima* of alchemy. The glyph at the bottom, though it resembles the Aquarius glyph, is more likely the alchemical sign for multiplication, a process by which the alchemical product becomes more voluminous. Or the four symbols may be elemental: mercury/air, sulfur/fire, salt/earth, wavy final glyph/water.

Atop the Wheel is the enigmatic sphinx. Modern tarot scholars consider the yellow descending serpent to be monstrous Typhon and the red "devil" figure to be jackal-headed psychopomp Hermanubis.

The Kerubic beasts from Ezekiel 10 occupy the card's four corners; their books may be the Gospels:

Lion = Leo = fixed fire = Regulus = Raphael = Mark

Eagle = Scorpio = fixed water = Antares = Uriel = John

Angel/Man = Aquarius = fixed air = Fomalhaut = Gabriel = Matthew

Bull = Taurus = fixed earth = Aldebaran = Michael = Luke[39]

Waite suggests that the wheel's inscriptions are the "divine intention within," while the living creatures manifest a "similar intention without."[40] While change is constant, it is also divinely intentional. But from a human perspective, is fortune scripted, haphazard, or both?

---

39. These are traditional Christian correspondences, not necessarily aligning with the Golden Dawn's directional and archangelic correspondences.

40. Waite, *Pictorial Key*, 108–11.

WHEEL OF FORTUNE

Even in this minimalist image, we see traces of Waite-Smith's Kerubic beasts as astrological glyphs. The iconic Wheel inscriptions also remain. (*Linestrider Tarot*)

THOTH SYMBOLISM

The Thoth version is lit by Jupiter's lightning bolts that "destroy, but also beget."[41] Jupiter correlates to Vishnu the preserver in Hinduism, but in a sense, he is all three aspects of the Brahma-Vishnu-Shiva trinity as the creator (staff of life), preserver (the mountain), and the destroyer (the thunderbolt).

The story of the revolving creatures is told in Crowley's enactment called the "Rites of Jupiter."[42] The creatures relate to the alchemical elements. Crowley refers to them as the gunas, or tendencies, of Hindu philosophy. They are said to be continually revolving, with nothing able to stay in each of the three states for long.

Hermanubis takes mercurial sattva, the mediating tendency of reason. Gaining knowledge is a pursuit that lifts one up from the mire, and thus he is shown rising. Typhon is the emotional heart shown descending. Typhon corresponds to salty tamas, the inclination toward inertia. He separates the ankh of life from the crook of Osiris, referring to his association with Set. Topside is rajas: Sphinx, describing the action of the four elemental powers. The sphinx is attributed to Malkuth: mankind and his quest for mastery of the four worlds. It is a reminder that here in the mundane lies

---

41. Crowley, *Book of Thoth*, 91.

42. Crowley, *Rites of Eleusis*.

fortune. Yet the card also tells us that what happens here on earth is mirrored in the heavens, for another wheel is reflected above.

At the apex of the pyramid behind, the hub of the wheel converges. In the Jupiter rites, there is an oracular figure called *centrum in trigono centri*. This hub is like that of the still point at the center, the axle that "moveth not" or the stillness sought in order to transcend the wheel of samsara and attain nirvana.[43] At the base of the wheel is a very small hand clenched into a fist, indicating the action of the hand, that of opening and closing, giving, receiving, and taking away.

RELATED CARDS

As Jupiter, the Wheel of Fortune rules Sagittarius and Pisces. Temperance (Sagittarius) reconciles the human paradox—part mortal, part eternal—in the same way the hybrid body of a centaur does. In the arrow's flight is a kind of spiritual striving—Jupiter's realms of belief, philosophy, and myth. The Moon card (Pisces) embodies Jupiter's fertility, dissolving of obstacles, and connection to the eternal imagination. If Temperance takes a vertical path to the sublime, the Moon suggests invisible worlds present right beside us.

Jupiter rules five of the thirty-six decans: as the 8 of Swords, or "Lord of Interference" (Gemini I), he is in detriment, waiting out fortune's ebbs and flows. As the 6 of Wands, or "Lord of Victory" (Leo II), he rules the moment of victory at the Wheel's apex. As the 4 of Swords, or "Lord of Truce" (Libra III), he provides equilibrium through the rule of law. As the 2 of Pentacles, or "Lord of Change" (Capricorn I), he eases travel and new enterprises. As the 9 of Cups, or "Lord of Happiness" (Pisces II), he rules both decan and sign; the "card of wishes" brings dreams to reality.

The 8, 9, and 10 of Wands (all Sagittarius cards) describe the legendary nature of a quest and its multiplication through strength and determination. In the 8, 9, and 10 of Cups (all Pisces cards), we navigate the great unconscious to escape nightmares and find dreams.

---

43. Crowley, *Book of Thoth*, 257.

Numerically, the Wheel, as 1 + 0, relates to the Fool and Magician, as well as the Sun via reduction (19; 1 + 9 = 10 = 1), cards holding secrets to the power of creation expressed through time.

ADVANCED CONCEPTS FOR FURTHER EXPLORATION

- Explore the difference and similarities between the three gunas of Hindu philosophy with the three primary elements and the elemental "powers of the sphinx" residing at the top of the wheel

- To understand the Thoth Wheel of Fortune card, read the full text of the "Rites of Jupiter" (part of the performances of planentary rituals called *The Rites of Eleusis*) and understand the relationship of Hermanubis, Typhon, and Sphinx on the rim with the *centrum in trigono centri* figure at the hub of the wheel

- The riddle of the sphinx in Sophocles's *Oedipus Rex*, speculated to be some version of this: "A thing there is whose voice is one; Whose feet are four and two and three. So mutable a thing is none That moves in earth or sky or sea. When on most feet this thing doth go, Its strength is weakest and its pace most slow." The answer is man—also symbolized by the sphinx

- Contemplate the idea of the 1 and the 0 (X as 10) as an axle and wheel, positive and negative polarities in fluctuation that create a perpetual motion machine, or a cosmic "on and off" button

- Magical Weapon: The Sceptre

- Magical Power: Power of Aquiring Political and other Ascendancy

JUSTICE/ADJUSTMENT
The Daughter of the Lords of Truth,
The Ruler of the Balance

Card Number: XI (RWS) VIII (Thoth)

Sign and Dignities: ♎ Libra, cardinal air. Ruler Venus, Saturn exalted;
Motto: "I balance"

Hebrew Letter: ל, *lamed*

Hebrew Letter Meaning: Simple letter *lamed*: Ox-Goad (Work); Value: 30

Path 22: Geburah (5, Severity/Strength—Mars) to Tiphareth (6, Beauty—Sun)

Color Scales in the Four Worlds: Emerald. Blue. Deep blue-green. Pale green

Themes and Keywords: Truths. Balance. Equilibration. Order. The dance. Cause
and effect. Action/reaction. Karma. Impartiality. Love (Venus) and law (Saturn).
Severity/mercy = tempered justice. Nature's exactitude. Structured air = music.
Weigh and prune versus continuously adapt. Time and timing.

ASTROLOGY/ELEMENT

"Weight, measure, and balance" describes the process of Libra, the Scales. Weight correlates to the word Libra, but also to Saturn, which is exalted in the sign. Venus, which rules the sign, describes measure and balance, or the idea of fairness proximate to justice.

Libra is the sign of partnership. It seems even the constellation doesn't like to be alone, for in antiquity it was considered merged with Scorpio; it functioned as the claws of the scorpion. From the second century, the claws evolved into a separate constellation the Greeks called *Zugón*, meaning the yoke or crossbeam of the balance, which connects things together. The yoke was also *jugum* (Latin), meaning pair, couple, and wedlock. *Libra* means weight or measure, the Scales; Libra's motto is "I balance."

This is the cardinal air sign, which initiates the element of air in the zodiac. The glyph of Libra looks like a stylized set of scales. It's a flat line (horizon) with something that looks like a capital omega over it. As the last letter of the alphabet, omega corresponds to the end, and thus the Universe card, which is the card of Saturn. Nature is not just, but it is fair—a concept of both Libra and Saturn. The glyph looks like a bird flying toward you over a horizon, above the earth and through the air, rising above in order to get a top down, impartial, balanced, dispassionate view. It also looks a little like a waist (the flat line or belt) with the line under the ribs above it—the diaphragm, the muscle that relaxes and contracts to create a vacuum (Fool).

While Justice's sword and scales are still clearly evident, this version has a particularly Venusian (for Libra) character. (*Pre-Raphaelite Tarot*)

MYTHOLOGY/ALCHEMY

Ma'at means "that which is straight"; that is, level and in balance. Her single feather represents her as the personification of truth, for it was her feather used as a unit of measure in the Egyptian ceremony of the weighing of the heart. In the Hall of Ma'at, also known as the Hall of Two Truths, the dead would need to profess their innocence of impure deeds before forty-two gods by name. Since the soul was thought to reside in the heart, the heart was weighed in the scales against the feather to see if there was balance. Anubis administered the test and Thoth recorded the results. If they passed, Osiris would admit them to the Field of Reeds, where they would be granted rebirth. Failure meant the heart would be devoured by the crocodile goddess Ammit, permanently condemning the soul.

The Titaness Themis is the Greek personification of law and divine order also associated with the scales. Themis governed right customs and proper procedures. Her sword represented her ability to separate fact from fiction. Knowing both cause and effect, she was valued as a seer of truth and justice. With Zeus, she bore the Horae (Hours), goddesses of the proper moment and the rightness of order unfolding over time, and the Moirai (Fates), the sisters who determined the destiny of gods and mortals alike.

Nemesis may have been a sister of the Fates (probably yet another progeny of Zeus). Her name relates to a word meaning "to give what is due" and shows her as the goddess of inescapable divine retribution for arrogance and crime.[44]

---

44. *Merriam-Webster*, s.v. "nemesis," accessed December 14, 2020, https://www.merriam-webster.com /dictionary/nemesis.

Sword, scales, crown, wings—this is Justice as the cardinal virtue, expressed in goddess-like form. (*Ancient Italian Tarot*)

QABALAH—PATH 22

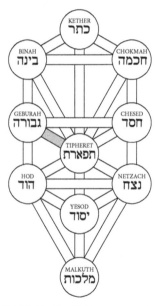

XI/VIII (11/8). Justice/Adjustment. Tree of Life.

The path of Justice/Adjustment runs from Geburah to Tiphareth. Geburah, sephira of Mars on the pillar of Severity, provides Justice's sword; Tiphareth, sephira of the sun on the Middle Pillar, provides Justice's balances. In a sense, Justice/Adjustment maintains the equilibrium of Tiphareth, weighing to establish fairness and then pruning away what is unneeded.

The single letter associated with Justice is ל *lamed*, meaning "to teach," or "ox-goad." If that sounds familiar, it's because א *aleph*, the Fool's letter, means "ox." Adjustment gives structure to the Fool's primal force; as Crowley puts it, she is the Fool's "dancing partner."[45] What's more, the two letters together form אל, one of the names of God. One might say this dynamic motion—the Fool providing the breath of life, Justice/Adjustment shaping and correcting it—makes our very world turn.

The relationship between Saturn and Venus (Libra's ruler) is profound. (In fact, the Empress's Hebrew letter, *daleth*, when spelled out—דלת—brings together these planets with Justice as intermediary: ד = Empress/Venus, ל = Justice, ת = World/Saturn. The restrictive sword of Justice gives rhythm to the air waves (the Fool is elemental air); this produces music. Careful weighing in Justice/Adjustment's scale promotes the symmetry of form we consider beautiful. In other words, beauty arises from the measurement, regulating, and adjustment of both time and space.

Unlike eternal Kether, Justice/Adjustment can only take place in actual time, balancing action and reaction. (To serve justice, one must "do" time.) Finally, the single-letter attribute of *lamed* is "work," the application of effort—through time.

---

45. Crowley, *Book of Thoth*, 87.

RIDER-WAITE-SMITH SYMBOLISM

Justice (*Rider-Waite-Smith Tarot*)

The minimalist surface of Pamela Colman Smith's Justice conceals some heavy-duty symbolism. In her left hand she holds the scales—the very ones which caused the Golden Dawn to switch Justice's numbering from eight to eleven.[46] If we place Justice along the path on the Tree of Life, the scales extend down toward Tiphareth and the sword upward toward Geburah. You could even call the crown Kether and the stone bench Malkuth.

The crown Justice wears is a "mural crown," like the one seen on the 4 of Pentacles—a type of crown typically depicted on the head of a genius loci or spirit of the city. This signifies Justice's crucial role in civil society. The purple veil behind Justice's throne sets apart the place of judgment as an objective arena or an examining room.

Waite says that Justice's pillars open to a world different from the Priestess's—perhaps the material world versus the divine world. (The square motifs on Justice's crown and robe, the robe's red color, and the white foot peeking out beneath it echo that idea of a pure intention steeped in a world of matter.) Unlike the dark and light pillars of the Priestess, Justice's are blank stone. This may refer to the "Hall of Two Truths" from one of the Golden Dawn's initiation rituals. In this enactment of the soul's judg-

---

46. The original sequence: VII The Chariot/Cancer, VIII Justice/Libra, IX the Hermit/Virgo, XI Strength/Leo. With the Justice-Strength switch, perfect zodiacal order became possible: VII/Chariot/Cancer, VIII/Strength/Leo, IX/Hermit/Virgo, XI/Justice/Libra.

ment by Ma'at, the initiate describes what inscriptions should be on the pillar; they are blank because it is a test!

THOTH SYMBOLISM

Crowley renamed this card "Adjustment" to differentiate the idea of human justice with that of the natural order: the cause and effect of nature and the idea that it is not just, but exact. Maintaining equilibrium is a dance, ever moving, an active process of infintitesimal corrections through time.

The goddess of Adjustment in the Thoth card, rather than holding the scales, *is* the scales. In the pans, the Alpha and Omega are perfectly balanced in bubbles of air. The body is the fulcrum, poised on its toes and the tip of a sword. The "chains of cause" are suspended from the feathered headdress of Ma'at. The figure is masked (impartial) but not blindfolded, dressed in Venusian greens and blues while the chains, pans, and sword have Saturnine black. The image is a description of Saturn's exaltation in Venus and of the Thelemic concept that love (Venus) is the law (Saturn).

Her sword placement between her thighs shows her to be the "woman satisfied" (who, in Crowley's deck, comes before the Hermit! Literally, since she is card VIII.) As the woman satisfied, the daughter (Malkuth) becomes the mother (Binah), Saturn's cycle of maturity. The sword itself is the same as seen in the Ace—the great sword of the Magician whose design embeds the seven planets and the Tree of Life.

She stands inside of a geometric vesica piscis, a large diamond, with smaller diamonds above. The diamond shapes refer to Kether as well as Adjustment's relationship to the Fool: the ox-goad, or prod, to his ox. The letters of the Fool and Adjustment (*aleph lamed*) spell the Hebrew words *AL* (God, all) and *LA* (not, or nothing). These polarities, in perfect balance, cancel each other out.

RELATED CARDS

The ruler of Libra (Justice/Adjustment) is Venus (the Empress). Though airy Justice/Adjustment may seem like a cerebral place to seek the goddess of love, her presence is everywhere. In her scales is not just the beauty of perfect proportion—it is equal opposites attracting: the Fool and Justice/Adjustment, Venus and Saturn, the first and seventh astrological houses. After all, what relationship—romantic or otherwise—can last without equality, fairness, and mutual trust?

Justice/Adjustment's three related decanic minors are the sword cards of Libra: the 2 of Swords (*Peace*—moon ruling Libra I), the 3 of Swords (*Sorrow*—Saturn ruling Libra II), and the 4 of Swords (*Truce*—Jupiter ruling Libra III). The story of these cards is that of the individual standing at a crossroads: at an impasse, torn between two equally good paths, realizing that action must be taken; finally, compromising to find liberation. You can also see the story of these three cards as one of interpersonal relationships: recognizing the Other, sacrificing one's ego for the benefit of the relationship, learning to compromise.

The court card corresponding to Justice/Adjustment is the Queen of Swords, who inhabits the first two decans of Virgo (the final decan belongs to the Prince (Thoth) or Knight (RWS) of Cups). Fierce lover of the truth, the Queen of Swords pierces all illusions. Interestingly enough (given that Justice is the Fool's dancing partner), she has enjoyed a long reputation in the cartomantic tradition as an excellent dancer.

ADVANCED CONCEPTS FOR FURTHER EXPLORATION

- In Justice/Adjustment—perhaps more than any other zodiacal major card—there is emphasis on the planet exalted in the sign, calling out Venus's relationship with Saturn. How does Venus (love) influence Saturn (law)?

- Note that the RWS figure is open-eyed and the Thoth figure is masked, but neither is blindfolded. The idea of blind justice as impartiality comes from early blindfolded representations of Justicia, or Lady Justice, with her sword and scales, who sometimes was portrayed as paired with Prudentia, whose iconography included a mirror (Venus) and serpent (Saturn)

- The woman of Justice/Adjustment is said to be the Fool's "goad" and dancing partner, for the Fool is *aleph*/ox, and Justice is *lamed*/ox-goad. Together these letters spell *AL*, god and all, and *LA*, not and nothing—an important relationship. Note that the foundational text of Thelema is the *Book of the Law* (*Liber AL*), and one of its central philosophies is "Love is the Law, Love under Will."

- *Daleth lamed tau* is *daleth* spelled in full. If *daleth* (Venus) is the Empress or mother, *tau* is both Saturn and the maiden of the universe, the daughter. *Lamed* connects them as the concept of the "woman satisfied" or the process of achieving that symbolic graduation from one to the other

- Mankind has progressed through the "ages," or Aeon, of Isis (matriarchal age) and Osiris (patriarchal age). Mankind is now said to be in the Aeon of Horus (the age of the "conquering child"). What does it signify that what follows is the Aeon of Ma'at?

- Magical Weapon: The Cross of Equilibrium

- Magical Power: Works of Justice and Equilibrium

THE HANGED MAN
The Spirit of the Mighty Waters

Card Number: XII

Element: ▽ Water

Hebrew Letter: מ, *mem*

Hebrew Letter Meaning: Mother letter: Water; Value: 40

Path 23: Geburah (5, Severity/Strength—Mars) to Hod (8, Splendor—Mercury)

Color Scales in the Four Worlds: Deep blue. Sea green. Deep olive green. White flecked purple

Themes and Keywords: Dissolution. Sacrifice. Renunciation. Redemption. Immersion. Baptism. Crucifixion. Listening. Change of perspective. Suspension. Time out. Cleansing. Earned or bought wisdom. Lucid dreaming. Stillness. Meditation. The power of water. Roads less traveled. Waiting. Self-abnegation. Annihilation of self in the beloved. Enlightment process.

ASTROLOGY/ELEMENT

Note that the esoteric title is the *Spirit* of the Mighty Waters. Our three primary elemental majors (Fool, Hanged Man, Judgement/Aeon) are the only ones thus named. The Hanged Man is the major representing the element of water, physical and astral. As an element, it is considered cold and wet, or phlegmatic in temperament. The phlegmatic nature is dispassionate, so though this is also the element of emotions, it is serenity, and rising above them.

The symbol of water is the downward-pointing triangle, showing that it has traits considered feminine, like receptivity and intuition. A downward-pointing triangle is also a very rough pictogram of the heart, as water as a symbol is associated with the feeling realms. Water is associated with consciousness itself, personified by the vastness of the sea, and the tranquilizing hush of endless waves upon the shore. Bodies of placid water present us with reflection, stillness, and depth. Water is the replenishing source that cleanses, purifies, baptizes, quenches, and conquers. It is the amniotic fluid of conception and life, yet the direction of the element, the west, is associated with endings and death.

This honey pot ant, a living reservoir of nectar and water for its community, reinterprets the Hanged Man's realm of service, sacrifice, and elemental water. (*Animal Totem Tarot*)

The Hanged Man as spiritualized water also has an affinity for Neptune the dissolver, the modern ruler of Pisces, and for twelfth house themes of transcendence, renunciation, and self-undoing. But as elemental water, it is associated with the entire

Cups suit and traits of all of the water signs: Cancer as birth and baptism, Scorpio as death and transmutation, and Pisces as sacrifice and resurrection.

MYTHOLOGY/ALCHEMY

Alchemically, water relates to dissolution, either the physical dissolving of the alchemical ash of calcination into water or, psychologically, the purification of the psyche through immersion in the unconscious. "Let go and let God," or going with the flow and remaining open to the previously rejected parts lurking in the unconscious mind. Treasures guarded by your demons surface, and you feel recharged and elevated.

The mythologies suited to this card are the dying gods of Frazer's *Golden Bough*, and the stories of sacrifice, resurrection, and redemption: Tammuz/Dumuzid, sent to the underworld for failing to mourn Inanna; Osiris slain by Set and reassembled by Isis; Jesus the crucified and resurrected; Lazarus who arose from the tomb; Attis the self-castrated; beautiful Adonis, slain lover of Aphrodite transformed by her tears; Dionysus slain by Titans and resurrected by Zeus; Mithras the savior, guardian of waters; and perhaps most fittingly, the Norse god Odin.

For nine days and nights Odin, wounded by a spear, willingly hung himself upon the world tree Yggdrasil without food or drink. He sacrificed himself to himself, or his lower self to his higher, in order to acquire the secret wisdom of the runes. In another tale, Odin sought Mimir's well at the roots of the tree Yggdrasil. Mimir, the rememberer, was the guardian of memory and knew all things. Odin sacrificed an eye for a taste of the water that granted wisdom. For Odin, no sacrifice was too great for knowledge and no price too steep for understanding. He gave up one way of seeing things (his eye) for another type of perception.

THE HANGED MAN

מ ▽

The Hanged Man is shown as Odin, who hung upon Yggdrasil and gave up his eye to Mimir for a taste of elemental water from the Well of Wisdom. (*Tabula Mundi Tarot*)

QABALAH—PATH 23

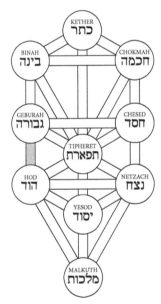

XII (12). The Hanged Man. Tree of Life.

The path of the Hanged Man runs from Geburah to Hod, along the Pillar of Form (or Severity) and directly below the path of the Chariot. In a sense, the Hanged Man floats inverted, with his head in mercurial Hod and nothing beneath—a suspension of rational intellect. You could say he is positioned, along with the equally watery Chariot, between the waters above and below, sky and sea (a reference to Binah, at the top of the Pillar, and possibly the watery paths of Death/Scorpio and the Moon/Pisces nearby on the lower Tree). Water requires a vessel to hold form, which perhaps explains the presence of these paths along the Pillar of Form; on this side descend the waters of divine grace, while its fiery spark descends on the opposite side of the Tree.

The Hanged Man corresponds to Hebrew Letter מ *mem* and elemental water. Unlike the other two mother letters, א *aleph* and ש *shin*, *mem*'s literal meaning is the same as the element it represents: water. In Jewish mysticism, *mem* can represent the "sea of Torah" or "ocean of wisdom." This thirst for spiritual connection with the divine accords with the Hanged Man's self-sacrificing quest for secret wisdom.

As trump 12, the Hanged Man connects numerically to trump 21, the World. In the Cube of Space (a representation of all twenty-two paths) the paths of the Hanged Man, the Fool, and Judgment form axes that intersect at a central point—the World. By closing letter ת *tav*, you can obtain the final form of ם of *mem*. The Hanged Man is the sacrifice of perfect purity; the dying god who redeems/reverses the wrongs of a broken World.

RIDER-WAITE-SMITH SYMBOLISM

The Hanged Man (*Rider-Waite-Smith Tarot*)

Hanging by the foot once was an intentionally humiliating form of administering justice. (Mussolini's corpse, for example, was hanged by the foot in 1945.) Although the Hanged Man had been equated with traitors and their punishment for centuries, the Waite-Smith deck instead depicted a sacred outcast, perhaps even a saint. The Hanged Man's halo is the most obvious clue, but—in her economical, not necessarily intentional way—Pamela Colman Smith left other clues as well.

The Hanged man's gibbet, a T-shaped *tau* cross, may have been the actual shape of the Holy Cross. It may refer to letter *tav*, once a cross-shaped hieroglyph and a signal of the card's connection to the World. Living ivy, a perennial assorted with immortality, bedecks the cross. This signifies that the Hanged Man's tree is a living tree, and his sacrifice—a form of inhibitory gnosis—serves eternal life.

Waite mentions that some believe the Hanged Man represents the "missing" cardinal virtue prudence (fortitude = Strength, and Justice and Temperance explain themselves).[47] He described Hanged Man's crossed legs as a "fylfot," i.e., a swastika, referencing the four of matter over the divine, triangular three formed by the figure's head and arms.

After the deck's 1909 release, the image would reverberate through popular culture. In T. S. Eliot's "The Waste Land," fortuneteller Madame Sosostris declares: "Here, said she / Is your card, the drowned Phoenician Sailor, / (Those are pearls that were his eyes. Look!)… I do not find / The Hanged Man. Fear death by water." In *Star Wars Episode V: The Emperor Strikes Back*, Luke Skywalker, hanged by the foot, reaches for his lightsaber with the Force.

THOTH SYMBOLISM

The drowned man and gallows of previous Aeons are superseded. Here the figure is suspended, crucified without suffering, by the nails (*vav*) of the Hierophant. With no support from below, he is dependent upon something higher, the inverted ankh. The ankh is a symbol of life equivalent to the Rose Cross, or the symbol of Venus (love, Tree of Life). It is also symbolic of the sandal strap representing the fifth power of the sphinx, "to go." Yet it is inverted; as of now, the Hanged Man isn't going anywhere.

---

47. Really, though, the World as Prudence makes a stronger argument. See "Rider-Waite-Smith Symbolism" in "The World/Universe."

He is communing with the highest divinity, shown by the white rays of light (Kether) through the green sky (Venus/love). His foot is attached by the coils of a serpent (wisdom), and a second serpent is coiled in a black chalice below. The black chalice represents the sea of mother Binah, the highest waters of understanding, and the serpent is the black and yellow of the utmost depths of the manifest world, daughter Malkuth in Assiah. Twenty-six rays come from his head (YHVH), with eighteen of them (lunar/water) entering the chalice.

His posture forms the cross above the triangle, an emblem of the Golden Dawn. This again could be Binah (triangle) and Malkuth (cross). Alternately, the cross is a symbol of Tiphareth, the son and realm of sacrificed gods, with the triangle representing the three supernals or divinity. Either way, it is a glyph of the unfolding of light in extension. Crowley calls the posture "the Sleep of Shiloam," a lucid sleep filled with clear light.[48] True to form, the card also hints at sex magic, exhaustion through sexual arousal leading to a state of communion, as well as the "sacrifice of a male child of perfect innocence (Fool) and high intelligence (Magus)" (proto life force lost to masturbation).[49]

RELATED CARDS

As the arcanum of "elemental water," the Hanged Man holds a connection to the three major arcana of water: the Chariot (Cancer), Death (Scorpio), and the Moon (Pisces). In that sequence unfolds his story of willing sacrifice: first, the Chariot's active pursuit (or "Grail quest"); next, Death as the sacrifice itself. Finally, the Moon grants the altered realities and secret visions that the Hanged Man sought from the start.

The story of the sacrificial quest for ascendance plays itself out in the minor arcana in the watery suit of Cups. Two different frameworks work equally well for this tale: the story of a savior's sacrifice and redemption, and the story of a quest for true or hidden knowledge. The Ace of Cups is the Grail itself; it is the Hanged Man's lifeblood that fills it. In the 2, 3, and 4 of Cups (*Love/Abundance/Luxury*) is the story of something precious, nurtured and protected; we see the nature of desire and seeking itself. In the 5, 6, and 7 of Cups (*Disappointment/Pleasure/Debauch*), that which is precious

48. Crowley, *Book of Thoth*, 98.

49. Crowley, 98.

is lost or given up willingly in exchange for something equally precious in an alchemical transaction. And in the 8, 9, and 10 (*Indolence/Happiness/Satiety*) is the gift that sacrifice has bought: regeneration and redemption.

The Hanged Man (12) also relates to the World/Universe (21) through numerical inversion and to the Empress (3) by enumeration (1 + 2 = 3)—suggesting that his sacrifice is integral to the continuous cycle of life in the world of matter. The connection between Empress and Hanged Man draws implicit parallels between sexual and spiritual gnosis.

ADVANCED CONCEPTS FOR FURTHER EXPLORATION

- Tibetan dream yoga, or apprehending the dream within the bardo of sleep

- The connection between the Watcher or Watchtower of the West, and the progression of XII to XIII; the Egyptian *Duat* and waters of *Amenti*

- The meditative trance or absorbtion of samadhi and the experience of the *jhana* states of consciousness

- The sound of *mem* as AUM and the waters of consciousness as astral fluid

- The "eye in the triangle" as related to both XII and in the opposite path of X: the stillness of XII and X as the stillness at the wheel's center surrounded by motion

- The cenotaph of the dying god and the redemption/resurrection formulas INRI/IAO

- The vow of the bodhisattva to work for the enlightenment of all sentient beings by practice and embodiment of the transcendent virtues

- Nirvana as liberation from samsara

- Magical Weapon: The Cup and Cross of Suffering, the Wine

- Magical Power: The Great Work, Talismans, Crystal-gazing

DEATH
The Child of the Great Transformers,
The Lord of the Gate of Death

Card Number: XIII

Sign and Dignities: ♏ Scorpio, fixed water. Ruler Mars (classical) Pluto (modern), Uranus exalted; Motto: "I desire"

Hebrew Letter: נ, *nun*

Hebrew Letter Meaning: Simple letter *nun*: Fish (Movement); Value: 50

Path 24: Geburah (6, Tiphareth—Sun) to Netzach (7, Victory—Venus)

Color Scales in the Four Worlds: Green-blue. Dull brown. Very dark brown. Livid indigo brown, like a black beetle

Themes and Keywords: Transformation. Putrefaction and regeneration. Inevitability. Rising again. Reaping and harvesting. Releasing and recycling nutrients (bioavailability). Surrender of desire nature.

ASTROLOGY/ELEMENT

Sex, death, and rebirth. As fixed water, Scorpio the Scorpion is one of the zodiac's most potent signs. There is no denying the shiver, the frisson, the intensity of the sign of Death. Though the sign is fixed, it isn't inactive; with Mars and Pluto ruling it, it has all the drive, power, and potential to deserve its reputation. Death doesn't give up its secrets so easily though. Scorpio keeps its powerful emotions hidden.

This is the only tripartite sign; there are three main archetypes associated with the three forms of water: ice, liquid, and steam. All are forceful, dominating, and physically magnetic. The base type is the scorpion, who is cunning, jealous, and vindictive. This type stings for pleasure, is a bit of a psychic vampire, and cannot be trusted to fight fair. The main theme is the serpent, transformative and healing, channeling its considerable powers into transmutation of self and others. The rarefied eagle type is subtle and noble, rising above mundane concerns to fly close to the sun.

Scorpio's motto is sometimes seen as "I create," but more often it is "I desire," showing the daring nature of Mars, Scorpio's classical ruler. Mars is aggressive, pursuing its passions with great force and imposing its will upon others. The glyph of Scorpio is an undulating "M" with a barbed tail, which can be the sting of the scorpion or the upraised sexual organ of Mars. Pluto is the modern ruler, expressing the regenerative powers of evolution.

The alpha star of Scorpio is the red heart of the scorpion, Royal Watcher of the West, Antares, meaning "Rival of Ares" (Mars). Like all the royal stars, Antares gives glory to those who overcome its downfall: a tendency toward obsessions and the seeking of intensity and extremes.

This skeleton wears the atef crown of Osiris and rides a composite beast comprised of the three forms of Scorpio: the eagle, serpent, and scorpion. (*Tabula Mundi Tarot*)

MYTHOLOGY/ALCHEMY

Alchemical *nigredo*, blackness or putrefaction, is a process of fermentation. The breaking down of the matter of a body after death leads to new life and the rise to a new state of being. It's not pretty—the ego is thrown into the cauldron of transformation and what bubbles up is disturbing. But fermentation "cooks" the material into something rich and fecund. It is an agent of change that leads to rebirth.

Osiris is the Egyptian god of an afterlife where one travels through the stars and reincarnates. He is shown partially wrapped like a mummy, for after his murder by his brother Set, he was dismembered—and reassembled and reanimated by Isis and Nephthys. Thirteen parts were found and wrapped together. Yet the last part, the penis, was never found because it was eaten by a fish! Isis fashioned him a new one out of clay, and once he was regenerated, they conceived Horus, the executor of his father's vengeance. Osiris's skin is often the green of new growth and life or black for the fertility of the Nile floodplains.

DEATH
THE WALK

**The skeleton wearing the serpent represents the widow Isis:
her husband Osiris was dismembered and thrown into the sea,
and only thirteen of the fourteen parts were found. (*Pharos Tarot*)**

Pluto is the Greek god who rules the underworld (Hades) and the afterlife. The Roman equivalent is *Dis Pater*, which translates to rich father, commonly shortened to Dis. Pluto is often associated with wealth and power due his conflation with the words *ploutos* (wealth) and *pleō* (to flow). As a chthonic god, he rules the underground realms where gems, metals, and mineral riches hide and fertile seeds await their time to grow.

The twin sons of Nyx (night) and Erebos (darkness) were Hypnos (sleep) and Thanatos (death)—a *memento mori* of the inevitable danse macabre.

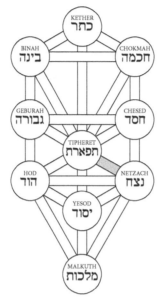

XIII (13). Death. Tree of Life.

The path of Death runs between Tiphareth and Netzach, the sixth and seventh sephiroth (6 + 7 = 13, Death's number). If the "transformers" are the realms above Tiphareth, Death acts as the release of the realms below. To achieve balance in Tiphareth, the desire nature of Netzach must be left behind. In his masterwork *Promethea*, Alan Moore shows his heroines on this path, reassuring each other that Death is "metaphorical." As they soon discover, that doesn't mean it isn't very real.

Like the Fool, the Empress, Strength, and Justice before it (and the Tower, the Sun, and the World after), Death lies on the Path of the Flaming Sword or Lightning Flash. It is an integral part of creation's energizing force.

Death corresponds to Hebrew letter נ *nun*, meaning "fish," dweller in the waters of *mem*, the preceding letter. The letters of the Greek word for "fish," ιχθυς, correspond to *Iēsous Christos, Theou Yios, Sōtēr* ("Jesus Christ, son of God, Savior")—that's why this symbol of wealth and luck also carries the redemptive connotations of Christian salvation theology. The single-letter attribute of *nun* is "movement" because fish are constantly in motion and because the cycle never ends. Life depends on death to recycle nutrients for growth.

Directly opposite the Lord of the Gates of Death on the Tree of Life is the Devil, Lord of the Gates of Matter. Where the Devil binds spirits to flesh, Death releases spirits from flesh; they balance each other.

RIDER-WAITE-SMITH SYMBOLISM

Death (*Rider-Waite-Smith Tarot*)

Pamela Colman Smith's Death, armored like the scorpion of this zodiacal sign, is more exoskeleton than skeleton. One has to ask: what does the armor protect? Nothing, perhaps—in which case it is a symbol of his office. His horse, with its pirate-themed bridle and inflamed eyes, alludes to the four horsemen of the Apocalypse: "And I looked, and behold a pale horse: and his name that sat on him was Death."[50] From Death's helm flies a familiar red feather; signifying life in the Fool and Sun cards, it now droops with spent force.

Emblazoned on Death's standard is Waite's "mystic rose," appearing as the white rose of York but also an emblem of life; Waite specifically describes Death as a card of renewal.

---

50. Rev. 6:8 (Authorized King James Version).

Borrowings from elsewhere in the deck abound. Before Death, four figures—perhaps suggesting the fourfold name—submit. A king lies fallen. A maiden looking very much like Strength turns away in a faint. A Hierophant-like figure, with a fish-head miter (recalling letter *nun*) pleads for intercession, though whether he is praying for life or soul, his own or others', is unclear. Only the child turns toward Death with joy.

In the background flows a river, the home of *nun* the fish. It conveys fixity, for it is always the same river, always running in the same direction. But also it conveys irreversible change, as the same water does not flow through a river twice. Between the pillars of the Moon, the sun of the Fool card is setting—or rising. Either way, it points to the journey into darkness we all must take, and the hopeful or dire certainty that the cycle shall begin again.

THOTH SYMBOLISM

Death here isn't perched on a stolid war horse or posed with his scythe—Death is moving, thrashing, dancing the dance of death, and churning the waters. He appears to be a marionette pulled on strings from the phallic region, resembling the helix of DNA. The bubbles he stirs up contain the dancing forms of new life. The skeleton wears the atef crown of Osiris, though both he and it are black instead of white. Crowley says that he represents Osiris in the waters of *Amenti*, also known as the *Duat* or realm of the dead, where each night, the sun god Ra sailed his barque from west to east.

Crowley considered this card more than just its zodiacal attribution, calling it "a compendium of energy in its most secret form." Though the sign of Scorpio has nothing to do with Saturn, the reaping skeleton with his scythe is a particularly Saturnine symbol of time. Saturn (Binah) represents form, the bones of things, the structure that cannot be destroyed and is left after all else has rotted away through the putrefaction process. In Death, (life) force transmutes to a different form. As Crowley says, "*Redeunt Saturnia Regna*"—the kingdom of Saturn returns.[51]

In the card we see the three scorpionic totems. The eagle flies above. The scorpion stands poised to sting below, between a lily shaped like an alpha and a lotus or poppy pod marked with omega. The flowers are connected, saying that beginnings and endings

---

51. Crowley, *Book of Thoth*, 100.

are inseparable. The serpent mediates between, entwined with the fish symbol that in essence is identical, both espousing the doctrines of regeneration and reincarnation. The serpent is Lord of Life and Death and an apt symbol for the male organ and its potency.

RELATED CARDS

In the Death card (Scorpio), Mars (the Tower) rules over his heavily armed night palace, reminding us that the river of our existence runs in only one direction, and that turning it back is not an option. A steady flood of water dissolves the structures of life we take for granted, releasing them to be rebuilt in new forms. There is no distraction, and there are no exceptions. Some modern practitioners ascribe Scorpio to Pluto, suggesting an affinity between Death and the refining fire of the Judgement/Aeon—in this model, heat and pressure create diamonds.

Death's three related decanic minors are the Scorpio cards in the Cups suit: the 5 of Cups (*Disappointment*—Mars ruling Scorpio I), the 6 of Cups (*Pleasure*—sun ruling Scorpio II), and the 7 of Cups (*Debauch*—Venus ruling Scorpio III). Imagine a compost heap, where cut-down vegetable waste, warmed by the sun, ferments into a new, fertile form. The 5, 6, and 7 of Cups confront the end of one existence and its alchemical transformation into the next.

Death's court card is the magnetic and fascinating Prince (Thoth) or Knight (RWS) of Cups. His are the first two decans of Scorpio; the final decan belongs to the Knight (Thoth) or King (RWS) of Wands. He has the ability to transform reality through his powers of enchantment: in other words, he can transfix his audience, alter consciousness, and create vastly different meanings from existing facts.

ADVANCED CONCEPTS FOR FURTHER EXPLORATION

- The five rivers of the Greek underworld (Acheron, Cocytus, Lethe, Phlegethon, Styx) as mind states associated with transformative processes (woe, lamentation, oblivion, burning, abhorrence)

- *Khenti-Amentiu*, "Foremost of the Westerners," as an epithet of Osiris and Abubis, and the *Duat* as the underworld waters through which the sun god Ra had to travel and battle Apophis, serpent of Chaos, as he underwent the transformation and revivication of his form from the aged Atum to the beetle Khepri

- In Crowley's *Book of Lies*, chapter 16 ("The Stag-Beetle") relates to his Death card as well as to his Tower card (Mars as ruler of Scorpio)

- The alchemical symbolism of fish as associated with primal waters and *prima materia* or "first matter" of alchemy, and the connection to salt and the Empress; salt as both corruption and regeneration

- Death as "Lord of the Gates of Death" and the opposite path of the Devil as "Lord of the Gates of Matter"—or life

- Death as a transition to the alchemical transformation that occurs in Temperance/Art

- Magical Weapon: The Pain of the Obligation

- Magical Power: Necromancy

TEMPERANCE/ART
The Daughter of the Reconcilers,
The Bringer Forth of Life

Card Number: XIV

Sign and Dignities: ♐ Sagittarius, mutable fire. Ruler Jupiter, Dragon's Tail (South Node) exaltation; Motto: "I aim"

Hebrew Letter: ס, *samekh*

Hebrew Letter Meaning: Simple letter *samekh*: Prop (Anger); Value: 60

Path 25: Tiphareth (6, Beauty—Sun) to Yesod (9, Foundation—Moon)

Color Scales in the Four Worlds: Blue. Yellow. Green. Vivid dark blue

Themes and Keywords: Alchemy. Tempering. Refinement. Calculation. Reconciliation of opposites. Synthesis of conscious and unconscious desires. The middle path. Aim and aspiration. Tension of the bowstring before release. Testing. Ordeals that strengthen. Moderation between extremes. Mixture. Covenants as promises within the self.

ASTROLOGY/ELEMENT

Sagittarius the Archer, or Centaur, is mutable fire, the fire of the sun ready to shift at December solstice. The energy of Sagittarius is refined, empyreal, and ethereal, like the rainbow.

The glyph looks like the flying arrow of the archer, the arrow of aspiration. Centaurs combine the speed of man's creative thought with the swiftness and strength of the horse's body to aim their bows heavenward. Their motto is "I aim," but it is sometimes given as "I perceive"—describing their reliable intuition and prophetic tendencies—or as "I seek," for they are the quintessential seekers. The archer aims his arrow toward the Milky Way's Galactic Center, located in the sign, along with the anomaly of the Great Attractor that everything is rushing toward as it follows something larger.

Sagittarius rules the hips and thighs, the part of the body that propels us into forward motion. Sagittarius needs freedom to roam, both physically and intellectually. It is all about the far view, eternally looking ahead while shooting for the stars. It's a paradox of resolved contradictions: unexpectedly brilliant, but fitful and prone to exaggeration; loyal and trustworthy, yet skittish of commitments; true to their word, but prone to procrastinate; strong powers of concentration, but must finish in one shot or is unlikely to resume; honest and refreshingly candid—or overly blunt; does poorly when listening to the advice of others!

With Jupiter as its ruler, Sagittarius is the picture of joviality, being happy-go-lucky explorers and dashing heroes of their own mind. As alchemists, the immortal Centaurs combine fire (will, force) and water (love, form), mingling contradictory elements to distill the hidden stone.

MYTHOLOGY/ALCHEMY

This is *the* card of alchemy, whether in the sense of tempering (Temperance) or in the pursuit of the Great Work, the Art of alchemy. Perhaps mixing fire and water (sulfur/mercury) creates the "salt" in the triad, the ash of the stone. Sagittarius is opposite the sign Gemini, so the *solve et coagula* marriage of the Lovers is consummated here. What was separated and then conjoined makes its way to the final stage of coagulation, the distillation of the red "powder of the sun" that can perfect all things it is added to. As an interior process, it creates a vehicle of will—an astral body of golden light through the action of light upon the pineal gland; a body that embodies one's highest aspirations. In the card too is the rainbow as a symbol of the putrefaction of the Death card, resulting in a stage of many colors or a vision of many-colored lights. It's all in service of the stone of the philosophers, the Universal Medicine.

Asclepius, son of Apollo and god of medicine, learned the art of healing from Chiron the Centaur. Chiron the wise was a healer, a master of arts and philosophy, and an oracle. He was the teacher of almost all the great heroes. Chiron was immortal but traded his immortality to save Prometheus, an immortal chained to a rock who had his liver eaten by an eagle every day for eternity as punishment for stealing fire for mankind.

Since Sagittarius is the Archer, like the Priestess this card is associated with Diana the huntress. The Greeks know her as lunar Artemis, twin sister of solar Apollo and goddess of night and the hunt.

Within the egg-shaped vessel of the crucible, nocturnal Artemis holds
the lunar bow and arrow and diurnal Apollo holds the solar lyre and horn;
they combine as a green-robed hermaphrodite. (*Pharos Tarot*)

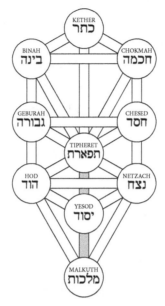

XIV (14). Temperance/Art. Tree of Life.

Three paths form the Middle Pillar: the High Priestess, Temperance/Art, and the World. Central Temperance extends from Tiphareth ("beauty," the sun) to Yesod ("foundation," the moon). Thus sun and moon represent alchemical opposites, brought together on this path. Many paths refer obliquely to the "Great Work," a central tenet of alchemy and the Golden Dawn's initiatory tradition—the ascent up the Tree to encounter the Holy Guardian Angel. This path does so directly, showing how that encounter is undertaken: through "the exchange and balance of opposites," or Spirit tempering consciousness.[52] Only thus can we know our "true will"—what our purpose is, and how to best attain it.

Temperance/Art is the "Daughter of the Reconcilers," but who are the reconcilers? They might be the supernal sephiroth, or they might be Geburah and Chesed, severity and benevolence, force and form, fire and water. Whichever it may be, Temperance reconciles them.

---

52. Wang, *Qabalistic Tarot*, 177.

Hebrew letter ס *samekh* means "prop," "tent peg," or "support"; like the ouroboros, it forms a closed loop. Its tensile strength holds up the dwelling we create for ourselves. *Samekh*'s attribute is "anger," but the actual Hebrew word, רוגז or *rogez*, once meant "quiver." Both senses can be found in the term "agitation."

Below Yesod, three paths or letters reach Malkuth: *qoph* (the Moon's path from Netzach), *shin* (Judgement/Aeon's path from Hod), and *tav* (the World/Universe's path from Yesod). These three letters converge to form *QShTh*—קשת—meaning "bow." This is (1) the rainbow formed when fire and water meet, and (2) the archer's bow shooting its Sagittarius arrow, Temperance/Art, between sun and moon. Temperance is a consummation as tense and quivering as the bowstring before release.

While far removed from esoteric tarot in many ways, this image retains one core symbol: the rainbow, symbol of reconciliation between opposites. (*Animal Totem Tarot*)

RIDER-WAITE-SMITH SYMBOLISM

Temperance (*Rider-Waite-Smith Tarot*)

Tree of Life references abound here. On the angel's forehead shines the glyph of the Sun, a reference to Tiphareth; at the angel's feet lie the waters of the Moon, a reference to Yesod. In the distance on the left, the light of a rising sun takes on the likeness of a crown—a reference to Kether at the top of the Tree; the path to reach it is the Middle Path. The mountains could be the Veil of Paroketh, which separates the lower sephiroth (Netzach, Hod, Yesod, Malkuth) from the higher. Irises adorn the banks: Iris equals "rainbow" in Greek, signifying not just the union of fire and water that makes a rainbow, but the archer's bow of Sagittarius, represented by קשת, *QShTh*, on the Tree of Life.

On the angel's robe, hidden in folds just below the neckline, is the Tetragrammaton. Below that is the "septenary," or triangle within the square. In this 4 + 3 form, it could be matter plus the divine. Or, more likely, the four cardinal (Prudence, Temperance, Fortitude, Justice) and three theological (Faith, Hope, Charity) virtues. The angel may be Michael (associated with fire in Golden Dawn rites) or Raphael, archangel of healing. It is certainly the Holy Guardian Angel of the Great Work.

The cups are solar gold; the physics-defying stream cascading between them, lunar blue. The action mimics tempering in the kitchen, where substances unlike in density or temperature must be carefully intermingled; it also recalls the extremes applied in, say, tempering a sword. The angel stands precariously—one foot on land, one foot in the water, with an expression of serenity or concentration—and is off-center on the card: maintaining balance requires both tension and attention.

THOTH SYMBOLISM

In the "Consummation of the Royal Marriage" of the Lovers, the dark king and light queen combine as one. Gold and silver have been exchanged. The red lion has become white and the white eagle red. The figure is dressed in the vegetal color of the green lion, the "vitriol" that devours the sun and purifies it into gold. The androgyne wears the bees and serpents of the Empress and Emperor. On "her" breast, a *lamen* (solar weapon of Tiphareth) of six spheres marks her as the many-breasted Diana of the Ephesians (lunar). The lamen is in the formation of the lower six planetary sephiroth. The arrow marks the upward path, and is the symbol of will, directed by love.

Reconcile and assimilate equal opposites, distilling them in the golden "cauldron" to remove the dross and realize the higher self. It's the process of rectification—purification of the philosopher's stone and the attainment of communion with the Holy Guardian Angel of Tiphareth.

The path lies between the sun and moon. The white left arm holds the cup of liquid gluten; the dark arm holds the lance with burning blood. The lunar fluids and solar fire coalesce to form the rainbow that follows putrefaction and the "little death" (death's head and raven on cauldron). The rainbow is inscribed VISITA INTERIORA TERRAE RECTIFICANDO INVENIES OCCULTUM LAPIDEM. "Visit the interior parts of the earth; by rectification thou shalt find the hidden stone." V.I.T.R.I.O.L., the universal solvent, is a balance of the three alchemical principles of Atus I, III, and IV. Crowley calls the stone of universal medicine "a talisman of use in any event, a completely elastic and completely rigid vehicle of the True Will of the alchemists."[53]

RELATED CARDS

As the sign of Sagittarius, Temperance/Art is ruled by Jupiter: the Wheel of Fortune. Where the Wheel of Fortune encompasses all the extremes life has to offer, Temperance

---

53. Crowley, *Book of Thoth*, 104.

seeks to reconcile those extremes. Whilst Fortune expands the scope of the journey, Art harnesses the potential energy, the power to travel great distances.

The three related decanic minors are the fiery cards of Sagittarius: the 8 of Wands (*Swiftness*—Mercury ruling Sagittarius I), the 9 of Wands (*Strength*—moon ruling Sagittarius II), and the 10 of Wands (*Oppression*—Saturn ruling Sagittarius III). As a metaphor, these describe the path of an arrow: its flawless trajectory; its unswerving force; its abrupt, ruthless, possibly fatal termination in its target. While this domineering sequence may not capture the refined aspiration of the Great Work, it does hint at the determination required of success—and the all-too-leaden source material that must be transmuted into gold.

The associated court card is the Knight (Thoth) or King (RWS) of Wands. His are the first two decans of Sagittarius; the final decan belongs to the Queen of Pentacles or Disks. Impetuous and charismatic, the Knight/King of Wands illuminates the way and inspires. Like a rainbow, his light fades quickly unless refueled.

The path of Temperance/Art meets the High Priestess on one end and the World/Universe on the other, emphasizing its critical role as a stairway one can take from mortal to divine realms. Fourteen reduces down to five, thus forming a connection to the Hierophant: he who promises to build a bridge between the same opposites Temperance/Art seeks to reconcile.

ADVANCED CONCEPTS FOR FURTHER EXPLORATION

- The Temperance/Art path as the middle path of the Middle Pillar, the arrow of the "bow" of *QShTh*—קשת on the Tree of Life

- The significance that this is the path that connects the sephira of the Sun (Tiphareth) with that of the Moon (Yesod), and that the sign Sagittarius is the exaltation of the Dragon's Tail or South Node, associated with solar and lunar eclipses

- The alchemical symbolism of the green lion that consumes the sun as a process of spiritual purification

- *Lapis philosophorum*, the "stone of the philosophers" of alchemy necessary to the Great Work of transmuting base metals to gold

- The transition from XIII to XIV and the Veil of Paroketh that separates Tiphareth and above from the rest of the Tree: XIV crosses this veil on the Middle Pillar while XIII crosses on the Path of the Flaming Sword

- The centaur of Sagittarius as a human-animal hybrid, and the centaur's association with healing

- Genesis 9:13 and the covenant of the rainbow

- Magical Weapon: The Arrow (swift and straight application of Force)

- Magical Power: Transmutations

THE DEVIL
The Lord of the Gates of Matter,
The Child of the Forces of Time

Card Number: XV

Sign and Dignities: ♑ Capricorn, cardinal earth. Ruler Saturn, Mars exalted; Motto: "I use"

Hebrew Letter: ע, *ayin*

Hebrew Letter Meaning: Simple letter: Eye (Mirth); Value: 70

Path 26: Tiphareth (6, Beauty—Sun) to Hod (8, Splendor—Mercury)

Color Scales in the Four Worlds: Indigo. Black. Blue-black. Cold, very dark gray

Themes and Keywords: Unlived potential. What draws soul to rebirth. Time. Forbidden knowledge. Temptation. Knowledge = power. Climbing. Shadows and light. The eye as mirror of the soul. Mind over matter. Matter over Spirit. Blind impulse. Unstoppable growth. Sex. Material mastery. Hidden structures of matter. Lust of result. Natural vigor.

ASTROLOGY/ELEMENT

Capricorn is the sign of the lusty goat. Capricorn's glyph represents the sea-goat, the head and horns of the goat followed by the curving fish tail. As the mountain goat, Capricorn climbs, gathering knowledge for his own ambitious purposes. As the sea-goat, Capricorn is the redeemer. The oceans hide precious ores churned from the mountains it has worn away. The sea-goat sacrifices his liberty, the mobility of the sea, and submits to the gravity of land to bring these building blocks to humanity.

Capricorn is cardinal earth, the impulse of matter to build, to live and rise. The sign embodies both the heights and the depths. It is placed at the zenith of the heavens, the top of the horoscope wheel. The sign begins at the winter solstice in the Northern Hemisphere, the darkest depths of the year. From there, the sun ascends from the underworld and light can only increase.

In the body, Capricorn rules the knees. The knee bends, allowing for climbing, making Capricorn industrious, insatiable, executive, and opportunistic. The knee bends to yield to divinity, making Capricorn prudent, trustworthy, and heavy with gravitas. Capricorn is serious, yet possessed of mirth and dry wit. It can be a rigorous taskmaster in service of prestige and property—or human betterment.

Capricorn's motto is "I use." Capricorn has self-respect and a strong sense of duty. It's not content to merely have, it seeks to put its resources to use and growth. It has all the desire nature of Mars, exalted in the sign. Yet with all its impulse for manifestation, its unlimited potential is subject to the structures of time and incarnation, imposed by planetary ruler Saturn.

The goat-horned satyr of Capricorn holds the hourglass of Saturn in one hand; in the other he holds a mirror shaped like an eye (*ayin*). (*Rosetta Tarot*)

MYTHOLOGY/ALCHEMY

When the Olympians were pursued by Typhon, Pan leapt into the Nile and changed himself into a goat-fish. Before Pan, there was another god whose emblem was the goat-fish. A third century BC text correlates Sumerian god Enki with Kronos (Saturn).[54] Enki (Ea in Mesopotamia) was a god of wisdom, fertility, and trickery.

Enki was known as the "Father of Light" and "Lord of the Sacred Eye." He lived in the fertile waters of the Abzu, the ocean beneath the earth. The water of the Abzu also represents semen, and portrayals of the god highlight his virility and masculinity. Enki's "water" fertilizes the fallow earth; as the Creator he formed humans of god blood, semen, and clay, intended to act as servants to the gods. His brother Enlil found humans too fertile and too noisy, with too many of them disturbing his sleep. When Enlil decided to wipe humanity off the face of the earth with a flood, Enki taught them to build an ark, thus saving humanity. In the end, the gods imposed restrictions; humans were no longer allowed to be as fertile, and their life spans were drastically shortened.

Ea/Enki was also associated with magic, incantations, and exorcism. Priests invoked him to remove and prevent evil, and for protection of kings. Because of Ea's

---

54. Kramer and Maier, *Myths of Enki*, 10.

role in recovering the "tablets of destiny" that controlled humanity's future, he was called on for purposes of divination, allowing them to see what was hidden. Enki is a precursor of the serpent of Eden. When given a choice between the will of the gods and the needs of the people, Enki always emerged as humanity's redeemer.

QABALAH—PATH 26

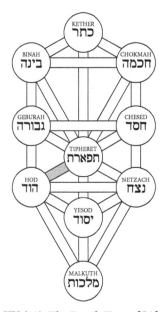

XV (15). The Devil. Tree of Life.

The path of the Devil runs from Tiphareth, the sephira of the sun (Beauty) to Hod (Splendor or Glory), the sephira of Mercury. Both capricious and mercurial, the Lord of the Gates of Matter is a deal-making, knowledge-loving trickster god. His path extends from the Pillar of Form to the Middle Pillar, illuminating the workings of the material world. It parallels the path of the Magician (Mercury) from Kether to Binah; it mirrors the path of the Lovers (Gemini, ruled by Mercury) from Binah to Tiphareth. As Saturn, Binah rules over the path and its tendency to express the confinements of form.

The Hebrew letter is ע *ayin*, meaning "eye" or "to see." (Some attribute the angel Uriel, said to be the sharpest-sighted angel in heaven, to this path.) In Hebrew it is a "silent" vowel. Thus, *ayin* concerns "seeing and not speaking," or understanding. It is twofold in nature—just as we have two eyes. *Ayin tov* ("the good eye") looks toward *samekh*, the supporting prop, and sees the good; the *ayin ra'a* ("the evil eye") looks toward *peh*, the consuming mouth, and sees evil. Thus this path concerns our choice: to see illusions, or to see *past* illusion to the true nature of reality.

A giant eye for Hebrew letter *ayin*, a Saturnine hourglass, and the double helix architecture of DNA accompany the Lord of the Gates of Matter. (*Tabula Mundi*)

The single-letter attribute given to *ayin* is שחוק *sechoq*, an idea encompassing happiness, laughter or light spirits (Hermetic Qabalists usually use the term "mirth"). It could be the laughter of disillusionment, madness, joy, or relief—depending on your point of view.

RIDER-WAITE-SMITH SYMBOLISM

The Devil (*Rider-Waite-Smith Tarot*)

In 1857, French occultist Éliphas Lévi published *Transcendental Magic: Its Doctrine and Ritual* (*Dogme et Rituel de la Haute Magie*), a treatise which would profoundly affect modern tarot. In it appeared a drawing of Baphomet, whom Lévi described as the "Goat of Mendes." Although that Egyptian cult figure was in fact a ram, Lévi's evocative image—a goat-man crouched on a rock and gesturing with his right hand—burned itself into popular consciousness. Eventually it would be officially co-opted by followers of Satanism. Its shadow is in Smith's Devil, whose grimacing face reflects a Japanese print style she knew well. The Devil's gesture mockingly recalls the Hierophant's two fingers up and two down, for the hidden versus the revealed. But here all is revealed—what you see is what you get. The gesture may also point upward to Tiphareth and downward to Hod, from a Tree's-eye view.

Like the Devils of the Tarot de Marseille tradition, this one is a chimera: bat wings, goat horns, clawed feet—an abomination of nature. Between his horns floats an inverse pentagram, signifying matter (four) over Spirit (one); it occupies the place where Kether would be. Beneath his feet lies a stone block which could be the Cube of Matter, or Malkuth. Some believe the Devil figure is to be Uriel; Waite says he is the "Dweller on the Threshold without the Mystical Garden [of Eden]." (Within the

Golden Dawn tradition, the remaining archangels show up in the Lovers/Raphael, Temperance/Michael, and Judgement/Gabriel.[55])

The card parallels the Lovers, almost suggesting a continuation of the same story. Eve has become a horned woman, her fruit-terminating tail reminiscent of the Tree of Knowledge; Adam is a horned man, his flaming tail recalling the Lover's Tree of Life as well as the Devil's torch.

THOTH SYMBOLISM

The Thoth card features Pan Pangenetor, the all-begetter, in the form of a goat in front of Priapus, an erect phallus. Pan Pangenetor *is* the All, the pure impulse to blindly create, appreciating all things and the ecstasy of every phenomenon, from depraved to sublime. *Hen to Pan*: All is One. The Devil is no less god than God. The divine name IAO, *yod-aleph-ayin*, refers to the trinity of creative masculine energy, Hermit-Fool-Devil, or the sperm, Spirit, and the eye of the phallus. Crowley says this is the Tree of Life against forms suggesting the divine madness of spring inherent in the depths of winter. Modeled upon early hand-drawn maps, these forms show the canals of Mars, exalted in the sign.

The crown of the Tree looks like the rings of Saturn. It represents the tip of the phallus penetrating the heavens or circumference of Nuit, transcending all limitations. The roots of the tree are transparent testes. On the left, four female figures pose, one prone while three adore the goat. On the right, a minotaur has climbed to the summit position, while the three other male figures either worship or attempt to supplant him. In each of the testes are the cells of life dividing and ten chromosomes; ten for *yod*, the spermatozoa.

The goat has horns that have grown in the spiraling form of all nature. Before him is the Wand of the Chief Adept, an icon of the divine will of creation. Crowned with the grapes of Bacchus, he smiles. His third eye is open.

---

55. Archangelic correspondences, it should be noted, differ widely across tarot.

RELATED CARDS

The Devil card corresponds to earth sign Capricorn; the World/Universe card is two-fold in attribution: Saturn and the element of earth. It comes as no surprise that, as Saturn, the World card rules over the quintessentially worldly Devil. The Devil binds our spirits to this world of matter—these bodies which sustain our physical being. We are imprisoned, but also vibrant and safe within our walls of flesh. As card fifteen, the Devil reduces to six, the Lovers—the path mirrored above it on the Tree of Life. Both the Devil and the Lovers raise powerful issues of choice and agency, perception and duality.

The Devil's three related decanic minors are those of Capricorn: the 2 of Pentacles (*Change*—Jupiter ruling Capricorn I), the 3 (*Work*—Mars ruling Capricorn II), and the 4 (*Power*—sun ruling Capricorn III). The suit of Pentacles tells a story of conducting the quest for prosperity and eventually transcending it. In the 2, 3, and 4, the engines of production start, work commences, and treasure begins to accumulate.

The associated court card is the Queen of Pentacles (RWS) or Disks (Thoth). She commands the first two decans of Capricorn; the final decan belongs to the Knight (RWS) or Prince (Thoth) of Swords. Resourceful and practical, this Queen climbs tirelessly to build her edifice—whether that is her home, her business, or the stable prosperity of her family.

ADVANCED CONCEPTS FOR FURTHER EXPLORATION

- The Tree of the Knowledge of Good and Evil and the Gnostic text *On the Origin of the World* describing the serpent as a savior sent by Sophia (Wisdom) to persuade and guide humankind toward enlightenment

- The metaphor of serpent to describe the Holy Guardian Angel; the Devil as a Prometheus figure or lightbringer

- Chapter 15 of Crowley's *Book of Lies*, "The Gun Barrel," expands the idea of the Devil as a Prometheus figure

- The "Path of the Serpent" on the Tree of Life: where the "Flaming Sword" is the downward path of the Divine becoming manifest, that of the Serpent is the upward path or the way of return as material existence reappraches its divine origins

- The Devil and the opposite path Death, together comprising the union of Hod, Tiphareth, and Netzach as the "City of the Sun"

- The Devil as the Lord of the Gates of Matter and the Child of the Forces of Time: the relationship between Time and Matter

- Chthonic gods, i.e., Hades, Typhon, Tartarus, and Mercurius

- The Devil as *force majeure*

- Magical Weapon: The Secret Force, Lamp

- Magical Power: The Witches' Sabbath so-called, the Evil Eye

THE TOWER
The Lord of the Hosts of the Mighty

Card Number: XVI

Planet and Dignities: ♂ Mars: rules Aries and Scorpio, exalted Capricorn; Day of the week: Tuesday

Hebrew Letter: פ, *peh*

Hebrew Letter Meaning: Double letter: Mouth (Grace—Indignation); Value: 80

Path 27: Netzach (7, Victory—Venus) to Hod (8, Splendor—Mercury)

Color Scales in the Four Worlds: Scarlet. Red. Venetian red. Bright red, rayed azure and emerald

Themes and Keywords: Martial force. War. The lightning flash of enlightenment. Fire of heaven. Purification by fire. Razing the ground for new construction. Penetration. Eruption. Deconstruction of self. Divine grace. Karmic rebalancing. Breakthroughs. Comeuppances. Revolution. Breaking fertile soil.

ASTROLOGY/ELEMENT

Mars! The red planet of force and drive is consummately masculine and unhesitatingly aggressive. It's always up for battle and action. Mars is what gives us energy to pursue what we desire. Associated with all things warlike in nature, it can also be a force for destruction. War can be experienced externally or internally, and through it is discovered the capacity for courage.

Mars's magical weapons are the sword and the lance, and the glyph of Mars looks like a shield and pointed weapon—or an erect penis! Mars is ruthless; it penetrates and breaks through as man asserts his singular ambitions upon his environment. While it is wrathful in nature, it is also a vehicle of energy that can bring changes that lead to growth, just as the plow rips through the earth before planting. There isn't much doubt that humankind as a whole can be destructive and barbaric. The Hebrew word for Mars, *Madim*, is associated with Adam, the first man of the creation myth, and a term also used in the collective sense for mankind.

Mars rules Aries, the sign of selfhood, and Scorpio, the sign of death (self-transcendence), and is exalted in Capricorn, who builds and climbs. "I am," "I desire," "I use": the mottos all apply. The purpose of Mars is to destroy outdated aspects of the self, so that more evolved elements of selfhood can arise. It is a dynamic force of creation and destruction, with the harsh flavor of the sephira Geburah, saying, "Let justice be done, though the heavens fall."[56]

MYTHOLOGY/ALCHEMY

Ares, the Greek god of war, is the son of Zeus, libertine thrower of lightning, and of Hera, well-known for her jealousy and temper. While Athena rules military strategy, Ares rules the physical violence of war. His Orphic hymn describes him as unbreakable and delighting in the fray of battle and bloodshed. His sister is Eris (Strife), the goddess of discord, whose name relates to a word meaning "to raise, to stir, to excite." She caused the Trojan War by throwing the apple of discord at a wedding party. His sons Deimos and Phobos (Fear and Fright) are also the names of the moons of Mars. His lover Aphrodite, the goddess of love, is also a goddess of war. Their son Eros, god

---

56. From the Latin legal phrase *Fiat justitia ruat caelum.*

of desire, was not above stirring up trouble between mortals with his arousing arrows. Watch out at their family reunion—all hell could break loose!

Dis is also known as Pluto, god of the infernal regions, and the planet co-ruling Scorpio along with Mars. The prefix dis means things like "apart, asunder, not, undo, remove, utterly, deprive, expel, release."

Shiva is one of the three fundamental deities of Hinduism, known as the Destroyer. Yet he also creates, protects, and transforms the universe. His name has connections with nothingness, with redness, with killing the forces of darkness, and with liberation. He is sometimes depicted with a third eye with which he burns desire to ashes. His body is shown covered with ashes to show that all material things are impermanent, and that the pursuit of spiritual liberation is more important. He is sometimes worshipped in the form of the phallic lingam. Five, the number of Mars, is his sacred number. It is said that when Shiva opens his eye, the universe will be destroyed.

QABALAH—PATH 27

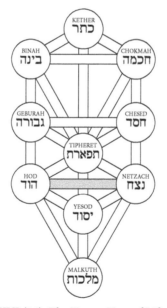

XVI (16). The Tower. Tree of Life.

The path of the Tower runs between Netzach (victory/eternity) and Hod (splendor/glory). The medieval Kabbalists described the God-name of Netzach as *Iehovah tzabaoth*; that of Hod as *Elohim tzabaoth*. That term, צבאות *tzabaoth*, means "armies" or "hosts"—hence the Tower's Hermetic title, "Lord of the Hosts of the Mighty." The path is the lowest of the three horizontal paths, beneath that of the Empress and Strength/Lust. Thus, the realms of Venus (Empress) and Mars (Tower) balance each other on the Tree. The Tower's explosive path serves to destroy the "false ego" that convinces us we are separate from one another.

The Tower corresponds to Hebrew double letter פ *peh*, meaning "mouth"—for several reasons. One of the Tower's source archetypes is the Tower of Babel, where to punish men for their overweening ambition, God confounded their speech: from one tongue to many. This is sometimes viewed as an act of grace, forcing men to work together again on agriculture and the arts of peace—destruction for the sake of unity. In Hod, sphere of the magician (Mercury), the uttered Word shakes the core of reality when vibrated or intoned in ritual. When performing the Lesser Banishing Ritual of the Pentagram, one stands at the intersection of *samekh* (Temperance) and *peh* (the Tower). Hovering just above Yesod and sometimes called the "roof of Yesod," the Tower path is a place of powerful transformation.

The double-letter attributes of *peh* are "grace" and "indignation." Grace, חן *chen*, can mean both elegance and gracious behavior or clemency. Indignation, כיעור *ki'ur*, is probably better translated as "ugliness" or "dirtiness." Here, as in the Babel story and Tower experiences generally, are two ways to interpret a difficult situation.

In the Tarot de Marseille's "La Maison de Dieu," the divine message appears as a multicolored plume, its corrective effect more startling than disastrous. (*Camoin-Jodorowsky Tarot de Marseille*)

By the nineteenth century, the plume had morphed into the catastrophic lightning flash familiar from today's Tower cards. (*Ancient Italian Tarot*)

RIDER-WAITE-SMITH SYMBOLISM

The Tower (*Rider-Waite-Smith Tarot*)

In Pamela Colman Smith's Tower card, a storm fills a blackened sky. In the many earlier versions of the Tarot de Marseille, a celestial plume descends to touch the Tower, suggesting the grace of God. Here the plume explicitly becomes a lightning flash: it is illumination and destruction, but the "lightning flash" is also the zigzag path down the Tree of Life, signifying creation. It terminates in the same arrow that terminates the glyph for Mars.

Further emphasizing the secret creative power of this disaster are twenty-two flaming yellow letter *yod*s, for the twenty-two letters of the Hebrew alphabet and the twenty-two major arcana. The crown at the top of the Tower is Kether, but it may also reference the rite of circumcision, a covenant between human and divine. The mountain at the base could be the structure of the human ego—its accomplishment, ambition, and pride—or it could be Malkuth. The Tower's three windows could similarly represent the three supernal sephiroth: Kether, Chokmah, Binah.

Two figures fall from the Tower. We could call them Netzach and Hod, or we could call them "Kings of Edom" as the Golden Dawn did. Rulers over a powerful kingdom conquered by the Jewish champion Judas Maccabeus, the Edomites represented a fallen order cleared away for a new beginning. In actual readings, though, it has to be noted that this card often calls out the exposure of an affair. Often clients identify the two falling figures as the two parties implicated in the aftermath.

THOTH SYMBOLISM

The Tower, also known as "War," is the orgasm that topples the phallus of the Devil.[57] All colors of red, of fire, are made striking by the use of black (Capricorn, where Mars exalts— and a color of Pluto (Dis)). Flames belch from the mouth (letter *peh*) of Dis, the hellmouth of the underworld. The background is an enormous lightning bolt issued from behind the eye of Shiva, reminding us that this is also a card of enlightenment, of the breaking down of the ego, and the complete realization of the doctrines of impermanence. From the eye, twenty-seven rays (path twenty-seven) shatter the picture plane into fragments.

The dove and serpent appear in chapter 1, verse 57 of the *Book of the Law*. Crowley calls them the two forms of desire, Schopenhauer's "Will to Live and Will to Die." The dove also relates to Venus, the Empress, and the lion-serpent to *teth*, the Lust card: the two other horizontal paths on the Tree of Life. Also, to Netzach (Venus) and Hod (endpoint of path twenty-seven), for the serpent wears a halo of fifteen rays (the number of Hod spelled out); alternately, the Devil's number (Capricorn exaltation). The dove carrying an olive branch is peace escaping the carnage of the Old Aeon, destroyed by Fire (the Aeon). The lion-serpent is identified as Abraxas, a god often seen with the head of a cock and carrying a whip and shield. The word may relate to an ancient Egyptian incantation, meaning "hurt me not."

The house of God is collapsing and four figures are thrown from the top. Their geometric form resembles salt crystals or units of matter. The ten-paned window and quartered-cross window (Malkuth) tell us that this collapse is felt in our material worlds.

RELATED CARDS

The Tower corresponds to Mars and thus also corresponds to the two Mars-ruled majors: the Emperor (Aries) and Death (Scorpio). In the Emperor we see the Tower's fiery, cardinal, initiating energy—the will to dominate and accomplish something of

---

57. Crowley, *Book of Thoth*, 107.

significance; the creative power of the lightning flash. In Death we see the Tower's devastating power to destroy, but also to renew. Mars exalts in Capricorn (the Devil)—where the Tower's potent utterances can reshape the material world. Finally as number sixteen, the Tower reduces to seven, the number of the Chariot. The Chariot's path connects to Geburah, the sphere of Mars, but Mars is in fall in its sign, Cancer, where the martial force is at best contained, internalized, and spiritualized.

Mars rules six of the thirty-six decans—one more than the other planets, for it both ends and begins the year. As 2 of Wands (*Dominion*—Aries I), he rules the generative urge to conquest. As 9 of Swords (*Cruelty*—Gemini II), he fathers Phobos and Deimos, Fear and Panic. As 7 of Wands (*Valor*—Leo III), he grants courage and the will to overcome obstacles. As 5 of Cups (*Disappointment*—Scorpio I), he spills blood and foments grief. As 3 of Pentacles (*Work*—Capricorn II), his tireless energy turns to productive ends. And as 10 of Cups (*Satiety*—Pisces III), he slakes his appetites before beginning the cycle anew.

In the 2, 3, and 4 of Wands (all Aries cards), Mars expresses his drive toward leadership; he who conquers must also rule. In the 5, 6, and 7 of Cups (all Scorpio cards), he underscores the sacrifices people make for what they love, and how ruination can turn to new life.

ADVANCED CONCEPTS FOR FURTHER EXPLORATION

- The horizontal paths on the Tree of Life, *Peh* (80), *Teth* (9), and *Daleth* (4), add up to 93—the *gematria* equivalent to the Thelemic current of love (*agape*) and will (*thelema*)

- The Tower (War/Mars) is the opposite path on the Tree of Life to that of the Empress (Love/Venus)—between them is Strength/Lust

- The Tower as the "Roof of Yesod" or the horizontal path over the sephira Yesod, the foundation

- The concept of the Tower as *La Maison Dieu*, the House of God—and the House of the Devil

- In the Lesser Banishing Ritual of the Pentagram, the adept is directed to stand symbolically at the intersection where the horizontal path of *peh* (the Tower) is crossed by the vertical path of *samekh* (Temperance/Art)

- Magical Weapon: The Sword

- Magical Power: Works of Wrath and Vengence

THE STAR
The Daughter of the Firmament,
The Dweller Between the Waters

Card Number: XVII

Sign and Dignities: ♒ Aquarius: ruler Saturn (classical), Uranus (modern); Motto: "I know"

Hebrew Letter: צ, *tzaddi* (RWS); ה, *heh* (Thoth)

Hebrew Letter Meaning: Simple letter *tzaddi*: Fishhook (Imagination); Value: 90; Simple letter *heh*: Window (Sight); Value: 5

Path 15 (Thoth): Chokmah (2, Wisdom—Zodiac) to Tiphareth (6, Beauty—Sun)

Path 28 (RWS): Netzach (7, Victory, Venus) to Yesod (9, Foundation—Moon)

Color Scales in the Four Worlds: Violet. Sky blue. Bluish mauve. White, faintly tinged purple

Themes and Keywords: Ideals. Hope. The future. Skies clearing. Clear vision. Unexpected help. Guiding light. Navigation. Freedom. Brilliance. Looking ahead. The true or naked self. The sea as sky and the sky as sea. Journeys of the goddess. Beauty in darkness. Distance. Power of the intellect.

ASTROLOGY/ELEMENT

The sign Aquarius is visionary and humanitarian. The constellation is called the Water Bearer, and usually is a kneeling man with a jug, or the jug itself, pouring waters into the area of the sky once known as "the sea." The ancient Sumerians saw Ea here with his twin streams of water. Yet it is an air sign, the fixed and stable center of the air trinity. There are seas of earth and there are seas of the aethyrs. The waters distributed are those of consciousness, understanding things instinctually known and gleaned through the airwaves. The wave-shaped glyph of its symbol shows twin streams of water in motion. The wave forms are also symbolic of all waves: airwaves, wavelengths, radio, electricity, light, brain waves, ESP.

Telephone, telegraph, television, and telepathy; all words whose prefix tele- means far, distant, especially in regard to transmission. This prefix comes from the Greek word *telos*, used by philosophers to denote end, goal, or purpose. Aristotle said that *telos* as purpose can encompass all human activity. The *telos* of Aquarius is "to know."

Aquarius *knows* that all people are one. Its comprehension of fraternity is innate; it senses the connection and communicates it to others. Yet Aquarius is also distant, known for being aloof, cool, and in a world of its own.

THE STAR

Here the traditional golden cup pours the setting sun, while her silver cup is the crescent moon pouring the celestial waters of Aquarius. (*Tabula Mundi Tarot*)

Aquarius has Saturn as traditional ruler and Uranus as modern ruler. Appropriate, for Saturn is tradition and Uranus modernity. Saturn favors structure, Uranus revolt.

Aquarius sees how the establishment can be improved and changed to approach its highest ideal form. What knowledge, inventions, vision, discovery, or social innovation will evolve us through time?

MYTHOLOGY/ALCHEMY

Some of the goddesses relevant include Inanna, Astarte, Venus, Binah, and Babalon, who will be seen in the iconography of the Star cards. The one goddess has many forms, but the goddess of stars personified is Nut.

After the *Inferno* (Tower), Dante sees the night sky. Ancient Egyptian *Nwt*/Nut/Nuit/Nuith is one of the Ennead of Heliopolis, the goddess of the sky and night sky. Thelemic Nuit is the sky goddess speaking in chapter 1 of Crowley's received text of the new Aeon, the *Book of the Law*. Hadit is the center to her circumference and together they create solar Horus.

Egyptian Nut was portrayed as a naked woman covered with stars, arching over the earth and personifying the night sky. Her name in Egyptian is often accompanied by the unspoken determinative symbol for sky. Her husband Geb personified the earth and was considered the father of snakes and creator of earthquakes and crops. With Geb, Nut procreated and made Osiris, Isis, Set, Nephthys, and some sources say Horus, though most say Horus is the son of Osiris and Isis.

Many themes remain consistent across all Star cards: the naked water bearer,
the starry night sky, even the bird (here an owl) on its tree. (*Ancient Italian Tarot*)

Some of Nut's epithets are: Mistress of All, She Who Bore the Gods, Coverer of the Sky, At Whose Feet Is Eternity, Brilliant One, Veil of Heaven, She Who Protects, and She Who Holds a Thousand Souls. She protected souls in the afterlife, and by arching over us kept the forces of chaos apart from the cosmos. At night her form was seen as the Milky Way; the sun and moon traveled through her body, passing through her belly to be reborn at dawn.

Aquarius contains the cross-quarter Gaelic holiday Imbolc, also concurrent with the Thelemic Feast of Stars celebration of Nuit. In the Northern Hemisphere, this is halfway between winter solstice and spring equinox and heralds the unseen, but palpable, awakening of seeds and increasing light.

QABALAH—PATH 15 (THOTH) OR 28 (RWS)

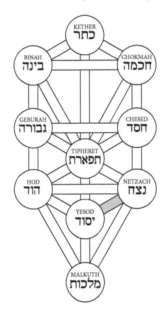

XVII (17). The Star. Tree of Life. Golden Dawn path attribution.

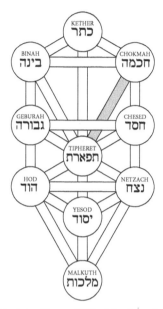

XVII (17) The Star. Tree of Life. Thoth path attribution.

Here is the same controversy first encountered with the Emperor: is the Star's path between Netzach and Yesod? Between Chokmah and Tiphareth? Letter ה *heh* or צ *tzaddi*?

Thoth's attribution comes from Crowley's 1904 vision in which his spiritual guide, Aiwass, declared: "*Tzaddi* is not the Star," leading Crowley to switch the Hebrew attributions of the Emperor and Star.[58] With the Star's placement between Chokmah and Tiphareth, a constellation of three goddesses above the abyss emerges: Priestess, Empress, and Star. Switching the Emperor and Star also balances Crowley's numerical switch of 8 (Lust) and 11 (Adjustment) on the opposite side of the zodiac. With primal and final ה now attributed to the Star and World, the divine name, יהוה, has two feminine and two masculine parts (*yod*, the Hermit, and *vav*, the Hierophant). Imagine the Star glimpsed through a window (*heh*) and offering visions, for the attribute of this letter is sight. The path also connects the Star with Chokmah, corresponding to the starry zodiac.

58. Crowley, *Book of the Law*, 26.

Apart from Crowley, the Golden Dawn's offshoot societies maintained the original attribution: the Star as *tzaddi*, its path between Netzach and Yesod. This maintains the orderly descent of the zodiacal cards down the Tree of Life, rather than jumping back above the abyss between the Devil/Capricorn and Moon/Pisces cards. It places the Star between the "feminine" sephiroth of Netzach and Yesod, leaving the Emperor between "masculine" Chokmah and Tiphareth.[59] *Tzaddi* is the "fishhook" angling in the sea (the Hanged Man/*mem*) for the fish (Death/*nun*); this describes the individual's place within collective consciousness, an Aquarian theme. It also relates to *tzaddi*'s attribute of imagination or thought. Finally, there is a mythic resonance: the Star evokes the passage of Inanna/Astarte to the underworld. There the goddess is hung on a hook by her sister/rival Erishkegal before her rescue, revival, and return.

RIDER-WAITE-SMITH SYMBOLISM

The Star (*Rider-Waite-Smith Tarot*)

"One big star plus seven smaller stars" is the longstanding formula for this card, visible in the earliest seventeenth-century woodcut decks. Why eight-pointed stars? Eight could refer to Mercury, the sephira Hod, the star of Lakshmi, the eightfold path, the compass rose, or spirit (a halfway point between matter, as square, and the divine,

---

59. Corresponding to Venus and the Moon. Chokmah and Tiphareth correspond to the zodiac itself and the Sun.

as circle). The smaller stars' position might represent the Pleiades formation, or a Saturnian scythe. The larger star may be Sirius, our brightest star.[60]

Who is the Star goddess? It could be the Great Mother, Binah (associated with Saturn, ruler of Aquarius), or the goddess Astarte, who in her descent to hell shed her garments at each of the seven gates. As with the Temperance angel, one foot rests on land and one in water; one vessel pours onto land and one into water. This, like the fishhook cast into the ocean, suggests individual versus collective consciousness. Poured from once separate vessels, the stream on land runs back to the sea.

The maiden (as Netzach/Venus) and her pool (Yesod/the Moon) could refer to the Star's path: Netzach. In the distance, what could be the "bird of Thoth" or ibis, which is said to have sung the world into being, rests on the Tree of the Knowledge of Good and Evil. This could refer to Hod, and the distant mountains to Malkuth. (As always, we read Tree of Life inferences as serendipitous rather than intentional. Although Smith received some direction from Waite, her influences came more from historical tarot than from the esotericism of her time.)

THOTH SYMBOLISM

"All I shall tell you is, there was the most beautiful goddess there ever was, and she was washing herself in a river of dew. If you ask her what she is doing, she says "I'm making thunderbolts."[61] We see in this card that beautiful goddess. To understand her fully, one must take in her words in the entirety of chapter 1 of the *Book of the Law*.

The junction of land and water represents the sea of the Great Mother Binah and the shores of the earth (daughter Malkuth), between them lies the Abyss, hidden by her clouds of hair. Behind is the celestial sphere: the primum mobile of Kether behind the zodiac of Chokmah. Her path runs from Chokmah, the zodiac (a sea of stars), to Tiphareth (sun—which is another star). Within the celestial sphere is a seven-pointed star of Venus; her nature is love. Beyond is the seven-pointed star of Babalon, a manifestation of Nuit. Crowley says that from this star, issues "the curled rays of spiritual

---

60. Each year in Egypt, Sirius's first appearance coincided with the flooding of the Nile, the return of fertility, and the full moon in Aquarius (opposite a Leo sun).

61. Crowley, *Konx Om Pax*, 20.

light. Heaven itself is no more than a veil before the face of the immortal goddess."[62] The spiral forms of light are the same shape as the energy of galaxies and nature.

She holds two breast-like cups. From the golden one she pours the ethereal waters of "inexhaustible possibilities" over herself, while with the silver she empties "the immortal liquor of her life" beneath.[63] Two cups, the mother above and the daughter below. The card is about distance and hope, ideals and goals. At the distant shore lies the City of the Pyramids, the penultimate attainment across the Abyss. Five butterflies of Spirit and soul and three (Binah) roses (Malkuth) appear to be crossing.

RELATED CARDS

Like the Devil/Capricorn, the Star/Aquarius answers to Saturn/the World or Universe. But where the Devil emphasizes matter's confinements (the ouroboros), the Star emphasizes spirit's freedom *within* matter; the central nude figure in the Star and World/Universe is the same. The Star's idealistic imagination transforms the World into a castle in the sky. As card seventeen, the Star reduces to eight—the number of Adjustment (Thoth) or Strength (RWS), which represent other aspects of the goddess. As Aquarius, the Star relates to the Fool (elemental air), providing a distant beacon for his quest.

The Star relates to the three decanic minors of Aquarius: the 5 of Swords (*Defeat*—Venus/Aquarius I), the 6 of Swords (*Science*—Mercury/Aquarius II), and the 7 of Swords (*Futility*—Moon/Aquarius III). In the great journey of air from intention to knowledge, these three cards describe the critical role of navigation, pursuing a fixed course through the steady application of the intellect. As in all 5-6-7 trios, the road is smoothest in the 6; the 5 shows the risk, the 6 provides the means, and the 7 confronts the bumps in the road.

The associated court card is the Knight (RWS) or Prince (Thoth) of Swords. The first two decans of Aquarius are his; the final decan belongs to the King (RWS) or Knight (Thoth) of Cups. This Knight or Prince, fierce in intellect, can envision any argument and fight for any principle. His tenacity makes him formidable in debate, for his goal is a Star that is always in his sights.

---

62. Crowley, *Book of Thoth*, 110.

63. Crowley, 109.

ADVANCED CONCEPTS FOR FURTHER EXPLORATION

- Her title as "Dweller Between the Waters" refers to terrestrial and celestial waters, seas of earth and seas of aethyrs, as well as *aqua vitae*, the waters of (universal) life: *amrita* (Sanskrit: nectar of immortality), *nepenthe* (Greek: medicine of forgetfulness for sorrow), *ambrosia* (Greek: immortality drink of gods served by Ganymede, the cupbearer personified in constellation Aquarius), and *alkhahest* (universal solvent of alchemy)

- Daughter of the Firmament as *heh*, window, and the view between the (Thoth-based) path from Chokmah (the zodiac) to Tiphareth (the sun, our star). Alternatively, as *tzaddi* (RWS), her path lies between the feminine sephiroth of Venus (Netzach) and the Moon (Yesod)

- The Star as related to the soul. The Egyptian word *khabs* translates as the unique individual expression of each person from the infinite possibilities of Nuit: "Every man and every woman is a star."[64]

- Magical Weapon: The Censer or Aspergillus[65]

- Magical Power: Astrology

---

64. Crowley, *Book of the Law*, 19.

65. Though listed as "Aspergillus" (a genus of mold) in Crowley's *777*, it is more likely that it should be "Aspergillum," an instrument for sprinkling holy water.

THE MOON
The Ruler of the Flux and Reflux,
The Child of the Sons of the Mighty

Card Number: XVIII

Sign and Dignities: ♓ Pisces, mutable water. Ruler Jupiter (classical) Neptune (modern), Venus exalted; Motto: "I believe"

Hebrew Letter: ק, *qoph*

Hebrew Letter Meaning: Simple letter *qoph*: Back of head (Sleep); Value: 100

Path 29: Netzach (7, Victory—Venus) to Malkuth (10, Kingdom—Earth)

Color Scales in the Four Worlds: Crimson ultraviolet. Buff, flecked silver white. Light pinkish brown. Stone

Themes and Keywords: Illusions. Subconscious realms. End of the zodiac. Witchcraft. The Crone. Taboo. Cycles, especially women's cycles. Fear of the feminine powers. Fluctuations. Changability/unreliability. Madness. Paradox. Sleep. Dreams true and false. Illness. Non-ordinary realities. Altered consciousness.

ASTROLOGY/ELEMENT

At the end of the zodiac we come to mutable water, Pisces the Fish. Mutable water is morphing, impressionable. Here at the last of the signs we come to the "dustbin" where unfinished karma and all of the accumulated debris of the human experience accumulates. Secrets swim in its waters. Pisces is the sign of the subconscious realms, the home of mediums, mystics, mediators, and monastics. Extremely sensitive to the currents of the emotional realm, Pisces are receivers of every vibration. Pisces is a sign of contemplatives, clairvoyants, and other travelers of the subliminal realms like artists of visions, music, theatre, and film. Pisces's motto is "I believe." This can be faith or folly.

Pisces is also known as a psychic sponge, needing to retreat from the world to purify itself. It has a tendency to escapism, avoidance, and overindulgent wallowing in senses. Temple or tavern? Serve or suffer? The fish can be slippery and water is wet. Pisces is hard to understand. Its glyph is two fishes tied together, swimming in different directions. The one that swims downstream is said to be the finite personality, while the other swims upstream and is the infinite soul of cosmic consciousness. Which fish will lead and which will submit to the stream?

Perilous subconscious crossings are illustrated by Greek mythological beings: Scylla, who is shown here as a sea monster with the heads of a dog, wolf, and crayfish-handed woman, and Charybdis, the whirlpool stairway leading into the depths of the subconscious (the sea). (*Rosetta Tarot*)

Jupiter rules Pisces, making them intrepid psychic explorers of the dream world and subconscious realms. Venus is exalted in the sign, giving universal love and compassion. Nebulous Neptune, the modern ruler, is the "higher octave" of Venus, allowing for the highest forms of self-sacrifice and transcendence, as well as themes of imagination, inspiration, fantasy, and deceit.

MYTHOLOGY/ALCHEMY

The dog and wolf of the Waite-Smith card become Anubis and the older deity Wepwawet in the Thoth deck. Both of these Egyptian gods have ties with the underworld and with secrets, thresholds, and secret places. Anubis is the Greek name for the Egyptian god Anpu, who was shown either in canine form or as a man with the head of a black dog. He was called "Foremost of the Westerners" (the dead) and "Master of Secrets." Wepwawet, also known as *Upuaut*, was depicted in jackal or wolf form or as a man with a jackal's head. They are often confused with each other. Both were symbolically colored black and carried the *was*-sceptre with the head of the Set animal. Both were considered either sons of Ra, of Set, or of Osiris with either Isis or Nephthys. Both are involved with leading the departed souls to Ma'at's Hall of Two Truths for the judgment and weighing of the heart test.

Together they are the loyal dog and the wily jackal. Anubis is the "Guardian of the Way" to the underworld and Wepwawet is the "Opener of the Way." As guardian, Anubis is a protective influence over more than just souls. As opener, Wepwawet opens more than just the underworld, but also possibilities and paths external and internal. Wepwawet also opened the way for the sun as he rode in the prow of the solar barque, and he is considered a revealer of religious mysteries and secret initiations.

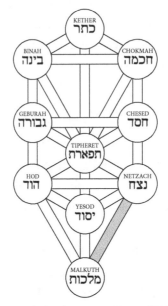

XVIII (18). The Moon. Tree of Life.

The path of the Moon runs from Netzach to Malkuth. It is the first path to connect to Malkuth, the world of the physical self and the senses that allow it to be perceived. This path crosses worlds, too, from the "formative" world of Yetzirah (which holds Netzach, Hod, and Yesod) to the "active" world of Assiah (Malkuth). One end lies in reality, the other in the underpinnings or backstage blueprint of reality. Netzach, meaning "victory" or "eternity," is the sephira of emotions; those traveling this path transcend beyond the ordinary world to the timeless forces that invisibly shape that world—the feelings, assumptions, and unexamined drives that make people act as they do.

Crowley suggested that in descending the Moon's path, the soul organizes the physical body (Malkuth) it will inhabit when incarnate. The Moon's Hermetic epithet is the "Child of the Sons of the Mighty," which the Golden Dawn glossed as the "creations of the created." These creations we can think of as the artifacts and illusions dreamed up by the human mind. One must know them for the phantoms they are before proceeding up the Tree.

The Moon's Hebrew letter correspondence is ק *qoph*, meaning "back of the head"— this is in contrast to *resh*, the head as the organ of thought, which we encounter next, on the Sun's path. The back of the head contains the cerebellum, which governs sense of balance, orientation, and coordination. This seems apt, since the Moon must keep its illusions well-regulated; otherwise, it is easy to become disoriented in reality. The single-letter attribute is Sleep, that nightly realm where people voyage within their own emotional landscapes and unconsciously re-shape their daylight world.

The barge of the moon travels the waters of sleep through the gates of horn
(hand of witchcraft, Neptune) and ivory (phrenology head, *qoph*),
which tell true dreams from false. (*Tabula Mundi Tarot*)

RIDER-WAITE-SMITH SYMBOLISM

The Moon (*Rider-Waite-Smith Tarot*)

While Pamela Colman Smith's illustration clearly hearkens back to the Marseille tradition (moon over two dogs and a crayfish in a pool!), it's also packed with symbols we can choose to read as esoteric. The Moon's face is asleep, the back of the head emphasized by elevation (both referring to Hebrew letter *qoph*). Thirty-two rays surround it, alluding to the the "thirty-two paths" (ten sephiroth plus twenty-two paths). What would be its downward diagonal gaze if the eyes were open could reflect the downward diagonal between Netzach and Malkuth.

If the distant mountains represent Malkuth, then the viewer this side of the pillars may stand in the lunar sephira, Yesod, represented by the pool at the base of the card. (The pool may also represent Pisces, the astrological correspondence of the card.) The two towers could be the Pillars of Force and Form—or, for that matter, the gates of horn and ivory. Fifteen *yod*s hang in the air between them; the fifteenth day of the twenty-eight-day lunar cycle brings us the light of the full moon. These towers are also seen on the Death card—a reminder that just as the light of vitality ends at death, so too must the solar intellect rest each night.

Two canine figures howl at the moon. The left one looks like a domesticated dog the right one like a wolf; our conscious and unconscious minds are close kin and can be stirred simultaneously by the imagination. The crayfish (besides possibly referring to its crustacean cousin, the lunar crab) may be our deepest, monstrous fears, reaching toward the dim illumination that dreams afford.

THOTH SYMBOLISM

Crowley says unconquerable courage is needed to tread this weird, deceptive path. For "the knight upon this quest has to rely on the three lower senses: touch, taste, and smell."[66] Crowley then refers to "Bortsch."[67] "Bortsch" (a deliberate re-spelling of *borscht*) refers to the crimson (ultraviolet) color of this card in the G. D. King Scales. This color is at the spectrum's end, just as Pisces is at the zodiac's end. "Bortsch" also refers to the "witch-moon of blood, eternal ebb and flow."[68] In "Bortsch," the speaker first takes an oath to endure in baffling the three Buddhist characteristics of anicca (impermanence),

---

66. Crowley, *Book of Thoth*, 112.

67. Bortsch is chapter 82 in Crowley's *Book of Lies*.

68. Crowley, *Book of Lies*, 174.

dukkha (suffering), and anatta (not self). Verse two says death is impotent against life. The conclusion says the solution is to accept things as they are and return to the path.

Canine and jackal twins, guardian and opener of the way, stand in the fog of the perilous path through the towers of the subconscious underworld. Each holds the *was*-sceptre. One holds a Mercury-like ankh (Hermanubis and detriment reference), the other a glyph combining Neptune (ruler) and Venus (exaltation).[69] Jackals wait to devour the impure. The towers also form the knees of a woman birthing the sun, referring to Egyptian Nut who birthed the sun daily. The beetle god Khepra who rolled the sun through the passage each night is shown at the critical juncture.

Above, we see the magic mirror, weapon of *qoph*, with rays of flux and reflux, and nine (Yesod) aborted *yod*-seed drops of "impure blood" (menstrual).[70] Below we see the brain waves of sleep. The solar consciousness is sleeping, descended into the dark waters of dreams, glamour, and demons of the subconscious mind. How dark, yet how splendid the adventure.

RELATED CARDS

The Moon card (Pisces) answers to the Wheel of Fortune (Jupiter). It shares with the Wheel a sense of constant motion and a sense of flux, as fortunes wax and wane. The Moon swims in the sea of the human emotional experience. It seeks to dissolve the boundaries between human and divine, rather than aspiring to fly past them like the Wheel's other avatar, Temperance/Sagittarius. Venus (the Empress) is exalted in Pisces, lending her grace to the many works of art produced here. The Moon card also relates to the Hermit in two ways: (1) the Hermit corresponds to Pisces's opposite sign, Virgo, and (2) the number of the Moon, eighteen, reduces to the number of the Hermit, nine. Body and soul depend on and nourish each other.

The Moon's three related decanic minors are the 8 of Cups (*Indolence*—Saturn in Pisces I), the 9 of Cups (*Happiness*—Jupiter in Pisces II), and the 10 of Cups (*Satiety*—Mars in Pisces III). In the Pisces cards we see the altered consciousness sought by the Hanged Man in the journey he first undertook in the Chariot and paid for with Death.

---

69. Mercury is in detriment in Pisces.

70. Crowley, *Book of Thoth*, 112.

In the 8, the things of this world are left behind; in the 9, personal bliss is attained; and in the 10, gifts are surrendered to the universe.[71]

The Moon's associated court card is the Knight (Thoth) or King (RWS) of Cups. He rules over the first two decans of Pisces; the final decan belongs to the Queen of Wands. A born spiritual leader, his rainbow visions shepherd his followers toward peace. These dreams are real in the same way ideals are—not because they can be actualized, but because without them we would be lost.

ADVANCED CONCEPTS FOR FURTHER EXPLORATION

- The "path perilous" is the trip through the "chapel perilous" in Sir Thomas Malory's *Le Morte d'Arthur*, in which a sorceress attempts to seduce Sir Lancelot as he proceeds on his quest. In psychology, "chapel perilous" is a term for a state of being unsure of whether events are being supernaturally influenced or are the product of imagination

- The "gates of horn and ivory" are a literary device that first appeared in Book 11 of the *Odyssey*; a play on the Greek words for "horn" as "fulfillment" and "ivory" as "deception"—the resulting phrase refers to true dreams as passing through the gates of horn, and illusions or false dreams through the gates of ivory

- *The Well at the World's End* by William Morris is perhaps the first fantasy novel, preceeding and influencing Tolkien's *Lord of the Rings*. It's applicable for themes of epic high fantasy, duplicity, wizardy, and romance—but also as a metaphor for water sign Pisces, the last sign of the zodiac

- The card's title as the Ruler of the Flux and Reflux has interesting connotations as both words contain "lux," or light. Flux also has applicable meanings of flow, fever, illness, and quicksilver

---

71. Confusingly, the major arcana associated with the planetary moon is the High Priestess, who has no particular astrological connection to the Moon as Pisces. However, they ply the same waters, the Priestess guarding mysteries that appear only as illusions to the rest of us.

- The opposite path of Judgement/Aeon as dealing with "awakening" versus the Moon card's "sleep"

- Magical Weapon: The Twilight of the Place and Magic Mirror

- Magical Power: Bewitchments, Casting Illusions

THE SUN
The Lord of the Fire of the World

Card Number: XIX

Planet and Dignities: ☉ Sun: rules Leo, exalted Aries; Day of the week: Sunday

Hebrew Letter: ר, *resh*

Hebrew Letter Meaning: Double letter: Head (Fertility-Barrenness); Value: 200

Path 30: Hod (8, Splendor—Mercury) to Yesod (9, Foundation—Moon)

Color Scales in the Four Worlds: Orange. Gold yellow. Rich amber. Amber, rayed red

Themes and Keywords: Creative life force. Illumination. Growth. Light. Visibility. Health. Strength. Royalty and centrality. Self-expression. Liberty. Fertility. Divine child(ren). Singleness versus doublings. The inner deity.

ASTROLOGY/ELEMENT

The sun gives us light, life, health, warmth, joy, and vitality. It's the fiery source we draw strength from, and it is the individuality of self. Solar fire is self-reliant. The sun represents the will to be and exist. It is the motivating factor of existence that generates life force and strength. The sun signifies creative abilities and the state of the constitution. It is the radiant, undying, and unchanging center of our external and internal worlds.

As the center, it also has to do with royalty, authority, and areas where the ego can shine. It's the activating male creative principle, both the father and the eternal child. As the "eye of the world" and emanator of light, it represents deity, and it has been worshipped as such throughout the ages. It's also the essence of mankind, Spirit or the god within.

The glyph of the sun is the circle of Spirit and infinity, the circumference infinitely expanding to contain the totality of the universe surrounding the dot in the center. The central dot can be seen as the seed that fertilizes the egg of the circle, or as the light of the sun itself in the circle of the solar system. The dot-in-circle is also the symbol of the element gold.

The sun rules fixed fire sign Leo, the height of summer in the Northern Hemisphere, and is exalted in cardinal fire sign Aries, the sign of spring and the start of the zodiac. As ruler of Leo it brings nobility, pride, fortitude, and vigor. Its exaltation sign, Aries, shows it as the igniting spark of the procreative force and the fount of courage and initiative.

At the juncture point of a solar analemma, two fingers inspired by Michelangelo's Sistine Chapel meet: the hand of God breathing life into his twin, Adam. (*Rosetta Tarot*)

MYTHOLOGY/ALCHEMY

Solar deities exist in every time and culture. Many were portrayed as the sun riding in a chariot, among them the Greek gods Helios and Apollo, the Roman Sol Invictus, Sumerian Shamash, and Hindu Surya. But the Egyptians had their sun deity ride the Atet, the solar barge also known as the Boat of Millions of Years. During the day, Ra drove the barque through the sky, providing light through the twelve Egyptian hours of the day. At night, the barque traveled the underworld through twelve gates overseen by protectors. Passing through these while battling destructive forces, the barque emerges at the sun's rising, born from the body of Nut.

In Egypt, the god Ra was the supreme ruler and creator. Like Horus, Ra has a falcon's head and wears the sun disk and serpent on his crown. They merge into one deity as Ra-Horakhty, whose name means Ra who is Horus of the Two Horizons (the rising and setting sun). In the New Kingdom, Ra and Amun were combined as Amun-Ra. As the disk of the sun itself, Ra was called Aten. In any form, Ra was revered as the giver of life; he created all things from his sweat and tears.

Thelemic Heru-Ra-Ha (literally "Horus sun-flesh") is a dual god comprised of active form Ra-Hoor-Khuit and passive form Hoor-Pa-Kraat. Active Ra-Hoor-Khuit is also known as *Ra-Horakhty* (Horus of the Horizons) and is the "crowned and conquering child," Lord of the current Aeon that began with the reception of the *Book of the Law*.[72] Aiwass, who dictated the work to Crowley, described himself as "the minister of Hoor-Pa-Kraat" (Horus the child).[73] The "babe in an egg of blue" also referred to the Greek form of Harpocrates, Lord of Silence.[74]

---

72. Crowley, *Gems from the Equinox*, 588.

73. Crowley, *Book of the Law*, 19.

74. Crowley, *Book of Thoth*, 61.

THE SUN

THE LAMP

The sun is shown as a lamp emblazoned with solar icons, the four stations of *Liber Resh*: Ra at dawn in the east, Hathor at noon on the zenith, Atum at sunset in the west, and Khepra at midnight below. (*Pharos Tarot*)

QABALAH—PATH 30

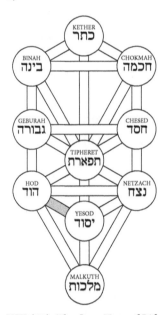

XIX (19). The Sun. Tree of Life.

The Sun card's path lies between Hod and Yesod, balancing the Star's path between Netzach and Yesod, for what is the sun but our own star? (If you place the Emperor along the path between Netzach and Yesod, as Crowley did, you can make a different connection: the sun is exalted in Aries, the Emperor's sign). Hod is Mercury's sphere, the place of the intellect, and Yesod is the moon's sphere, the place of unconscious physical processes. What is the sun doing here? You could say that it is the Sun's role to create harmony between body and mind.

The Hebrew letter associated with the Sun is ר *resh*, meaning "head"; other meanings are "chief," "first," and "top." The sun rules our lives and acts as leader of the planetary forces, just as the head rules the rest of the body through its powers of organization and centralization.

Like the other six "planets," the sun's associated letter is double, meaning that it originally had both a hard and a soft pronunciation. All double letters, as we have seen, bear opposing double attributes. The Sun's pair of opposites is "fertility" and "barrenness." The word for fertility, זרע *zera*, means "seed" or "to sow." The word for barrenness, שממה *shamemah*, translates more accurately as "wasteland." The comparison here is between rich soil, ready for planting, and land that has no productive "use." It's worth remembering that no crop grows without sunlight. (Ultimately, if you descend through the food chain to photosynthesis, the truth is that we all eat mainly sunlight!) But the sun can also bake the soil dry so that nothing may sprout; so too may our powers of reason devastate where they are meant to support.

RIDER-WAITE-SMITH SYMBOLISM

The Sun (*Rider-Waite-Smith Tarot*)

A sun, beaming directly at us, a stone wall, and a child: Smith's card shows clear influences from the Tarot de Marseille image. The Sun's direct face corresponds to *resh*, the Hebrew letter for head (just as the sideways, sleeping face of the Moon corresponded to *qoph*, back of the head). Its twenty-two rays refer to the twenty-two major arcana or Hebrew letters; the alternating straight and wavy rays suggest a balance of male and female.

Depicting one child rather than the two shown in earlier decks may represent a preference toward the light over a balance of light and dark. The child's wreath has six flowers (Tiphareth is the sixth sephira of the Sun/Son). The Fool's red feather (last seen drooping in the Death card) and a bright red banner (taken from Éliphas Lévi's conception of the card) bear the hue of life and passion. Of the horse, Waite said: "The mind leads forth the animal nature"; Apollo's chariot was also said to be drawn by white horses. Like the Lovers, the Star, and the World, the child is nude, having no need for disguise or alteration.

Between the sun and the child lies a stone wall surmounted by four sunflowers (four for the divine name, the four worlds, or perhaps the four elements). Sunflowers not only resemble the sun, they turn toward it; once they mature, they remain facing east to maximize their sun exposure. The wall may represent the "Veil of Paroketh" separating Tiphareth from the lower sephiroth. Waite conceived this as the "walled garden of the sensitive life," from which the enlightened mind can emerge into freedom.

THOTH SYMBOLISM

Egyptian rites dedicate each part of the body to a god or goddess, saying of the face (*resh*, head or face) "my face is the face of Ra."[75] Here we see the face of the sun shining out as the center of a picture described as being Crowley's heraldic family crest, the "sun charged with a rose on a *mont vert*" (green mountain).[76] It's a form of the Rose Cross of manifestation, but here the rays of the Cross have broadened from the limitation of four to the twelve that represent the zodiac, the body of Nuit, and the realm of complete freedom of expansion. The twelve are further divided into thirty-six decans, or the 360 degrees of totality. The green mountain is the fertility of the earth rising up toward the heavens; the wall crowning it represents the control of the will.

At the base of the hill, two disks are inscribed with a figure upon a cross. From the blue disk of water, a red, butterfly-winged child of fire arises. From the green disk of earth comes the yellow child of air. Air and fire elementally feed each other to create the "fire of the world." The card as a whole is Heru-Ra-Ha, divided into Ra-Hoor-Khuit (red for fire) and Hoor-Pa-Kraat (yellow, connecting him to the Fool). Speech and silence, energy and stillness—"twin forms of thy play."[77] The twin children dance with joy in their liberation. Their butterfly wings represent the spirit—that which remains. In the new Aeon, old ideas of the restrictions of sin and death are abolished, and mankind is free—the soul is immortal.

RELATED CARDS

Like the moon, the sun rules only one sign: Leo. It's interesting to note that the moon's sign, Cancer, corresponds to an armed warrior in the Chariot card—but the sun's sign, Leo, corresponds to an unarmed (and, in some versions, unclothed) woman. Even when they switch genders, the sun and moon remain opposites! Strength/Lust

---

75. Budge, *Book of the Dead*, 355.

76. Crowley, *Book of Thoth*, 113.

77. Crowley, *Book of Thoth*, 259.

represents the sun as the life force incarnate; the physical joy of existing in a natural state of health. The sun's exaltation in Aries gives the Emperor his gifts of leadership and preeminence.

The sun rules five of the thirty-six decans: As 3 of Wands, or "Lord of Virtue" (Aries II), he confers wisdom and promotes the balanced application of the intellect. As 10 of Swords or "Lord of Ruin" (Gemini III), his harsh light casts a world in black and white. As 8 of Pentacles or "Lord of Prudence" (Virgo I), the sun promotes health and productivity and plays a divinatory role supported by Mercury's rulership. As the 6 of Cups or "Lord of Pleasure" (Scorpio II), he watches altruistically over children and communities of mutual support. As 4 of Pentacles or "Lord of Power" (Capricorn III), he confers wealth and grants access to those who govern. In the 5, 6, and 7 of Wands (all Leo cards), we see the individual's fight to rise to eminence, their luminous public face, and their struggle to retain prominence of place.

The Sun's number, nineteen, reduces to ten (the Wheel of Fortune) and then to one (the Magician). Their connection speaks to the hidden mechanisms that drive a world in constant motion.

ADVANCED CONCEPTS FOR FURTHER EXPLORATION

- Explore the Golden Dawn rose and cross symbol as the intersection of the body and the individual's expansion of consciousness, as well as a symbol of the dawn of eternal life

- Leonine solar twins, the Aker, called *Duaj* and *Sefer* ("yesterday" and "tomorrow"); related to Heru-Ra-Ha with aspects passive and active, as Ra-Horakhty or "Horus of the Two Horizons"

- Consider the solar symbolism in the Egyptian text *Pert m Hru*, the "Book of Coming Forth by Day" known as the *Book of the Dead*, where the deceased is made to live again and arise reborn with the morning sun: i.e., this excerpt from chapter 17: "I am Yesterday, I know Tomorrow"[78]

---

78. Budge, *Book of the Dead*, 282.

- Crowley's sun adoration ritual *Liber Resh vel Helios*, which focuses the mind on the center of our solar system at dawn, noon, sunset, and midnight and eliminates the fear of death

- The opposite path on the Tree of Life is either the Star (RWS) as another Sun, or the Emperor (Thoth) as Aries, the sign of the sun's exaltation

- Magical Weapon: The Lamen or Bow and Arrow

- Magical Power: The Red Tincture, Power of Acquiring Wealth

JUDGEMENT/AEON
The Spirit of the Primal Fire

Card Number: XX

Element: △ Fire & ○ Spirit

Hebrew Letter: ש, *shin*

Hebrew Letter Meaning: Mother letter: Tooth; Value: 300

Path 31: Hod (8, Splendor—Mercury) to Malkuth (10, Kingdom—Earth)

Color Scales in the Four Worlds: Fire: Glowing orange scarlet. Vermillion. Scarlet, flecked gold. Vermillion, flecked crimson and emerald. Spirit: White fading to gray. Dark purple, nearly black. Seven prismatic colors with violet outside. White, red, yellow, blue, with black outside

Themes and Keywords: Fire and Spirit. The trinity. Major cycles. A new age. The long view; the large perspective. Synthesis. Self-becoming; self-awareness. The light of the spirit. Awakening on all levels. Redemption. Epiphanies.

ASTROLOGY/ELEMENT

This is one of two cards with dual attributions, for it represents the element of fire, but also the fifth element of Spirit. It's the "Spirit of the Primal Fire," and in a sense, fire *is* Spirit, or the closest element to it. Yet Spirit is also like air, as it is like breath. It gives life, it takes life; yet Spirit remains. It directs the orbits of the lights of sun and moon just as it animates beings incorporeal and incarnate.

As fire element, it is the animating force, corresponding to the power "to will." It enlivens. As Spirit, it is the culmination and combination of all of the other elements, the force that gives divinity the power "to go."

Fire is what gives the sun its light, and is that which gives the signs Aries, Leo, and Sagittarius vitality and passion. It is idealistic and visionary, ardent and energizing. It creates and destroys. Spirit directs the Fool on the Fool's journey to continually evolve, change, and grow. It's the egg of Akasha: the immutable source of creation. Together fire and Spirit break down the old and usher in the new. The Fool awakens to a whole new world and exults in it, taking a definite step as the magnitude of a greater series of cycles is revealed.

Modern astrology sometimes assigns the planet Pluto here, probably a reference to both the fiery depths of hell and to the underworld in general as the place for souls in transition.

MYTHOLOGY/ALCHEMY

Who is the angel of the Waite-Smith Judgement card? Michael of the fiery sword or Gabriel with his horn? Crowley's *777* lists the Golden Dawn's traditional description: "Israfel blowing the Last Trumpet. The dead arising from their tombs. An angel blowing a trumpet, adorned with a golden banner bearing a white cross. Below a fair youth rises from a sarcophagus in the attitude of Shu supporting the Firmament. On his left a fair woman, her arms giving the sign of Water—an inverted ▽ on the breast. On his right a dark man giving the sign of Fire—an upright △ upon the forehead."[79]

---

79. Crowley, *777*, 34, 146.

This angel could be Gabriel with his horn or Michael with his sword, flying above a prophet who climbs out from under the rubble on Judgment Day. (*Tarot Egyptiens*)

Israfel, "the Burning One," is one of four Islamic archangels. His task is to wait for God's command, when he will blow his horn announcing the Day of Resurrection. But it's said he corresponds to Raphael, so the confusion continues! To occultists, Israfel is associated with Crowley's invocation of Thoth, called *Liber Israfel* (aka *Liber Anubis*). Thoth himself is the lord of the tarot (thus *Book of Thoth*) and *Liber Israfel* is composed of twenty-two verses.

In the Thoth card there isn't an angel in the same sense, yet Crowley describes the card as a form of Heru-Ra-Ha (as in the Sun card) and says that Heru is cognate with HRU, the Golden Dawn's Great Angel of the Tarot. *Heh-resh-vav*: the revealer of the solar mysteries. HRU, who in the *Book of the Dead* and on the Stele of Revealing, "goes forth by day."[80] In Egyptian, HRU also simply means day, life, and light. The same number of beings exist in the Thoth card as the traditional version, but has them as the Thelemic deities Nuit, Hadit, and the dual forms of Horus, who is also Heru.

---

80. HRU translates as "coming (or going) forth by day" and is seen in the hieroglyphs on the Egyptian artifact known to Thelemites as the Stele of Revealing. *Pert m Hru*, the Egyptian name for the *Book of the Dead*, translates as the "Book of Coming Forth by Day."

QABALAH—PATH 30

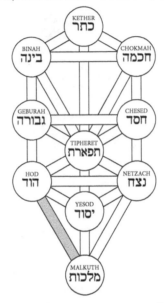

XX (20). Judgement/Aeon. Tree of Life.

The path of Judgement/Aeon runs from Hod (Glory) to Malkuth (Kingdom). Hod is the sephira of the intellect, associated with Mercury; it is the final expression of Binah, or the "will to form," on the Pillar of Severity. Malkuth represents the physical world we can know and touch. The refining fire of Judgement allows intellect to transcend the confines of the physical form, just as the Moon card (between Netzach and Malkuth) allowed emotions to dissolve the illusion of separateness from one another.

Judgement's Hebrew letter is ש *shin*, one of the three mother letters. The others are א *aleph* (the Fool), corresponding to primal air, and מ *mem* (the Hanged Man), corresponding to primal water. *Shin* corresponds to primal fire; the word for fire, אש or *esh*, draws on two of the mother letters. According to the *Sefer* Yetzirah, the head derives from fire, the chest from air, the belly from water. Alchemically, *shin* compares to sulfur, the fiery life force, where *mem* compares to salt and *aleph* to mercury. The word *shin* means "tooth," "sharp," or "to press." Its three prongs may represent the three bumps of a molar. It suggests the consumption of the physical body by a refining fire, leaving behind pure spirit.

If you add *shin* שׁ to the fourfold name, יהוה, you arrive at the name יהשוה, *Yeshua*. By adding Spirit to the name of God, you arrive at the son. Also, *shin* begins the god-name *Shaddai*, and when a priest lifts his hands in blessing, his arms and head form the letter *shin*.

RIDER-WAITE-SMITH SYMBOLISM

Judgement (*Rider-Waite-Smith Tarot*)

Like so many of her trumps, Smith's Judgement resembles its Tarot de Marseille predecessors. The same red wings seen on the Temperance angel seem to reflect a fiery light upon the angel's hair. The angel is likely Gabriel, who plays a role as truth-revealer in several different versions of scripture. Although the Bible never actually mentions Gabriel sounding a horn on Judgment Day, this trope has taken hold over the centuries and likely is the source for the card image. (If you have an early RWS edition, you may notice that the first section of the horn has a disturbingly Freudian flesh color—corrected in later printings.) From the banner hangs the equal-armed red cross of St. George, once carried by the crusaders.

Three main figures rise from their tombs, recalling the three-pronged form of letter *shin*; Paul Foster Case suggests their gray color suggests we are on a non-physical plane.[81] Others have suggested their bodies, upside down, form the letters LVX or LUX. Another significant group of three is less obvious: the elements of the three mother letters. Here in the last of three baptisms—by air, water, fire—the fiery-winged angel hovers above the sea of the end times, the sound of his trumpet ringing through the air. The seas may also be those glimpsed descending from the robe of the High Priestess, who represents the middle path straight up to the divine source. The pale mountains in the back may be those of Malkuth.[82]

THOTH SYMBOLISM

This card is a masterful attempt to incorporate the entire doctrine of the tenets of Thelema into pictorial form. In 1904 Crowley was led, by his mediumistic wife Rose, to a message from the god Horus. She identified him on a stele in the Cairo museum, stele 666 (a solar number). The Stele of Ankh-ef-en-Khonsu was made to commemorate the death of a priest of that name. It is known to Thelemites as the Stele of Revealing, as through it, the Law of Thelema was revealed, inaugurating the new Aeon of approximately 2,000 years.

On front, priest Ankh-ef-en-Khonsu makes offerings to the falcon sun god Ra-Horakhty: Ra-Hoor-Khuit, chief god Ra as Horus of the Two Horizons. Above arches the body of night sky goddess Nut; beneath her is the winged disk representing Horus-of-Behdet (Hadit). The background has symbols of the west, place of the dead. The stele's text consists of a prayer the deceased makes to the great god.

An entire book could be written about this card alone—and in a sense, there was one. Over three subsequent days, Crowley's guide Aiwass dictated the holy text of Thelema, known as *Liber AL*, the *Book of the Law*. Aiwass speaks in each of the three chapters as a different god form: in the first as Nuit, in the second as Hadit, and in the third as Horus. This divinely received text conveys their roles and teachings about cosmic concepts, universal and within the self.

---

81. Case, *The Tarot*, 200.

82. Wald Amberstone (*Secret Language of Tarot*) suggests they are the ice-cold intellect of Hod, which none may encounter without the elemental fire of *shin* as protection.

THE AEON

ש   ○   △

Themes of major cyclic change abound: solar analemma, lunar Aubrey holes, Omphalos/Orphic egg, sprouting seed, comet, flaming keyhole tomb opening, Stonehenge sunrise, ouroboros, and the glyphs of the signs at the end and beginning of the zodiac. (*Tabula Mundi Tarot*)

We see Nuit arching overhead as the circumference of the infinite sphere. Below is winged Hadit, everywhere that is the center. Falcon-headed Ra-Hoor-Khuit faces you enthroned. Inside, the ethereal child Hoor-Pa-Kraat making the gesture of silence. He stands on the letter *shin* that encloses three adoring figures: father, mother, and the conquering child of this new Aeon of fire.

RELATED CARDS

Judgement/Aeon, repository of elemental fire, relates to the three fiery zodiacal majors: the Emperor (Aries), Strength/Lust (Leo), and Temperance/Art (Sagittarius). This sequence spells a journey toward self-knowledge, the inner alchemy by which one discovers one's true will and purpose. The Emperor exerts his life force outward as rulership; Strength/Lust awakens the divine fire within; Temperance/Art introduces the knowledge and conversation of the Holy Guardian Angel. As the card of Spirit, Judgement/Aeon also can be said to relate to all majors.

The minor wands cards tell a story of aspiration too, but on a human scale and with human consequences. The Ace of Wands is the mysterious flame of life driving each of us to seek our life purpose. The 2, 3, and 4 of Wands (*Dominion/Virtue/Completion*) tell a story of conquest, rulership, and civilization. The 5, 6, and 7 of Wands (*Strife/*

Victory/Valor) describe the will's self-assertive determination to overcome all rivals and obstacles to achieve glory. And in the 8, 9, and 10 of Wands (*Swiftness/Strength/Oppression*) we see a drive to expand beyond one's own domain, either due to a sense of purpose or simply naked ambition. Just as the 10 of Swords unveils a dark side of the power of choice, the 10 of Wands reveals a shadow in the quest for purpose. The Lovers and Temperance/Art, respectively, suggest ways these powers may be turned to better use.

By reduction, Judgement/Aeon relates to the High Priestess. In Thelema, the formula 0 = 2, where duality cancels itself into nothingness or wholeness, suggests a connection with the Fool (which in some earlier decks actually occupied this penultimate position in the sequence of trumps): the refining fire (19) suggests a secret path (2) to beginning anew (0).

ADVANCED CONCEPTS FOR FURTHER EXPLORATION

- The fifth elemental power or fifth element of Spirit, associated with the power "to go" in the way of gods, and the connection with the first elemental power of fire, "to will"

- The color scales for the Spirit element of this card are particularly appropriate for contemplation

- The entire text of Crowley's *Book of the Law* explains the cosmic concepts of inner and outer space as the Thelemic trinity Nuit, Hadit, and Horus

- The Thoth Aeon card makes clear that this card is a continued expression of the solar force in the preceeding Sun card, showing Nuit, Hadit, and Horus as a circle, a point, and their union

- This card has connections with the Egyptian and Thelemic concepts of *Khabs* and *Khu* as the light of the spirit; Khabs as the internal star or light of consciousness within the Khu, or spiritual garment, identity, or astral form one takes

- Both the Sun card and the Judgement/Aeon card are associated with Heru, who is speculated to have a connection with HRU, the Golden Dawn's angel of tarot. *Pert m Hru*, the Egyptian "Book of Coming Forth by Day," is also relevant to the themes of this card

- Other connections exist between this card and the Sun card; i.e., consider the meaning behind the variations in their esoteric titles

- The opposite path of XVIII, the Moon, as the subconscious forces as opposed to the expression of conscious awakening in this card

- Magical Weapon: The Wand or Lamp, Pyramid of △

- Magical Power: as fire—Evocation, Pyromancy; as Spirit—Invisibility, Transformation, Vision of the Genius

THE WORLD/UNIVERSE
The Great One of the Night of Time

Card Number: XXI

Planet and Dignities: ♄ Saturn: rules Capricorn and Aquarius, exalted Libra; Day of the week: Saturday

Element: ▽ Earth

Hebrew Letter: ת, *tav*

Hebrew Letter Meaning: Double letter: Cross (Power-Servitude); Value: 400

Path 32: Yesod (9, Foundation—Moon) to Malkuth (10, Kingdom—Earth)

Color Scales in the Four Worlds: Saturn: Indigo. Black. Blue black. Black, rayed blue. Earth: Citrine, olive, russet, and black. Amber. Dark brown. Black, flecked yellow

Themes and Keywords: Completion and renewal. Matter and time. Eternity. Returning. Closure. Unfolding. Wholeness. Where the journey leads. Beginnings and endings. The ultimate. The least and the greatest. Complete narratives/stories. Imagined worlds within worlds. Confinement = freedom. Going, and to stop. All and one.

ASTROLOGY/ELEMENT

At the end of the sequence of trumps, the World card takes on the correspondences of the outermost and slowest classical planet, Saturn, and the heaviest element, earth. Earth is associated with the sephira Malkuth, terminus of the card's path. We can begin in Malkuth and rise, yet the path of the World is both the beginning and the end. Malkuth is the daughter, connected to Binah the mother through Saturn. It represents commitment to completion, or the ultimate aspiration of initiation to the Great Work, to rise from the mundane and connect to the divine supernal realm.

Saturn, the "Keeper of the Records," rules both Capricorn and Aquarius. Capricorn provides the building blocks and blueprints, while Aquarius provides the vision of how they can be evolved and improved. Both are working with the structures imposed by matter and time (Saturn). Saturn's exaltation in Libra shows his role as the Lord of Karma, as Saturn's law will benefit those who operate from Libra's place of love and partnership with the world.

Saturn rules the bones. Its glyph looks like a small letter *h* topped and weighted by the cross of matter. Matter hangs heavy upon it. Hard hours hatch the harvest. It looks much like the inversion of Jupiter's symbol, and appropriately represents the forces of contraction and limitation that provide boundaries and counterforce to Jupiter's expansion. In the end, we are bound by the way we experience time in the material world. Time can be a perceived restriction, or with appropriate conservation and use of energy, it can be a process of gaining wisdom through its passage.

MYTHOLOGY/ALCHEMY

The World maiden suggests Persephone, who descended and rose again in eternal cycles. Yet the figure is said to be hermaphroditic. Consider the "magical images" of the sphere of Saturn, with both male and female variant: the Ancient and the Celestial Queen.

The Ancient, with long robes and beard, reminds us of Father Time, the reaper known as self-born Chronos (Aion). In the Orphic tradition, Chronos produced the primordial deities Aethyr, Chaos, and the World-Egg that contained the god Phanes. He emerged from the egg entwined with a serpent, crowned with a nimbus of light. Phanes was made from the intersection of time (Chronos) and necessity (Ananke).

Quite a parental legacy to live up to! Phanes's name means, "to bring light"; his consort Nyx brought night.

Chronos is conflated with the Greek god Kronos (Saturn), son of the titans of heaven (Ouranos) and earth (Gaea). Kronos, upon wife Rhea, sired Zeus and his siblings. Fearing his overthrow, he swallowed each of his children except Zeus. Rhea and Zeus fooled him, causing him to disgorge the other Olympians, who did indeed ultimately depose and castrate him just as he had done to his father Ouranos. Saturn's karma in action!

The Celestial Queen image is even more fitting for the maiden. Isis, Nut, Astarte, Ishtar, Inanna, Hera, Juno, Kali, and others have all borne the title Queen of Heaven, all forms of she called the Great Goddess, primordially Eurynome who once ruled the world with serpent Ophion. As the Great Work portrayed involves uniting will and love, we must include Aphrodite *Ourania*, meaning heavenly, said to be born of the foam from when Ouranos's genitals were cast into the sea. This is the celestial aspect of the love goddess, counterpart to the more familiar earthly Aphrodite *Pandemos* (of the people).

The maiden of the Universe twirls spiral galaxies, manipulating "*dextro* and *laevo* rotary" cyclic forces, and, like Eurynome, stands poised above the head of the serpent Ophion of creative force.83 (*Rosetta Tarot*)

---

83. Crowley, *777*, 146.

QABALAH—PATH 32

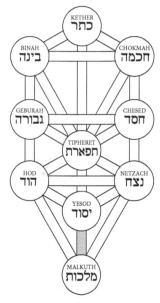

XXI (21). The World/The Universe. Tree of Life.

The path of the World/Universe runs between Yesod and Malkuth. In some Tree versions, this is the only path leading out of Malkuth (i.e. the only way for us to transcend the world of our senses). Of the four Kabbalistic worlds—Atziluth, Briah, Yetzirah, and Assiah—the first three each host three sephiroth. Assiah is the lowest of the worlds, and its one and only sephira is Malkuth. Separateness is in its nature.

Here we encounter archetypal mothers and daughters; Malkuth is the sephira of the Page/Princess in the same way that Binah is the sephira of the Queen. In traditional Kabbalah, Malkuth is the home of the *Shekhinah*, feminine aspect of the divine, compassionately dwelling among us as a human. She is the eternal bride (malkah) longing to be reunited to her divine bridegroom in Tiphareth. Once wed, the bride and bridegroom ascend the Tree to become Queen (Binah) and King (Chokmah) before starting the cycle anew. Thus, the World card corresponds to Saturn as well as Earth, for it too is an expression of Binah/Saturn.

The world of Yetzirah holds Netzach, Hod, and Yesod. When we rise from Malkuth to Yesod, we cross worlds: from Assiah to Yetzirah, from the ordinary realm to the "astral plane." This is where we go in dreams, meditation, journeys, and trance states.

Double letter ת *tav* (mark), last of the alphabet, corresponds to this path. According to Ezekiel, *tav* marked the foreheads of those deemed worthy by angels to save.[84] The first, middle, and last letters of the Hebrew alphabet spell the word for truth, אמת *amet*.[85] *Tav*'s double attribute is עבדות / ממשלה, "power and servitude" or "dominance and subjugation"; modern translations might be "government and slavery." This is apt, for the World/Universe confines us in a way we may experience as safe and liberating—or as a prison.

RIDER-WAITE-SMITH SYMBOLISM

The World (*Rider-Waite-Smith Tarot*)

Pamela Colman Smith's World dancer derives from the Marseille tradition. She is the figure of Prudence, the last and "highest" of the four cardinal virtues (the others being Strength, Justice, and Temperance).[86] This prudence is not "cautiousness"; it's the self that understands its connection with the world surrounding it. We might also call the World's dancer Sophia ("wisdom") or the *anima mundi*, the soul of the world; Renaissance-era mystics believed our connection with the divine was held by the *anima mundi*. Waite says

---

84. Ezekiel 9:4 (Authorized King James Version).

85. The initial *aleph* in *amet* is crucial and signifies the cycle must begin again. Without *aleph* you spell *met*, death.

86. Place, *Tarot, Magic, Alchemy, Hermeticism, and Neoplatonism*, 498.

the card refers "to that day when all was declared to be good," i.e., the final day of creation. She is the soul, present and free yet contained in the body.

The wreath signifies many things: it is a *vesica piscis*, which can be the fish symbol some equate with salvation or a representation of the womb. It may be the ouroboros, the serpent devouring his own tail which represents the world's continuous regeneration (Prudence is sometimes depicted as a woman stepping on the head of a serpent). It could be the Fool's eternal zero, marking a cyclical end and beginning.

The model for the dancer is said to be Florence Farr—actress, Golden Dawn initiate, and friend of Smith's.[87] Farr's initiatory name was *Sapientia Sapienti Dona Data*, "wisdom is a gift given to the wise." The figure's nude form recalls the Star (corresponding to Saturn-ruled Aquarius); her two batons share the same form as the Magician's baton.

Finally, the four creatures at the card corners are the same four creatures of Ezekiel, or Kerubic beasts, we saw in the Wheel of Fortune. Besides hinting at the elements, directions, gospels, fixed zodiac signs, and divine name, they convey the sense that all is in it right place.

Even this nineteenth-century design shows the four Kerubic beasts.
The ribboned ovoid of the wreath prefigures Waite-Smith, though
the nude dancer bears no wands. (*Ancient Italian Tarot*)

---

87. Katz and Goodwin, *Secrets of the Waite-Smith Tarot*, 201.

THOTH SYMBOLISM

Crowley's *777* says the traditional design should include the "quadrature of the circle."[88] It's why most World cards show the maiden (final *heh* of Tetragrammaton) enclosed in some form of wreath cornered by the four Kerubic beasts. Her crossed legs form the cross (*tau*) in the circle's center—the quartered circle as Malkuth's symbol. The circle of Spirit has been squared by the cross of matter. The circle can be seen as letter O and the cross as letter X, together spelling ox, the translation of *aleph*, the Fool's letter. Look back at Thoth Fool—his body forms an X bursting through a semicircular portal. The light of Kether is now fully, infinitely extended in fourfold division: "nothing"—in complete expansion.

Crowley's *777* also tells us the "wreath" should be 400 circles—the number of *tau*. Here, though, it has seventy-two sections further divided into three, representing the Shemhamphorash hidden name of God formed from seventy-two letter triads, each representing an individual angel. Seventy-two also represents astrology's quintile aspect—a division of the circle's 360 degrees by five, the fifth element of Spirit.

The four beasts are in the same switched positions as in the Hierophant, but the hollow-eyed masks have come to life. The daughter (Eurynome), crowned with a square nimbus of light, wrestles—or dances in celebration—with the serpent (Ophion) as Heru-Ra-Ha. Her foot standing upon his head recalls the words of magician Éliphas Lévi, who claims that the crux of the magical work involves setting our foot upon the head of the serpent of "that blind force" and leading it where we will.[89] She pokes at the eye of Horus/God with the butt-end of Saturn's sickle. Below her is a celestial diagram showing the bones or chemical elements of the "House of Matter." It's superimposed on three pyramids—Giza, or the "City of the Pyramids" of Binah, the "Night (Nox) of Time (Saturn/Pan)." In Crowley's words, "This is she that is set upon the Throne of Understanding"; purpose accomplished.[90]

---

88. Crowley, *777*, 34.

89. Lévi, *Transcendental Magic*, 242.

90. Crowley, *Book of Thoth*, 144.

RELATED CARDS

Traditionally, Saturn rules both Capricorn and Aquarius. Thus, the World/Universe as Saturn rules the Devil and the Star. If the World's wreath forms a "wall," the goat structures and follows the rules within, while the water bearer reaches for utopian ideals outside it. The Devil binds us to worldly things, but the Star prompts us to dream new worlds. One governs material structures and space; one governs intellectual structures and time. As Saturn, the World exalts in Justice/Adjustment, where its balancing act is a dance that shapes the music of the spheres.

As Saturn, the World/Universe occupies five of the thirty-six decans. Here we mainly see Saturn as teacher: As 7 of Pentacles (*Failure*—Taurus III), he teaches us the patience to repair what has gone wrong. As 5 of Wands (*Strife*—Leo I), he swallows his children like Kronos, fostering a contest where the strongest prevails. As 3 of Swords (*Sorrow*—Libra II), he keeps oaths, teaching us wisdom from our mistakes. As 10 of Wands (*Oppression*—Sagittarius III), he confers a punishing work ethic. As 8 of Cups (*Indolence*—Pisces I) he establishes strong boundaries, teaching us to walk away. In the 2, 3, and 4 of Pentacles (all Capricorn cards), the World/Universe is a kingdom to be won, built, and then fortified. In the 5, 6, and 7 of Swords (all Aquarius cards), the World/Universe demarcates boundaries, determining who's in and who's out, which rules to follow, and where the loopholes are.

Besides Saturn, the World/Universe represents elemental earth. Thus, it relates to the three earthy zodiacal majors: the Devil, the Hierophant, and the Hermit. This sequence traces a journey from the material to the divine (reminiscent of *tikkun olam*, the restoration of the world). The Devil/Capricorn shows mastery over the world of matter; the Hierophant/Taurus builds a bridge between the mundane and the divine; the Hermit/Virgo looks to the world's legacy and realms beyond.

The suit of earth abounds with metaphors of production. In the 2, 3, and 4 of Pentacles (*Change/Work/Power*), industry takes root and begins to prosper. The 5, 6, and 7 of Pentacles (*Disappointment/Success/Failure*) seize the perfect moment and foster growth. In the 8, 9, and 10 (*Prudence/Gain/Wealth*), we see the final product multiplied, reaped, and monetized; as currency it goes on to new life and purpose in the material world.

The World/Universe, as card twenty-one, reduces to three, the number of the Empress—who as Mother Nature presides over all cycles of life, growth, death, and renewal.

ADVANCED CONCEPTS FOR FURTHER EXPLORATION

- The evolutionary cyclic connection between Atu 0, the Fool, and XXI, the World/Universe as formlessness versus form

- The connection between light and night, the three negative veils of existence, and the magical formulas and signs of LVX and NOX

- The concept of the climax of the descent into matter as the signal for "redintigration" of Spirit (restoration to wholeness)

- The World/Universe card as the daughter Malkuth, and the Empress as the mother Binah

- The concept of time as the house of matter

- The *anima mundi*, or soul of the world

- The Hindu concepts of prakriti and purusha as material form and spirit consciousness, the feminine and masculine components of all reality

- Magical Weapon: as Saturn—A Sickle; as earth—The Pantacle or Salt

- Magical Power: as Saturn—Works of Malediction and Death; as earth— Alchemy, Geomancy, Making of Pantacles

MINOR ARCANA

COMPONENTS OF THE MINOR ARCANA

Each minor card can be considered as a combination of:

- Number symbolism relating to the ten sephiroth of the Tree of Life and their planetary rulers
- The suit and the related element and Qabalistic world

For the minors 2 through 10, there is the additional consideration of:

- The zodiacal sign (including the nature of the sign's planetary ruler)
- The planet ruling the card's particular ten-degree segment of the sign, known as a decan

ELEMENTS AND THE MINOR ARCANA

In Golden Dawn–based decks, the four suits of the minor arcana correlate to the four elements in the following way:

Wands = fire

Cups = water

Swords = air

Pentacles/Disks = earth

Other esoteric systems assign the four elements to the four suits in different ways—in particular, fire and air often exchange places, a trade which mirrors the Knight-King swap in the court cards. If you look at the history of esoteric tarot pre-Golden Dawn, in fact, the only really consistent correspondence seems to be Cups = water.

However, if we are using decks based on the Golden Dawn's tarot system or its offspring (the Rider-Waite-Smith and Thoth decks), it's essential to use the correspondences as given above. They are the basis for understanding Qabalistic references in the minors (including the four Qabalistic worlds and the four letters of the Tetragrammaton). They are also the basis for understanding astrological references in the minors, for each suit contains the three signs sharing the same elemental triplicity. For example, all fire signs occur in the Wands suit—Aries in the 2, 3, and 4; Leo in the 5, 6, and 7; and Sagittarius in the 8, 9, and 10.

Generally speaking, fire is active or *yang*, associated with exercising the will, with passion, creativity, and intention. Water is receptive or *yin*, associated with experiencing the emotions and reflective inner journeys. Air results from a mixture of fire and water, associated with mental attitudes, qualities of reason and thought, speech and expression, and visualization. It is active, associated with movement and occasionally conflict. Earth combines the three preceding elements. It's considered passive, complex, solid, and associated with physical manifestations such as the body and material resources.

QABALAH OF THE MINOR ARCANA

The minor arcana of the tarot, as in a playing card deck, form a decimal system: 1 to 10. So do the ten sephiroth of the Tree of Life. What we know about each of the ten sephiroth can inform our understanding of each of the ten numbered cards of each suit. The fifth sephira, Geburah or "severity," tells us something about the harsh, imbalanced character of each five in the minor arcana. Each sephira is associated with an astrological correspondence, and the "severity" of Geburah is well matched to the warlike nature of planet Mars.

TEN SEPHIROTH

1. Kether, "crown": the source that contains all things, the number which contains all other numbers, energy without form, creator gods; the primum mobile

2. Chokmah, "wisdom": the male principle, expansion, the idea of direction, the impulse to being, sky gods; the zodiac and fixed stars

3. Binah, "understanding": the female principle, the idea of restriction, the impulse to form; mother goddesses, Saturn

4. Chesed, "mercy": the source of the knowable world, structure and increase, growth, father gods; Jupiter

5. Geburah, "severity": destruction and separation, restraint, the force of division, war gods; Mars

6. Tiphareth, "beauty": the place of harmony, the meeting of above and below, balance, sacrificial solar gods; sun

7. Netzach, "victory": eternity, emotional connection, instinct, the will to endure and to connect, the force of attraction, goddesses of love; Venus

8. Hod, "glory": the intellect, the system, the rational mind, invention, travel between worlds, gods of mind; Mercury

9. Yesod, "foundation": imagination, the backstage of reality, the astral plane, the place of magic, lunar gods and goddesses; moon

10. Malkuth, "kingdom": the physical world, home of the Shekhinah or feminine aspect of God, manifest reality, the body, daughter goddesses; Earth

FOUR WORLDS AND THE TETRAGRAMMATON

The four suits of the minor arcana correspond not only to the four elements, but to the four "Qabalistic worlds." These worlds represent stages of creation, from conception and gestation through differentiation and actualization. In Qabalah, these abstract notions take the following structure, which descends from the sublime and numinous to the real and tangible:

Fire = Atziluth, the world of archetypes (Wands)

Water = Briah, the world of creation (Cups)

Air = Yetzirah, the world of formation (Swords)

Earth = Assiah, the world of action (Pentacles/Disks)

Thus, when we speak about the four suits, we can view them each as having characteristics taken from the corresponding world. While Swords have something to do with the way we *think* about doing things, Pentacles have something to do with simply doing them.

The four worlds can also be thought of as an expression of the elements on the vertical plane, as opposed to the horizontal distribution of all four elements in each sephira. Atziluth can be assigned to the three upper sephiroth (the supernal triangle), Briah to the next three, the lower three sephiroth to Yetzirah, and the last sephira, Malkuth, to Assiah.

The elements and worlds also can be correlated in the above order to the letters of the Tetragrammaton YHVH (*yod*-primal *heh-vav*-final *heh*). (In Greek, *tetra-* means "four" and *gramma-* means "letters.") These four Hebrew letters were considered an unpronounceable divine name of God. Hermetically speaking, it represents the *logos* as expressed on four planes below that of the highest: the division of unity or the "unmanifest" as it expresses itself in four tendencies or directions. These four tendencies can also be thought of as expressions of will, love, reason, and action.

Hermeticists also call upon one more set of four—the four powers of the sphinx: *velle* ("to will"), *audere* ("to dare"), *scire* ("to know"), and *tacere* ("to keep silent"). Crowley posited that these four powers taken together give rise to a fifth: *ire* ("to go").

ACES VERSUS "DECANIC" MINORS

Each of the four Aces is called the "root of" the related element of the suit, and can be considered the fourfold division of the divine name YHVH, as unity takes an initial step toward one of the suits or Qabalistic worlds. The Aces are seed ideas. As a "root," the Ace draws from the tendency of the element, but does not yet show growth. That growth will happen in the minors 2 through 10.

In the Golden Dawn's system, the "2 through 10" minors correlate to the decans, 10° arcs which cover a third of each 30° zodiacal sign; there are thirty-six of them in total. Decanic minors, as their name implies, enjoy a one-to-one correspondence to the zodiacal decans. The sequence begins with the 2 of Wands (the first decan of Aries) and concludes with the 10 of Cups (the last decan of Pisces).

These decanic minors are each associated with one of the twelve zodiacal signs and one of the seven traditional planets. The planet that rules that particular decan may be different from the planet that rules the sign itself. For example, the 7 of Cups's decan is ruled by Venus, but its sign, Scorpio, is ruled by Mars. Because each sign and planet has its own associated major arcanum, each minor card expresses the combined forces of its two related majors. In the case of our 7 of Cups, the major associated with Venus is the Empress; the major associated with Scorpio is Death. By juxtaposing the Empress and Death, we learn something about the character of the 7 of Cups.

The decanic minors are also groupable by quadruplicity (see the Major Arcana section for explanation of this term). The 2, 3, and 4 cards are always the initiating cardinal signs of the suit; the 5, 6, and 7 cards are the stable middle, or fixed, signs of the suit; and the 8, 9, and 10 cards are the final transmuting, or mutable, signs of the suit.

Aces, as the root from which the entire sequence flows, cannot be confined to a single decan, or indeed, a single sign. The Golden Dawn conceived of the Aces as revolving around the North Pole, bringing the force of their suit from the astral to the material plane. Each Ace has a special relationship with the Page or Princess of its suit. So, the Page or Princess of Swords is said to rule from 0° Capricorn to 30° Pisces; the "throne of the Ace" is a 45° swath in the center of that domain, enclosing the sign of Aquarius.

PLANETARY ORDER OF THE DECAN RULERS

In the sequence of decan rulerships, the seven traditional planets appear in a set order: Saturn, Jupiter, Mars, Sun, Venus, Mercury, Moon. This "Chaldean" (or Ptolemaic or "descending") order and derives from these bodies' apparent orbital speed around the earth. Saturn appears to be the slowest, and the Moon appears to be the swiftest. Because there are thirty-six decans—one more than thirty-five, which would be a multiple of seven—one planet must occur an extra time. In the Chaldean ordering scheme for the decans, that planet is Mars, which begins the series with the first decan of Aries and ends it with the last decan of Pisces. For a clear visualization of the sequence of decans and their rulers, see the "Table of Decans" chart in the Tables and Diagrams section at the end of this book.

Traditionally, the start of the zodiac is 0° Aries, the vernal equinox or first day of spring in the Northern Hemisphere. However, in the Golden Dawn manuscript *Book T*, the decans and corresponding "angels" of the decanic minors begin the series with the first decan of Leo. This may be because of the sun's centrality to the zodiac, the importance of the solar force, and the solar symbolism of Leo as important to the "Golden Dawn." It may correlate to the Egyptian start of the zodiac. But it is also the sidereal position of the Royal Watcher star Regulus, the Heart of the Lion. These Royal stars associated with the Kerubic, fixed signs can also be correlated to the four worlds, four letters, four elements, and four Powers of the Sphinx. Regulus would thus correspond to the first of these, fire and the power of will.

"QABALISTIC DOUBLES"

There are seven (or possibly eight) decanic minor cards that qualify as what we call "Qabalistic doubles," where each decan ruler matches the planet corresponding to the sephira it rules, thus enhancing the influence of that planet (for better or worse):

- 3 of Swords: decan ruler Saturn also rules sephira three, Binah

- 4 of Swords: decan ruler Jupiter also rules sephira four, Chesed

- 5 of Cups: decan ruler Mars also rules sephira five, Geburah

- 6 of Cups: decan ruler the Sun also rules sephira six, Tiphareth

- 7 of Cups: decan ruler Venus also rules sephira seven, Netzach

- 8 of Wands: decan ruler Mercury also rules sephira eight, Hod

- 9 of Wands: decan ruler the Moon also rules sephira nine, Yesod

You could also argue the 10 of Wands is a Qabalistic double, if you think of decan ruler Saturn as linked to ten, Malkuth.

GOLDEN DAWN TITLES

In 1887, Samuel MacGregor Mathers of the Hermetic Order of the Golden Dawn compiled a series of unpublished order documents that together comprised what is known as *Book T*, a treatise on the esoteric aspects of tarot. Each of the decanic minors was here given a title designating it as a "lord" of something, for the Golden Dawn saw the cards as being invested with a connection to a personality of sorts. Each of the thirty-six minors 2 through 10 is connected to an innate intelligence that encompasses two "angelic" beings: one during the hours of light, and one during the hours of night. These seventy-two are the angels of the *Shemhamphorash*, or "Great Name of God," composed of seventy-two triads of letters derived from the letters of three verses in Exodus (xiv, 19–21), written boustrophedonically (i.e., written in alternating directions: right-to-left, then left-to-right, and so on).

These Golden Dawn "lord" names or "Hermetic titles" describe the intrinsic nature of the essence of the expression or spiritual intelligence of each card. In a sense, each card is a living force that can relate, interact, and be influenced by other cards it connects to.

In many instances, Crowley condensed or changed these Golden Dawn names to a single word that he felt best encapsulated the card's essence. In Crowley's Thoth deck, what many people consider as divinatory keywords are actually references to these Golden Dawn titles.

ACE OF WANDS
Root of the Powers of Fire

Dates:[91] June 21–September 21 (summer in the Northern Hemisphere)

Astrology: Cancer-Leo-Virgo quadrant, emphasizing the Kerubic fire sign Leo

Element: Fire and Spirit. All Aces are associated with Spirit, but the fire Ace is doubly so

Sephira/World: Kether in Atziluth

Color(s): Brilliance

Associated Majors: Judgement/Aeon as the elemental trump of fire (and Spirit)

Associated Minors: Page/Princess of Wands

Themes: Creativity and potential. Highest divinity. Initiation. Blind force. Primum mobile. First swirling of manifestation. One in all and all in one. Will. Force that leads to form.

---

91. Dates vary annually. All Ace dates listed in this book are based on 2019–2020 dates.

ASTROLOGY/ELEMENT

Aces are tendencies for unity to divide itself by stepping away in one of four directions. The Judgement/Aeon card is the "Spirit of the Primal Fire," and this Ace is the root source of the element itself.

Aces are nascent beginnings in the world of the element. The fire realm has themes of life force and will: inspiration and passion, conquest and principled leadership, courage under pressure leading to victory, and the virtues of speed, flexibility, and strength. Fire is also associated with Spirit, so this first Ace expresses the closest connection with divinity.

This Ace's Cancer-Leo-Virgo quadrant of space is a fertile astrological sequence. In Cancer we see that nurturing with enclosure and protection leads to a creative birth. Sun-ruled, fixed fire sign Leo at the center of the triad best resonates with the Ace. Here the individual is given a chance to struggle and to shine. Last, we have Virgo, showing that the ultimate goal of the creative projects we start with this Ace is manifestation.

MYTHOLOGY/TIME OF YEAR

In a sense, all creation myths have some resonance with the Ace of Wands, because it connects to the element of Spirit as well as fire. Whether the universe began with a big bang or a lightning flash, it is the story of the first spark of existence from nothing. No beginning, you say? Then the Ace of Wands is the arbitrary beginning of a never-beginning, never-ending cycle.

Aces each encompass an entire quarter of the year.[92] The Ace of Wands gets the June solstice through the September equinox. In the Northern Hemisphere, this is the solar height of summer, the hottest and most fertile season.[93] Yet the light, which peaked at the June solstice, is now decreasing. The light is a stand in for both fire and Spirit. All beginnings are progressions that lead toward endings, yet all endings are deaths that lead to rebirths. At the summer solstice, the holly king returns to do battle with the reigning oak king, who rises again.

---

92. Aces, however, rule quadrants of space, rather than time.

93. For Southern Hemisphere equivalent, see the Ace of Swords.

This naturalistic Ace clearly shows its tree-borne origins, but the living leaves and nuts can also remind us of the Wands' eternal life force. (*Ancient Italian Tarot*)

QABALAH

The Ace of Wands is known as Kether in Atziluth. All Aces correspond to the first sephira, Kether (כתר) or "crown." Kether is associated with the primum mobile, or "first motion," a force thought responsible for the motion of all the planets and stars across the sky. In Kether, the crown, is contained all that will follow. The divine name associated with Atziluth is *Adonai* ("Lord").

All Wands correspond to the first of four worlds, Atziluth ("proximity" or "emanation"), which is also called the archetypal world. In Atziluth is the will to form. Thus, Kether in Atziluth represents the driving force which gives momentum to all of creation. In a sense, it contains everything—but only in potential form. Atziluth also corresponds to י *yod*, the first letter of the divine name. The tip of letter *yod* is said to reside in Kether. Expressed in Tree of Life terms, the Ace of Wands is the source and cause of all creation, as well as the movement which impels it.

ACE OF WANDS
ROOT OF THE POWERS OF FIRE

The hints of form coalescing in the bark are the "first swirlings" of manifestation, while the ancient bearded face evokes the many titles of Kether like the Most High, the Head That Is Not, and the Vast Countenance. (*Tabula Mundi Tarot*)

RIDER-WAITE-SMITH SYMBOLISM

Ace of Wands (*Rider-Waite-Smith Tarot*)

Like the other Aces in the deck, this one strongly resembles its counterpart in the Tarot de Marseille. A right hand, its palm facing the viewer, grasps a phallic staff of living wood with green and vibrant leaves. The hand issues out of nothingness from the right, perhaps a reference to the right-to-left spelling of the divine name in Hebrew,

יהוה. In place of the yods on the Ace of Swords and droplets on the Ace of Cups are eighteen leaves (the Hebrew word חי *chai*, meaning "life," adds up to eighteen through gematria). According to the Golden Dawn, the Ace of Wands represents "natural" force, as opposed to the Ace of Swords' "invoked" force.

In the far distance rises a phantasmal castle—a representative of the physical world, Malkuth, at the other end of creation. In between we see all four elements—sunlight as fire, river water, air cloud, hills of earth, because the Ace of Wands contains all while also being only the beginning of the journey.

THOTH SYMBOLISM

This Ace represents natural force arising as opposed to invoked force. Crowley describes it as a "solar-phallic outburst."[94] The wand issues eighteen lightnings, the number of the Hebrew word *chai*, meaning life. The flashing colors of red and green scintillate to create an artistic interpretation of the Golden Dawn color for the card which, like deity itself, is described only as "brilliance."[95]

The primordial force of the divine is making itself manifest, yet at "so early a stage that it is not yet definitely formulated as Will." It is coming forth as the wand, the tool through which the adept works; the power of will awaits the hand. The fire is incipient, not materialized. Yet it is the spark that leads ultimately to all creation, so the ten *yod* shaped flames are in the form of the Tree of Life. Kether is said to reside at the tip of the *yod* of YHVH as it begins to issue forth. The *yod* is also a seed, like the first Ace.

RELATED CARDS

While the Ace of Wands, in a Qabalistic sense, contains all cards, it especially refers to the complete suit of Wands. It is the first letter of the divine name; the other Aces are the remaining letters. As both "crown" and "root," the Ace is the throne of its Page or Princess. Because Thoth Knights/RWS Kings reside in Chokmah and represent the *yod* (whose tip is in Kether), they also relate to the Ace.

---

94. Crowley, *Book of Thoth*, 188.

95. Crowley, 188.

All Aces are said to revolve around the North Pole, but the "throne of the Ace" lies at the heart of the Page/Princess' domain; for the Princess of Wands, that is the heart of the Cancer-Leo-Virgo quadrant (Chariot-Strength/Lust-Hermit).[96] Thus, the Ace of Wands has a particular connection with Strength/Lust. As the "Root of the Powers of Fire," it also especially relates to Judgement/Aeon, the trump for the element of fire (and Spirit).

---

96. The Page/Princess is said to rule 0° Cancer to 30° Virgo; the Ace occupies the central 45° from 22°30' Cancer to 7°30' Virgo.

2 OF WANDS
Lord of Dominion

Dates:[97] March 20–March 30 (includes the March equinox)

Astrology: Aries, the sign ruled by Mars, with Sun exalted

Element: Cardinal fire

Decan: 0°–9° Aries; Aries I, the decan ruled by Mars

***Picatrix* Image:** A black man, with a large and restless body, having red eyes and with an axe in his hand, girded in white cloth

***Picatrix* Significations:** Strength, high rank, wealth without shame

Agrippa Image: A black man, standing and clothed in a white garment, girdled about, of a great body, with reddish eyes, and great strength, and like one that is angry

Agrippa Significations: Boldness, fortitude, loftiness, and shamelessness

Sephira/World: Chokmah in Atziluth

Color(s): Pure soft blue, plus the colors of the associated majors

Associated Majors: The Emperor and the Tower

---

97. Dates vary annually. All decanic minor dates listed in this book are based on 2019–2020 dates.

Associated Minors: Queen of Wands holds the decan; relates to King/Knight as a two

Themes: Manifest fire. Rulership via conquest. Mastery of all directions. Penetration. Initiating. Breaking ground. Affirmation of will. Resolve and resolution. Old and new worlds.

ASTROLOGY/ELEMENT

The card covers the Ram's decan I. The decan, and Aries itself, is ruled by militant Mars. The sephira is ruled by the entirety of the zodiac. Thus, we see in the card a message of domination over all things. The fire that was pending in the Ace now issues forth in its highest untainted form. Fire force is at heart a quality of inspirational leadership. Aries is the groundbreaking pioneer. With the addition of Mars, we add conquest.

The images of this face were said to grant victory and ascendancy. The ancients relate the decan with dark and powerful men, red-eyed and wielding weapons. They are described as ferocious, fiery, and furious. The force that was nascent in the Ace's wand now is wielded as the warriors grab hold of axes and spears. Here at the beginning of the zodiac, the infant Aries swings his blade to sever himself from the collective at the end of the zodiac and heads out newly born to conquer the world.

A fiery ram's head and wands shaped like Mars glyphs underscore
the Mars-in-Aries decan rulership of this card. (*Rosetta Tarot*)

MYTHOLOGY/TIME OF YEAR

One might expect the double martial influence to color this card with tales of bloodshed, but this isn't a card of the savagery of war. While it describes dominion and conquest, it is not born of cruelty. Fire at its first appearance is so full of life force that it can only burst forth and embark upon a course of invasion into new territory. Perhaps myths more appropriate here are the epic tales of heroes setting out to accomplish incredible feats; we could reference Alexander the Great or the Greek myths of the nearly invulnerable Achilles, the travels of Odysseus, Perseus rescuing Andromeda, Hercules and his twelve labors, and Jason in search of the Golden Fleece.

TWO OF WANDS

In modern tarot, a globe has come to signify the concept of "dominion" and the idea that a new year and a new world begin together. (*Linestrider Tarot*)

The time of year spans approximately ten days following the March equinox. In the Northern Hemisphere this is the first day of spring, when day and night are equal but the balance shifts toward light.[98] The fires of spring have kindled. The seed breaks open, is penetrated by the light, and grows.

---

98. The Southern Hemisphere equivalent is the 2 of Swords.

QABALAH

The 2 of Wands corresponds to Chokmah in Atziluth. All twos correspond to the second sephira, Chokmah (חכמה) or "wisdom," which corresponds to "the zodiac."[99] Chokmah is the wellspring of the Pillar of Force; its "wisdom" is a flash of insight appearing from nothingness, just as Chokmah appears from the empty point of Kether.

All Wands correspond to the first of four worlds, Atziluth ("proximity" or "emanation"), also called the "Archetypal World" in Hermetic Qabalah. Chokmah in Atziluth represents dawning potential, the intimation or awareness of everything to come, though none of it shall take form until the next sephira, Binah.

Atziluth also corresponds to י *yod*, the first letter of the divine name. The tip of letter *yod* is said to reside in Kether, the body in Chokmah. All twos relate to Chokmah: *Dominion* (Atziluth), *Love* (Briah), *Peace* (Yetzirah), and *Change* (Assiah) all begin with perceiving and acting upon a world outside oneself.

RIDER-WAITE-SMITH SYMBOLISM

© 1971 U.S. GAMES SYSTEMS, INC.

2 of Wands (*Rider-Waite-Smith Tarot*)

---

99. In the Ptolemaic concentric model, the twelve signs inhabit a sphere of their own—below the primum mobile, but above the orbits of the seven traditional planets, which descend from Saturn to the Moon.

Themes of looking forward and back dominate this image (sight is a trait of the Emperor). A magisterial figure looks out over a globe as if seeking new territory; Waite ascribed to him the "sadness of Alexander" upon learning there were no new worlds to conquer. He holds one wand whilst the other is fixed—perhaps they are the will and the means to accomplish what he desires. Or they could be the past and future, as he stands at the threshold of the zodiacal New Year. In the distance, as far away as Malkuth is from Chokmah on the Tree, are the houses and hills of his kingdom.

Below his left hand and adorning the crenellated parapet, a plaque displays roses and lilies in a saltire formation. In tarot language, these represent opposites: passion and purity, will and love, fire and water. They could even refer to the Pisces-to-Aries transition. This is their only appearance in the numeric minors.

THOTH SYMBOLISM

To Crowley, the card represents "ideal Will, independent of any given object."[100] The picture is of two crossed Tibetan *dorjes*. The *dorje*, or vajra, meaning both diamond and thunderbolt, is a ritual weapon with the strength and hardness of the diamond and the irresistible force of the thunderbolt. It is related to a root word meaning "the axe of the godhead," with which Indra destroyed the ignorant. One of the most powerful weapons in the universe, it represents firmness of purpose, spiritual power, indestructibility, directed will, endless creativity, and skillful activity. It symbolizes the destructive force necessary for creation, such as the sperm penetrating the ovum in order to fertilize it.

Six flames (a reference to the sixth sephira, solar Tiphareth) radiate out from the center, symbolizing the solar force. The sun is exalted in Aries and is the source of the will force and that inner directive which guides it. The flames and vajra are in the flashing colors of fire against a background of the sky blue of Chokmah and fatherly sky gods.

---

100. Crowley, *Book of Thoth*, 189.

RELATED CARDS

The 2 of Wands correlates to the first decan of Aries, ruled by Mars. The Emperor (Aries) and the Tower (Mars) together signify an implacable will to break new soil; the first decan of the zodiacal New Year sparks beginnings of all kinds.

As the Queen of Wands' middle decan (her others are 10 of Cups/Pisces III and 3 of Wands/Aries II), the indomitable 2 of Wands connects Self and Other, lending the Queen a charisma that can inspire both lust and fighting spirit.

Aces contain the full potential of the suit; twos reflect that potential into conscious awareness. The 2 of Wands becomes conscious of worlds to dominate; the 2 of Cups becomes emotionally conscious of the Other; the 2 of Swords becomes aware of other thoughts and opinions; the 2 of Pentacles becomes aware of other ways of living.

Kings (RWS)/Knights (Thoth) reside in Chokmah, Qabalistically; the King/Knight of Wands shares the same brilliant insight of Chokmah that erupts in the 2 of Wands.

3 OF WANDS
Lord of Virtue (Established Strength)

Dates:[101] March 31–April 9

Astrology: Aries, the sign ruled by Mars, with Sun exalted

Element: Cardinal fire

Decan: 10°–19° Aries; Aries II, the decan ruled by the Sun

Picatrix **Image:** A woman dressed in green clothes, lacking one leg

Picatrix **Significations:** High rank, nobility, wealth, rulership

Agrippa Image: A woman, outwardly clothed with a red garment, and under it a white, spreading abroad over her feet

Agrippa Significations: Nobleness, height of a Kingdom, and greatness of dominion

Sephira/World: Binah in Atziluth

Color(s): Crimson, plus the colors of the associated majors

Associated Majors: The Emperor and the Sun

---

101. Dates vary annually. All decanic minor dates listed in this book are based on 2019–2020 dates.

Associated Minors: Queen of Wands

Themes: New growth. Quickening of creative projects. Dignity. Virility. Performance. Benevolent rulership. Good governance. Nobility. Right action. Guesthost relationship. Watch and wait.

ASTROLOGY/ELEMENT

The 3 of Wands covers Aries decan II. This face is both ruled by the Sun and contains the degree of its exaltation, giving it extra dignity. Threes are associated with the planet Saturn, the Lord of Karma who rewards those who step up and refuse to shirk responsibility. With virtue comes influence, and with influence comes accountability. In this card, one rises to the occasion, discovering their true inner nobility by developing strength of character. Through right action, poise, and decorum, an individual cultivates sovereignty of self, establishing undeniable strength and the regal bearing of a genuine leader.

Though we think of Aries and the sun as inherently masculine, the decan images of *Picatrix* and Agrippa are both female, perhaps due to the influence of Saturn's association with the Great Mother. In one image, a woman dressed in green has only one visible leg, suggestive of a sprouting plant. In another, she is dressed in a red garment over a white, the colors implying purity underlying passion.

The woman in green stands with one leg visible, as described in the decan image of *Picatrix*, but her head is that of a heron, associated with the Bennu bird. (*Liber T: Tarot of Stars Eternal*)

MYTHOLOGY/TIME OF YEAR

The Egyptian god Amun-Ra is a match for Aries's solar decan. This god form combines Amun and Ra into one supreme deity. Both were portrayed as ram-headed, suggesting virility. Amun was known as "the Hidden One," a primeval creator god who also was self-born; a good parallel for the theme of self-sovereignty. As *Amun Kematef*, "Amun who has completed his moment," he was seen as a snake which renewed itself. Known as the "Lord of All," Amun gave form to all things seen and unseen and his presence was invisible yet everywhere. Ra is the visible sun who ruled in all parts of creation: the sky, the earth, and the underworld. Together as Amun-Ra they combine two principal deities, one visible, one invisible. The fertile ram god was said to father the Pharaoh, known as "Son of Ra, Beloved of Amun."

The wands topped with pine cones are symbols of the pineal gland that
receives light at the center of the head: a reference to *resh*, the letter
of the Sun card that rules the decan. (*Tabula Mundi Tarot*)

The time of year, around the first ten days of April, heralds solar heat and growth in the Northern Hemisphere. Seeds begin to sprout and things quicken.

QABALAH

The 3 of Wands is Binah in Atziluth. Binah (בימה), the third sephira, translates as "understanding" and corresponds to the slowest, outermost classical planet, Saturn.

Sometimes referred to as a "palace of mirrors," where Chokmah's insight may be reflected and amplified, Binah begins the Pillar of Form. It is the first experience of separateness—sea from sky, inside from outside, above from below. With Binah, reality begins to take literal form; hence Binah is also called the Great Mother.

All Wands correspond to the first of four worlds, Atziluth (meaning "proximity" or "emanation"), also called the Archetypal World. "Binah in Atziluth" receives the flash of insight from Chokmah and differentiates and processes it. Father Chokmah and mother Binah produce the son (Tiphareth); it is like the inception of an undertaking whose consequences will unfold throughout a lifetime. As the Lord of Virtue, Binah expresses the natural drive of wands to create; as *Abundance*, *Sorrow*, and *Work*, Binah will seek to connect, recognize, and fabricate.

RIDER-WAITE-SMITH SYMBOLISM

3 of Wands (*Rider-Waite-Smith Tarot*)

In this tranquil, sunlit scene, a figure stands with his back to us, relaxed and trusting in the gentle breeze. Ships set out across the sea below him; his three staves rise naturally from the earth. Where the martial 2 of Wands set out to conquer, the solar 3 observes a more patient time frame, watching and waiting as his kingdom develops.

According to Waite, this "calm and stately personage" sends his ships out to sea laden with merchandise. We can read into his body language his concern, his sense of accomplishment, his hope for a good return on his investment. If all goes well, the value of his goods will be multiplied in Binah's "palace of mirrors." It takes the wealth of a kingdom to assume such a risk, and it takes secure sovereignty to negotiate with foreign lands as an equal. The enterprising spirit of the wands looks ahead, long term, to seeing its potential made manifest in cold, hard pentacles.

THOTH SYMBOLISM

Threes formulate a stable triangle, a portal through which things are made manifest. In this case it is the will which has been given form. Sol in Aries is associated with the I Ching hexagram 11, *tai*. In Crowley's translation of the *Book of Changes*, *tai* is called the "Yoni of Lingam," consisting of open (yin) lines over solid (yang) lines. It fits for a card that combines the masculine Aries and Sun within the feminine sephira Binah. The text speaks of fortune through seeking the virtues of patience and self-reliance.

Because this is a card of spring forces, the lotus wand of great mother Isis is depicted. The wand is the magical weapon of solar Tiphareth in the Golden Dawn Adeptus Minor ritual and is traditionally consecrated upon its creation with an invocation to Aries. Ten curved and ten straight flames flare from the background. Ten is the number of *yod* and twenty is *yod* spelled fully (*yod-vav-daleth*), hinting at the secret seed and the hand of creation.

RELATED CARDS

In the 3 of Wands we encounter the second decan of Aries, ruled by a sun exalted by sign and face. The Emperor (Aries) and the Sun combine to form the picture of a well-run kingdom, where benevolence and mutual respect characterize the relationship of citizen and state. As in the guest-host relationship, each willingly undertakes responsibilities to the other.

Threes firmly shape the essence of their suit. The 3 of Wands gives ambition and creative force a channel to act upon the world. The 3 of Cups supports circles of mutual affection; the 3 of Swords harbors irreversible insights; the 3 of Pentacles converts matter into products.

The 3 of Wands connects to Queens two different ways: (1) it is the Queen of Wands' final decan, where creative communities form; and (2) Queens reside in Binah; Queen of Wands shares the same faith in the creative process we see in the 3.

Finally: three, Binah, and the World/Universe are the number, sephira, and path of Saturn—all expressing themes of closure and realization.

4 OF WANDS
Lord of Completion (Perfected Work)

Dates:[102] April 10–April 19

Astrology: Aries, the sign ruled by Mars, with Sun exalted

Element: Cardinal fire

Decan: 20°–29° Aries; Aries III, the decan ruled by Venus

***Picatrix* Image:** A restless man, holding in his hands a gold bracelet, wearing red clothing, who wishes to do good, but is not able to do it

***Picatrix* Significations:** Subtlety, subtle mastery, new things, instruments and similar things

Agrippa Image: A white man, pale, with reddish hair, and clothed with a red garment, who carrying on the one hand a golden Bracelet, and holding forth a wooden staff, is restless, and like one in wrath, because he cannot perform that good he would

Agrippa Significations: Wit, meekness, joy, and beauty

Sephira/World: Chesed in Atziluth

---

102. Dates vary annually. All decanic minor dates listed in this book are based on 2019–2020 dates.

Color(s): Deep violet, plus the colors of the associated majors

Associated Majors: The Emperor and the Empress

Associated Minors: Shadow decan of the Knight of Pentacles/Prince of Disks

Themes: Creative checkpoint. Manifest will. Force and form. Perfect pairings. Marriage. Power couples. Order and fulfillment. Fleeting unions. Temporary refuges.

ASTROLOGY/ELEMENT

Aries decan III is a perfect pairing of a sign ruled by Mars and a decan ruled by consort Venus. Four gives the influence of magisterial Jupiter, officiating the marriage and wrapping up what was initiated. In Aries I the unadulterated energy of fire sprang forth in a martial spirit of independent conquest. The dominion won was established in Aries II through solar wise action. In Aries III, the charms of Venus yoke even Mars, exchanging might for works of peace and social graces.

Both *Picatrix* and Agrippa describe an Aries type of man, restless, clothed in red, wearing Venusian golden bracelets, unable to do some form of good he wishes. Perhaps this lack comes from the impermanence of the final decan, or perhaps this shows Venus's detriment in Aries, or that the stability of fours is short-lived. Venus can beguile Mars for only so long before he turns his energy once more to approaching strife. Meanwhile, though, we can enjoy the bright beauty of harmonious union.

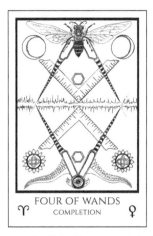

FOUR OF WANDS
COMPLETION

Structure (the measuring tools of the Emperor-Aries) and nature (the honey and bees of the Empress-Venus) complete each other. (*Tabula Mundi Tarot*)

MYTHOLOGY/TIME OF YEAR

While the decan and its ruler give us the obvious dynamic of Ares and Aphrodite, there are numerous others who fill the roles of Emperor and Empress. Primordial Greek gods Gaea, the personified earth, and Ouranos, who embodied the sky, came together to create the Titans. The Titans bore siblings Zeus and Hera, the ultimate power couple, King and Queen ruling the gods of Mount Olympus.

In Egypt, sky goddess Nut each night merged with the earth god Geb. Their four children were power couples as well: Isis, Queen of Heaven paired with Osiris, King of the Gods and the Underworld. Nephthys, goddess of water, birth, and death, paired with Set, god of chaos and fire.

The Hindu trinity of Venusian goddesses chose their gods. Lakshmi, goddess of fortune, who rose from the sea like Venus, wed Vishnu the preserver. Parvati, goddess of love, espoused Shiva the destroyer. Saraswati, goddess of the arts, was partnered with Brahma the creator.

QABALAH

The 4 of Wands is Chesed in Atziluth. Chesed חסד, the fourth sephira, translates as "mercy" or "loving kindness" and corresponds to generous, expansive Jupiter. It's also called *Gedulah*, "greatness."[103] Chesed's counterpart is Geburah, the fifth sephira; one gives, one takes away.

As the first sephira below the supernal triad and the abyss of Da'ath, Chesed is sometimes called the "Kether of the lower sephiroth." Everything that we can comprehend as human beings emanates from Chesed. God as a loving, patriarchal creator abides here, as does the first day of creation.

In the background is a castle compound (fours, Chesed) and a tower (Mars, ruler of Aries) with five (Mars) circular rings, seven (Venus) levels in all, and topped by a flag decorated with the salamander, a symbol of the fire element. (*Mystical Tarot*)

All Wands correspond to Atziluth ("proximity" or "emanation"), the Archetypal World. "Chesed in Atziluth" provides a moment of benevolent ease, providing all one needs for creative acts to follow.

As the Lord of Completion, Chesed ensures all is ready; as *Luxury*, *Truce*, and *Power* it will offer points of emotional, intellectual, and material respite before the rigors of Geburah.

---

103. The names of the seven lower sephiroth derive from 1 Chronicles 29:11: "Thine is the greatness, and the power, and the glory, and the victory, and the majesty … thine is the kingdom."

RIDER-WAITE-SMITH SYMBOLISM

4 of Wands (*Rider-Waite-Smith Tarot*)

Although Waite describes "two female figures" raising their bouquets, it's easy to imagine the red- and blue-draped forms as Emperor and Empress. The castled heights in the background resemble those protected by the Chariot, as well as the little towns depicted throughout the Pentacles suit. It could even be the castle on which the 2 of Wands stands. The rounded bridge half-obscured by foliage may be Maidstone Bridge in Kent, the same bridge pictured in the 5 of Cups.[104]

While the bridge may signal either welcome or leave-taking, the garlanded staves strongly recall the huppah, the bridal structure erected over the newlyweds in a traditional Jewish wedding. This temporary construction symbolizes the home; its unification of natural and built elements recalls the Empress as Mother Nature and the Emperor as the great architect. As a "stage" card, the 4 of Wands represents a temporary stop on the journey or roles its protagonists play for a time.

THOTH SYMBOLISM

Four wands revolve in a wheel, invoking Chesed/Jupiter (the Wheel). Fours are emblems of the Demiurge, who thinks himself God because he is first below the abyss,

---

104. Katz and Goodwin, *Secrets of the Waite-Smith Tarot*, 277.

unaware of those above who made him. Fire here is content, thinking itself completely manifest yet unaware that creation continues its inexorable course.

The wheel is also a circle, the universal symbol of something complete in itself, yet limited by its boundary. The ram-headed wands signify Aries and Jupiter in the form of Amun-Ra, the ram-headed father god. The other wands bear doves, symbols of Venus. Martial red wands shadowed in Jupiter's violet flash against a Venusian green background.

Crowley tells us that Venus's rulership of Aries's decan signifies that one cannot complete one's work without diplomacy and tact. The card is a complete glyph of the Thelemic saying "Love is the Law, Love under Will," as will can be thought of as the initiative of Aries, love as the occupation of Venus, and law as the domain of Jupiter.

RELATED CARDS

The 4 of Wands unites the Emperor (Aries) and the Empress (Venus). For a moment, the Empress's infinite natural grace and the Emperor's orderly structure complement each other; their rites of union legitimize the kingdom established in the 2 and 3 of Wands. The wedding does not equal the marriage, however, and the 4 of Wands' pleasures may be fleeting.

Fours gather together an abundance of their suit resources. The 4 of Wands publicly aligns community interests. The 4 of Cups holds a fullness of feelings; the 4 of Swords holds thoughts gathered in stillness; the 4 of Pentacles holds amassed treasures.

4 of Wands is also the first or shadow decan of the Knight of Pentacles/Prince of Disks, who is well-acquainted with its laurels and rarely content to rest on them; in the 5 and 6 of Pentacles, he will do all he can to forestall scarcity.

Finally, four, Chesed, and the Wheel of Fortune are the number, sephira, and path of Jupiter—each expressing security and fullness in its own way.

5 OF WANDS
Lord of Strife

Dates:[105] July 23–August 1

Astrology: Leo, the sign ruled by the Sun

Element: Fixed fire

Decan: 1°–9° Leo; Leo I, the decan ruled by Saturn

***Picatrix* Image:** A man wearing dirty clothes, and the image of a rider looking to the north, and his body looks like the body of a bear and the body of a dog

***Picatrix* Significations:** Strength, generosity, and victory

Agrippa Image: A man riding on a lion

Agrippa Significations: Boldness, violence, cruelty, wickedness, lust and labors to be sustained

Sephira/World: Geburah in Atziluth

Color(s): Orange, plus the colors of the associated majors

Associated Majors: Strength/Lust and the World/Universe

---

105. Dates vary annually. All decanic minor dates listed in this book are based on 2019–2020 dates.

Associated Minors: Knight of Wands

Themes: Incompatibility. Pressure. Testing. Will under restriction. Upheaval. Purification by fire. Striving. Overcoming constraint. Competition and attention. Drama. Motion and activity. Compression and release.

ASTROLOGY/ELEMENT

Leo decan I: Leo is ruled by the Sun, while the decan ruler is the sun's nemesis, Saturn. Darkness tries to smother light. To top it off, the card is a five, whose sephira is ruled by the other malefic, Mars, adding *Sturm und Drang* ("storm and drive"). The sun's energy is strong in fixed Leo. Martial drive suits it. Yet it is being restrained by leaden Saturn, creating a powder keg ready to blow.

Agrippa's image for this decan is a man riding a lion, appropriately oppressive labor for the lion. The *Picatrix* has a man wearing dirty clothes, the weight of unwanted earth. It separately mentions a rider, looking to the north, the direction of winter (Saturn). The rider appears ready for winter, for his body looks like two types of wild animal: a bear and a dog. Oddly enough, the signification descriptions are "strength, generosity, and victory," which seem to foreshadow the decan to come, suggesting that the restricting blockage introduced by Saturn is blowing open.

The wands have the red ribbons of elemental fire, while the badger is black (Saturn) and known for its aggression (fire). (*Animal Totem Tarot*)

MYTHOLOGY/TIME OF YEAR

Pele is a Hawaiian goddess of volcanoes, fire, lightning, and wind, known as "She Who Shapes the Sacred Earth." Through the action of fire and earth, she created the islands. She is noted for her power and passion, but also for her unpredictability and jealousy. She was a rival of the snow goddess Poli'ahu. They battled fire against snow until earthquakes shook the land. Eventually the snow mantle of Poli'ahu chilled and hardened Pele's lava, confining her to the southern portion of the land.

The Buddhist wrathful gods and goddesses who destroy the obstacles to enlightenment apply. These fierce beings appear demonic, adorned with terrifying expressions, charnel ornaments, and sexually suggestive elements. Yet they guard against the very demons they resemble, representing harnessed obstacles as a force of liberation.

Lion goddess *Sekhmet* (meaning "power") is the daughter of solar Ra. This lion-headed goddess led the pharaohs in warfare. Pasht or *Pehkhet*, meaning "she who scratches," was also known as the "night huntress with sharp eye and pointed claw."

This decan contains 5° Leo, the start of the Golden Dawn zodiacal year.

Mesopotamian deity Zurvān is shown carrying the *tau* cross and flanked by scythes; his form combines the lion of Leo with parts of the other Kerubic beasts (Saturn). (*Tabula Mundi Tarot*)

QABALAH

The 5 of Wands is Geburah in Atziluth. Geburah (גבודה), the fifth sephira, translates as "severity," "strength," or "restraint," and corresponds to fierce Mars with his cutting sword. Geburah acts as a corrective restraining the free flow of Chesed; Chesed and Geburah act as the inviting and repelling arms of divinity. Also known as *Din* ("judgment") and *Pachad* ("fear"), Geburah separates individuals, giving each room to breathe; it is associated with the second day of creation, when God divided the "waters from the waters," creating the sky above and sea below.[106] It is this separating, testing, subjectively challenging nature of Geburah/Mars that gives the fives of tarot their conflictual nature.

All Wands correspond to Atziluth ("proximity" or "emanation"), the Archetypal World. Geburah in Atziluth applies heat and pressure, ensuring that only the fittest contender in the creative process survives.

As the Lord of Strife, Geburah literally pushes us to strive; as disappointment, defeat, and worry, Geburah forces us to confront and deal with emotional loss, unfairness, and actual poverty.

RIDER-WAITE-SMITH SYMBOLISM

5 of Wands (*Rider-Waite-Smith Tarot*)

---

106. Genesis 1:6 (Authorized King James Version).

Waite emphasizes the playful nature of this card, calling it "mimic warfare." Five youths contend on uneven ground, "as if in sport or strife." Although the contestants bear a family resemblance to one another, their variously colored garments suggest that this is not a team—it's every person for themselves. The irregular angles of the staves suggest many agendas at odds with each other.

Like all fives, this one is forward-looking. Every sport has a goal or standard, however contrived, by which one determines the winner. Who will be crowned and recognized in the 6 of Wands? The spirit of the card is not hostile, but Saturn's pressure does not encourage sharing: it encourages each to shine at maximum luminosity, even though the spotlight will only highlight one. The five-six sequence (from Saturn in Leo to Jupiter in Leo) recalls Zeus's liberation of his siblings from his father Kronos's belly before taking his place as King of the Gods.

THOTH SYMBOLISM

The central solid wand is that of the Chief Adept, topped by a caduceus with winged disk. The twinned serpents below the sun disk are wearing the crowns of Upper and Lower Egypt. The disk is marked with Crowley's personal sigil as signature, for this decan contains his ascendant degree. The sigil combines the "Mark of the Beast" (male solar influence), conjoined with the "Star of Babalon" (female Saturn influence).

The smaller flanking wands are the phoenix and lotus wands used in the Adeptus Minor Ritual of the Golden Dawn. The wand coloring chosen by Lady Harris is purposefully elementally discordant, set against a backdrop of fiery yellow-orange. The wands clash as the phoenix wand relates to purification by fire, while the lotus wand relates to water and to the universe between spirit and materiality—or the zodiac between heaven and earth.

Crowley remarks upon the lion goddess Pasht as hailed as *saeva et ferox* (cruel and fierce) and upon Geburah's disturbance as issuing from Binah's seemingly maternal depths.[107]

---

107. Crowley, *Book of Thoth*, 191.

RELATED CARDS

In the 5 of Wands, the World/Universe (Saturn) meets Strength/Lust (Leo), a card which can convey either bravery or physical vigor. On the one hand, Saturn's spatial confinement and the five's heat create a hothouse environment; on the other, Saturn's time pressures motivate those who dare to compete. As the Knight/Prince of Wands's central decan, the five makes him strive to shine. It's not enough for this Knight to excel; he must be the best! When everyone recognizes that, he will have achieved the victory of the 6 of Wands.

Fives create motion and imbalance. The 5 of Wands sets our ambitions alight. The 5 of Cups deprives us of emotional security. The 5 of Pentacles of our material resources. The 5 of Swords disrupts our thought patterns, our perception of "the rules."

Finally, five is the number of Geburah, the sephira of Mars—the corresponding path is the Tower, source of life-altering, character-developing challenges that knock you out of your comfort zone!

6 OF WANDS
Lord of Victory

Dates:[108] August 2–August 12 (includes the cross-quarter holiday)

Astrology: Leo, the sign ruled by the Sun

Element: Fixed fire

Decan: 10°–19° Leo; Leo II, the decan ruled by Jupiter

Picatrix **Image:** A man who wears a crown of white myrtle on his head, and he has a bow in his hand

Picatrix **Significations:** Beauty, riding, the ascension of a man who is ignorant and base, war and naked swords

Agrippa Image: An image with hands lifted up, and a man on whose head is a crown; he hath the appearance of an angry man, and one that threateneth, having in his right hand a sword drawn out of the scabbard, and in his left a buckler

Agrippa Significations: Hidden contentions, and unknown victories, and upon base men, and upon the occasions of quarrels and battles

---

108. Dates vary annually. All decanic minor dates listed in this book are based on 2019–2020 dates.

Sephira/World: Tiphareth in Atziluth

Color(s): Clear pink rose, plus the colors of the associated majors

Associated Majors: Strength/Lust and the Wheel of Fortune

Associated Minors: Knight of Wands

Themes: Harmony. Honors. Royalty. Triumph with peace. Successful climax. Pride and recognition. Self-expansion. Excellence.

ASTROLOGY/ELEMENT

Leo decan II combines our fiery central sun (Leo) with the decan ruler Jupiter, king of the gods. The sun is doubly emphasized as the sixes are all associated with the solar sephira Tiphareth.

Picatrix mentions a man who wears a crown of white myrtle on his head, reminiscent of the laurel crowns of the victor. The hero carries a bow, like the sun lord Apollo. The additional comment reads "the ascension of a man who is ignorant and base," showing the shadow side of any rise, as all beings are base to some degree. The signification is said to be "Beauty, riding … war and naked swords"—which, like all sixes, does sound sexual.

Agrippa's man is also crowned and threatening, raising up his hands with a drawn sword and buckler. The signification speaks to victories over base men and battles hidden and unknown overcome. It fits well with the idea that the strife of the preceding fifth card leads to the glories of the sixth.

In this heraldic image, the "lion sejant" of Leo wears the laurel wreath and poses in shared victory with the crowned owl "in its vigilance" from the top of Fortune's wheel (Jupiter) in this deck. (*Tabula Mundi Tarot*)

MYTHOLOGY/TIME OF YEAR

The ancient Olympic Games were held in honor of Zeus (Jupiter). The competitors sought to emulate the virtues of their heroes as they strove for excellence, hoping to display the fortitude of Ajax, the potency of Achilles, the acumen of Odysseus, and the cunning morality of Diomedes. The victors were awarded the laurel crown, but more importantly, they battled for something priceless: *kleos aphthiton*, undying glory. The winners were revered with congratulatory odes celebrating their vigor and tracing their lineage to deity, giving them instant demigod status.

SIX OF WANDS

This monumental figure, bearing the usual laurels of Jupiter, shows one facet of *Victory*:
fame. The falling leaves and spectral sidekick ask: Will it last? (*Linestrider Tarot*)

The athletes were devoted to Eris (Discordia), the goddess of strife. While Eris is more commonly known for sowing discord, she has a constructive aspect that fosters excellence and inspires self and communal betterment. The "good strife" is beneficial, motivating the athletes to strive toward distinction and favor from Nike (Victoria), goddess of victory.

Leo II begins just after Lughnasadh/Lammas (August 1), a cross-quarter Pagan holiday of first harvest, feasting, ritual athletics, and mountain climbing. "Old Lammas" is celebrated when the sun reaches 15° Leo.

QABALAH

The 6 of Wands represents Tiphareth in Atziluth. Tiphareth (תיפארת), the sixth sephira, is the "heart" of the Tree, balanced not only between the pillars of mercy and severity, but also between Kether and Yesod/Malkuth. Hermetic Qabalists translate Tiphareth as "beauty," but "splendor" or "glory" (terms usually associated with Hod) would be equally apt. Tiphareth corresponds to the sun and the third day of creation, when God brought the land forth from the waters and made it fruitful. By bringing opposing forces into proportion, Tiphareth nurtures life on earth just as our sun does. This benign creative force gives the sixes of tarot their clear sense of purpose.

All Wands correspond to Atziluth ("proximity" or "emanation"), the Archetypal World. In Tiphareth in Atziluth, the drives and life force of the Wands have found a collective purpose.

As the Lord of Victory, Tiphareth gives us a sense of heroic belonging; as pleasure, science, and success, Tiphareth grants us emotional fulfillment, solutions to tough problems, and tangible achievements.

RIDER-WAITE-SMITH SYMBOLISM

6 of Wands (*Rider-Waite-Smith Tarot*)

Waite suggested that the "laurelled horseman" might be read in many ways that share an exultant theme: a "victor triumphing," "great news," "the crown of hope," and most evocatively, "expectation crowned with its own desire." His gaze looks forward, although his horse turns to the viewer with a knowing expression. (Much has been made of this, as if the skeptical mount knows the moment cannot last.)

The 5, 6, and 7 of Wands read as a sequential triptych: the 5 shows the contest, the 6 shows the winner, and the 7 shows his battle to retain his status. In this sequence, there is also a changing relationship between the people pictured in each card: all five are at odds at first, but they come to fall in step with their leader, all wands aligned, before arraying themselves against him in the final scene. Finally, there is a rise in altitude: scrapping at ground level, elevated on horseback, and defending the high ground.

THOTH SYMBOLISM

The same wands as in the 5, but within the 6 of Wands symmetry is restored to the design, as all sixes reflect the centering influence of the sephira Tiphareth. Instead of one wand of the Chief Adept dominating the others, two are crossed at the summit, and all the wands are of similar girth. The phoenix wands now face inward toward the Chief Adept Wands, rather than outward against the lotus wands.

Winged disks top the central wands, with the sun disk red (fire) and wings blue (water and Jupiter). The fiery solar colors are against the clear pink rose of solar dawn, shaded with the violet of Jupiter (and Yesod). The cool pinks and violets seem to add a feminine balance to cool the masculine fire. Fire here is perfectly balanced, on the middle pillar and at the center. The 6 of Wands is like the sun, center stage with the spotlight of glory shining upon it. Nine steady flames foreshadow the next balanced wands card, the nine or Lord of Strength.

RELATED CARDS

In the 6 of Wands, the Wheel of Fortune (Jupiter) and Strength/Lust (Leo) combine good luck and public visibility. The Wheel shows figures in all conditions, but the 6 highlights a victor at the top of the wheel, solar glory glinting off his crown. The contests of the previous card have produced a winner whose moment of recognition has arrived.

This is the Knight/Prince of Wands' final decan—what he has been aiming for all along. Brought up in *Luxury* (4 of Cups), he has sought through *Strife* (5 of Wands) to prove himself. His adoring public now gives him his longed-for validation.

Sixes bring purpose and harmony to their suit. The 6 of Wands creates a sense of belonging (patriotism, for example). The 6 of Cups fosters altruism; the 6 of Swords resolves conflicts; the 6 of Pentacles shares its success with others.

Finally, six, Tiphareth, and the Sun are the number, sephira, and path of the Sun. Each harmonizes imbalances; each helps us find meaning and purpose in life.

7 OF WANDS
Lord of Valor

Dates:[109] August 13–August 22

Astrology: Leo, the sign ruled by the Sun

Element: Fixed fire

Decan: 20°–29° Leo; Leo III, the decan ruled by Mars

Picatrix **Image:** A man who is old and black and ugly, with fruit and meat in his mouth and holding a copper jug in his hand

Picatrix **Significations:** Love and delight and food trays and health

Agrippa Image: A young man in whose hand is a whip, and a man very sad, and of an ill aspect

Agrippa Significations: Love and society, and the loss of one's right for avoiding strife

Sephira/World: Netzach in Atziluth

Color(s): Amber, plus the colors of the associated majors

Associated Majors: Strength/Lust and the Tower

---

109. Dates vary annually. All decanic minor dates listed in this book are based on 2019–2020 dates.

Associated Minors: Shadow decan of the King of Pentacles/Knight of Disks

Themes: Prevailing toward a goal. Regaining balance. The good fight. Offense versus defense. Overcoming stiff opposition. Proving oneself. Having backbone. Difficulty is opportunity for courage. No guts, no glory.

ASTROLOGY/ELEMENT

Leo III shows the first signs of degeneration hitting the fire suit. The decan combines the Sun (Leo), decan ruler Mars, and Venus as seven. It's passionate, but it's a struggle for Venus to try and balance all of this masculine energy from an off-balance position. Mars wants to be on the offensive and strives toward the goal with solar force behind it. Venus would prefer to collaborate but instead must take the defensive role. The challenge is to find a way to regain the poise and honors experienced in the six.

With a brave heart, one must rise to these tests. Agrippa's image depicts a young man with a whip and a sad and ill man, seemingly indicating someone goaded against their will. The young man represents the trying force that has arisen, driving the reluctant other man toward uncertain outcome. *Picatrix* has an old and ugly man (Mars) with fruit (Venus) and meat (Mars) in his mouth and a jug of copper (Venus) to sustain him.

The foreground's flaming torch evokes the classic theme of "one against many"; in the background, a martial homage to the Waite-Smith Tower looms. *(Tabula Mundi Tarot)*

The central wand is a blunt object of martial force, while the innermost
flanking pairs of wands are ceremonial daggers shaped like the glyph of Mars
and decorated with the lions of Sekhmet (Venus and Leo). (*Rosetta Tarot*)

MYTHOLOGY/TIME OF YEAR

The goddess Nike, personification of victory, was the daughter of Titan Pallas, sometimes also said to be the daughter of Ares (Mars). Her brothers were *Zelos* (zeal) and
Kratos (strength), and her sister was *Bia* (force). In some myths, Nike was the half-sister
of Athena, goddess of wisdom and warfare, fathered upon Metis by Pallas, though
Zeus bore her.

Winged Nike's name comes from a root meaning "first," as in victor. She was said
to grant speed, valor, strength, and success in quests undertaken. She holds the laurel
wreath crown of the victorious and positions her wings outspread over the victor in
any contest. She carries the palm branch of peace, a Venusian offering that insinuates
that peace comes after the battle is won. As Zeus's divine charioteer, she helped him
overthrow his father Kronos.

QABALAH

The 7 of Wands is Netzach in Atziluth. Netzach (נצח) and Hod (הוד), the seventh and
eighth sephiroth, work together in Kabbalah. Some call them the "armies/hosts" of
God, the "sources of prophecy," or the "tactical sephiroth." They are channels through

which we can receive divine guidance. We think of Netzach as the emotional and Hod as the intellectual sphere. Hermetic Qabalists tend to translate Netzach as "victory," but a more accurate translation is "eternity" or "endurance." Netzach, ruled by Venus, is a place of passions and quests, where one finds the inspiration to follow through on what they love.

All Wands correspond to the first of four worlds, Atziluth (meaning "proximity" or "emanation"), also called the Archetypal World. Netzach in Atziluth feels daring and driven; it leads to a desire to do the impossible. This is clearly seen in the Lord of Valor. As *Debauch* (*Illusionary Success*), *Futility* (*Unstable Effort*), and *Failure* (*Success Unfulfilled*), Netzach offers up phantasmal dreams, elaborate plans, and the stamina to prevail through hardship.

RIDER-WAITE-SMITH SYMBOLISM

7 of Wands (*Rider-Waite-Smith Tarot*)

A young warrior is beset by six opposing staves; as Waite observes, he occupies the "vantage point," which gives him an edge over his enemies. He wears one boot and one shoe. Some have suggested that this trope—the mismatched footwear—derives from Smith's intimacy with Shakespearean theatre: in *The Taming of the Shrew*, the character Petruchio arrives at his wedding in similar garb.[110] It is a deliberate act of provocation, intended to give offense. The 7 of Wands stands upon the heights he summited in the 6 of Wands. The breeze is brisk here, stirring his hair. His expression is one of determination; he will willingly die before giving up.

If we superimpose the image on the Tree of Life, the angle of the young man's staff extends from 5 (Geburah/Mars) to 7 (Netzach/Venus); his heart (Tiphareth) is at the center. If he can maintain his balance (Tiphareth), he shall prevail in the end.

THOTH SYMBOLISM

The balanced wands of the 6 are relegated to the background, while in the foreground a looming club is the seventh that opposes them. The background is the deep purple color of Leo in the Queen Scale, while the color of the wands is now veering toward the red of Mars. The club is crude and blunt, a martial weapon without finesse. The club's ten segments suggest that the disorder coming to the suit is due to its increasing materialization. The key is not to waste the energy that the fire force still has, but to direct it before it dissipates.

Sevens represent what is needed to achieve victory (Netzach) in each suit. In fire, what is needed is valor and ardor, zeal and enthusiasm for the challenge and opposition at hand. The combination of Venus and Mars brings passion, while Mars and Leo give backbone. But though there is courage, the battle is disorganized. The flames that were steady in the 6 are disordered here, and the astrological symbols are thrown off-center.

RELATED CARDS

Mars rules the third decan of Leo in the 7 of Wands. Here the disruptive force of the Tower (Mars) combines with the lion's brute force (Strength) to produce courage and desperate measures. Opposition is strong, but so is the determination to overcome enemies within and without through heroic, individual effort.

Sevens are cards of quests and seeking. The 7 of Wands defends what his ambition has secured; the 7 of Cups escapes into fevered visions; the 7 of Swords schemes and

---

110. Katz and Goodwin, *Secrets of the Waite-Smith Tarot*, 243.

acts on plan B; The 7 of Pentacles evaluates and tries to recuperate or improve previous efforts.

As the first (or "shadow") of his three decans, the 7 of Wands motivates the King of Pentacles/Knight of Disks to stabilize his kingdom and ensure its profit and prosperity. He knows violent confrontation leads to oppression, and his best self avoids heated arguments.

Finally, seven, Netzach, and the Empress are the number, sephira, and path of Venus. Together they represent the unconquerable force of desire, prevailing over common sense.

8 OF WANDS
Lord of Swiftness

Dates:[111] November 21–November 30

Astrology: Sagittarius, the sign ruled by Jupiter

Element: Mutable fire

Decan: 0°–9° Sagittarius; Sagittarius I, the decan ruled by Mercury

***Picatrix* Image:** The bodies of three men and one body is yellow, another white and the third is red

***Picatrix* Significations:** Heat, heaviness, growth in plains and fields, sustenance and division

Agrippa Image: A man armed with a coat of mail, and holding a naked sword in his hand

Agrippa Significations: Boldness, malice, and liberty

Sephira/World: Hod in Atziluth

Color(s): Violet, plus the colors of the associated majors

---

111. Dates vary annually. All decanic minor dates listed in this book are based on 2019–2020 dates.

Associated Majors: Temperance/Art and the Magician/Magus

Associated Minors: King/Knight of Wands

Themes: Movement. The "light bulb" moment. Brilliant yet fleeting. Messages in motion. Divine inspiration. Vehicles of will. The speed of light. Express package delivery.

ASTROLOGY/ELEMENT

Sagittarius decan I combines Jupiter, ruler of Sagittarius, with Mercury, ruler of the decan. As an eight, it has a doubled Mercury influence. Though Mercury is in detriment in Sagittarius, it's supported by this twinning. In the sign of the traveling archer, Mercury is the wand: direct, on the move, and not stopping to nitpick details.

Mutable fire has become empyrean. Aries bursts out of the gate. Leo burned bright and true. Sagittarian fire has refined itself, dispersing through the expanding and far-reaching nature of Jupiter. It's as delicate as a rainbow or the filament of a light bulb. Add Mercury and the mind becomes visionary and fleet as the archer's arrow speeding toward the target.

Picatrix gives an image of the bodies of three men, one yellow, one white, and one red, colors of fire and Spirit. The indications are of heat and growth. Agrippa's image is of a man armed with mail, holding an unsheathed sword. It suggests someone bold who won't be tied down.

EIGHT OF WANDS
SWIFTNESS

The doubling of mercurial influence is shown by the caduceus and talaria (winged sandals) of Hermes (Mercury), while the rainbow of Temperance/Art references the sign of Sagittarius and the idea of heavenly messages and ephemeral fire. (*Tabula Mundi Tarot*)

MYTHOLOGY/TIME OF YEAR

With all this Mercury energy, one could tell of messenger goddess Iris who traveled on the rainbow or perhaps speak of *Aeolus* ("swift-moving"), keeper of the fleet *Anemoi*, the gods of the winds. There were eight wind gods, one for each direction of the compass: Boreas (North), Notus (South), Eurus (East), Zephyrus (West), plus four lesser gods for the between directions.[112]

With Jupiter-ruled Sagittarius and doubled Mercury, tales of Zeus and Hermes are appropriate. Hermes was the messenger and son of Zeus. His mother was Maia, the eldest of the Pleiades sisters. He was a brilliant and precocious child. By noontime of the first day of his birth, he had invented the lyre and sung his own commemorative birthday hymn. He was mischievous and thieving, stealing Apollo's cattle that very evening. Yet while he was a handful, he was beloved by the other gods and a favorite of Zeus, assisting him in his numerous trysts and always on hand to provide his father with brilliant insights, assistance, and advice.

---

112. Sometimes conflated with Apeliotes (Southeast).

Here the Lord of Swiftness is a horse, an apt representative for Sagittarius, the half-equine centaur figure of mythology. (*Animal Totem Tarot*)

QABALAH

The 8 of Wands is Hod in Atziluth. Netzach נצח and Hod הוד, the seventh and eighth sephiroth, work together in Kabbalah and are sometimes known as the "armies/hosts" of God, the "sources of prophecy," or the "tactical sephiroth." They are channels for divine guidance, Netzach in the emotional and Hod in the intellectual sphere.

Translated as "splendor," "majesty," or "glory," Hod houses the intellect, the crowning feature of humanity. Hod, sphere of Mercury, gives us rationality, logic, and the means to communicate. In prophecy, Hod gives speech to the felt sense of Netzach.

All Wands correspond to the first of four worlds, Atziluth ("proximity" or "emanation"), also called the Archetypal World. As Lord of Swiftness, Hod in Atziluth bestows a sure sense of direction. As *Indolence* (*Abandoned Success*) in Briah and *Prudence* in Assiah, Hod's sensible voice tells us when it is time to move on and how to organize our lives into feasible steps. In airy Yetzirah, however, it may overanalyze, leading to *Interference* (*Shortened Force*).

RIDER-WAITE-SMITH SYMBOLISM

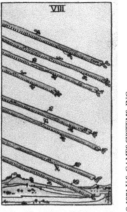

8 of Wands (*Rider-Waite-Smith Tarot*)

According to Waite, these wands in flight are descending, not ascending; they "draw to the term of their course. That which they signify is at hand." No sooner do we anticipate the event than it occurs! Because their arrival is imminent, the length of their flight is immaterial—only their direction/vector matters.

Excluding the Aces, the 8 of Wands and the 3 of Swords are the only minor cards in the Waite-Smith deck which feature no human figures, giving them an air of abstraction. Like the Wheel of Fortune/Jupiter which rules Sagittarius, this card is impersonal, referring more to the swift communication of ideas and things than the people who give and receive them.

The river and buildings beyond it can be interpreted Qabalistically as Yesod (the moon) and Malkuth (earth). The 8 of Wands descends at an angle, as if from Hod (eight) to Malkuth (ten). Or, viewed from within the Tree rather than facing it, they could describe the Magician's path from Kether to Binah.

THOTH SYMBOLISM

The eight wands are no longer material wooden staves but instead are red rays of electricity, waves traveling at the speed of light. In Crowley's text, he says that in the

8 of Wands the fire is "no longer conjoined with the ideas of combustion and destruction" and represents energy at its most exalted and tenuous, such as electric current and pure light, as well as Hod's attributes of thought and speech.[113] The rays are fitting tribute to Mercury's skills of transmission, and the arrowheads on the rays tell of Sagittarius's far-reaching expansion. Above the vibrating rays, light divides into the colors of the spectrum, which "exhibit interplay and correlation."[114]

Unlike the other Wands cards, there are no flames, for their energy has been siphoned to produce the rays. Behind is a geometric crystalline form that looks like a pyramid (symbol of Chesed/Jupiter) and its reflection. It overlaps another pyramid seen from above but off-centered (off middle pillar). The eight arrowheads mark the pyramid's visible corners.

RELATED CARDS

The 8 of Wands, ruled by Mercury, is the first of three Sagittarius minors.[115] In the 8, the Magician (Mercury) and Temperance/Art (Sagittarius) produce swift communication, instant messaging, and express package delivery! Though Sagittarius is one of Mercury's signs of detriment, eight is Mercury's number. So even if the Magician's effects rebound or evanesce, they are speedy and true in direction.

Eights offer system-based steps that help you find your way toward external and internal realizations. In the 8 of Wands, information finds its audience at the speed of light. The 8 of Cups walks away from drowning in its own feelings. The 8 of Swords analyzes the unanalyzable, and the 8 of Pentacles organizes your practical life.

The 8 of Wands, the central decan of the King (RWS) or Knight (Thoth) of Wands, gifts him with quick reflexes, flashes of insight, and an unhesitating management style.

Eight is the number and Hod is the sephira of Mercury. His rulership of the decan makes the 8 of Wands doubly mercurial.

---

113. Crowley, *Book of Thoth*, 184.

114. Crowley, 193.

115. In the 8, 9, and 10 of Wands, the zodiacal archer's action can be deconstructed: the speeding arrow, the bow's tensile strength, and finally, the impact on the stricken target.

9 OF WANDS
Lord of Strength

Dates:[116] December 1–December 10

Astrology: Sagittarius, the sign ruled by Jupiter

Element: Mutable fire

Decan: 10°–19° Sagittarius; Sagittarius II, the decan ruled by the Moon

Picatrix Image: A man leading cows and in front of him he has an ape and a bear

Picatrix Significations: Fear, lamentations, grief, sadness, misery and troubles

Agrippa Image: A woman weeping, and covered with clothes

Agrippa Significations: Sadness and fear of his own body

Sephira/World: Yesod in Atziluth

Color(s): Indigo, plus the colors of the associated majors

Associated Majors: Temperance/Art and the Priestess

Associated Minors: King/Knight of Wands

---

116. Dates vary annually. All decanic minor dates listed in this book are based on 2019–2020 dates.

Themes: Power in flexibility. Regaining health. The "green fuse" or force of nature. Aspiration. Flowing with change. Aim and release. Balance. The middle path. Rallying the will. Align mind and body with intention. Resilience. Tensile strength.

ASTROLOGY/ELEMENT

Sagittarius II combines Sagittarian Jupiter with a double dose of lunar energy: the Moon ruling the decan and nines. Mutable fire has stood up to everything the suit has progressed through, achieving fire's penultimate stance. It's a place of strength, even after challenge. The centaur stands at the ready, bow quivering with just the right tension and aiming at the goal. The doubling of the lunar energy gives the flexibility to flow with anything coming.

Yet lunar forces also bring instability and adversarial conditions. *Picatrix* shows a man leading cattle, faced by an ape and bear, which sounds like the mind and body causing the troubles he portends. Agrippa's image is a weeping woman covered with clothes, which he says indicates bodily fear. The trials of opposition may cause fear but are an opportunity to rise to the occasion, rallying and strengthening the will force; overall, it is a strength. Sagittarius is about juggling lunar and solar forces, flexing mind and body, unconsciousness and consciousness, with equilibrium and grace.

MYTHOLOGY/TIME OF YEAR

As the apotheosis of Sagittarius—whose path joins the sephira of the Sun with that of the Moon—and a doubly lunar card, it has myths common to Temperance and the Priestess. Who fits better than Artemis, lunar goddess of the silver bow, twin to solar Apollo with his golden lyre? Artemis, virgin who guarded the chastity of her body as inviolate, the wild huntress who yet helped women with the travails of childbirth. Her virginity signifies her autonomy, which justifies the fierceness with which she guards it.

Artemis's half-sister is Persephone; they are both daughters of Zeus (Jupiter). Her Hades ordeal certainly was an opportunity for her to be strong and adaptable. She prevailed, coming into her role as the venerable and formidable Queen of the Underworld. With her rise, the sap rises and things blossom; at her descent, things wither.

Whether this decan is a period of withering or blossoming depends on hemisphere. Though a beautiful maiden of spring, she isn't trifling—she also carries out the curses of men to punish the dead.

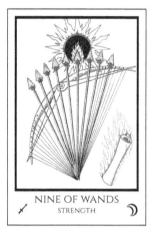

Bow imagery is a constant in esoteric tarot cards related to fiery Sagittarius; the Priestess's scroll symbolizes the inner knowledge or certainty underlying *Strength*. (*Tabula Mundi Tarot*)

QABALAH

The 9 of Wands is Yesod in Atziluth. Yesod יסוד, the ninth sephira, translates as "foundation" or "basis"—that which lies beneath the real world, Malkuth.[117] Here the light of the previous sephiroth gathers, to be expressed in Malkuth. The sixth day marked the creation of humans; thus Yesod corresponds to sexual intercourse. But also it signifies the moon, the unconscious, the imagination, magic, and the first step on any spiritual journey. All nines are places of power.

Wands correspond to Atziluth ("proximity" or "emanation"), the Archetypal World. Yesod in Atziluth is the moment in the creative process when one's art is fully realized in the mind. Action (Malkuth) brings it into reality. Because the moon rules its decan as well as Yesod, the 9 of Wands is doubly lunar; as Lord of Strength, it is potent, flexible, and tensile. As *Happiness*, *Cruelty* (and *Despair*), and *Gain*, Yesod exerts maximum

---

117. In Hebrew, the yesodot are the elements of the periodic table. Yesod is also sometimes called *tzaddik*, the "righteous one."

motivation on the human character, causing us to act in different ways depending on the suit.

While the moon rules this card's decan, the sun also appears—a reference to Temperance/Art (Sagittarius)'s path between Sun and Moon on the Tree of Life. (*Rosetta Tarot*)

RIDER-WAITE-SMITH SYMBOLISM

9 of Wands (*Rider-Waite-Smith Tarot*)

A strongly built figure holds his baton with an embattled expression "as if awaiting an enemy." Anticipating trouble already on the way, he looks up to the left as if gazing at the wands descending from the previous card, or from Hod (8) to Yesod (9) on the Tree of Life. His bandaged brow speaks to previous confrontations. Waite describes the wands behind him as a "palisade," a defensive formation of upright stakes. This recalls two of the meanings of *samekh*, the Hebrew letter corresponding to Temperance/Sagittarius: "support" or "prop"; and "quivering" or "anger."

Among the Waite-Smith nines, the 9 of Wands is the only "stage" card, emphasizing the reactive role its hero must play. What he does next depends on someone else's actions, as he will not act unless provoked. He draws from long experience to assess the coming threat. In Tree of Life terms, the green hills beyond can be read as Malkuth. Are they the home he has sworn to protect?

THOTH SYMBOLISM

Crowley writes extensively about the antinomy and resolution of change and stability; the axiom that stability is guaranteed by change is a law governing all of nature. He remarks that the moon, weakest of all planets, is in Sagittarius, most elusive of the signs, yet still dares to call itself strength. "Defense, to be effective, must be mobile."[118]

The card shows nine arrows as archers are the ultimate form of mobile defense. The shafts of the arrows are fiery red. Eight of the arrows are crossed, terminated by lunar crescent arrowheads with the lit or waxing end forward. The central ninth's arrowhead is a crescent with the dark or waning side forward. It has the sun at the fletching end. The sun has eighteen rays, a lunar number. Nine are rayed, nine straight. Sagittarius's path travels between Sun and Moon, the conscious and unconscious. The symbol of Sagittarius is on the dark side of the moon. The symbol of the moon is included only as the central arrowhead.

RELATED CARDS

The 9 of Wands, ruled by the Moon, is the second of three Sagittarius minors. Here the High Priestess and Temperance/Art join in the tensile strength of the archer's bow, chief weapon in the sure and secret hunt for divine knowledge. Like the Moon, the 9 travels far and experiences extremes. These trials lend it strength.

---

118. Crowley, *Book of Thoth*, 186.

In nines, each suit achieves the peak of its power. The 9 of Wands burns with determination, the 9 of Cups brims with joy, the 9 of Swords seethes with despair, and the 9 of Pentacles capitalizes on its work. A secret to each 9 can be found in the corresponding 3: if threes are the seed, then nines are the fruit.

The 9 of Wands is the final decan of the King (RWS) or Knight (Thoth) of Wands. His ability to drive a point home, seeing it forcefully through to its target, originates here. But it must happen quickly, or not at all!

Nine is the number and Yesod is the sephira of the Moon. The Moon's rulership of this decan makes the 9 of Wands doubly lunar.

10 OF WANDS
Lord of Oppression

Dates:[119] December 11–December 20

Astrology: Sagittarius, the sign ruled by Jupiter

Element: Mutable fire

Decan: 20°–29° Sagittarius; Sagittarius III, the decan ruled by Saturn

Picatrix **Image:** A man with a cap on his head, who is murdering another man

Picatrix **Significations:** Evil desires, adverse and evil effects, and fickleness in these and evil wishes, hatred, dispersion, and evil conduct

Agrippa Image: A man like in color to gold, or an idle man playing with a staff

Agrippa Significations: Following our own wills, and obstinacy in them, and activeness for evil things, contentions, and horrible matters

Sephira/World: Malkuth in Atziluth

Color(s): Yellow, plus the colors of the associated majors

---

119. Dates vary annually. All decanic minor dates listed in this book are based on 2019–2020 dates.

Associated Majors: Temperance/Art and the World/Universe

Associated Minors: Shadow decan of the Queen of Pentacles/Disks; relates to Page of Wands as a ten

Themes: Weight. Dampening of creative force. Industrial cogs. Shouldering a burden. Tyranny. Authority abuse and greed. Unchecked ambition. Obligations and endurance. Taking responsibility. Will under pressure. Working class struggles. Powering through.

ASTROLOGY/ELEMENT

In Sagittarius decan III, buoyant Jupiter has to carry the burden of Saturn squared, as Saturn rules both the decan and the tens as well as earth. In addition, the fire force comes in contact with ten, the end of the line and a big load of lead and earth and water smothering the ethereal fire. It's not all bad, as Saturn rewards those who carry more than their fair share of burden. But it sure feels oppressive. Saturn constricts and Jupiter expands. But Jupiter is outnumbered.

Picatrix describes a man with a cap on his head, who is murdering another man. Perhaps the cap disconnects him from divinity. Evil is mentioned four times; there is definite chance of being taken advantage of here. Agrippa's image is more benign, showing "a man golden in color, or an idle man playing with a staff." The significations are contentions, actively evil things, and "horrible matters." But they also mention following one's will with obstinacy, which seems to be the way through.

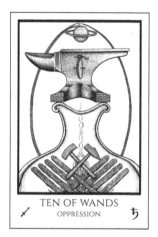

TEN OF WANDS
OPRESSION

The card is doubly saturnine, shown by the hammer and pick of
the oppressed working classes and the heavy anvil weighing down the
alchemical vessel from Sagittarius's Temperance/Art card. (*Tabula Mundi Tarot*)

MYTHOLOGY/TIME OF YEAR

Atlas *Telamon* (enduring Atlas) was a Titan who sided with the Titans in their war
with the Olympians. He is often portrayed as holding the earth on his shoulders, but
his burden was heavier than that. When the Titans lost the war, Zeus (Jupiter) sen-
tenced Atlas to stand at the edge of Gaea (Earth) and hold up the entire celestial
sphere of the universe on his shoulders.

King Sisyphus was covetous and deceitful. He took pleasure in violating Zeus's law
of *xenia*, protection and hospitality offered to travelers, killing guests for his own profit.
He further angered the gods by imprisoning Thanatos (Death) through duplicity, taking
relief away from those suffering and denying gods their sacrifices. Sisyphus had hubris,
claiming to be cleverer than Zeus. His punishment was rolling a boulder uphill for eternity. The boulder, charmed by Zeus, rolled back down each time it reached the top.

The time period covers the ten days preceding the December solstice, when the
sun in the Northern Hemisphere approaches maximum darkness.

QABALAH

The 10 of Wands is Malkuth מלכות in Atziluth. Malkuth is a separate vessel, hanging
alone at the base of the Tree. Co-terminous with the fourth world, Assiah, Malkuth

receives the outpouring of its predecessors. It corresponds to the Sabbath, the restful final day of creation, and the *Shekhinah* (divine feminine aspect). Translated as "kingdom" or "kingship," Malkuth's separateness is a blessing and a curse. It is humanity's fate to live apart from the divine, but only through our reconciling actions can the creation's wholeness be restored. In esoteric tarot, this is the return of the daughter to the mother, Binah.[120] In the tens of tarot, the ripe fruit bursting with seeds falls to the ground; the cycle ends only to begin again.

All Wands correspond to Atziluth ("proximity" or "emanation"), the Archetypal World. Malkuth in Atziluth, Lord of Oppression, brings the passions of the Wands to a closure so forceful it sows the seeds of its own overturning. As *Satiety*, *Ruin*, and *Wealth*, Malkuth's overflow leads to extremes: emotional repleteness, intellectual fanaticism, vast inheritances.

RIDER-WAITE-SMITH SYMBOLISM

10 of Wands (*Rider-Waite-Smith Tarot*) (left)
On the right is the 10 of Swords, not Wands, from the *Sola Busca Tarot*. Nevertheless, its influence on the Waite-Smith 10 of Wands is self-evident. (*Sola Busca Tarot*)

---

120. Malkuth represents the final *heh* in the Divine Name, יהוה, as Binah represents the primal or first *heh*. The restoration of creation's wholeness is the concept of *tikkun olam*, familiar to all who study Jewish mysticism.

"The place which the figure is approaching may suffer from the rods that he carries," says Waite.[121] There are two ways to read the Waite-Smith 10 of Wands: the most familiar one concerns heavy burdens; too much to do. Another reading is the determination to achieve success, no matter what the cost to all concerned. Waite observes that "fortune, gain, success" may accompany this card—but so may their price. The 10 of Wands believes the ends justify the means!

As has been widely observed, Smith based her version of the 10 of Wands on the fifteenth-century *Sola Busca Tarot*, whose 10 of Swords shows a man similarly weighted down. In both cases, it is an awkward bundle, held as if by one at the end of his strength, blinded by single-minded purpose. The "stage" division underscores the role he is to play in the lives of those he is about to encounter. The town he approaches, in Tree of Life terms, might be Malkuth.

THOTH SYMBOLISM

All the way down in Malkuth, fire has separated itself from Spirit, becoming a blind force unchecked and destructive. The double influence of Saturn, slow and heavy, is the antithesis of swift, ethereal Sagittarius. Crowley tells us that the fires still have enormous power as their energies complete, "but they have lost their patents of nobility."[122]

The eight background Wands are still crossed, each with clawed ends showing their lack of intelligence. In front of them, the dorjes from the 2 of Wands have lengthened into prison bars, a "stupid and obstinate cruelty from which there is no escape." The bars are the black of Saturn and Earth (Malkuth), and the suit symbols are captive, penned in by them while the flames attempt a breakout. There is still will force, but it has committed the crime of being bound to shallow purpose and lust of result. The consequence of using force and nothing but force is a harsh and relentless burden: excessive responsibility that one must bear with endurance.

---

121. Waite, *Pictorial Key*, 178.
122. Crowley, *Book of Thoth*, 194.

RELATED CARDS

In the 10 of Wands, the World/Universe (Saturn) meets Temperance/Art (Sagittarius). Obdurate Saturn lends its weight to the archer's arrow, which buries itself in the target with a sickening thud. Saturn's only expression as a ten, this card has an inarguable finality. Saturn confers endurance for great burdens, but also rigidity. Jupiter (ruler of Sagittarius) ensures this traveler and his heavy task go the distance. In the 2 of Pentacles, we can look for a turn in fortunes.

As the Queen of Pentacles' first or shadow decan, the 10 of Wands grants reservoirs of ambition, motivating her engines of progress (the 2 and 3 of Pentacles); at weak moments, the tyranny of the to-do list may make her despotic.

Tens bring endings and beginnings. The 10 of Wands is ambition's goal—great accomplishment, sometimes brutal. The 10 of Cups promises love handed across generations; the 10 of Pentacles promises resources. The 10 of Swords shows an argument taken to its final conclusion; surrender makes a reset possible.

ACE OF CUPS
Root of the Powers of Water

Dates:[123] September 22–December 20 (autumn in the Northern Hemisphere)

Astrology: Libra-Scorpio-Sagittarius quadrant, emphasizing the Kerubic water sign Scorpio

Element: Water. All Aces are also associated with Spirit

Sephira/World: Kether in Briah

Color(s): White brilliance

Associated Majors: The Hanged Man as the elemental trump of water

Associated Minors: Page/Princess of Cups

Themes and Keywords: Emotional seeding. Heart opening. Devotional quests. Flow and abundance. Romance and nascent stirrings of love. Unconditional love. Spiritual healing. Sacrifice. Purification.

---

123. Dates vary annually. All Ace dates listed in this book are based on 2019–2020 dates.

ASTROLOGY/ELEMENT

At the Ace of Cups, totality steps in the direction of the water element. As godhead splits into a fourfold form, this Ace takes on the role of primal *heh* in the divine name. As "Root of the Powers of Water," the Ace of Cups is the wellspring, the source of that "Spirit of the Mighty Waters" seen in the elemental trump of the Hanged Man.

Elemental water provides compassion and understanding. The water signs are romantic and creative as well as sensitive, impressionable and more than a little psychic. Water focuses attention on feelings. The Ace begins a suit that encompasses the entire emotional range.

This Ace rules the quadrant of space centered around the fixed water sign Scorpio. The Libra-Scorpio-Sagittarius trinity exemplifies the transmuting qualities of emotion on the seekers journey. Libra begins the quadrant with a focus on the Venusian qualities of love, Sagittarius shows the aspirational and expansive quality of the heart's mission, and central Scorpio provides the transformative and penetrating power of emotional depth.

MYTHOLOGY/TIME OF YEAR

The Ace of Cups bears an image that embodies the Holy Grail, icon of the spiritual quest. The Grail is an elusive object venerated and sought after for its limitless powers as a fount of joy and devotion and as a metaphor for the pure heart.

The Grail is kept in the castle of the Fisher King, last of his line. The king has been wounded in the "thigh," implying that he has been wounded in the groin and thus cannot father a successor. He has been punished thus for wooing a woman he was not free to pursue. Since the fertility of the kingdom is tied to that of the king, the land suffers. The king is a stand in for spiritual authority which has been compromised by excess. He awaits an untarnished hero to achieve the Grail, ask the right question, and bring healing to king and kingdom.

ACE OF CUPS
ROOT OF THE POWERS OF WATER

**The Ace as the Holy Grail and cup of Babalon: the waters
form the symbol of *heh* primal. (*Tabula Mundi Tarot*)**

The time of year extends from the September equinox through December solstice, as the equality of light and darkness morphs toward distinct polarity.

QABALAH

The Ace of Cups is Kether in Briah. All Aces correspond to the first sephira, Kether (כתר) or "crown," while Kether corresponds to the primum mobile, first motion, the force that moves the planets and stars across the sky. Kether, the crown, contains all that follows.

All Cups correspond to the second of four worlds, Briah (in Hermetic Qabalah, "Creation" or the "Creative World"), as well as primal *heh*, the first letter ה in the Divine Name, יהוה. In Briah, the idea of form arises—"something from nothing." In the next world, Yetzirah, form will differentiate. Kether in Briah represents the all-encompassing mind that comprehends all that follows. In Hermetic Qabalah, it is also the seat of the emotions.[124]

The Golden Dawn's diagram of the "Cup of Stolistes" represents the Tree of Life (minus Kether) as three connected forms: a crescent (water), a sphere (air), and a triangle (fire); the watery crescent extends from Atziluth to Briah. This they likened to "Moses's laver" and Solomon's "brazen sea"—both objects used for ritual lustration and purification.

---

124. The divine name Eheieh (היהא) associated with Briah means "I shall be."

RIDER-WAITE-SMITH SYMBOLISM

Ace of Cups (*Rider-Waite-Smith Tarot*)

Given its themes of divine love, sacrifice, and purification, the Ace of Cups recalls all vessels used in a spiritual context: the grail, the chalice, the font. Sacred fluids consecrate rites of joining (i.e., baptism or communion), just as the fountain spills back into its source. As in all Aces, a right hand holds the object, palms facing the viewer. The dove of Spirit or divine grace descends, holding in its beak the cross in a circle (be it Communion wafer, symbol of earth, or Malkuth in Kether). What first seems to be a "W" for water on the cup also resembles an "M" for Mary or *mem*, Hebrew for water.

ACE OF CUPS

Echoes of Waite-Smith's Ace of Cups: the inverted "M"
(or upright "W") and the quartered circle symbol. (*Linestrider Tarot*)

Twenty-six droplets descend (יהוה, the Divine Name, enumerates to 26; 10 + 5 + 6 + 5). Five streams—which could be Christ's wounds, the four elements and Spirit, or the senses—return endlessly to the water beneath. Perhaps the red water lilies floating within this infinite cycle symbolize human life arising out of eternal life.

THOTH SYMBOLISM

The Ace of Cups represents the feminine complement of lunar yoni to the phallic solar Ace of Wands; grail to the lance. The Holy Grail of the old Aeon becomes the cup of Babalon in the new. Thus, the three interlocking rings of the Aeons are engraved on the bowl, perhaps also referencing the Holy Trinity.

The cup floats upon the dark sea of fertile mother Binah, emerging from a lotus that has eighteen visible petals, the number of the Moon card. Crowley says the lotus fills the cup with life fluid as water, wine, or blood, according to purpose.[125] He mentions the dove of the Holy Ghost descending upon it to consecrate it, yet all that is visible is a stream of white brilliance, the color of the card, representing the purity of Kether in Briah.

---

125. Crowley, *Book of Thoth*, 195.

Scalloped rays of light radiate above and are reflected in the ripples vibrating the water below. The same Venusian scallop forms adorn the dress of the Princess of Cups, who represents the Ace's throne.

RELATED CARDS

The Ace of Cups corresponds first and foremost to the complete suit of Cups. It also relates to primal *heh* ה, the second letter of the Divine Name. As both "crown" and "root," the Ace is the throne of its Page or Princess. Because RWS Kings/Thoth Knights reside in Chokmah and represent the *yod* (whose tip is in Kether), they also relate to the Ace.

All Aces are said to revolve around the North Pole, but the "throne of the Ace" lies at the heart of the Page/Princess's domain.[126] For the Page/Princess of Cups, that domain encompasses Libra, Scorpio, and Sagittarius. Her corresponding major arcana are Justice/Adjustment, Death, and Temperance/Art. Thus the heart of the Ace of Cups lies in Death/Scorpio, the sign of fixed water. As the "Root of the Powers of Water," the Ace is elementally akin to the Hanged Man, the trump of water. The Hanged Man, Death, and the Ace and Page/Princess of Cups share themes of love and sacrifice.

---

126. The Page/Princess is said to rule 0° Libra to 30° Sagittarius; the Ace occupies the central 45° from 22°30' Libra to 7°30' Sagittarius.

2 OF CUPS
Lord of Love

Dates:[127] June 21–July 1 (includes the June solstice)

Astrology: Cancer, the sign ruled by the Moon, with Jupiter exalted

Element: Cardinal water

Decan: 0°–9° Cancer; Cancer I, the decan ruled by Venus

***Picatrix* Image:** A man whose fingers and head are distorted and slanted, and his body is similar to a horse's body; his feet are white, and he has fig leaves on his body

***Picatrix* Significations:** Instruction, knowledge, love, subtlety and mastery

Agrippa Image: A young virgin, adorned with fine clothes, and having a crown on her head

Agrippa Significations: Acuteness of senses, subtlety of wit, and the love of men

Sephira/World: Chokmah in Briah

Color(s): Gray, plus the colors of the associated majors

Associated Majors: The Chariot and the Empress

---

127. Dates vary annually. All decanic minor dates listed in this book are based on 2019–2020 dates.

Associated Minors: Queen of Cups holds the decan; relates to Knight/King as a two

Themes and Keywords: Nurturing. *Agape* versus *Eros*. Preparing for pregnancy. Maternal care. Pledging troth. Entwining. Union of polarities and the result. Romance. Harmony of male and female. Partnership. Mirroring. Mutual attraction. Interest/excitement.

ASTROLOGY/ELEMENT

Cancer decan I combines the motherly moon as ruler of cardinal water sign Cancer, with feminine Venus as ruler of the decan. Cancer is a protective and maternal sign, associated with the womb and breasts. Venus is the goddess of love and attraction, encouraging harmonious union. Yet as a two, it is also associated with the supernal masculine, as well as with themes of polarities encountering each other. This merger of the sexes is bound to be fruitful.

Agrippa's decan image is appropriately feminine and Venusian, featuring a youthful crowned virgin in fine clothes. The signification speaks of acute senses, perhaps the feeling nature of Cancer, and mentions specifically the love of men. The *Picatrix* imagery is less clear, telling of a man with distorted fingers and head, perhaps a supernal reference to *yod* and Kether, from which the twos descend. His horse-like body could relate to the seas of Cancer, and his white feet and fig leaves are vaguely Venusian. The significations at least mention love.

Dolphins are associated with Venus and the womb (Cancer); here they
are paired as *argent* (silver) and *or* (gold). (*Rosetta Tarot*)

MYTHOLOGY/TIME OF YEAR

Untainted love stories are appropriate here. Homer's *Odyssey* tells of Penelope's marital fidelity to Odysseus and her determination to preserve both her marriage and her son's legacy despite Odysseus's long absence.

Venus's maternal side shows in Aphrodite's protectiveness toward her son Eros. The mortal Psyche had offended Aphrodite, who sent her son Eros to cause Psyche to fall in love with something hideous. But Eros fell prey to his own arrows and fell deeply in love with Psyche. After many trials from Venus, the tale has a happy ending when Psyche is made immortal and allowed to wed Eros.

Silver (lunar) and gold (solar) cups, red and white roses: symbols of the alchemical marriage or union of opposites traditionally associated with the card. (*Universal Wirth Tarot*)

Goddesses who protect children also apply. Hindu Parvati was the wife of Shiva, and goddess of love, children, marriage, and devotion. Parvati and Shiva are often portrayed as the *Shiva linga*, the conjoined yoni and lingam that represent the interdependence of the male and female forces in the regenerative process of life. Parvati's prakriti (feminine nature) joins Shiva's purusha (male consciousness).

The decan begins at June solstice, when baby animals flourish.[128]

---

128. Northern Hemisphere orientation. The Southern Hemisphere equivalent is the 2 of Pentacles.

QABALAH

The 2 of Cups corresponds to Chokmah in Briah. All twos correspond to the second sephira, Chokmah (חכמה) "wisdom." Chokmah is associated with "the zodiac."[129] As the wellspring of the Pillar of Force, Chokmah's "wisdom" is the flash of insight appearing as if from nowhere, in the same way that Chokmah erupts from ineffable Kether.

All Cups correspond to the second of four worlds, Briah (the Creative World), and primal *heh*, the first letter ה in the Divine Name, יהוה. In Briah, the idea of form, or "something from nothing," arises. Chokmah in Briah represents the first awareness of the Other. The Empress and Chariot are the majors associated with the 2 of Cups. They correspond to letter *daleth* ("door") and *cheth* ("enclosure"). Thus this card can represent an opening within the self-contained vessel of perception.

Because of Chokmah's quality of conscious awareness, all twos—dominion, love, peace, and change—begin with perceiving and acting upon a world outside oneself.

RIDER-WAITE-SMITH SYMBOLISM

2 of Cups (*Rider-Waite-Smith Tarot*)

---

129. In the Ptolemaic concentric model, the twelve signs inhabit a sphere of their own—below the primum mobile but above the orbits of the seven traditional planets, which descend from Saturn to the Moon.

The influence of Venus is instantly evident in this card. Two complementary figures approach each other in a spirit of attraction or tenderness. Above them hovers the red winged lion of alchemy, which may signify the spiritualization of base instinct. Along with the intertwined snakes below, it forms the caduceus of Hermes, a symbol of opposing forces reconciled. (Also, it graphically alludes to the intertwined, curving shapes found on earlier 2 of Cups cards.) The contrasting apparel of the couple underscores their complementary nature, though they share the white sleeves of pure intention found elsewhere in the deck.

The couple in question stand apart from the background, making this a "stage" card. You can argue all the Waite-Smith twos are "stage" cards, in fact. This seems apt, given the consciousness of others that erupts in the two: it is the introduction of an audience that causes us to play a role. In the distance, a tiny house suggests their ultimate destination in Malkuth.

THOTH SYMBOLISM

The image contains dolphins representing *argent* (silver) and *or* (gold) from the card's Golden Dawn description. The twos represent the first and purest manifestation of the water element, showing us that the highest expression of the emotional realm is love. Crowley tells us that because the twos represent the will, the two in water is a perfect example of the Thelemic axiom "Love under Will." Here the male and female forces are in perfect equilibrium, blessed and fortunate in their union since Jupiter is exalted in the sign.

The cups overflow with water. They are being filled with clear water from one lotus that rises from another. The dolphins are entwined around the stem as the water baptizes them. The dolphin is associated with foam-born Aphrodite and sea god Poseidon. Alchemically, the dolphin is related to the womb and the feminine principles of procreation, yet their bodies are in solar colors of rose and gold. The theme of perfect pairing is echoed by the parallel placement of the astrological symbols.

RELATED CARDS

The 2 of Cups corresponds to the first Venus-ruled decan of cardinal, watery, Moon-ruled Cancer. The Chariot (Cancer) and the Empress (Venus) produce a creative, nurturing energy; an awareness of and tenderness for someone other than oneself. This interest may be maternal or romantic depending on context.

As the Queen of Cups' middle decan (her others are 10 of Swords/Gemini III and 3 of Cups/Cancer II), the 2 of Cups represents her profound empathy; like a mirror, she perfectly reflects the emotional world of her partner.

As the sephira Chokmah, the 2 of Cups relates also to Kings (RWS)/Knights (Thoth). Thus the King/Knight of Cups enjoys flashes of insight into the human heart—insights which he may develop into a spiritually evolved worldview.

The tarot twos seek the balance of the Other: *Dominion* (Wands) seeks a partner to conquer; *Love*, one to cherish (Cups). *Peace* (Swords) holds two ideas in equilibrium, and *Change* (Pentacles) unites two parties in transactions.

3 OF CUPS
Lord of Abundance

Dates:[130] July 2–July 11

Astrology: Cancer, the sign ruled by the Moon, with Jupiter exalted

Element: Cardinal water

Decan: 10°–19° Cancer; Cancer II, the decan ruled by Mercury

***Picatrix* Image:** A woman with a beautiful face, and on her head she has a crown of green myrtle, and in her hand is a stem of the water lily, and she is singing songs of love and joy

***Picatrix* Significations:** Games, wealth, joy, and abundance

Agrippa Image: A man clothed in comely apparel, or a man and woman sitting at the table and playing

Agrippa Significations: Riches, mirth, gladness, and the love of women

Sephira/World: Binah in Briah

Color(s): Black, plus the colors of the associated majors

---

130. Dates vary annually. All decanic minor dates listed in this book are based on 2019–2020 dates.

Associated Majors: The Chariot and the Magician/Magus

Associated Minors: Queen of Cups

Themes and Keywords: Time of rejoicing. Fleeting sense pleasures. Shared celebrations. Female threefold nature. Fertile enclosures. Impermanent gratification. High point in a cycle.

ASTROLOGY/ELEMENT

In Cancer II a lunar sign combines with decan ruler Mercury and the influence of Saturn as a three (Binah). Cancer's nurturing energies combine well with the Great Mother energy of the third sephira, as both define protective boundaries within which the many blessings of Mercury can be received. Mercury's childlike wonder at all the abundance of worldly delights is given free rein in a fertile enclosure.

Yet with Saturn, one must also recognize limits and endings (Mercury rides in Cancer's Chariot to Saturn's realm in his role as a psychopomp) and that the Buddhist doctrine of *anicca* (impermanence) is inherent in existence. Good things arise and they pass away. The key is to fully enjoy them in the moment and be present without clinging.

Along with the three light phases of the moon, symbols of abundance
(golden apple, pomegranate, wheat) are held up from hands within cups
(from the Magician card, Mercury). (*Tabula Mundi Tarot*)

Picatrix has a beautiful woman crowned in greenery singing of love and joy. Agrippa has a finely dressed man or a couple sitting at table and playing. Both significations speak of light and pleasant times, mirthful games and wealth.

MYTHOLOGY/TIME OF YEAR

Persephone, Demeter, and Hecate are the goddess-in-triad as Maiden, Nymph, and Crone, representing the green corn, the ripe ear, and the harvested grain. Almost all know of mother Demeter, whose daughter Persephone was abducted by Hades and brought to the underworld in his chariot (Cancer). Persephone's father Zeus sent Mercury in another chariot to retrieve her, but not before she tasted the sweet seeds of a pomegranate, binding her to the Underworld for certain months of the year. For the remaining time, mother and daughter—and the entirety of nature—rejoiced in earth's abundance. Their Eleusinian and Thesmophorian rites involve feasting, dancing, sexuality, and fertility.

The Three *Charities* or Graces were daughters of the Oceanid Eurynome, a lunar mermaid daughter of Titans *Oceanus* (salt water) and *Tethys* (fresh water). Her name may mean "widely distributed." With Zeus (of course), she bore *Aglaea* (Splendor), *Euphrosyne* (Cheer), and *Thalia* (Festivity). The Charities also have chthonian associations. Fertility and death coexist, just as certain times of year have either summer growth or winter withering, depending on hemisphere.

QABALAH

The 3 of Cups is Binah in Briah. Binah (בימה), the third sephira, translates as "understanding" and is associated with the slowest, outermost classical planet, Saturn. Sometimes referred to as a "palace of mirrors," Binah is the wellspring of the Pillar of Form and the first experience of separateness—sea from sky, inside from outside, above from below. With Binah, the Great Mother, reality begins to take literal form.

All Cups correspond to the second of four worlds, Briah (the Creative World), and primal *heh*, the first letter ה in the Divine Name, יהוה. Binah in Briah multiplies the emotional recognition of the Other conceived in Chokmah. It corresponds to letters *beth*/"house" (the Magician), and *cheth*/"enclosure" (the Chariot). Thus, themes of protection and quickening characterize this card.

As the Lord of Abundance, Binah expresses the natural capacity of Cups to connect and nurture; as virtue, sorrow, and work, Binah seeks to create, recognize, and fabricate.

RIDER-WAITE-SMITH SYMBOLISM

3 of Cups (*Rider-Waite-Smith Tarot*)

Waite describes "maidens in a garden-ground with cups uplifted, as if pledging one another." He describes their celebration as a matter concluded in "perfection" and "plenty." Profoundly feminine, even maternal, the 3 of Cups recalls Hermes's journey to unite Persephone and Demeter and the abundance following their reunion. The iconography of three dancing women also recalls other trios of classical antiquity: the Graces, the Fates, and the thrice-three Muses. The colors of the women's tunics—red, yellow, and white—recall the colors of the sephiroth (Geburah, Tiphareth, and Kether) touched by the Magician's and Chariot's paths. Meanwhile, their upraised cups recall the configuration of the three supernal sephiroth at the top of the Tree of Life.

On the ground, surrounding the women's dancing feet, clusters of fruit and gourds lie strewn in a display of harvest bounty. These perhaps symbolize the mature and ripe potential of the 3. Like an egg or nesting doll, each self-sustaining fruit contains the seed of its daughter.

THOTH SYMBOLISM

The cups arise from the placid seas of Binah, being filled by golden lotuses. The clear waters flow in opulent cascading waterfalls, creating ripples in the calm sea. The cups are made of wine-red pomegranate seeds, for Crowley states that this is a card of Demeter and Persephone, indicating the spiritual basis of all fertility as well as the principle that all things have their season. The good things in life can be enjoyed, but they cannot be trusted, as all things wither in time (Saturn).

Marseille versions of the 3 of Cups traditionally bear pomegranates in their arabesques. Did this influence Lady Frieda Harris's Thoth painting? (*Camoin-Jodorowsky Tarot de Marseille*)

The eight golden lotuses represent the Word or *logos* of Hermes (Mercury) landing and seeding the receptive waters of Cancer with the blessings of creation. Hermes's "all-access" pass to all realms allows for his travel to retrieve the treasures of the depths, just as he brought the maiden Persephone back to the world and to her mother Demeter. When they are apart, she is in winter's mourning. According to Hermetic Qabalah, she is then the dark sterile mother Ama; when they are together, she is the bright fertile mother Aima seeded by the *yod*.

RELATED CARDS

The 3 of Cups brings us to the second decan of Cancer, ruled by Mercury. The Magician/Magus (Mercury) and the Chariot (Cancer) together provide a protected space where communication flourishes, souls quicken, and one's heart may be spoken.

Threes firmly shape the essence of their suit, tracing a path from recognition to reality as two turns into three. The 3 of Cups supports circles of mutual affection, while the 3 of Wands gives ambition a channel to act upon the world. The 3 of Swords gives rise to irreversible insights, while the 3 of Pentacles converts matter into products.

The 3 of Cups connects to Queens two different ways: (1) it is the Queen of Cups' final decan, where love turns into festivity; and (2) Queens reside in Binah; giving the Queen the same formative, nurturing capacities seen in the 3.

Finally, three, Binah, and the World/Universe are the number, sephira, and path of Saturn—all expressing themes of closure and realization.

4 OF CUPS
Lord of Luxury (Blended Pleasure)

Dates:[131] July 12–July 22

Astrology: Cancer, the sign ruled by the Moon, with Jupiter exalted

Element: Cardinal water

Decan: 20°–29° Cancer; Cancer III, the decan ruled by the Moon

***Picatrix* Image:** A celhafe [turtle] with a snake in his hand, who has golden chains before him

***Picatrix* Significations:** Running, riding, and acquisition by means of war, lawsuits, and conflict

Agrippa Image: A man, a hunter with his lance and horn, bringing out dogs for to hunt

Agrippa Significations: The contention of men, the pursuing of those who fly, the hunting and possessing of things by arms and brawlings

Sephira/World: Chesed in Briah

---

131. Dates vary annually. All decanic minor dates listed in this book are based on 2019–2020 dates.

Color(s): Blue, plus the colors of the associated majors

Associated Majors: The Chariot and the Priestess

Associated Minors: Shadow decan of Knight/Prince of Wands

Themes and Keywords: Comfort with slight discomfort. The womb. Plenty yet discontent. World grown small. More than enough. Four noble truths of Buddhism. Outgrowing limitations. Irritation builds pearls. Moods and emotions. The container. Safety versus stagnation.

ASTROLOGY/ELEMENT

Can there be too much of a good thing? In Cancer III, the fickle Moon is both sign and decan ruler, inflated by ever-expansive Jupiter ruling the fours. This a fortunate pairing, but with too much water. Sometimes even comfort comes with a vague sense of underwhelm perhaps due the stagnation of fours. Ironically, having too much often leads to dissatisfaction and yearning for the next thing. Like Siddhartha, one can only tread a path of affluence for so long before thinking that surely there is more to life than acquisition.

Both decan signification descriptions speak of riding out, pursuing and forcefully acquiring and possessing through contention. *Picatrix* describes an enigmatic *celhafe*, probably an alternate transliteration of *salihafa*, the Arabic word for "tortoise," which is associated with Cancer. A turtle carries its self-sufficient albeit constricting home upon its back. The *celhafe* holds a snake and has golden chains before him. Snakes are symbols of transformation, and chain—however golden—are confining. Agrippa's image is a hunter with lance, horn, and hunting dogs, chasing after the ever-elusive prey.

A rare sighting: the central figure as a turtle warrior, the "celhafe" (Arabic: *salihafa*, سلحفاة) described in *Picatrix*. (*Liber T: Tarot of Stars Eternal*)

MYTHOLOGY/TIME OF YEAR

Zeus (Jupiter) had dalliances with countless women (lunar beings). For Hera, his libido was too much of a good thing. Zeus gamboled with the priestess Semele, who confided to a disguised Hera the identity of her lover. Hera planted seeds of doubt and dissatisfaction, leading Semele to request that Zeus prove his divinity after he swore to grant her anything. Sadly, mortals cannot look upon even his smallest thunderbolt without perishing. The result of their union was twice-born Dionysus, who is killed ritually with a thunderbolt in the seventh month following December solstice, the time of this decan.

Three of the four Galilean moons of Jupiter were named for Zeus's lunar-themed lovers. Callisto was a follower of Artemis/Diana. Europa was seduced by Zeus in the form of a white bull. Lunar goddess Io was a nursemaid and consort of Zeus to whom he gave the horn of cornucopia that filled with any food or drink desired. Of course, Hera turned her into a white heifer, chased by a gadfly.

QABALAH

The 4 of Cups is Chesed in Briah. Chesed (חסד, also known as Gedulah/"greatness") the fourth sephira, translates as "mercy" or "loving kindness" and corresponds to expansive Jupiter. Chesed's counterpart is Geburah, the fifth sephira; one gives, one holds back. The first sephira below the supernal triad, Chesed presents the divine in a form comprehensible to humans: for example, a loving patriarchal God.

Cups correspond to the second of four worlds, Briah (the Creative World), and primal *heh*, the first letter ה in the Divine Name, יהוה. At Chesed in Briah, one can enjoy a moment of maximum emotional sustenance and saturation before leaving the familiar behind and descending the Tree, further into mundane reality. As the moon in Cancer, the 4 of Cups also bears a connection to letters *gimel*/"camel" (the High Priestess) and *cheth*/"enclosure" (the Chariot), conveyances for bearing precious waters far from their source.

The fence of *cheth* (Cancer) is a wave of cardinal water surrounding the
four phases of the moon and the pearl in its enclosure. (*Tabula Mundi Tarot*)

As *Completion*, *Luxury*, *Truce*, and *Power*, Chesed offers points of creative, emotional, intellectual, and material respite before the rigors of Geburah.

RIDER-WAITE-SMITH SYMBOLISM

4 of Cups (*Rider-Waite-Smith Tarot*)

A hand looking very much like the one in the Ace offers a young man a cup, which he either ignores, refuses, or does not see. The three cups so joyously uplifted in the previous card have been set aside; our insensible friend desires nothing further. The very weather seems stagnant and still, and the leaves of what appears to be an oak hang motionless in the air. The tree, symbol of life and knowledge, is in full late-summer leaf; it can grow no more this season. Something must soon change.

Waite says the figure's expression is "one of discontent with his environment." The seated figure beneath the tree is powerfully reminiscent of the Buddha as young Prince Siddhartha, whose life of curdled luxury eventually led him to seek freedom from attachment. Is this a refusal of divine grace or a refusal of material luxury? The answer is ambiguous—but it is certainly an inflection point in the Cups' journey toward emotional fulfillment.

THOTH SYMBOLISM

Crowley tells us that by the time the water element reaches the four, purity has somehow been lost in pursuit of satisfaction, introducing the seeds of decay to the fruit of pleasure. Due to the double lunar component of the card, he remarks upon the parallels with the geomantic figures *Via* and *Populus* and the idea that while in nature change equals stability, the four is resistant to change. He calls it a dead end, a number that cannot form a magic square and whose magic number (ten, the "end") folds in upon itself in the form of the tetractys.

The cups have square stable bases but the lower cups show their instability by being tipsily perched upon the stems rather than the leaves of a lotus, above an undulating sea. The top cups are filled by a somewhat-wilted lotus blossom and spill water into the bottom cups, which—though full—stagnate and do not flow into the sea. In the background, a storm appears imminent.

RELATED CARDS

As our third card of Cancer (the Chariot), the 4 of Cups is powerfully lunar, for the moon (High Priestess) rules both sign and decan. The 4 of Cups unites two vertical paths on the Tree: the Priestess symbolizes the invisible forces governing natural cycles, while the Chariot navigates the lunar tides. If 2 and 3 represent conception and quickening, 4 represents the confinement before birth. Overfull, with nowhere to go, we are driven on our quest for meaning.

Fours gather together an abundance of their suit resources. The 4 of Cups collects a surplus of feelings; the 4 of Swords, thoughts gathered in stillness; the 4 of Pentacles, amassed treasures. The 4 of Wands publicly aligns community interests.

The 4 of Cups is the first or shadow decan of the Knight (RWS) or Prince (Thoth) of Wands; having fully experienced its padded luxuries, he is eager to prove himself in the 5 and 6 of Wands.

Finally, four, Chesed, and the Wheel of Fortune are the number, sephira, and path of Jupiter—each expressing security and fullness in its way.

5 OF CUPS
Lord of Disappointment (Loss in Pleasure)

Dates:[132] October 22–October 31

Astrology: Scorpio, the sign ruled by Mars (classical) and Pluto (modern)

Element: Fixed water

Decan: 0°–9° Scorpio; Scorpio I, the decan ruled by Mars

Picatrix **Image:** A man with a lance in his right hand and in his left hand he holds the head of a man

Picatrix **Significations:** Settlement, sadness, ill will and hatred

Agrippa Image: A woman of good face and habit, and two men striking her

Agrippa Significations: Comeliness, beauty, and strifes, treacheries, deceits, detractions, and perditions

Sephira/World: Geburah in Briah

Color(s): Scarlet red, plus the colors of the associated majors

---

132. Dates vary annually. All decanic minor dates listed in this book are based on 2019–2020 dates.

Associated Majors: Death and the Tower

Associated Minors: Knight/Prince of Cups

Themes and Keywords: Discontent. Emotional dryness. Martial excess. Disruption of the emotional realm. Disturbance of ease. The Buddhist concept of the "hungry ghost." Not being satisfied. Loss of connection. The river of letting go.

ASTROLOGY/ELEMENT

It's another case of excessive planetary influence: overmuch malefic Mars. Scorpio's classical ruler is Mars. Decan I is ruled by Mars. Mars rules all fives. With fiery Mars for sephira, decan, and sign, all the moisture in the Cups has evaporated, symbolic of lost or disrupted emotional connection—too much in the 4, not enough in the 5. To solve? "Just add water"—otherwise known as reviving emotion. Scorpio is emotionally deep. Here there isn't enough water for Scorpio to swim in and emotional connectivity is lost. What waters do exist in the card are analogous to the rivers of Hades.

The decan image from *Picatrix* has a man holding a lance (weapon of Mars) and a male severed head (Mars is associated with both dismemberment and the head). The significations are settlement, sadness, ill will and hatred. Agrippa's image is of a woman being struck by two men. It echoes the theme of the feminine force (Cups/water) being outnumbered and battered by toxic masculinity. The significations speak of beauty (Cups) and perditions in the archaic sense of destruction (Mars/Tower) and loss (Scorpio/Death).

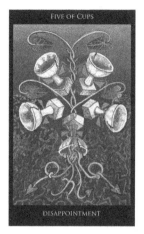

The lotus plant has roots tracing the glyphs of Mars and Scorpio;
the seabed is dry and there are no flowers. (*Rosetta Tarot*)

MYTHOLOGY/TIME OF YEAR

Ares, the Greek Mars, was Aphrodite's lover. Her cuckolded husband, Hephaestus, has an appropriate mythic tale. Hephaestus was the blacksmith who made all the gods' weapons. He is known, like Geburah/fives, for being associated with the idea of motion, for he was such a skilled craftsman that his statues could move.

Yet Hephaestus had a lot to be disappointed about. It's said that Hera self-generated him in jealous response to Zeus's gestating Athena without her. Hephaestus was born ugly and with a shriveled foot. Disappointed Hera disowned him, casting him from Olympus in disgust. He was rescued and raised by sea nymph Thetis and Oceanid Eurynome.

Hephaestus wanted Athena's hand in marriage. Though Zeus agreed, Hephaestus was never able to consummate the marriage because Athena rejected him. Instead, he married the beautiful Aphrodite, who proceeded to be unfaithful to him with Ares and, well, just about everyone.

Scorpio's modern ruler, Pluto, brings myths about the waters of Hades, the five rivers Styx, Lethe, Cocytus, Acheron, and (especially) flaming Phlegethon.

QABALAH

The 5 of Cups is Geburah in Briah. Geburah (גבורה), the fifth sephira, translates as "severity," "strength," or "restraint," and corresponds to fierce Mars's cutting sword. Geburah "corrects" or controls the free flow of Chesed; these sephiroth are the inviting and restraining arms of divinity. Geburah separates individuals, giving each room to breathe (it is associated with the second day of creation, the division of sky from sea). It is this separative, subjectively challenging nature of Geburah/Mars that gives fives their conflictual tone.

The parched setting and fish skeleton (Hebrew letter *nun*, corresponding to Death/Scorpio) emphasize the dry, destructive tendencies of Geburah as a five. (*Tabula Mundi Tarot*)

Cups correspond to the second of four worlds, Briah (the Creative World), and primal *heh*, the first letter ה in the Divine Name, יהוה. The martial character of Geburah in Briah deprives people of emotional supports they have grown to depend on, forcing them to grow in character to compensate.

As the Lord of Disappointment, Geburah pushes us to confront loss; as *Strife*, *Defeat*, and *Worry*, Geburah forces us to literally strive, as well as to confront unfairness and material uncertainty.

RIDER-WAITE-SMITH SYMBOLISM

5 of Cups (*Rider-Waite-Smith Tarot*)

A central dark-cloaked figure mourns over three spilled cups, though two remain upright behind him. The spilled liquids, in the lurid red and green of Mars and Venus, could be blood, wine, or poison—it's impossible to know. According to Waite, "It is a card of loss, but something remains over."[133]

Rivers, such as the one pictured just beyond, run in only one direction, recalling the fixed-water nature of Scorpio and the phrase "water under the bridge"—in this case, the Maidstone bridge in Kent, seen in happier circumstances in the 4 of Wands and the site of many memories for the artist.[134]

Despite their bleakness, there is more than one way to read these symbols: the castle could be all that has been lost, or it could be a safe harbor. The bridge could lead away or toward. The blackness of the cloak could telegraph mourning or fertility. The cups might be more than half empty or still nearly half full.

---

133. Waite, *Pictorial Key*, 216.

134. Katz and Goodwin, *Secrets of the Waite-Smith Tarot*, 277.

THOTH SYMBOLISM

The water has turned stagnant, the sea becoming what Crowley calls a North African "*chott.*" A chott is a salt lake that is dry for most of the year, only receiving water in winter. What little water there is is colored the green-brown colors of Scorpio, showing the putrefying action of Scorpio as associated with Death. The lotuses shrivel. Without taking in water they droop and wither. Their stems are fiery against a reddish background, the colors of the Tower and Mars.

The cups are positioned like an inverted pentagram signifying the four elements of matter subjugating Spirit. They are watery blue and shaped as the Golden Dawn ritual Cup of the Stolistes, yet they are empty and contain no water to purify the temple.

Crowley comments that the attribution of Mars in Scorpio is associated with the geomantic figure *Rubeus*. When *Rubeus* appears ascendant in a geomantic map, it is considered to be such an ill omen that the figure is destroyed and the divination abandoned for several hours.

RELATED CARDS

The 5 of Cups brings together a formidable pair: Death (Scorpio) and the Tower (Mars)! With Mars ruling the decan, sign, and sephira, the card brings us an especially pure expression of the war god's power. Its ordeal is a real-life expression of the Tower's life-altering, character-developing challenges. Mars governs separation, whether through cutting away or burning off. While all cards of Death (the 5, 6, and 7 of Cups) teach us about inevitable, cyclical change, the Tower's presence in the 5 makes it the most likely to speak of sudden loss.

Central decan of the Knight (RWS) or Prince (Thoth) of Cups, the 5 accounts for his ability to transform profound feeling into artistry. No stranger to tragedy, this prince seeks in the 6 to draw meaning downstream from the blood and tears shed earlier.

Fives create motion and imbalance. The 5 of Cups deprives us of emotional security and the 5 of Pentacles of material resources. The 5 of Wands sets our ambitions alight and the 5 of Swords disrupts our perception of "the rules," stirring minds to envious hostility.

6 OF CUPS
Lord of Pleasure

Dates:[135] November 1–November 10 (includes the cross-quarter holiday)

Astrology: Scorpio, the sign ruled by Mars (classical) and Pluto (modern)

Element: Fixed water

Decan: 10°–19° Scorpio; Scorpio II, the decan ruled by the Sun

Picatrix **Image:** A man riding a camel, holding a scorpion in his hand

Picatrix **Significations:** Knowledge, modesty, settlement, and of speaking evil of one another

Agrippa Image: A man naked, and a woman naked, and a man sitting on the earth, and before him two dogs biting one another

Agrippa Significations: Impudence, deceit, and false dealing, and for to send mischief and strife amongst men

Sephira/World: Tiphareth in Briah

Color(s): Yellow gold, plus the colors of the associated majors

---

135. Dates vary annually. All decanic minor dates listed in this book are based on 2019–2020 dates.

Associated Majors: Death and the Sun

Associated Minors: Knight/Prince of Cups

Themes and Keywords: Freedom and joy. Innocent and sexual pleasures. Balance. Warm emotional connection. Harmony. Ease. Sexual will. Well-being and satisfaction. Nostalgia. Childhood.

ASTROLOGY/ELEMENT

It's ruled by fiery Mars, yet Scorpio is a water sign. In the Scorpio decans, the 5 has deficient water and excessive Mars, while the 7 has putrid water due to Venus's "internal corruption."[136]

The 6 is the point of emotional balance, hitting the sweet spot. Plentiful water is warmed by the radiant and life-giving sun, which rules both the decan and the sephira. The element water is inherently lunar, providing the perfect medium for fertilization by the sun.

Picatrix shows a man riding a camel and holding a scorpion. "A man" can be symbolic of Mars or the Sun; the camel he is conjoined with is lunar; and a scorpion relates to the sign. Agrippa has a man and woman naked, and a man sitting on the earth before two dogs biting one another. The naked couple invokes the solar/lunar twins and a suggestion of innocence or knowledge. It also invokes sexual pleasure. While the "two biting dogs" imagery contradicts the harmonious message, it resonates thematically, as "two dogs" are lunar and biting is martial.

---

136. Crowley, *Book of Thoth*, 199.

A solar *yantra* glows in the center of six golden cups filled by gold lotuses, whose roots form the glyph of Scorpio. *(Rosetta Tarot)*

The twelve-pointed symbol of the Sun rises as the eagle of Scorpio glides. *(Tabula Mundi Tarot)*

MYTHOLOGY/TIME OF YEAR

The flaming and purifying rivers of Hades seen in the 5 lead to Elysium in the 6. The Elysian plain was an underworld place of perfect happiness; originally a paradise for heroes who had been made immortal (and those favored by and related to the gods), it evolved into a haven for all virtuous dead. In Virgil's *Aeneid*, the hero is guided to

Elysium by the priestess of the Apollonian oracle to bring the underworld's queen a golden bough.

The Isles of the Blessed were located far west of the great ocean. Bucolic and temperate, the isles were a place free from sorrow and toil. Only those reincarnated three times, with each life gaining admittance to Elysium, were granted passage to the Fortunate Isles.

The Scorpio decans of the 5 and 6 contain celebrations of the dead. The pagan sabbath Samhain (All Hallows' Eve), when the veil is thin, is followed by the Christian All Souls' Day and the Mexican *Dia de Los Muertos*.

QABALAH

The 6 of Cups represents Tiphareth in Briah. Tiphareth תיפארת, usually translated as "beauty," is the sixth sephira and the "heart" of the Tree, balanced not only between the Pillars of Mercy and Severity, but also between Kether and Yesod/Malkuth. Tiphareth corresponds to the Sun and the third day of creation, when God brought forth and fructified the land. By bringing opposing forces into proportion, Tiphareth nurtures life on earth just as our sun does. This benign creative force gives the sixes of tarot their clear sense of purpose.

Cups correspond to the second of four worlds, Briah (the Creative World), and primal *heh*, the first letter ה in the Divine Name, יהוה. Tiphareth in Briah helps us see purpose in our emotional world: caring for others as we were once cared for.

As the Lord of Pleasure, Tiphareth gives our hearts a sense of belonging; as victory, science, and success respectively, Tiphareth grants us heroic fulfillment, solutions to tough problems, and tangible achievements.

RIDER-WAITE-SMITH SYMBOLISM

6 of Cups (*Rider-Waite-Smith Tarot*)

The 6 of Cups is the "Lord of Pleasure," but Waite dwelt on the nostalgic aspect of that pleasure: "Enjoyment," he writes, "but coming rather from the past; things that have vanished."[137] Two children face each other in a courtyard suffused with the light of the "golden hour." It might be the same sunset seen in the Death card, Scorpio's major arcanum. To the left, an obscure adult figure recedes from view, for his time has passed.

The architecture of the little village is reminiscent of Smallhythe Place, the country home of Smith's good friend Ellen Terry.[138] The flowers on display are five-petaled and white: five often symbolizes the microcosm or human world, six the macrocosm or divine. But they are cut flowers, beautiful for just a day when arranged in their vases. They are sacrifices, serving a purpose when one wishes to express love or show caring for another human being. They call to mind the white rose on Death's banner.

---

137. Waite, *Pictorial Key*, 214.

138. Katz and Goodwin, *Secrets of the Waite-Smith Tarot*, 274.

THOTH SYMBOLISM

The purification process of Scorpio II is a distillation that yields gold. The cups are shining trophies being filled by waters gushing from six golden lotuses. They do not overflow but are filling. The cups are arranged in hexagonal formation with the sun at the center. Their bases are formed of five spheres (for Mars, ruler of Scorpio) and are of the golden metal of the sun. The stems arch with beautiful symmetries. The waters are blue, clear, and undulating gently as the sun shines upon them.

Crowley tells us that Sol in Scorpio represents fulfillment of the sexual will. He correlates the twentieth I Ching hexagram *Kwan* (*Kuan, Guān*), sun over earth, with connotations of both contemplation and manifesting, as well as the process of a union that is fertile. *Kwan* shows the priest who has ceremonially purified himself and is ready to present his offerings. He does so by contemplating heaven above and that which is below.

Crowley speaks of putrefaction as sacrament and formulas of sexual magic and initiation that precede the sacrifice of orgasm.

RELATED CARDS

The 6 of Cups brings together the Sun and Death (Scorpio). Six and Tiphareth are the number and sephira of the Sun, making this card particularly solar. The golden luminary shines in its fullness in the Sun card and sets or dies in the Death card. In this solar story is the secret message of the card. The sun is sacrificed and redeemed each night; so too do people sacrifice themselves for those they care for, thus renewing love's infinite cycle.

Sixes harmonize the essence of their suit, drawing out its practical purpose in life. The 6 of Cups fosters our sense of altruism; the 6 of Wands inspires a sense of belonging (e.g., patriotism). The 6 of Swords resolves conflicts; the 6 of Pentacles shares its success with others.

Sixes also correspond to Knights (RWS) or Princes (Thoth). Acquainted with tenuous peace from the 4 of Swords and loss from the 5 of Cups, in this decan the Knight stirs our feelings through his fictive arts and works of beauty.

7 OF CUPS
Lord of Debauch (Illusionary Success)

Dates:[139] November 11–November 20

Astrology: Scorpio, the sign ruled by Mars (classical) and Pluto (modern)

Element: Fixed water

Decan: 20°–29° Scorpio; Scorpio III, the decan ruled by Venus

Picatrix **Image:** A horse and a rabbit

Picatrix **Significations:** Evil works and flavors, and forcing sex upon unwilling women

Agrippa Image: A man bowed downward upon his knees, and a woman striking him with a staff

Agrippa Significations: Drunkenness, fornication, wrath, violence, and strife

Sephira/World: Netzach in Briah

Color(s): Emerald, plus the colors of the associated majors

---

139. Dates vary annually. All decanic minor dates listed in this book are based on 2019–2020 dates.

Associated Majors: Death and the Empress

Associated Minors: Shadow decan of the King/Knight of Wands

Themes and Keywords: Apparitions. Delirium. Imagination versus illusion. Magic and glamour. "Fantasy Island." Dreams and indulgences. Enchantment. Corruption of purity. Fairy favors. Elusive visions. Distortion versus reflection. Being enamored. Sirens and succubae. False lights. Fertile imaginings. Ensoulment of images. Shameful secrets. Creative work. The magic lasso. Compost.

ASTROLOGY/ELEMENT

All Scorpio decans have a potency caused by doubling planetary influences. Scorpio is ruled by Mars, but both decan and sephira of the seven are ruled by Venus. Scorpio Venus is a siren, glamorous, deep, and dark. Here she's a debased courtesan decadent to the point of degeneration and debauchery. Venus's function is to attract. Her magic mirror shows what you wish to see, compelling illusions that draw you toward her. When you awaken will they be fertile visions or fantasies?

Picatrix has the seemingly innocent image of a horse and a rabbit, yet these animals are both associated with sexual deviations. The signification is of evil works and flavors and sex forced upon women. This shares with the 7 of Cups the idea of apparitions and desires, leading one to some form of degradation. Agrippa's image is similarly somewhat perverse. A man bows down on his knees before a woman striking him with a staff. The signification specifically mentions drunkenness and fornication. On the morning after, the enchantment may fade.

MYTHOLOGY/TIME OF YEAR

Lethe ("Oblivion") was both a goddess and a river that traversed Hades through the cave of Hypnos, god of sleep. The shades of the dead are given the waters of river Lethe to forget their earthly life. The Orphics taught initiates to instead drink from the adjacent pool of *Mnemosyne* ("Memory"), to achieve omniscience.

Glamorous Aphrodite, goddess of beauty and laughter, also has a dark side revealed in some of her epithets: *Skotia* "Dark One," *Melainis* "Black One," *Anosia* "Unholy,"

Androphonos "Killer of Men," *Tymborychos* "Gravedigger," *Cloacina* "of the Sewers," and *Apaturus* "Deceptive One."

The 7 gives us old and new tales of sirens and succubae. Famous femme fatales beguile; Miss Havisham and her wedding cake decay. *Ignus Fatuus*, foolish fire, leads travelers astray. Whether it is Roman Black Sea wars won with poisoned honey, the debauchery of Venus and the satyrs, spirits in the Dead Marshes of Mordor beckoning, the spells of Circe, or Satan tempting Eve in the form of the will-o'-the-wisp, the common theme is of sweet, dark ensnarement.

QABALAH

The 7 of Cups is Netzach in Briah. Netzach (נצח) and Hod (הוד), the seventh and eighth sephiroth, work together in Kabbalah and are sometimes known as the "armies/hosts" of God, the "sources of prophecy," or the "tactical sephiroth"—in other words, channels for divine guidance. We think of Netzach as the emotional and Hod as the intellectual sphere. In Hermetic Qabalah, we tend to translate netzach as "victory"; a more accurate rendering is "eternity" or "endurance." Netzach, ruled by Venus, is a place of passions and quests, where one finds the inspiration and tenacity to pursue what they love.

Cups correspond to the second of four worlds, Briah (the Creative World), and primal *heh*, the first letter ה in the Divine Name, יהוה. Netzach in Briah creates fantasy, longing, phantasmal dreams, and transformative visions. As *Valor*, *Futility* (*Unstable Effort*), and *Failure* (*Success Unfulfilled*), Netzach provides us with daring and drive, elaborate plans, and the stamina to prevail through hardship.

RIDER-WAITE-SMITH SYMBOLISM

7 of Cups (*Rider-Waite-Smith Tarot*) (left)
On the right, the Venusian illusions suggested by the Waite-Smith 7 of Cups take on
nuances from another mythic archetype: Pandora's box. (*Pre-Raphaelite Tarot*)

Seven numinous cups hang in the air before a bedazzled seeker. Waite calls them "strange chalices of vision," denoting "imagination."[140] What archetypal qualities do these symbols express? Perhaps they are beauty, danger, power, wealth, fame, heroism, the divine—or perhaps they are the seven stages of alchemical transformation. The psychedelic character of the card certainly brings to mind the *cauda pavonis*, or "peacock's tail"—an alchemical stage in which, it is said, one becomes aware that existence itself is a dream.

The dark form of the seeker could indicate the chaotic potential of the card, or the shadow self, projected as in a dream onto the mind's eye. The angelic head could signal the presence of decan ruler Venus. The truth of these symbols is in the eye of the beholder, but one thing is certain: they are objects of fear and desire—the emotional depth charges of Netzach—inspiring us and drawing us toward eternity in act, speech, and thought.

---

140. Waite, *Pictorial Key*, 212.

THOTH SYMBOLISM

The impure tiger lilies found on the Thoth card here become
putrefying corpse (Scorpio) lilies (Venus). (*Rosetta Tarot*)

Crowley informs us of Venus's correspondence with copper, a metal of "external splendor and internal corruption."[141] The lotuses have been corrupted, becoming tiger lilies—carnality versus purity. Lilies are pure, but tigers terrify and fascinate; they symbolize urges out of control, dangerous and instinctive impulses that harrow us. False pleasures lure people; some willingly consume poison for pleasure and risk madness. The lilies drip viscous green slime that overflows from the cups, making the sea, in Crowley's words, a "malarious morass" that looks poisonous, or like the bottom of the sewer drain.[142]

The cups are iridescent to convey the beguiling nature of Venus: beauty found in an oil slick. They are arranged in two descending triangles (feminine symbols of water and Venus) over a bloated and much larger lower cup. Overall the formation suggests the Tree of Life below the supernal triad or being out of touch with the divine. Detached and off the Middle Pillar, the holy mysteries of nature are profaned, becoming shameful secrets with demoralizing ease.

---

141. Crowley, *Book of Thoth*, 199.

142. Crowley, 199.

RELATED CARDS

Here Venus rules the third decan of Scorpio, bringing together the Empress and Death—the great forces of *eros* and *thanatos*. This potent combination produces a *pharmakon* which may be medicine or poison; a deadly addiction or the world-altering visions of art. Those under its influence may appear to long for death or, equally, to transcend it.

Sevens are cards of quests and seeking. While the 7 of Cups escapes into fevered images, the 7 of Wands defends what his ambition has secured; the 7 of Swords schemes and acts on plan B; the 7 of Pentacles evaluates and tries to recuperate or improve previous efforts.

As the first (or "shadow") of his three decans, the 7 of Cups lurks in the underbelly of the King/Knight of Wands' brilliant charisma. He does well to forgo its dark glamour for more forward-looking and well-lit enterprises.

Finally, seven, Netzach, and the Empress are the number, sephira, and path of Venus. Together they represent the unconquerable force of desire, ever prevailing over reason.

8 OF CUPS
Lord of Indolence (Abandoned Success)

Dates:[143] February 19–February 28

Astrology: Pisces, the sign ruled by Jupiter (classical) and Neptune (modern). Venus exalted

Element: Mutable water

Decan: 0°–9° Pisces; Pisces I, the decan ruled by Saturn

Picatrix **Image:** A man with two bodies, who looks as though he is giving a gesture of greeting with his hands

Picatrix **Significations:** Peace and humility, debility, many journeys, misery, seeking wealth, miserable life

Agrippa Image: A man carrying burdens on his shoulder, and well clothed

Agrippa Significations: Journeys, change of place, and in carefulness of getting wealth and clothes

Sephira/World: Hod in Briah

---

143. Dates vary annually. All decanic minor dates listed in this book are based on 2019–2020 dates.

Color(s): Orange, plus the colors of the associated majors

Associated Majors: The Moon and the World/Universe

Associated Minors: King/Knight of Cups

Themes and Keywords: Confusion and self-undoing. Treasure hunts abandoned. Loss of heart. Culpability. Sloth. Spiritual depression. Giving up or transcending. Resignation. Impediments over time. Stagnation. Introspection. Decline and melancholy. Disinterest. Renunciation. Dark night of the soul. Wandering the labyrinth.

ASTROLOGY/ELEMENT

Pisces's classical ruler is buoyant Jupiter, planet of long-distance travels and spiritual quests, but modern ruler Neptune reveals some of Pisces's tendency to become lost, the quality of self-undoing. Mercury is the planet of the eights, of the mind, and of short journeys. Jupiter and Mercury want to progress, to travel and move freely; Pisces wants to transcend. But the first decan of Pisces is ruled by Saturn, a planetary influence that acts as a dead weight in the absence of initiative. Saturn's discipline has nothing to ground on in ethereal Pisces.

Picatrix and Agrippa speak of journeys and seeking wealth and give images of cryptic contradictions. A man is well clothed yet carries burdens on his shoulder (Agrippa). In *Picatrix* there is a man with two bodies, which seems to correspond to the dual nature of Pisces as well as the idea of the duplicitous double. The man "looks as though he is giving a gesture of greeting with his hands." The deception in "looks as though" is implied.

A silver salmon for Pisces swims upstream beneath a luminous moon; the Moon major arcanum corresponds to Pisces. (*Animal Totem Tarot*)

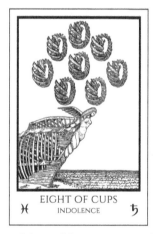

EIGHT OF CUPS
♓ INDOLENCE ♄

The barge of the Moon card (Pisces) has run aground (Saturn) on the shores, bordering the ocean of the brain waves of sleep (Pisces). (*Tabula Mundi Tarot*)

MYTHOLOGY/TIME OF YEAR

Neck, *Nix*, *Nixe* and many other similarly named creatures are of the fathomless waters of Pisces. These shapeshifting water spirits, mermen and mermaids, call to mind the nicors (sea monsters) that Beowulf, wearing full armor, battled in the deep. All are related to root words meaning "naked" and "to wash." Some of these beings were malicious, others harmless. The sirens seen in the 7 here in the 8 use Neptunian charms, making enthralling music to cause one's will to drift away. One such was the German/Celtic folk story of the Lorelei, who lured ships and men to their deaths through song. The name comes from old German *lurein*, "murmuring," and *ley*, "rock." Sailors had to turn away to escape the haunting sound that made them abandon sense and become heedless of the destination. The careless would thus meet the Saturn figure or Devil of sailors, called *Nekken* in the Scandinavian countries or Davy Jones in more recent times, whose "locker" was the bottom of the sea.

QABALAH

The 8 of Cups is Hod in Briah. Netzach (נצח) and Hod (הוד), the seventh and eighth sephiroth, are sometimes known as the "armies/hosts" of God, the "sources of prophecy," or the "tactical sephiroth." They are channels of divine guidance, Netzach in the emotional and Hod in the intellectual sphere.

Cups correspond to the second of four worlds, Briah (the Creative World), and primal *heh*, the first letter ה in the Divine Name, יהוה. Hod (translated as "splendor" or "glory") houses the intellect, the crowning feature of humanity. In the world of Briah, Hod gives us the perspective and humility to recognize our own stagnant emotions. Hod's rationality and logic act as a corrective to and an exit route from the phantasmal visions of Netzach in Briah.

As *Indolence/Abandoned Success*, Hod in Briah helps us move on. As *Swiftness* (Atziluth), *Interference/Shortened Force* (Yetzirah), and *Prudence* (Assiah) respectively, Hod confers a sure sense of direction, a weakness for overanalysis, and powers of organization.

RIDER-WAITE-SMITH SYMBOLISM

8 of Cups (*Rider-Waite-Smith Tarot*)

In the 8 of Cups, Waite says a "man of dejected aspect is deserting the cups of his felicity."[144] He picks his way through rock-strewn waters. The landscape might be the Romney Marshes, an ill-reputed Sussex wasteland in Pamela Colman Smith's time.[145] In the night sky an eclipse is taking form, signaling a time of great moment or great trial; even a dark night of the soul. From a Tree of Life perspective, the forbidding hills and moon may signify Malkuth and Yesod, endpoints of the World's path.

The figure's boots and cloak are red, colors of passion and life, as if to reassert his place in the vibrant world after a period of gloom. Also, the 8 of Cups is a stage card, but our protagonist is exiting stage right. Perhaps he is relinquishing a role which he has outgrown. Perhaps the staff supporting him is one of the World card's batons—symbols of power and agency.

THOTH SYMBOLISM

The cups have shallow bowls and are rusted and dented, conspicuously missing chunks from their handles, making them impossible to wield. It's a metaphor for emo-

---

144. Waite, *Pictorial Key*, 210.

145. Katz and Goodwin, *Secrets of the Waite-Smith Tarot*, 269.

tions that slip away and aren't connected with. There are only two lotuses that offer water, and the lotuses look droopy and spotted. Only two of the cups overflow, two are only half filled, and the three highest and central lowest are empty. The water is strangely becalmed, dark and stagnant; the lagoons of the badlands where nothing may grow. The sky is leaden with deep gloom, leaving only a trickle of yellowish light on the horizon.

Crowley says the 8 of Cups is the "Garden of Kundry" to the "Palace of Klingsor" expressed in the 7.[146] He describes it as most unpleasant due the influence of Saturn, who causes time and sorrow to descend upon pleasure, with no recourse due the weakness of the water element when low and imbalanced. It's described as a planned party that never happens; somehow, it's the host's own fault.

RELATED CARDS

The 8 of Cups, ruled by Saturn, is the first of three Pisces minors. In this card, the World/Universe (Saturn) and the moon (Pisces) combine their influences. While Saturn bears down on us with relentless pressure, the moon creates uncertainty and strong moods. As they join forces, a sense of intolerable claustrophobia and stagnation arises. The future may remain unclear, but one thing's for certain—we can't stay here! (Eight is also the number of ever-adaptable Mercury.) The path of the World is a first step from Malkuth (Saturn/Earth) to Yesod (the Moon), a similar journey between realms.

While the 8 of Cups helps people rescue themselves from drowning, other eights show the mind seeking out solutions in different ways. The 8 of Wands delivers information at the speed of light, the 8 of Swords analyzes the unanalyzable, and the 8 of Pentacles organizes practical lives.

The 8 of Cups is the central decan of the King (RWS) or Knight (Thoth) of Cups— the dark night of the soul that gives him his compassion and insight into human nature.

---

146. Crowley, *Book of Thoth*, 200.

9 OF CUPS
Lord of Happiness

Dates:[147] February 29–March 9

Astrology: Pisces, the sign ruled by Jupiter (classical) and Neptune (modern). Venus exalted

Element: Mutable water

Decan: 10°–19° Pisces; Pisces II, the decan ruled by Jupiter

Picatrix **Image:** A man upside down with his head below and his feet raised up, and in his hand is a tray from which the food has been eaten

Picatrix **Significations:** Great reward, and strong will in things that are high, serious and thoughtful

Agrippa Image: A woman of a good countenance, and well adorned

Agrippa Significations: To desire and put oneself on or about high and great matters

Sephira/World: Yesod in Briah

Color(s): Violet, plus the colors of the associated majors

---

147. Dates vary annually. All decanic minor dates listed in this book are based on 2019–2020 dates.

Associated Majors: The Moon and the Wheel of Fortune

Associated Minors: King/Knight of Cups

Themes and Keywords: Penultimate bliss as the best kind. Luck. Wish fulfillment. Magic. Truth and ideals. Toasting good fortune. Rewards without effort. The good life and rich living. Material and spiritual harmony. True contentment. Satisfaction. Being well-fed.

ASTROLOGY/ELEMENT

When Pisces is good, it's very, very good; the sum total of karmic reward. Fortunate and expansive Jupiter rules both the sign and the decan, so it can't help but be good. Add to this the moon as ruler of the nines. The moon is quite comfortable with watery Pisces. The combination with Jupiter brings out the moon's role as the bearer of fruit and granter of fulfillment and favor. Water's penultimate expression gives emotional satisfaction, the sort of happiness and contentment that enriches the soul.

The three creatures from *Tabula Mundi*'s Fortune card (Jupiter) get the bigger half of the wishbone and celebrate among the nine lucky fish of Pisces. (*Tabula Mundi Tarot*)

Agrippa's image is a well-adorned woman of good countenance. The decan image from *Picatrix* has a man upside down with his feet raised above his head, holding a tray from which food has been eaten. It calls to mind the Hanged Man card of elemental water. His feet—corresponding to the last sign Pisces—are above his head (a symbol of the first sign, Aries). This inversion places the spiritual over the cerebral, yet the food tray offers material rewards and sustenance.

MYTHOLOGY/TIME OF YEAR

Where does one turn for their heart's desire? Find a genie, toss a coin into the wishing well, catch a mermaid or a river nymph? If one is appealing to the classical Greek gods for wish fulfillment, then Zeus (Jupiter) is always a good choice.

In Buddhist and Hindu tradition there is a relic called the *Cintāmaṇi*, or wish-fulfilling jewel, from the head of either the great fish, Makara, or the serpentine Naga King, containing the teachings of Buddha. In the Western tradition it has overlap with the concept of the philosopher's stone. The Japanese goddess *Kisshōten* (Auspicious Heavens), was a goddess of happiness, fertility, and beauty, adapted from the Hindu Lakshmi, goddess of fortune. Like the Bodhisattvas, she is sometimes depicted holding the *Cintāmaṇi* gem in her hand. It was said to be a luminous pearl that arrived in a chest that fell from the sky. Anything one wished could be manifested through it: treasure, clothing, food, sicknesses cured, or waters purified.

QABALAH

The 9 of Cups is Yesod in Briah. Yesod (יסוד), the ninth sephira, translates as "foundation" or "basis"—that which lies beneath the real world, Malkuth. Here the light of the previous sephiroth gathers in preparation for birth. Yesod is the sphere of the Moon and creation's sixth day (the making of humans); thus it corresponds to sex, the unconscious, the imagination, magic, and the first step on any spiritual journey. All nines are places of power—motivations acting upon us just behind the surface of our apparent reality.

Cups correspond to the second of four worlds, Briah (the Creative World), and primal *heh*, the first letter ה in the Divine Name, יהוה.

In Yesod in Briah, our emotions have power. Our hopes and fears become reality—one reason why the 9 of Cups is sometimes called the "card of wishes." In Atziluth, Yetzirah, and Assiah, Yesod activates different facets of the human character: *Strength,*

Cruelty, and acquisitiveness (*Gain*). In each case, the fruits of these motives will be found in Malkuth, the ten.

RIDER-WAITE-SMITH SYMBOLISM

9 of Cups (*Rider-Waite-Smith Tarot*) (left)
Many readers describe the smug Waite-Smith 9 of Cups as the cat eating the canary.
In the image on the right, that phrase has been made literal. (*Linestrider Tarot*)

An uncommonly well-fed and pleased-looking figure sits facing the viewer, knees splayed and arms crossed over his ample belly. Behind him, nine cups set upon a high draped counter overlook the scene. Fortune has smiled upon him and, according to Waite, the cups in reserve indicate "the future is also assured." The curved, protective form of the counter recalls the round forms of both the Wheel of Fortune and the Moon. The figure's plumed red bonnet suggests satisfaction, wish fulfillment, and enthusiastic participation in life's pleasures. (We've seen similar red plumage on the Fool, the Sun, and—albeit wilting—Death.)

It's generally believed that Smith based her design at least in part on the jovial, bombastic Falstaff character of *Henry IV*.[148] Modern readers, however, sometimes read a degree of shadow into this card, perhaps thinking of Falstaff's eventual dissolu-

---

148. Katz and Goodwin, *Secrets of the Waite-Smith Tarot*, 267.

tion and downfall. Some see its central figure as insufferably smug. What could he be hiding behind that nicely arranged blue tablecloth?

THOTH SYMBOLISM

Nine cups in Dionysian and Jovian purple, also corresponding to the color of lunar Yesod, completely fill the picture plane. Their three-by-three formation is utterly stable. Every cup is filled; nine golden lotuses spill water that looks like a net of golden light poised to capture blessings. Crowley practically gushes at this card, calling it a "pageant of the culmination and perfection of the original force of Water" and "an ordered banquet of delight, True Wisdom self-fulfilled in Perfect Happiness."[149]

Of course, he's also a realist. He reminds readers earlier in the text on the nines that even fortune isn't permanent as "there is no rest from the Universe."[150] Still, you can't do much better than this card, for water is at its strength: in a lunar sephira, balanced on the middle pillar, and twice given Jupiter's benediction. Crowley equates it with the geomantic figure *Laetitia*, joy and gladness, which he calls the best, most powerful, and least ambiguous of the sixteen figures.

RELATED CARDS

The 9 of Cups, ruled by Jupiter, is the second of three Pisces minors. Here the Moon and the Wheel of Fortune shower you with lottery winnings, full nets, and your heart's desire. Fortunes wax and wane, but when the Moon is well-aspected, swift and joyous fulfillment follow. As they say in the state lottery, "Someone's gotta win!"

In nines, each suit achieves the peak of its power. While the 9 of Cups brims with joy, the 9 of Wands burns with determination. The 9 of Swords seethes with despair; the 9 of Pentacles capitalizes on its work. A secret to each can be found in the corresponding 3—threes are the seed, nines are the fruit.

This is the final decan of the King (RWS) or Knight (Thoth) of Cups. A philosopher of the human heart, this King knows isolation from his prior experience in the

---

149. Crowley, *Book of Thoth*, 201.

150. Crowley, 186.

7 of Swords and 8 of Cups. He knows that true joy, found within oneself, cannot be exhausted.

Finally, nine is the number and Yesod is the sephira of the Moon, suggesting further links to the Moon trump.

10 OF CUPS
Lord of Satiety (Perfected Success)

Dates:[151] March 10–March 19

Astrology: Pisces, the sign ruled by Jupiter (classical) and Neptune (modern). Venus exalted

Element: Mutable water

Decan: 20°–29° Pisces; Pisces III, the decan ruled by Mars

Picatrix **Image:** A sad man full of evil thoughts, thinking of deception and treachery, and before him is a woman with a donkey climbing atop her, and in her hand is a bird

Picatrix **Significations:** Advancement and lying with women with a great appetite, and of quiet and seeking rest

Agrippa Image: A man naked, or a youth, and nigh him a beautiful maid, whose head is adorned with flowers

Agrippa Significations: Rest, idleness, delight, fornication, and embracings of women

---

151. Dates vary annually. All decanic minor dates listed in this book are based on 2019–2020 dates.

Sephira/World: Malkuth in Briah

Color(s): Citrine-olive-russet-black, plus the colors of the associated majors

Associated Majors: The Moon and the Tower

Associated Minors: Shadow decan of the Queen of Wands; relates to Page/Princess of Cups as a ten

Themes and Keywords: Fleeting sweetness. Transcending. Oblivion and surrender. Over consumption. Illusion of perfection. The pipe dream. Overripe fruits and the seed within. Building and dissolving. Ephemeral fulfillment. Dream within a dream. Sacrifices for perfection. "Picture perfect" projections.

ASTROLOGY/ELEMENT

It's the final decan of the zodiac. Fortunate Jupiter rules Pisces, but Mars is ruler of the decan, the first of the double Mars decans that stitch together the zodiacal cycle. Mars is the lesser malefic, which is a hidden thorn among the graces inherent in Jupiter-ruled Pisces. There are pleasant dreams before the war drums beat at the subsequent first decan of Aries.

TEN OF CUPS
SATIETY

Poppy pods evoke the narcotic mists of the Moon (the major governing the Pisces decans). A martial griffin presides over the year's dissolute end. (*Tabula Mundi Tarot*)

TEN OF CUPS

SATIETY

The cups are shaped like rams' heads (Mars as ruler of Aries) and all are
satiated, as they each are biting (Mars) the fish of Pisces. (*Rosetta Tarot*)

Tens bear the influence of material Earth and greater malefic Saturn. This ten is the culmination of water and the zodiac itself in a Jupiter-ruled sign—so it's quite satisfied. Yet it's the end of the line for the element and the calm before the storm of the Swords suit to come.

Agrippa's image is a pleasant one, involving a man naked with a beautiful maid in a flower crown. *Picatrix*'s image is decidedly negative and disturbing, with talk of evil thoughts as a man watches a woman mounted by a donkey. The significations are contradictory: advancement and appetites, yet quiet and seeking rest.

MYTHOLOGY/TIME OF YEAR

The gods associated with these planetary influences are all closely related: one big happy family. Ares (Mars, decan ruler) was the son of Zeus (Jupiter, Pisces ruler), nephew of Demeter (tens/Earth), and both half-brother and cousin to Persephone (tens/Earth-Saturn). The legacy passes from progenitors Kronos (Saturn) and Rhea (Earth).

Ares was an Olympian, disliked by the other gods. Even his own parents (Zeus and Hera) despised the god of war. He was considered disrespectful, loving bloodshed and killing. His warlike nature destroyed the creations—life itself—of Zeus and Demeter. Zeus forced himself upon Demeter, mother of Persephone, who became Queen of the Dead. Due to her own "abduction" to the underworld, she is the personified embodiment of her annual rise: winter turning into spring. The decan covers the last days of Pisces and culminates at the vernal equinox, the first day of spring.[152] Though spring always comes, she is forever in a cycle where descent follows ascendance; the barbs of winter (Saturn) concealed in spring (Mars).

QABALAH

The 10 of Cups is Malkuth מלכות in Briah. Hanging alone at the base of the Tree, Malkuth is a sphere apart, receiving the outpouring of its predecessors. It corresponds to the final day of creation and the divine feminine aspect. This separate "kingdom" is a blessing and a curse. Fated to live apart from the divine, creation's wholeness is only restored through reconciling actions. In Qabalistic tarot, this is the return of the daughter to the mother, Binah. In all tens, the ripe, seed-laden fruit falls to the ground; the cycle ends only to begin again.

Cups correspond to the second of four worlds, Briah (the Creative World), and primal *heh*, the first letter ה in the Divine Name, יהוה.

In Malkuth in Briah, the Lord of Satiety, the emotional world spills over. In its tears, joy and sorrow are indistinguishable, and this love will reproduce itself in the next generation. As *Oppression*, *Ruin*, and *Wealth*, Malkuth's overflow leads to extremes: the tyranny of ambition, intellectual fanaticism, vast inheritances.

---

152. In the Northern Hemisphere.

RIDER-WAITE-SMITH SYMBOLISM

10 of Cups (*Rider-Waite-Smith Tarot*)

In the 10 of Cups is a vision that is almost too good to be a true—a perfect rainbow of cups arching over a picture of familial happiness. "It is contemplated in wonder and ecstasy by a man and woman below, evidently husband and wife…the two children dancing near them have not observed the prodigy but are happy after their own manner," according to Waite.[153] A small home in the distance may represent Malkuth, as the hills in the 10 of Swords and the town in the 10 of Wands do. (In the 10 of Pentacles, one is in the middle of Malkuth!)

But the 10 of Cups is a stage card. While those on stage may fully inhabit their roles for the moment, all that can change the moment the curtain falls. Indeed, the 10 of Cups can often signify the illusion of happiness. This, however, does not diminish its power—since a hopeful imagination is often the surest guide toward true happiness.

THOTH SYMBOLISM

The cups are arranged in a Tree of Life. The paths are formed by the stems and tendrils of a large lotus in martial red upon a scarlet background. The flower of the lotus contains the three supernals. All of the waters descend from Kether, with the cups on the

---

153. Waite, *Pictorial Key*, 206.

Middle Pillar overflowing and cascading into the next. The further down the Tree of Life and off the Middle Pillar one gets, the more tilted and unstable the cups become. The cups' curling handles resemble rams' horns.

Crowley tells us that a disturbance is due since the water element's work is complete. The shake-up is coming in the form of Mars "which inevitably attacks every supposed perfection."[154] The ethereal and spiritualized water of Pisces is not well matched with martial energy. We are warned with Proverb 7:23 ("until a dart strike through his liver") that the impulse to chase pleasure can be a trap, or as Crowley says, "Having got everything that one wanted, one did not want it after all."[155]

RELATED CARDS

Fire and flood! In the 10 of Cups, the flaming Tower (Mars) meets the watery Moon (Pisces), giving rise to a rainbow apparition just before the story's end. Mars in Pisces leads immediately to Mars in Aries (2 of Wands), for the Tower destroys and creates in the same burst of energy. The Moon, archetype of swift change, ushers the old year out in her tides.

As the Queen of Wands' first (shadow) decan, the 10 of Cups may represent illusions she destroys as a conquering goddess in the 2 and 3 of Wands—or her longing to surrender control.

Tens bring endings and beginnings. The 10 of Cups promises emotional connections outliving the limits of a human lifespan. The domineering 10 of Wands seeds its own overthrow; the 10 of Pentacles safeguards legacy capital for its descendants; the 10 of Swords shows an argument concluding in the "death" of the losing viewpoint.

Among court cards, tens correspond to Pages/Princesses—culmination of their suit and the guarantee it will be renewed even as it ends.

---

154. Crowley, *Book of Thoth*, 202.

155. Crowley, 187.

ACE OF SWORDS
Root of the Powers of Air

Dates:[156] December 21–March 19 (winter in the Northern Hemisphere)

Astrology: Capricorn-Aquarius-Pisces quadrant, emphasizing the Kerubic air sign Aquarius

Element: Air. All Aces are also associated with spirit

Sephira/World: Kether in Yetzirah

Color(s): White brilliance

Associated Majors: The Fool as the elemental trump of air

Associated Minors: Page/Princess of Swords

Themes and Keywords: Will as purpose grasped. Dual nature for good or evil. Conquest versus defense. Invoked versus natural power. Free will. Fixity of purpose. Magic: the ideas of one world = the reality of the next. Mind as interpreter of symbols. Self-directed thought.

---

156. Dates vary annually. All Ace dates listed in this book are based on 2019–2020 dates.

ASTROLOGY/ELEMENT

The winds blow as unity now goes forth in the direction of the air element. The divine brings forth and grasps the Sword of reason. This Ace is the root source of the energy inherent in mental processes. First came fire (force) which descended upon the primal waters (form). The heated waters created the winds, birthing the son, air. The combination of fire (will/creativity) and water (love/emotions) yields air (reason/mind): thought as the precedent to action. While the first two Aces are naturally arising energies, the Ace of Swords is consciously invoked. Form is force directed into matter; thought is the director.

Elemental air governs internal and external communications, connecting the energies of inspiration and emotion (fire, water) to the material world of action (earth). It conceives of and disseminates ideas. The Ace represents the inception of the delineating principles of thought. The air signs are Gemini (idea analysis), Libra (idea balance and sharing), and Aquarius (inventive ideas and ideals).

This Ace rules the Capricorn-Aquarius-Pisces quadrant of the year, centered on Kerubic air sign Aquarius.

MYTHOLOGY/TIME OF YEAR

One of the most loved and well-known sword myths is the tale of the "Sword in the Stone" of Arthurian legend. In the story a sword appears embedded in an anvil resting upon a stone in a churchyard on Christmas Eve. The wizard Merlin foretells that only the true and rightful king, the heir of Uther Pendragon, can remove the sword and become ruler of Britain. Thus Arthur obtains the kingship and the sword, which in some versions is conflated with the magical sword Excalibur he was later given by the Lady of the Lake. Excalibur was inscribed on one side "Take Me Up" and on the other, "Cast Me Away," illustrating the idea of a force invoked with purpose and sovereignty.[157]

This Ace rules the quarter from the December solstice through the March equinox. This spans the darkest day of winter through the first day of spring, when light and darkness are again in balance.[158] The increasing light leading to balance is a metaphor for mental clarity.

---

157. Tennyson, *Idylls of the King*, 9.

158. In the Northern Hemisphere.

QABALAH

The Ace of Swords is Kether in Yetzirah. All Aces correspond to the first sephira, Kether (כתר) or "crown," while Kether corresponds to the primum mobile, that force which moves the planets and stars across the sky. Kether, the crown, contains all that follows.

The upraised sword points at the crown of Kether (Fool, air) marked with the letters: *aleph* is hidden and *lamed* is central; these are *AL* (God) and *LA* (not or naught). (*Tabula Mundi Tarot*)

What we now call the "crown of Kether" has long been part of the Ace of Swords; here, oak and laurel replace palm and olive. (*Ancient Italian Tarot*)

All Swords correspond to the third of four worlds, Yetzirah (in Hermetic Qabalah, "Formation" or the "Formative World") and *vav*, the third letter in the Divine Name, יהוה. The character ו represents a tent peg or nail—that which is used to join two disparate elements, such as heaven and earth. Kether in Yetzirah represents the intellect consciously reaching from the earthly to the spiritual realm; i.e., the act of invocation.

Briah, Yetzirah, and Assiah are related terms, but they can be translated slightly differently, as "created," "formed," and "made." In Yetzirah—"formed"—form is differentiated; it shall become manifest and tangible in Assiah. The part of the soul associated with Yetzirah is the *ruach* ("breath"), which contemplates creation with awe.

RIDER-WAITE-SMITH SYMBOLISM

Ace of Swords (*Rider-Waite-Smith Tarot*)

Like all of Smith's Aces, the Ace of Swords bears a strong resemblance to its Tarot de Marseille predecessors—even down to which hand grasps the sword, and how. All are right hands, but the Aces of Cups and Wands show us the soft palm, while the Aces of Swords and Pentacles show the hand's hard back. (The Ace of Swords represents "invoked" force to the Ace of Wands' "natural" force.) The sword's blade shows a sharp contrast of light and shadow, suggesting its role as a weapon of either great good or evil.

From the crown (perhaps signifying Kether), two fronds descend: an olive branch signifying peace, and a palm branch signifying suffering. Six *yod*s flank the blade, bringing to mind the sixth sephira, Tiphareth, which, like the suit of Swords and world of Yetzirah, corresponds to the third letter of the Divine Name. Finally, like all Aces, this one subtly alludes to its element; the background features nothing but air above a minimalist, low mountainscape.

THOTH SYMBOLISM

Crowley makes sure to instruct us that the air element (thought) is extremely powerful but has no self-generated impulse. The *ruach* (the "breath of Spirit" and the intellect) is centered in Tiphareth, home of the son and the HGA. The intellect can be a wielded weapon, powerful when it is set in motion by its elemental parents. In other words, thought is manifestly powerful only when directed by will and love. Properly wielded it is the *logos*, the Word that represents the divine wisdom of creation.

Sun (fire) and water combine in the background to form clouds (air). The sword depicted represents the magical weapon the "Great Sword of the Magus."[159] The blade is inscribed with θέλημα (*thelema*), meaning "will." As a noun, it means the true will, but it is derived from the verb *thelō* as in "to will," reminding us to grasp hold of our purpose. The sword is shown piercing a crown (Kether) of twenty-two points, colored white outside (Kether, or divinity) and yellow inside (Tiphareth, or the adepts' connection with will).

RELATED CARDS

The Ace of Swords naturally corresponds first and foremost to the suit of Swords. As both "crown" and "root," the Ace is also the throne of its Page or Princess. And because Kings (RWS) and Knights (Thoth) reside in Chokmah and represent the *yod* (whose tip is in Kether), they too have a relationship to the Ace.

All Aces are said to revolve around the North Pole, but the "throne of the Ace" lies at the heart of the Page/Princess's domain; the quadrant of Capricorn, Aquarius, and Pisces; their respective majors are the Devil, the Star, and the Moon.[160] The Ace of

---

159. See Crowley's *Book 4, Part II* for a full description.

160. The Page/Princess is said to rule 0° Capricorn to 30° Pisces; the Ace occupies the central 45° from 22°30' Capricorn to 7°30' Pisces.

Swords centers on the Star/Aquarius, the sign of fixed air. As Root of the Powers of Air and first of its suit, the Ace always has an affinity for the Fool, the trump for the element of air. The Fool, the Star, and the Ace and Page of Swords share themes of the use of one's free will, attainment of knowledge, and the journeys one undertakes to do so.

2 OF SWORDS
Lord of Peace (Peace Restored)

Dates:[161] September 22–October 1 (includes the September equinox)

Astrology: Libra, the sign ruled by Venus, with Saturn exalted

Element: Cardinal air

Decan: 0°–9° Libral; Libra I, the decan ruled by the Moon

***Picatrix* Image:** A man with a lance in his right hand, and in his left hand he holds a bird hanging by its feet

***Picatrix* Significations:** Justice, truth, good judgment, complete justice for the people and weak persons, and doing good for beggars

Agrippa Image: An angry man, in whose hand is a pipe, and the form of a man reading in a book

Agrippa Significations: Justifying and helping the miserable and weak against the powerful and wicked

Sephira/World: Chokmah in Yetzirah

---

161. Dates vary annually. All decanic minor dates listed in this book are based on 2019–2020 dates.

Color(s): Blue pearl gray, like mother-of-pearl, plus the colors of the associated majors

Associated Majors: Justice/Adjustment and the High Priestess

Associated Minors: Queen of Swords hold the decan; relates to King/Knight as a two

Themes and Keywords: Equanimity and equilibrium. Restorative justice. Transcendent mind states. Balance of dualities. Stilling the mind. Fair relationships. Justice as a fair and balancing force. Acceptance of all doctrines. Accommodating other perspectives. Truth leading to peace. Equality.

ASTROLOGY/ELEMENT

Libra is ruled by Venus, decan I is ruled by the Moon, and twos correspond to the Zodiac itself. Libra is about balance while the moon is known for fluctuation. Somehow in the exalted space of the zodiac, the lunar conditions achieve a moment of stasis under the harmonious influence of conciliatory Venus. The properly wielded mind balances dualities and reaches equanimity. The mind weighs and adjusts, obtaining equilibrium. While the Swords suit is by nature conflicted due to the chaotic qualities of the mind, here in the first manifestation it is as pure and tranquil as things get.

In *Picatrix*, a man holds a lance in his right hand and a bird in his left, perhaps representing balance between male and female forces. Agrippa has an angry pipe-wielding man and the form of a man reading a book. The contrast between anger and calm rationality also emphasizes a sort of balance. The significations of these images both reference the idea of justice as a beneficial balancing force.

The light man holds a bird and pipe and the dark man holds a lance and book, interchanging the decan imagery from *Picatrix* and Agrippa. (*Liber T: Tarot of Stars Eternal*)

MYTHOLOGY/TIME OF YEAR

The scales of Libra are the only stars of the zodiacal belt that represent an inanimate object. Libra is poised between Virgo the virgin and Scorpio's scorpion. The stars of Libra have at times been considered the claws of the scorpion sent to kill Orion. Other myths have them as scales held by the maiden Astraea, the celestial virgin of Virgo who was the daughter of Themis (justice). Either way, there is an association with the idea of divine justice. The association with Astraea shows the purity that is necessary for truth and true fairness.

The scales of justice are an emblem of Themis or Dike, as is the sword. The sword and scales are also seen held by Lady Justice, Roman Justitia, the blindfolded personification of the virtuous moral force of the judicial system and due process.

The season of Libra begins at the September equinox, when night and day are of equal lengths. The scales of the constellation were said to weigh the light against the darkness, balancing them perfectly.

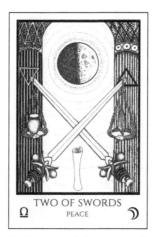

TWO OF SWORDS
PEACE
Ω   ☽

Below the dark and light moon, the two swords become scales of Justice/Adjustment (Libra), between the pillars and above the scroll—emblems of the Priestess (moon). (*Tabula Mundi Tarot*)

QABALAH

The 2 of Swords corresponds to Chokmah in Yetzirah. All twos correspond to the second sephira, Chokmah (חכמה) or "wisdom." Chokmah is associated with the zodiac, a celestial sphere or layer where the twelve constellations revolve above the orbits of the seven traditional planets. Chokmah's "wisdom" is the flash of insight that appears as if from nowhere, just as Chokmah appears from the empty point of Kether.

Swords correspond to the third of four worlds, Yetzirah (the World of Formation). They also correspond to (and resemble) *vav*, the third letter in the Divine Name, יהוה. Swordlike *vav* ו takes the form of a fastener, used to join two disparate elements, such as heaven and earth.

Chokmah in Yetzirah can represent the intellect's grasp of polarity; the insight that if there is one point of view, there must be an opposite one. Chokmah's gift is the quality of conscious awareness. Thus *Dominion* (Atziluth), *Love* (Briah), *Peace* (Yetzirah), and *Change* (Assiah) all begin with perceiving and acting upon a world outside oneself.

RIDER-WAITE-SMITH SYMBOLISM

2 of Swords (*Rider-Waite-Smith Tarot*)

"A hoodwinked female figure balances two swords upon her shoulders," says Waite; the term "hoodwinked" (as opposed to "blindfolded") is one used in Masonic circles.[162] It signals to us that a form of initiation is occurring, in which the novice sets aside her individual perspective in favor of someone else's. The idea of peace emerges as a visual metaphor in the equipoise it takes to hold the swords in balance. Still, Waite cautions against reading too much ease into the card, given the inherently conflictual character of swords.

A waxing crescent moon hangs in the sky, indicating that this is the onset of a longer process. The rock-strewn waters could extend directly from the backdrop of the High Priestess card; they are calm but not motionless, reflective of a mind making room to accommodate larger ideas.

The 2 of Swords is a "stage" card, suggesting that this figure is taking on a chosen, conscious role rather than acting on impulse or instinct.

THOTH SYMBOLISM

Swords unite in a state of equilibrium. At the crossing point, a rose blooms in peaceful blues: the pale blue of the moon, the blue-green tones of Libra, and blue-gray of

---

162. Waite, *Pictorial Key*, 250.

Chokmah. Crowley tells us that the rose represents the harmonizing influence of the mother (Venus and Moon). The intricate hilts of the swords have a central motif of a dove (symbol of Venus, ruler of Libra), with praying angelic figures tranquilly kneeling along either side.

The whirling pinwheel forms are a snapshot temporarily stilling the constant motion of the mind. Here we see the swirling swastikas as perfectly balanced mirror images of each other. They whirl over a background the color of Netzach (Venus, ruler of Libra) in Yetzirah (Swords). Yet, as Crowley tells us, "The energy abides above the onslaught of disruption."[163]

There are also two tiny swords, air daggers, at the top and bottom of the card. Each is the fulcrum of balance, with the lunar crescent balanced above and the scale glyph of Libra below.

RELATED CARDS

The 2 of Swords corresponds to the first decan of cardinal, airy, Venus-ruled Libra. The moon rules this decan, bringing together the High Priestess (moon) and Justice/ Adjustment (Libra). While Justice/Adjustment emphasizes an equal balance of two points of view, the realm-crossing Priestess mediates between them; her flexible perspective mirrors the waxing and waning moon.

As the Queen of Swords' middle decan (her others are 10 of Pentacles/Virgo III and 3 of Swords/Libra II), the 2 of Swords represents this Queen's flawless comprehension of dueling perspectives, which allows her to weigh accurately before taking sides.

As the sephira Chokmah, the 2 of Swords relates also to Kings (RWS) and Knights (Thoth). This airy sovereign possesses keen insight into the intellect's abstractions; he discriminates in both positive and negative ways.

The tarot twos seek the balance of the Other: *Dominion* (Wands) seeks a partner to conquer; *Love*, one to cherish (Cups). *Peace* (Swords) holds two ideas in equilibrium, and *Change* (Pentacles) unites two parties in transactions.

---

163. Crowley, *Book of Thoth*, 204.

3 OF SWORDS
Lord of Sorrow

Dates:[164] October 2–October 11

Astrology: Libra, the sign ruled by Venus, with Saturn exalted

Element: Cardinal air

Decan: 10°–19° Libra; Libra II, the decan ruled by Saturn

Picatrix **Image:** A black man, a bridegroom having a joyous journey

Picatrix **Significations:** Tranquility, joy, abundance and good living

Agrippa Image: Two men furious and wrathful and a man in a comely garment, sitting in a chair

Agrippa Significations: Indignation against the evil, and quietness and security of life with plenty of good things

Sephira/World: Binah in Yetzirah

Color(s): Dark brown, plus the colors of the associated majors

Associated Majors: Justice/Adjustment and the World/Universe

---

164. Dates vary annually. All decanic minor dates listed in this book are based on 2019–2020 dates.

Associated Minors: Queen of Swords

Themes and Keywords: The universal sorrow. Sublime melancholy. Truth that leads to enlightenment. Karmic coupling. Contracts. Love that binds. Self-knowledge and commitment. Love and time. Realizations that can't be unrealized.

ASTROLOGY/ELEMENT

In the middle decan of Libra, the Venusian ruler of Libra meets a double dose of Saturn, as Saturn rules the decan *and* corresponds to the threes. Libra is all about partnerships, as Venus is the goddess that couples or brings things together. Saturn is the Lord of Karma, and a force of restrictions, contracts, and bindings. Yet Saturn is exalted in Libra. The karmic trials and tribulations encountered here are also sublime insights, sacred promises, and knowledge leading toward enlightenment. Whether these swords bind or sever, it is a dark and melancholic state. Truth is often painful. One must to some degree let go of reason in order to truly know themselves or commit to another.

While the idea of sorrow is weighty, the significations of both *Picatrix* and Agrippa both speak of good things. The *Picatrix* image of a black man, a bridegroom having a joyous journey, references both the blackness of Saturn/Binah and the bridegroom as a combination of contractual Saturn and partnering Libra.

THREE OF SWORDS
♎   SORROW   ♄

Amongst various Saturn symbols, the cracked heart jar of Ma'at (Libra) is upon the tripod of the Delphic oracle, whose motto is "Know thyself." (*Tabula Mundi Tarot*)

MYTHOLOGY/TIME OF YEAR

The 3 of Swords brings us stories of dark and sorrowful wives and mothers. Venus as Libra's ruler gives us Demeter, who so lamented the loss of her daughter that the earth itself grew dark and cold. Persephone's marriage bound her forever to spend half the year in the underworld—yet gave her queenship of that powerful realm.

In the most influential of Egyptian myths, Isis has a role as the chief mourner for her husband and brother Osiris, who was killed and dismembered by their brother Set (another Saturn figure). Isis wanders the earth, giving voice to her grief over the loss of her husband and sibling. She expresses her sorrow, her anger, and her desire for him, all in hopes that these thought-forms and emotions will stir him. In the *Lamentations of Isis and Nephthys*, Isis and her sister, Set's wife, call to Osiris's soul and entreat him to rejoin the living. They find and bind his parts back together, and Isis conceives her son Horus.

QABALAH

The 3 of Swords is Binah in Yetzirah. Binah (בימה), the third sephira, translates as "understanding" and is associated with slow, distant Saturn. Sometimes referred to as a "palace of mirrors," Binah begins the Pillar of Form and the experience of separateness—sea from sky, inside from outside, above from below. With Binah, the Great Mother, reality begins to take literal form.

Airy Yetzirah (the Formative World) is the third of four Kabbalistic worlds, and the one corresponding to the suit. *Vav*, the third letter in the Divine Name, יהוה, also corresponds to Swords; it resembles a tent peg or nail—that which joins two disparate elements, whether physical or metaphysical.

Binah in Yetzirah brings permanent recognition to the intellectual insights of Chokmah. The 3 of Swords also corresponds to *tav*—"mark" or "sign" (the World/Saturn) and *lamed*—"ox-goad" (Justice/Adjustment). A mark confirms what we know; an ox-goad corrects. Confirmation plus correction equals understanding!

As the Lord of Sorrow, Binah recognizes what cannot be denied; as *Virtue, Abundance* and *Work*, Binah seeks to create, connect, and fabricate.

RIDER-WAITE-SMITH SYMBOLISM

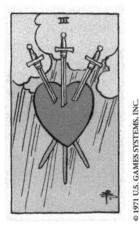 

3 of Swords (*Rider-Waite-Smith Tarot*) (left)
The card that launched a billion tattoos! The image on the right is likely the inspiration
for Pamela Colman Smith's iconic 3 of Swords design. (*Sola Busca Tarot*)

Waite suggested that this image of a pierced heart was really "too simple and obvious to call for specific enumeration," though he mentions it might signify "removal, absence" or "rupture." The design seems to be a stylized version of the 3 of Swords from the fifteenth-century *Sola Busca Tarot* (the first tarot deck to include scenic pips). A 1907 exhibit at the British Museum featured photographs of the Sola Busca deck, and it seems likely that Pamela Colman Smith had the opportunity to view the exhibit before beginning work on her own card images in 1909.[165] While the joyous decan images and the low-spirited Waite-Smith card differ greatly, both emphasize the idea of marriage, for the relationship forms a third entity that arises between two parties.

The 3 of Swords and the 8 of Wands are the only minor cards to feature no human figure, lending them a certain abstract clarity. The 3 of Swords is also the only card in the deck to show rain, which accounts for its uniquely somber cast.

---

165. Kaplan et al., *Pamela Colman Smith*.

THOTH SYMBOLISM

Crowley's solar degree falls in this decan. He mentions Binah in her aspect as the dark sterile mother Ama and the mourning of Isis. He tells us that this is not the mundane sorrow we expect but rather the *Weltschmerz*, a German term for world weariness about the imperfections of existence, much like the melancholy trance of enlightenment leading to the Buddhist realization that everything is unsatisfactory (*dukkha*) and impermanent (*anicca*).

A third sword thrusts itself between the matched swords of the 2 of Swords. It pins the rose in place as the other swords tear it asunder. The swords are Venusian green set against a background the black and dark colors of Saturn. The background mesmerizes, looking at once like storm clouds and the roiling dark sea of Binah. Crowley calls it the "womb of Chaos," whose children are both monstrous and yet the supreme transcendence of the natural order of things.[166] He refers us to Aethyr 14, a vision of the black serpent, the Great One of the Night of Time (Saturn/Universe).[167]

RELATED CARDS

With the 3 of Swords, we arrive at the second decan of Libra, ruled by Saturn. The World (Saturn) brings two entities together into a defined space, and Justice/Adjustment (Libra) officially binds them into a third entity—a new structure that can be undone only with pain and effort.

Threes firmly shape the essence of their suit. The 3 of Swords fosters irreversible insights. The 3 of Cups supports circles of mutual affection; the 3 of Wands gives ambition a channel to act upon the world; the 3 of Pentacles converts matter into product.

The 3 of Swords connects to Queens two different ways: (1) it is the Queen of Swords' final decan, where vows are sealed and sundered; and (2) Queens reside in Binah; giving the Queen the same formative capacities we see in the three.

Finally, three, Binah, and the World/Universe are the number, sephira, and path of Saturn—all expressing themes of closure and realization.

---

166. Crowley, *Book of Thoth*, 204.

167. Crowley, *Gems from the Equinox*, 496.

4 OF SWORDS
Lord of Truce (Rest from Strife)

Dates:[168] October 12–October 21

Astrology: Libra, the sign ruled by Venus, with Saturn exalted

Element: Cardinal air

Decan: 20°–29° Libra; Libra III, the decan ruled by Jupiter

***Picatrix* Image:** A man riding a donkey with a wolf in front of him

***Picatrix* Significations:** Evil works, sodomy, adultery, singing, joy and flavors

Agrippa Image: A violent man holding a bow, and before him a naked man, and also another man holding bread in one hand, and a cup of wine in the other

Agrippa Significations: Wicked lusts, singings, sports, and gluttony

Sephira/World: Chesed in Yetzirah

Color(s): Deep purple, plus the colors of the associated majors

Associated Majors: Justice/Adjustment and the Wheel of Fortune

---

168. Dates vary annually. All decanic minor dates listed in this book are based on 2019–2020 dates.

Associated Minors: Shadow decan of the Knight/Prince of Cups

Themes and Keywords: Temporary stabilization. Structure as refuge. Rest from mental chaos. Isolation and convalescence. Laws as protection. Keeping vigil. Meditation.

ASTROLOGY/ELEMENT

This is a case where we see something very subtle. The decan is ruled by Jupiter, in a Jupiter-ruled sephira, in a sign ruled by Venus. Two doses of the greater benefic, in the sign of the lesser. Double Jupiter with Venus, but it isn't a big payoff. It's merely "truce," which says much about the mind. Truce is a valuable rest from the strife of the suit of Swords, which has very few resting places. The subtle lesson is again about the nature of mind and its pitfalls.

The significations are a mix of savage and savory, speaking of evil works and lusts but also singing, joy, and feasting. *Picatrix*'s man rides a donkey and is behind a wolf, both animals symbolizing mankind's base natures. Agrippa has a violent man with a bow facing a naked man while another man holds bread and wine. The implied evil is the destructiveness of the mind, which can take a break even while facing the naked truth.

Leaves from Jupiter's oak float within the safe space described by the swords—
almost certainly an astrological coincidence. (*Ancient Italian Tarot*)

MYTHOLOGY/TIME OF YEAR

There is a famous truce between Aphrodite (Venus) and Persephone (daughter of Demeter, also Venusian). Persephone is a maiden (Venus), but also saturnine due to her association with the underworld. Persephone and Aphrodite fought over mortal Adonis, a beautiful youth from an incestuous union. His mother Myrrha was cursed into incest by Aphrodite. Myrrha's mother had boasted about Myrrha's beauty, so Myrrha was cursed into sleeping with her father. She persuaded the gods to transform her into a myrrh tree as both punishment and a sort of salvation. Myrrh has an association with Saturn, exalted in this decan.

Adonis was born from the trunk of myrrh, and Aphrodite rescued the beautiful infant, entrusting it to Persephone. Aphrodite fell in love with him as he grew, yet Persephone refused to give him back. They had to have Zeus (Jupiter) intervene. Zeus sought a second opinion, that of the muse Calliope, a Venusian figure and muse of poetry and eloquence. Her advice was that there should be a balance—a truce, even: that Adonis should divide his time equally between Aphrodite, Persephone, and himself.

QABALAH

The 4 of Swords is Chesed in Yetzirah. Chesed (חסד, also known as Gedulah, "greatness") the fourth sephira, translates as "mercy" and is the sphere of Jupiter. Chesed's counterpart is Geburah, the fifth sephira; Chesed gives, Geburah restrains. The first sephira below the supernal triad, Chesed presents the divine as a loving father figure.

The third of four worlds is Yetzirah (the Formative World), which hints at the power of swords/the mind to form reality. Swords also correspond to *vav*, the third letter in the Divine Name, יהוה. *Vav* ו represents a peg or nail—that which joins two disparate elements—while also, serendipitously, resembling a sword.

Chesed in Yetzirah signifies the generous accommodation of other viewpoints. Its connection to *kaph*/palm (Wheel of Fortune) and *lamed*/ox-goad (Justice/Adjustment) suggests a spacious approach to course correction—reaching one's open hands to the sides to balance on a narrow path.

As *Completion*, *Luxury*, *Truce*, and *Power*, Chesed offers moments of creative, emotional, intellectual, and material respite before the rigors of Geburah.

RIDER-WAITE-SMITH SYMBOLISM

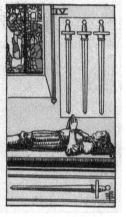

4 of Swords (*Rider-Waite-Smith Tarot*)

The figure of the recumbent knight has caused many to wonder *Is he sleeping, or is he dead?* Waite indicates that the design suggests both "tomb" and "effigy," but also the knight's vigil. His prayerful pose brings to mind Jupiter as a patron of religion.

The knight lies at a remove from the vibrant bustle of life: most of the card's color is sequestered in the stained-glass window at left and above; on close inspection, one can discern the word PAX, "peace," inscribed in what looks like a halo. Smith's inspiration might have been Winchelsea Church, a site famed for its medieval tombs, although the church's famed stained-glass windows arrived after Smith designed the deck.[169]

Three swords hang suspended above the knight; one sword lies empaneled beneath him. Although one cannot know Smith's intentions, it's compelling to imagine the knight may have found in his meditations the clarity (Ace of Swords) to face sorrow (3 of Swords).

THOTH SYMBOLISM

Crowley tells us that this is a refuge from mental chaos, and one that has been chosen subjectively. He refers to intellectual authority and the establishment of law, as well

---

169. Katz and Goodwin, *Secrets of the Waite-Smith Tarot*, 309.

as the masculine idea of protection through vigilance. The peace thus won is a temporary compromise, certain to be disturbed by the approaching 5 of Swords—but for now, there is a static sort of harmony based on conciliation and tacit agreement.

The swords meet where they point inward in a St. Andrew's cross formation, also known as a *saltire*, a heraldic form seen on the Scottish flag and many coats of arms. Crowley describes it as rigid. It's also sometimes used as a protective hex sign on doorways, lintels, and fireplaces to prevent witches from entering. Each sword hilt has a different elemental motif. The points meet at a rose of forty-nine petals, which also makes the entire design into a form of the rose cross. Forty-nine is Venus's number—seven, times itself—and the rose implies social harmony.

RELATED CARDS

As Libra's final decan, the 4 of Swords enjoys Jupiter's decan rulership and number, four. It brings together the Wheel of Fortune (Jupiter) and Justice/Adjustment (Libra). The 2, 3, and 4 of Swords all concern balance. The 2 of Swords stresses perspectives equal in weight; the 3 of Swords addresses the bonds that codify fairness. But the 4's balance is a still point within motion, a stable axis because of the whirling mass surrounding it.

The vajra, Jupiter's weapon, weaves between the swords while the feathers of Justice/Adjustment (Libra) write the alpha and omega. (*Tabula Mundi Tarot*)

Fours gather together an abundance of their suit resources. The 4 of Swords gathers thoughts in stillness. The 4 of Wands aligns public interests. In the 4 of Cups a surplus of feelings collect; in the 4 of Pentacles, treasures amass.

The 4 of Swords is the first or shadow decan of the Knight (RWS) or Prince (Thoth) of Cups. Rising beyond its temporary truce, he will learn to handle loss through self-sacrifice and redemption in the 5 and 6 of Cups.

Finally, four, Chesed, and the Wheel of Fortune are the number, sephira, and path of Jupiter—each expressing its own form of stability.

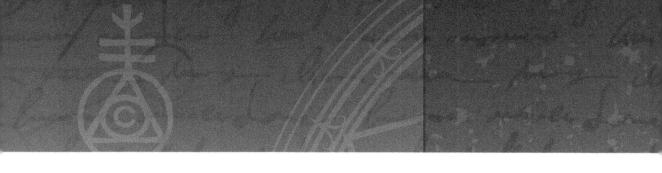

5 OF SWORDS
Lord of Defeat

Dates:[170] January 20–January 29

Astrology: Aquarius, the sign ruled by Saturn (classical) and Uranus (modern)

Element: Fixed air

Decan: 0°–9° Aquarius; Aquarius I, the decan ruled by Venus

Picatrix **Image:** A man whose head is mutilated and he holds a peacock in his hand

Picatrix **Significations:** Misery, poverty, and slavery

Agrippa Image: A prudent man, and of a woman spinning

Agrippa Significations: The thought and labor for gain, in poverty and baseness

Sephira/World: Geburah in Yetzirah

Color(s): Bright scarlet, plus the colors of the associated majors

Associated Majors: The Star and the Empress

Associated Minors: Knight/Prince of Swords

---

170. Dates vary annually. All decanic minor dates listed in this book are based on 2019–2020 dates.

Themes and Keywords: Passivity leading to surprise attack. Failure of good intentions. Lack of defense. Detachment and pacifism. Winners and losers.

ASTROLOGY/ELEMENT

Aquarius is classically ruled by Saturn, and the first decan is ruled by Venus. These two are a difficult pairing, as Venus's natural warmth and desire for connection is chilled by dour Saturn. Add disruptive Mars for the corresponding sephira and this is a situation where Venus is overwhelmed; a stranger in a strange land. Aquarius is a rebel, often known for cool aloofness and going their own way. Venus's natural inclination is to seek harmony and companionship, but perhaps here she would be better off going on the offensive, or at least putting up a better defense.

Picatrix shows a man with a mutilated head, implying he has been attacked somehow, and he holds a peacock, a Venusian symbol. Agrippa's image is more cryptic, showing a prudent man and a woman spinning. Both significations mention poverty, showing Venus's association with money being limited by Saturn and cut by Mars. But Agrippa also mentions thought (Aquarius) and labor (Saturn) for gain (Venus), which is perhaps the best manifestation of this combination.

The "beheaded man with a peacock" image from *Picatrix*, signifying tough times and an arduous path for all. (*Liber T: Tarot of Stars Eternal*)

MYTHOLOGY/TIME OF YEAR

Here is a story of Venus or Aphrodite's defeat, which didn't happen often! Yet she was thwarted in her love for Ares (Mars) and forced to marry Hephaestus. As the blacksmith, Hephaestus's emblems are fire (Mars) and the anvil (Saturn), the two malefic planetary influences disturbing Venus in this card.

Hephaestus is primarily a saturnine figure, being both lame and ugly. He was sometimes said to be parthenogenetically conceived by Hera, a goddess of Saturn. Hera disowned him for his disfigurement. As revenge, Hephaestus trapped Hera in a magic golden throne. In order to secure her release, Hera and Zeus promised Hephaestus the hand of beautiful Aphrodite. This was against Aphrodite's will, as the goddess of beauty wanted nothing to do with the grotesque blacksmith.

Aphrodite still went on to commit adultery with Ares and was trapped, thwarted, and humiliated yet again by Hephaestus, who set an invisible net and caught the lovers *in flagrante delicto*. Hephaestus then displayed them naked for the amusement of the gods.

The dove of Venus is attacked by the raptor of Aquarius
and the red sword of Mars. (*Tabula Mundi Tarot*)

QABALAH

The 5 of Swords is Geburah in Yetzirah. Geburah (גבורה), the fifth sephira, translates as "severity" or "restraint," and corresponds to Mars's fierce sword; Geburah and Chesed are the inviting and restraining arms of divinity. Geburah separates individuals so each can breathe; it is associated with the second day of creation, when God divided the sky above and sea below. The separative, subjectively challenging nature of Geburah/Mars gives fives their conflictual tone.

Swords correspond to the third of four worlds, Yetzirah (the Formative World), suggesting their role in forming or shaping reality through our mental perspective. They also correspond to *vav*, the third letter in the Divine Name, יהוה, which itself resembles a sword, while ideographically representing a nail, that which joins two disparate elements.

In Yetzirah, all of creation's variety exists conceptually before taking form in Assiah. Geburah in Yetzirah underscores the inequities perceived and imposed by the mind. As the Lord of Defeat, Geburah forces us to confront imbalances of power; as *Strife*, *Disappointment*, and *Worry*, Geburah forces us to face competition, loss, and material uncertainty.

RIDER-WAITE-SMITH SYMBOLISM

5 of Swords (*Rider-Waite-Smith Tarot*)

In Pamela Colman Smith's 5 of Swords, ragged, scuttling clouds reflect the native disruptions of the five cards; the very air is disturbed! (This is the central decan of the Knight of Swords, whose backdrop features similarly blustery skies.) Waite describes the foreground fighter as the "master in possession of the field" and those glimpsed beyond as "retreating and dejected." Whether the three are allies or foes, it is clear that hard feelings rule the day. We can perhaps read the three swords held by the victor as the "sorrow" (3 of Swords) he inflicts; the two on the ground as the "peace" (2 of Swords) that has been lost.

The 5 of Swords is a stage card, suggesting the role is a temporary one. We can also view the troubled waters beyond as a roiling unconscious, from which our gloating protagonist is deliberately setting himself apart. Should he continue to ignore these turbulent depths in his determination to win, further confrontations are inevitable!

THOTH SYMBOLISM

The five swords are arranged in a sinister pentagram, symbolic of the elements of matter triumphing over spirit. The central and only straight sword stands for spirit, for the hilt is decorated with the crown symbol of Kether. It has been attacked by the other swords, for the blade has a missing chip. The surrounding swords are bent and marked with designs representing the four elements: a fish for water, a red flame for fire, a green serpent for earth, and a swirl that looks like a 6 or 9, but likely represents a swirling cloud or gust of wind for air.

The central rose we saw in the four, representing Venus, has been completely destroyed. The forty-nine petals (Venus's 7 x 7) are all that remain, marking out the averse pentagram. Love, or at least pacific sentiment, has been dismantled by intellect. The swastika shapes that were so ordered and symmetrical in the two (*Peace*) are here chaotic and disrupted against a background of Venusian colors darkened by saturnine black.

RELATED CARDS

The 5 of Swords brings together the Empress (Venus) and the Star (Aquarius), a pacific combination which esoteric tarot generally considers no match for the rough edges of a five. One role of a star is to guide us away from familiar comforts; here dangerous frontiers, quixotic quests, and pyrrhic victories might be found. Central decan of the Knight (RWS) or Prince (Thoth) of Wands, the 5 creates tensions the 6 must solve.

Faced with apparent disaster, he will navigate forbidding terrain to safe harbor—or greener pastures.

Fives create motion and imbalance. The 5 of Swords disrupts thought patterns, the perception of "the rules." The 5 of Wands sets ambitions alight, while the 5 of Cups removes emotional security and the 5 of Pentacles removes material resources.

Finally, five is the number and Geburah is the sephira of Mars. Its corresponding path is the Tower, source of life-altering, character-developing discomforts which spur us on to new paths and accomplishments.

6 OF SWORDS
Lord of Science (Earned Success)

Dates:[171] January 30–February 8 (includes the cross-quarter holiday)

Astrology: Aquarius, the sign ruled by Saturn (classical) and Uranus (modern)

Element: Fixed air

Decan: 10°–19° Aquarius; Aquarius II, the decan ruled by Mercury

Picatrix **Image:** A man who looks like a king, who permits much to himself and abhors what he sees

Picatrix **Significations:** Beauty and position, having what is desired, completion, detriment, and debility

Agrippa Image: A man with a long beard

Agrippa Significations: Understanding, meekness, modesty, liberty, and good manners

Sephira/World: Tiphareth in Yetzirah

Color(s): Rich salmon, plus the colors of the associated majors

Associated Majors: The Star and the Magician/Magus

---

171. Dates vary annually. All decanic minor dates listed in this book are based on 2019–2020 dates.

Associated Minors: Knight/Prince of Swords

Themes and Keywords: Innovation and ingenuity. Seeking ideals. Movement and working toward betterment. Navigation. Invention. Evolution and goals. Problem solving.

ASTROLOGY/ELEMENT

Here we are reminded that while Aquarius's classical ruler is Saturn, the modern rulership is given to Uranus, planet of inventive genius. It is joined by brilliant Mercury, ruler of the decan and well-placed in the sign, and the Sun, our own personal star and ruler of the sixes. Because of the importance of the sun, all sixes show some form of success. The original Golden Dawn title of this card is "Earned Success": a success earned through the combination of Saturn's fixity of purpose, the inspiration of Uranus, and the ingenuity of Mercury. Mercury also adds the idea of travel, with the idea of movement toward the Aquarian ideal, that which somehow benefits humanity.

Picatrix offers the image of a kingly man "who permits much to himself" (sun) and "abhors what he sees." The significations speak of beauty and attainment—yet some debility, due to Saturn's influence. Agrippa's image of a man with a long beard also sounds both saturnine and solar. The significations indicate liberty and understanding: two attributes of Mercury in Aquarius.

These scientific tools are mercurial: the orrery is also solar (six) and the sextant navigates the stars (Aquarius). (*Tabula Mundi Tarot*)

MYTHOLOGY/TIME OF YEAR

Ganymede, cupbearer of Olympus, is thought to be the water bearer of constellation Aquarius. When Zeus instructed him to flood the earth, only two mortals survived, Deucalion and Pyrrha. Deucalion was the son of Prometheus, the mercurial figure who brought fire to mankind, and Hesione Pronoia, goddess of foresight. Pyrrha was the daughter of Pandora (she of the infamous box who released the world's evils, keeping only hope contained) and Epimetheus, both associated with hindsight. Prometheus warned his son of the coming devastation, so Deucalion ingeniously built a floating chest.

This decan of Aquarius contains one of the cross-quarter holy days, halfway between equinox and solstice. Christians celebrate Candlemas, the Feast of the Blessed Virgin. Pagans celebrate Imbolc, dedicated to the goddess Brigid. Thelemites celebrate the Feast of Stars, which goes back to ancient Egypt as the Feast of Nut—or Nuit, the goddess of "Infinite Space, and the Infinite Stars thereof."[172] The date also aligns with secular holidays devoted to weather divination, such as Groundhog Day.

QABALAH

The 6 of Swords represents Tiphareth in Yetzirah. Tiphareth תיפארת, the sixth sephira, is the "heart" of the Tree, between both the Pillars of Mercy and Severity, and Kether and Yesod/Malkuth. Hermetic Qabalists translate Tiphareth as beauty; it corresponds to the sun and the third day of creation, when God brought the land forth and made it fruitful. Tiphareth's benign creative presence brings opposing forces into proportion, giving sixes their sense of purpose.

Yetzirah, the third of four worlds, is the "World of Formation" in Hermetic Qabalah and the realm of swords. *Vav* ו, the third letter in the Divine Name, יהוה, also corresponds to and resembles swords. *Vav* is said to mean "nail" or "tent peg"—that which joins two disparate elements, such as heaven and earth. Tiphareth in Yetzirah signifies the intellect reaching toward beauty: the love of science and natural law, what Pythagoras called the "harmony of the spheres."

---

172. Crowley, *Book of the Law*, 21.

The 6 of Swords brings together letters *beth*, "house" (the Magician) and either letter *heh*, "window" or *tzaddi*, "hook" (the Star).[173] Either interpretation suggests the mind's power to draw distant things closer.

As the Lord of Science, Tiphareth grants solutions to tough problems; as *Victory*, *Pleasure*, and *Success*, it brings heroic belonging, emotional fulfillment, and tangible achievements.

RIDER-WAITE-SMITH SYMBOLISM

6 of Swords (*Rider-Waite-Smith Tarot*) (left)
Over the years, the Waite-Smith deck's influence has made the 6 of Swords' iconic "journey in a boat" the defining feature on modern versions of the card. (*Linestrider Tarot*) (right)

Waite describes a "ferryman carrying passengers in his punt," a small, flat-bottomed boat used in shallow waterways.[174] The pole is the boat's means of propulsion, planted on the river bottom on the downstroke and trailed behind as a steering rudder on the upstroke. Like the Magician's wand, it symbolizes the will and means to direct one's

---

173. The Golden Dawn originally assigned *tzaddi* צ to the Star, and that is the correspondence Waite would have had in mind for the *Rider-Waite-Smith Tarot*. When Crowley, however, "received" the *Book of Thoth*, he was told that "*Tzaddi* is not the Star," leading him to assign *tzaddi* to the Emperor instead and *heh* ה to the Star.

174. Waite, *Pictorial Key*, 242.

own fate. In tarot, the color black can signify potential; the black pole suggests possibilities opening as the mind works toward a solution. Ripples in the foreground passing into smooth waters ahead may represent the troubled times one leaves behind.

Water and sky, flying and floating—visual themes of the card—remind us of its connection to air sign Aquarius, the water bearer. Water also may represent the unconscious realms of sleep, dream, death. The ferryman could be Charon or the conscious mind traversing the waters of the unknown through journeying. Perhaps this passage takes us through the non-ordinary reality of Yetzirah, shaping the destiny that will materialize on that farther shore, the kingdom of Assiah.

THOTH SYMBOLISM

Crowley has renamed the Thoth card "Science," as the pursuit of science is how humanity earns its success, using reason and experimentation to evolve.

Lady Frieda's exhibition notes explain the background of radiating geometrical star-like patterns. She describes them as a fencer's diagram, worked out scientifically to show the positions in which a fencer can stand invulnerable. With Aquarian logical assessment, mercurial inventiveness and agility, and Tiphareth's balance, the fencer executes a sublime series of moves with the speed of thought. That the diagram is all about steps toward a goal enhances the themes of Mercury, the travel god, and Aquarius, the star.

The background contains the "circle squared"—also present on Saturn's card, ruler of Aquarius. It represents using the mind to stretch toward goals seemingly out of reach. The swords' points converge at the center of a rose cross of six golden squares, a symbol of the sun and Tiphareth. The hilts are colored to represent the classical planets.

RELATED CARDS

In the 6 of Swords, the Magician/Magus (Mercury) and the Star (Aquarius) join forces to produce an intellect of exceptional sharpness and clarity. The Magician embodies the idea of as above, so below, pointing to the stars and the earth and forming connections between them. The mind leaps across untraveled expanses to find solutions.

As the Knight/Prince of Swords' final decan, the card represents his best self—the power struggles of the 4 of Pentacles and the ruthless battles of the 5 of Swords finally resolve. Steady reasoning charts his course like a fair wind.

Sixes emphasize harmonious resolutions. While the 6 of Swords resolves conflicts, the 6 of Wands creates a sense of belonging (e.g., patriotism). The 6 of Cups fosters a sense of caring; the 6 of Pentacles altruistically shares its success with others.

Six is the sun's number and Tiphareth the Sun's sephira. Itself a star, the Sun represents the hopes of the Star, brought near.

7 OF SWORDS
Lord of Futility (Unstable Effort)

Dates:[175] February 9–February 18

Astrology: Aquarius, the sign ruled by Saturn (classical) and Uranus (modern)

Element: Fixed air

Decan: 20°–29° Aquarius; Aquarius III, the decan ruled by the Moon

***Picatrix* Image:** A man having a mutilated head, and an old woman is with him

***Picatrix* Significations:** Abundance, accomplishing of will, giving offense

Agrippa Image: A black and angry man

Agrippa Significations: Insolence and impudence

Sephira/World: Netzach in Yetzirah

Color(s): Bright yellow-green, plus the colors of the associated majors

Associated Majors: The Star and the Priestess

Associated Minors: Shadow decan of the King/Knight of Cups

---

175. Dates vary annually. All decanic minor dates listed in this book are based on 2019–2020 dates.

Themes and Keywords: Survival skills. Moral ambiguity. Insincerity. Strategy and slyness. Shrewd maneuvering. Vacillation and over-compromise. Rogues and transgressions. Divided mind. Resourcefulness.

ASTROLOGY/ELEMENT

Aquarius decan III combines a Saturn (and Uranus) ruled sign with a moon-ruled decan in a Venusian sephira. Like the five, the 7 of Swords is another flavor of imbalance. The moon and the sevens are known for instability and approaching change, so the steady effort required for saturnine success isn't being easily supported. Vacillation—and passive insincerity—struggles with sustained exertion and tends toward compromise, if not outright victimization. If victory is to be won, it will be through shrewd surprise maneuvers.

Like in the 5, *Picatrix* also mentions a man with a mutilated head, perhaps an indication that there has been an attack that involves state of mind. This time he is with an old woman, which implies feminine infirmity and could be an indicator of Venus or the moon associated with a dissipating decan. The significations do mention "will accomplished" but also somehow giving offense. Agrippa's image is wrathful; the man is described as black and angry. The significations are of improper attitudes: insolence and impudence.

MYTHOLOGY/TIME OF YEAR

Trickster and shape-shifter figures of mythology and folklore like Loki, Coyote, Puss in Boots, Puck, and Brer Rabbit exemplify the sly craftiness associated with this card. Greek mythology has Odysseus, *The Odyssey*'s eponymous hero, known as "Odysseus the Cunning" for his guile and strategies. The Greeks respected his wiliness, but the Romans, with their sense of honor and virtue, considered him reprobate, degenerate, and deceitful. Whichever moral opinion one holds, he was known for repeatedly escaping situations through last-minute, devious scheming.

The moon's ascendancy and the sun's closed eyes suggest
subterfuge under cover of night. (*Universal Wirth Tarot*)

But in the tale that started him on his long odyssey, he was unsuccessful through
vacillation, though his hesitation was understandable under the circumstances. When
Helen of Troy was abducted, her husband called upon Odysseus to help wage war
upon the Trojans. Odysseus, wishing to avoid involvement, feigned lunacy. He hitched
a mismatched team to his plow and began sowing his fields with salt. His strategy was
exposed when someone put his infant son in front of the plow.

QABALAH

The 7 of Swords is Netzach in Yetzirah. Netzach נצח and Hod הוד, the seventh and
eighth sephiroth, work together in traditional Kabbalah. Sometimes known as the
"armies/hosts" of God, or "tactical sephiroth," they are channels for divine guidance. Considering Netzach the emotional and Hod as the intellectual sphere, Hermetic Qabalists tend to translate Netzach as "victory" (more accurately, "eternity" or
"endurance"). Netzach, ruled by Venus, is a place of passions and quests where we find
the inspiration to pursue what we love.

The suit of Swords corresponds to the third of four worlds, Yetzirah (the Formaitve
World). In fact, when the four worlds are mapped onto a single Tree, Yetzirah corresponds to the seventh, eighth, and ninth sephiroth—giving the 7, 8, and 9 of Swords a
special resonance with its formative aspect. *Vav* ו, the third letter in the Divine Name,

יהוה, corresponds to swords and represents a nail, emphasizing its connective properties: it joins two disparate elements, such as heaven and earth, even though the sword serves as a tool of separation on the mundane plane. In Yetzirah lie the ingenious, various blueprints for all creation, and in Netzach the motivation to fabricate.

Netzach in Yetzirah, the Lord of Futility, gives rise to elaborate plans and schemes. As *Valor*, *Debauch* (*Illusionary Success*), and *Failure* (*Success Unfulfilled*), Netzach gives daring and drive, phantasmal dreams, and the stamina to prevail through hardship.

RIDER-WAITE-SMITH SYMBOLISM

7 of Swords (*Rider-Waite-Smith Tarot*) (left)
The dramatically furtive body language of the figure in the right image may
well have inspired Smith's own thieving protagonist. (*Sola Busca Tarot*)

The body language of Smith's 7 of Swords strongly recalls its counterpart in the *Sola Busca Tarot*; in each, a furtive figure advances, his arms full of swords and his forward knee raised, as if leaving the image stage left. His head faces back over his shoulder with the furtive demeanor of a criminal checking for witnesses. The encampment and clustered silhouettes in the background suggest soldiering operations, adding to the suggestion of subtle, undercover tactics. Visible on the nearest tent are glyphs of the Moon and Aquarius—the only such explicit astrological reference in Smith's minor arcana. The yellow skyscape is unusual for the cool-toned Swords suit; this brazen act takes place in broad daylight.

Despite his militaristic environs, our thief is dressed as a civilian. His fur-trimmed hat and boots call to mind a kind of animal cunning, or perhaps the shape-shifting magic of a trickster archetype. Beneath his feet is one of Smith's "stages," suggesting his role is one taken on for expediency's sake.

THOTH SYMBOLISM

Against asymmetric background forms, six swords with planetary symbols point downward in a lunar crescent formation, arranging themselves at a central sword representing the sun. The Sun is in fall in Aquarius, and its association with Tiphareth aligns it with the *ruach*, the part of the soul that distinguishes between good and evil. The intellect (*ruach*) must defend itself against the intrusions of the animal part of the soul, the *nephesh*, and the emotions associated with the moon and Netzach.

Crowley describes this as a contest wherein one is outnumbered and struggles in vain. He calls the "intellectual wreckage" of the card not as extreme as that seen in the five, yet also says that in certain circumstances it is more disastrous than ever.[176] He says that here is always doubt as there are obstinate forces that will attempt to take it as "natural prey."[177] But the opposing swords are described as six feeble against one strong, so there is wiggle room to be had. A clever one can perhaps slip the noose.

RELATED CARDS

In the 7 of Swords, the Moon rules the final decan of Aquarius. The High Priestess (Moon) illuminates the distant goal of the Star (Aquarius) in hidden, flexible ways; schemes which demonstrate great resourcefulness while risking collapse from their own precarious complexity.

Sevens are cards of quests and seeking. While the mentally hyperactive 7 of Swords has a plan for every eventuality, the 7 of Wands defends what his ambition has secured.

---

176. Crowley, *Book of Thoth*, 207.

177. Crowley, 207.

The 7 of Cups escapes into fevered visions, while the 7 of Pentacles assesses where previous efforts have gone astray.

First (or "shadow") of the King (RWS) or Knight (Thoth) of Cups' three decans, the 7 of Swords represents the mind's war with itself. He must rise above the mind's mazy contortions to achieve the heart-centered, compassionate mysteries which are his birthright, as seen in the 8 and 9 of Cups.

Finally, seven, Netzach, and the Empress are the number, sephira, and path of Venus. Together they represent the unconquerable force of desire; life's will to regenerate.

8 OF SWORDS
Lord of Interference (Shortened Force)

Dates:[178] May 21–May 31

Astrology: Gemini, the sign ruled by Mercury

Element: Mutable air

Decan: 0°–9° Gemini; Gemini I, the decan ruled by Jupiter

Picatrix Image: A beautiful woman, a mistress of stitching, two calves and two horses

Picatrix Significations: Writing, computation and number, giving and taking, the sciences

Agrippa Image: A man in whose hand is a rod, and he is, as it were, serving another

Agrippa Significations: Wisdom, and the knowledge of numbers and arts in which there is no profit

Sephira/World: Hod in Yetzirah

Color(s): Russet, plus the colors of the associated majors

---

178. Dates vary annually. All decanic minor dates listed in this book are based on 2019–2020 dates.

Associated Majors: The Lovers and the Wheel of Fortune

Associated Minors: King/Knight of Swords

Themes and Keywords: Unexpected snags. Need for cerebral sharpening. Mental paralysis. Lack of intellectual persistence. Necessary untangling. Obstruction and hindrance. Unforeseen bad luck and minor accidents. Finding a way. Trivial incidents that yet alter one's course. Excessive force applied to small things. Delays and timing issues. Fate versus free will.

ASTROLOGY/ELEMENT

The sign of the twins, Gemini, is ruled by Mercury, and so are the eights. The decan is ruled by Jupiter. It's an interesting pairing of the largest planet with the smallest. Jupiter is in detriment in both of Mercury's signs; his force is "shortened" (the Golden Dawn's Hermetic title for the 8 of Swords of *Shortened Force*). Yet even hamstrung, the Greater Benefic isn't that difficult. It merely means that mercurial skills will be required to untangle unexpected snags. As always, Jupiter brings plenitude and luck and Gemini offers variety. But an abundance of choices leads to paralysis, and unanticipated twists of fortune aren't always beneficial.

Picatrix gives a decan image of a beautiful, skilled seamstress, the twinning concept is expressed as pairs of domestic beasts. Agrippa's image is of a man serving while holding a rod in his hand, which implies a unit of measurement. In each case the significations are of mercurial proficiency: numbers, measures, writing, and the granting of wisdom and aptitude. Yet *Picatrix* indicates a certain capriciousness, mentioning both giving and taking away, and Agrippa indicates arts without profit.

EIGHT OF SWORDS
Ⅱ   INTERFERENCE   ♃

The twins of Gemini are represented by the alchemical lion and eagle from a medieval illustration called the *Battle of Sol and Luna*, and the decan rulership of Jupiter is shown by the thread of the spinning wheel and the four-pronged vajra (Jupiter). (*Tabula Mundi Tarot*)

MYTHOLOGY/TIME OF YEAR

Hermes (Mercury), the son of Zeus (Jupiter), was a mischievous child whose meddling began on the very day of his birth. He immediately began causing trouble for his own amusement, inventing and pioneering along the way. On his first day, he invented the lyre and composed a hymn to himself. He stole his brother Apollo's cattle, cleverly hid his tracks, and in order to cook the first sacrifice to the gods, discovered fire and fashioned the first fire-starting bow drill. He divided two of the cows into twelve parts even though the Olympic gods numbered eleven, for naturally, he allotted himself a portion.

Zeus knew right away that he had to intervene to curb his child's propensity for interference and keep him as busy as possible. Zeus cleverly made his precocious son his right-hand man and the messenger for all the gods. Further occupying his restless nature, at Zeus's direction Hermes took on guardianship of the world's flocks and canines and assumed the never-ending task of guiding souls to the underworld.

QABALAH

The 8 of Swords is Hod in Yetzirah. Netzach נצח and Hod הוד, the seventh and eighth sephiroth, are counterparts channeling divine guidance, Netzach in the emotional and Hod in the intellectual sphere.

Translated as "splendor," "majesty," or "glory," Hod houses the intellect. In the sphere of Mercury, it governs reason and communication. In prophecy, Hod gives speech to the felt sense of Netzach. It corresponds to the fifth day of creation—the branching of nature into many species.

Qabalists call Yetzirah the "World of Formation," hinting at the power of airy swords to shape our perception. Swords also correspond to *vav* ו, the third letter in the Divine Name, יהוה. On the one hand, *vav* resembles its corresponding suit emblew, the sword which separates. On the other, *vav* ideographically refers to "nail," that which joins two disparate elements. In Yetzirah lie the countless, varied blueprints for creation, and in Hod the mental impulse to enumerate them. Hod's powerful analytic proclivities in Yetzirah can lead to interference (*Shortened Force*).

In Atziluth, Hod bestows a sure sense of direction, as the Lord of Swiftness. As *Indolence* (*Abandoned Success*) in Briah and *Prudence* in Assiah, Hod tells us when it is time to move on and how to organize our lives into feasible steps.

RIDER-WAITE-SMITH SYMBOLISM

8 of Swords (*Rider-Waite-Smith Tarot*) (left)
On the right, a mole takes the place of the traditional blindfolded victim. He feels his way
through darkness and uncertainty without the benefit of sight. (*Animal Totem Tarot*)

"Temporary durance rather than irretrievable bondage," Waite says of this card, suggesting that one can wait out its frustrations; the next turn of the wheel may bring liberation! The figure stands in watery mud, surrounded by swords—a picture of the mind literally stuck, its conscious workings mired in an encroaching unconscious. If the earth represents what is known and stable in life, the water is the unacknowledged emotional power that threatens to dissolve certainty. Clothed in the red of life's passions with her sight occluded, the prisoner cannot decide in what direction safety lies. In the background, a castle rises; perhaps it is the kingdom of Malkuth.

The "bound and hoodwinked" 8 of Swords is one of only two cards featuring a blindfold; like the other card, the 2 of Swords, it may have an initiatory quality. Perhaps this trial is the price of entry into mental clarity. The process of learning to deal with frustration may be an ordeal of choice!

THOTH SYMBOLISM

Two long swords are placed with their points facing down, often a negative connotation. They block a cultural (Jupiter) variety (Gemini) of short swords: "the Kriss, the

Kukri, the Scramasax, the Dagger, the Machete, and the Yataghan." These daggers are shortened varieties of swords, an allusion to the Hermetic title originally assigned by the Golden Dawn, the "Lord of Shortened Force." Force is will. The mind faces a diverse array of choices that create a paralysis, or at least a temporary disturbance. Jupiter's detriment in flighty Gemini offers too many distractions, diluting the Greater Benefic's expansive nature and diminishing its natural munificence.

Crowley tells us that here there is a lack of intellectual persistence in matters of contest, yet that Jupiter still confers a bit of luck despite weakened efforts and accidental setbacks. These indicators of mental interference are placed against a background of blue and orange pinwheels. While these are colors of Jupiter and Gemini respectively; they are also the flashing colors of water. What is needed is patient application of intellectual skill in the face of emotional disturbance.

RELATED CARDS

The 8 of Swords, ruled by Jupiter, is the first of three Gemini minors. Jupiter is in detriment in Gemini and not at home in the sephira of Mercury.[179] Here the ever-spinning Wheel of Fortune (Jupiter) runs into the forced choice of the Lovers (Gemini). The result is not unlike what happens when you poke a sword into a moving bicycle wheel.

Eights offer systematic efforts toward real-world solutions. The 8 of Swords attempts to analyze the unanalyzable. The 8 of Wands speeds along information at the speed of light, the 8 of Cups walks away from drowning in its own feelings, and the 8 of Pentacles organizes our practical lives.

Central decan of the King (RWS) or Knight (Thoth) of Swords, the 8 of Swords gives him the thankless ability to process massive quantities of information, which he will wield ruthlessly in the 9 of Swords.

Eight is the number and Hod is the sephira of Mercury, giving the messenger a strong presence in this first card of his day sign.

---

179. It's interesting to contrast the 8 of Swords (Jupiter in Mercury's sign) with the 8 of Wands (Mercury in Jupiter's sign). Gemini and Virgo, Mercury's signs, directly oppose Sagittarius and Pisces, Jupiter's signs)—meaning each planet is in detriment in the other's signs. Why do we find an easier experience in the 8 of Wands (*Swiftness*) than in the 8 of Swords (*Interference*)? Perhaps because eight is Mercury's number, giving the planet greater comfort as a decan ruler. Or perhaps we are overlooking the 8 of Swords' redeeming qualities and its precocious mental activity!

9 OF SWORDS
Lord of Cruelty (Despair and Cruelty)

Dates:[180] June 1–June 10

Astrology: Gemini, the sign ruled by Mercury

Element: Mutable air

Decan: 10°–19° Gemini; Gemini II, the decan ruled by Mars

Picatrix **Image:** A man whose face is like an eagle and his head is covered by linen cloth; clothed and protected by a coat of leaden mail, and on his head is an iron helmet above which is a silk crown, and in his hand he has a bow and arrows

Picatrix **Significations:** Oppression, evils, and subtlety

Agrippa Image: A man in whose hand is a pipe, and another being bowed down, digging the earth

Agrippa Significations: Infamous and dishonest agility, as that of jesters and jugglers; labors and painful searching

Sephira/World: Yesod in Yetzirah

---

180. Dates vary annually. All decanic minor dates listed in this book are based on 2019–2020 dates.

Color(s): Very dark purple, plus the colors of the associated majors

Associated Majors: The Lovers and the Tower

Associated Minors: King/Knight of Swords

Themes and Keywords: Anxiety and irreconcilable thoughts. Self-castigation. Separation. Guilt, shame, jealousy, fear, remorse. Nightmare, sleeplessness, anguish. The mind consuming itself. Persecution. Cutting words.

ASTROLOGY/ELEMENT

Gemini II uncomfortably combines Mercury, ruler of Gemini, with Mars, ruler of the decan, and the Moon, ruler of nines. Gemini (Mercury) relates to the mind, as does the sharp suit of Swords. The mind, with all its chaotic propensity, becomes a dangerous place when pitiless Mars unleashes his fury in the realm of the moon, the subconscious and the astral. Gemini is gifted with speech and idea, but Mars is barbarous and the moon is unstable. Merciless thoughts and words, whether directed at the self or outward, can cause pain.

The swords' hilts have glyphs of Gemini and Mars and
form the teeth of a gaping mouth (*peh*, Mars). (*Rosetta Tarot*)

Picatrix describes a man whose head (a part ruled by martial Aries) is covered by linen cloth, calling to mind a shroud. His face is like an eagle and he wears an iron helmet, silk crown, and leaden mail. He carries a weapon of piercing. Agrippa shows one man holding a pipe and another bowed down, digging. His significations describe "dishonest agility," one of the more destructive aspects of Mercury, as well as painful searching, a theme of the card.

MYTHOLOGY/TIME OF YEAR

The cruelty of war god Ares (Mars) is well-known. His Orphic hymn calls him "the horrifying one," delighting in obscene carnage, along with his twin (Gemini) sons *Phobos* (fear) and *Deimos* (dread). The combination of Mars, Moon, and Gemini might also bring to mind Hecate, the three-faced night goddess of necromancy and sorcery. Deities of nightmare also apply: *Phobetor*, the Frightener, brother of Morpheus; Celtic triune goddess the Morrigan, foreteller of doom in battle; the Tenebrae, daughters of *Erebus* (darkness) and *Nyx* (night); *Achlys*, the poisonous personification of misery and sadness.

Then there are the *Erinyes*, known as the Furies, goddesses who punished oathbreakers and were said to embody the act of self-cursing. They were born from blood drops spilled from Uranus's castration. They had bat wings, snakes for hair, and bleeding eyes, and they carried scourges with which they castigated wrongdoers. *Alecto* (the unremitting) punished moral misdeeds with madness. *Megaera* (the jealous one) caused envy and condemned acts of infidelity. *Tisiphone* (the "venger") was Tartarus's blood-cloaked guardian and denizen of Dis who punished crimes of homicide.

QABALAH

The 9 of Swords is Yesod in Yetzirah. Yesod יסוד, the ninth sephira, translates as "foundation" or "basis"—that which lies beneath the real world, Malkuth.[181] Here the light of the previous sephiroth gathers before taking physical form. Yesod corresponds to sex, the moon, the unconscious, the imagination, magic, and the first step on spiritual journeys. All nines are places of power.

---

181. In Hebrew, the *yesodot* are the elements of the periodic table. Yesod is also sometimes called *tzaddik*, the "righteous one."

Swords correspond to Yetzirah (the Formative World), third of four worlds, and *vav* ו, the third letter in יהוה. *Vav*, "nail," joins two disparate elements. Yetzirah holds the intellect's blueprints for creation, endlessly created and destroyed in Yesod's imagination. The soul-part of Yetzirah is the *ruach*, or breath. According to Crowley, the *ruach* consumes itself in the 9 of Swords.[182]

As the Lord of Cruelty, Yesod shows the mind's fearful power to create our reality. But as *Strength*, *Happiness*, and *Gain*, Yesod exerts equal motivation on the human character in ways that are likely to be perceived as more constructive.

RIDER-WAITE-SMITH SYMBOLISM

© 1971 U.S. GAMES SYSTEMS, INC.

9 of Swords (*Rider-Waite-Smith Tarot*) (left)
In the rendition on the right, the nocturnal whip-poor-will, bane of insomniacs, gives form to the cruel, sleep-depriving voices implied in the Waite-Smith 9 of Swords. (*Animal Totem Tarot*)

"Utter desolation," reads Waite's description of the 9 of Swords.[183] A figure clothed in the white garb of good intentions sits upright, her hands holding her head. The nine parallel swords above her point toward the future anxiety or past regret; they seem

---

182. This act of "consuming the breath" reminds us that letter *peh* ("mouth") corresponds to Mars and letter *zain* ("sword") to Gemini. It also brings to mind the hyperventilation that often goes with panic.

183. Waite, *Pictorial Key*, 236.

almost enmeshed, like patterns of self-sustaining, destructive thought. The black background, borrowed from the Tower card, suggests this is a night terror.

On the left lower panel of the figure's bed, we see a scene apparently featuring two combatants. This recalls the martial figures of the hunt seen in many decan descriptions of Gemini II. Some have suggested this could be the myth of Cain slaying Abel with the jawbone of an ass, or Juliet's anguished cogitations as she contemplates her sleeping draught in *Romeo and Juliet*.[184]

Despite her mental torment, our heroine is safe—the coverlet strewn with roses and zodiacal signs perhaps represents the security blanket of Malkuth; the difference between mental constructs and physical reality.

THOTH SYMBOLISM

Crowley tells us that this card is described well by the distressing poem by Thomson, "The City of Dreadful Night," which makes for bleak reading. Not even the return to the Middle Pillar can save us here, for the suit of Swords is inherently full of conflict, and this is its penultimate expression. He calls it the world of the psychopath and the fanatic, where rage and hunger operate without check or balance. Nine swords of inconstant lengths all point in the negative direction. The swords are rusty and blood stained (attributes of Mars) and drip an effluvium of poison, representing toxic thought.

In the background, the whirling winged forms of the suit inevitably descend toward darkness at the bottom of the card. The sigil of Mars is bloodred while the sigil of Gemini is the noxious green of venom. Malicious words and virulent thoughts lead to pain. We are told the only recourse is resignation to martyrdom or, calling to mind the Furies, implacable revenge.

RELATED CARDS

The 9 of Swords, ruled by Mars, is the second of three Gemini minors. The destructive Tower combines with the Lovers' power of agency, unleashing a cascade of devastat-

---

184. Katz and Goodwin, *Secrets of the Waite-Smith Tarot*, 300.

ing effects: blame is cast, affairs exposed, cycles of guilt and anxiety plague the mind, sharp words cut, speech and writing cause torment.

In nines, each suit achieves the peak of its power, driving the human psyche to great heights and depths. As the 9 of Swords seethes with despair, the 9 of Wands burns with determination. The 9 of Cups brims with joy as the 9 of Pentacles hungers for acquisition. A secret to each nine can be found in the corresponding three—threes are the seed; nines, the fruit.

The 9 of Swords is the final decan of the King (RWS) or Knight (Thoth) of Swords, lending this formidable figure his sharp tongue and quick judgement. His failure complex (from his first decan, the 7 of Pentacles) can fuel his martial ruthlessness.

Finally, nine is the number and Yesod is the sephira of the Moon, underscoring the inconstant nature of this placement.

10 OF SWORDS
Lord of Ruin

Dates:[185] June 11–June 20

Astrology: Gemini, the sign ruled by Mercury

Element: Mutable air

Decan: 20°–29° Gemini; Gemini III, the decan ruled by the Sun

Picatrix **Image:** A man clothed in mail, with a bow, arrows, and quiver

Picatrix **Significations:** Audacity, honesty, division of labor, and consolation

Agrippa Image: A man seeking for arms, and a fool holding in the right hand a Bird, and in his left a pipe

Agrippa Significations: Forgetfulness, wrath, boldness, jests, scurrilities, and unprofitable words

Sephira/World: Malkuth in Yetzirah

Color(s): Citrine-olive-russet-black, all gold flecked, plus the colors of the associated majors

---

185. Dates vary annually. All decanic minor dates listed in this book are based on 2019–2020 dates.

Associated Majors: The Lovers and the Sun

Associated Minors: Shadow decan of the Queen of Cups; relates to Page/Princess of Swords as a ten

Themes and Keywords: The dark before the dawn. Death of one choice. Expulsion from the garden. Toil and trouble. Too much knowledge. End of illusions. Darkness and light. Depression. Fanaticism.

ASTROLOGY/ELEMENT

The last decan of the mercurial twins is ruled by the sun, bringer of light. But tens are ruled by the sun's antithesis Saturn, planet of darkness, and the weighty world of Earth. The sun, or ego, gets along fine with Mercury, the mind. Yet in the last card of a difficult suit, the element has degraded. It's about to move from the lightness of air to the density of earth, a difficult transition that requires something to be released with finality.

Picatrix's image shows a man well-prepared for any conflict. "Audacity, honesty, division of labor, and consolation" imply discipline: one is ready for anything in body and mind. Agrippa's image of a man "seeking for arms" and a fool holding a bird and a pipe is more cryptic. Seeking arms implies impending conflict, and the "fool" shows a deterioration of reason. That he holds an emblem of air and one of earth or Saturn is fitting. The significations show the consequences of the degradation of the suit.

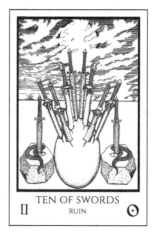

The sword-in-the-stone motif references Gemini (*zayin*); the swords pierce the twin serpents (Gemini and solar twins). (*Tabula Mundi Tarot*)

MYTHOLOGY/TIME OF YEAR

To the Egyptians, this was the final decan of the zodiac, bringing endings before the sun rose in the new year. Solstice nears, accompanied by tales of darkness and light.

Phaethon, son of sun god Helios, wanted proof of his divine parentage. Helios made a vow to give him anything—and to his chagrin, Phaethon insisted on driving the solar chariot. Flying too high, he froze the earth; when he flew too close, he scorched all living things, leading Zeus to strike him down.

Similarly, there's Icarus, son of inventive Daedalus, who built the labyrinth for King Minos. After Minos imprisoned Icarus and Daedalus to prevent knowledge of the labyrinth from spreading, they escaped using wings ingeniously constructed of wax. Icarus ignored his father's warning to not fly too close to the sun; his wings melted and he plummeted to the earth.

In another tale of solar ruin, Eos, goddess of the dawn, asked Zeus to make her lover Tithonus immortal but forgot to ask for his eternal youth. He couldn't die but aged, withered, and shrunk, transforming into an immortal cicada.

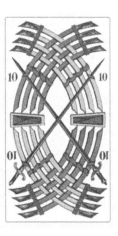

Only in the 10 of Swords do straight swords cross in Tarot de Marseille–derived decks. This is a duel to the death, and the enmeshed swords in the background admit no mediation. (*Ancient Italian Tarot*)

QABALAH

The 10 of Swords is Malkuth in Yetzirah. Malkuth ("kingdom") hangs alone at the base of the Tree, co-terminous with the fourth world, Assiah, and receives the outpouring of its predecessors. It corresponds to the Sabbath and the Shekhinah (divine feminine aspect). Malkuth's separateness is a blessing and a curse: people live apart from the divine, but reconciling actions restore creation's wholeness. In esoteric tarot, this is the "return of the Daughter" to the Great Mother, Binah. In all tens, the ripe fruit bursting with seeds falls to the ground; the cycle ends only to begin again.

Swords correspond to Yetzirah, third of four worlds, called the "Formative World" in a nod to the reality-shaping power of perception. Swords further correspond to *vav* ו, the third letter in the Divine Name, יהוה. *Vav*, "nail," joins two disparate elements, such as the imagined and actual worlds. Malkuth in Yetzirah can represent a collapsing of Yesod's infinite possibilities into a single reality.

As Lord of Ruin, Malkuth's forceful closure can foment intellectual fanaticism. As *Oppression*, *Satiety*, and *Wealth*, Malkuth drives each suit to its logical conclusion: tyranny that sows its own undoing, emotional repleteness, vast inheritances.

RIDER-WAITE-SMITH SYMBOLISM

© 1971 U.S. GAMES SYSTEMS, INC.

10 of Swords (*Rider-Waite-Smith Tarot*)

"It is not especially a card of violent death," writes Waite, as if anticipating the terror of later generations of card readers first laying eyes on this card.[186] Subsequent tarot scholars have suggested the card depicts Thomas Becket, twelfth-century Archbishop of Canterbury, gruesomely martyred in a similar manner.[187] The figure's white sleeves and red outer garment recall the Hierophant's ecclesiastical robes, as does the gesture made by his right hand. Is it the papal benediction, whose two-up, three-down configuration signifies the double human/divine nature of Christ and the Holy Trinity? Does it represent "as above, so below"? The *prana mudra* that mobilizes the body's energy?

Beneath a black sky, dawn breaks over the river, highlighting the contrast between the flowing current of the unconscious and the conscious light of the mind—and suggesting one fate that may arise, at least metaphorically, when they cannot be reconciled. But many also see it as "the darkness before the dawn," or simply a completion of the mind's tasks.

THOTH SYMBOLISM

The swords are arranged as a Tree of Life with their hilts as the sephiroth. The heart sword at the sixth sephira, Tiphareth, has been shattered by the points of swords one through five and seven through nine. The tenth sword at Malkuth is splintered. The hilt has a pentagram, for the five senses of man, and a crescent, symbol of the subconscious. Normally the lunar sephira is Yesod, but here the symbol has descended. The Yesod sword is decorated with a sphere and dot that resembles the sun symbol; the decan ruler has dropped from its normal position in Tiphareth.

The other swords have emblems of Saturn, ruling the tens; the scales at Kether for Saturn's exaltation; Binah and Chokmah with an architectural compass over an hourglass; and the rest are some form of crosses for Saturn's letter *tav/tau*. It's clear Crowley and Harris are emphasizing that the destructiveness of this card comes from Saturn, as this is a ten and the last of the combative Swords suit.

---

186. Waite, *Pictorial Key*, 234.

187. Katz and Goodwin, *Secrets of the Waite-Smith Tarot*, 297. In particular, it was said one sword was driven through his head, bringing to mind the Sun's Hebrew letter, *resh*, "head"; also present may be the Sun's red banner of life.

RELATED CARDS

In the 10 of Swords, the Sun meets the Lovers (Gemini), reminding us that the noon-day sun divides all appearances into bright surface and stark shadow. Here our mythical twins must part, as one is sacrificed on the altar of choice. In the garden, Eve takes her bite of knowledge and Eden is history! The 10 of Swords forces us to face a decision, abandoning all alternatives and leaving us prostrate, unable to see the light at the end of the tunnel.

As the Queen of Cups' first or shadow decan, the 10 of Swords sounds a desperate note. Her gifts of love and communion (the 2 and 3 of Cups) redeem its black depths, which, as a wounded healer, she knows all too well.

Tens bring endings and beginnings. In the 10 of Swords, an argument has been brought to its desperate conclusion. The 10 of Wands' outcomes are great accomplishment—or tyranny. The 10 of Cups promises love handed across generations; the 10 of Pentacles does the same for resources.

ACE OF PENTACLES
OR ACE OF DISKS
Root of the Powers of Earth

Dates:[188] March 20–June 20 (spring in the Northern Hemisphere)

Astrology: Aries-Taurus-Gemini quadrant, emphasizing the Kerubic earth sign Taurus

Element: Earth. All Aces are also associated with Spirit

Sephira/World: Kether in Assiah

Color(s): White, flecked gold

Associated Majors: The World/Universe as the elemental trump of earth

Associated Minors: Page/Princess of Pentacles

Themes and Keywords: Creation. Embodiment. Sleep and awakening. Seeds. The start of something material. Taking action. Body and Spirit conjoined. Material opportunities. Incipient resources. Incarnation and becoming. Seed money.

---

188. Dates vary annually. All Ace dates listed in this book are based on 2019–2020 dates.

ASTROLOGY/ELEMENT

Heavenly unity takes a final trajectory, its expressed tendency now moving toward a last objective: to take shape and form as the element of earth. In earth all previous elements combine and solidify. This is the suit where mankind sleeps and is awakened. This Ace is the supply point for the last of the elemental powers, "to keep silent," which is a precursor to the synthesis of all: the fifth power "to go," or to take action in the material world.

Elemental earth creates both the organic matter and the opportunities for activity: getting things done, providing practical necessities, and working with tangible resources. All beings desire the security, physical pleasure, and fulfillment this realm has to offer. Earth is the place where the complexities of life emerge and evolve.

The Ace represents initiation into this material realm of substance. Earthy Taurus is concerned with holding value and assets, Virgo with analyzing and perfecting them, and Capricorn with their use and responsible stewardship.

This Ace rules the Aries-Taurus-Gemini quadrant, centered around fertile Taurus.

The "Root of the Powers of Earth," represented as the complete
cosmos and reposing among literal roots. (*Universal Wirth Tarot*)

MYTHOLOGY/TIME OF YEAR

The cup and the disk are joined in myth, just as in the Tetragrammaton. They share the letter *heh* and the story of the daughter who becomes the mother in the Qabalistic fairy tale. For the cup of the Holy Grail was said to be fashioned from a green stone, a luminous gem loosened from Lucifer's crown when he fell from heaven. This stone was called the *tzohar*, which like the letter *heh*, has a possible translation of "window" in Genesis, where the term describes either a window or a gem providing a source of light within the Ark. Either way, there is a connotation of light, which can be taken as a metaphor for awakening.

The *tzohar* was bright as the sun, capable of illuminating the world. It was retrieved by an angel and given to Adam and Eve when they were expelled from the Garden of Eden. The Talmudic version of the legend said that the stone also functioned as an astrolabe for star viewing.

QABALAH

On the Tree of Life, the Ace of Pentacles or Disks is Kether in Assiah. All Aces correspond to the first sephira, Kether כתר or "crown." Kether is associated with the primum mobile, or first motion, a force thought responsible for the motion of all heavenly bodies. Kether contains all that will follow.

All Pentacles correspond to the fourth and last of the four worlds, Assiah (meaning "doing" or "action"), the World of Action. In Assiah we recognize something very familiar; the world perceived with all five ordinary senses. Kether in Assiah represents the physical seed or root of matter—the tiniest particles which eventually constitute the largest forms. It sets concrete reality in motion.

A cross section of a tree, interlocking Trees of Life, eyes, and maple keys
all echo themes of sun, earth, growth, and becoming. (*Rosetta Tarot*)

Assiah corresponds to final *heh* ה, the last letter of Tetragrammaton, indicating that it is the ultimate expression of creation. It corresponds also to the divine name AGLA, which is a notariqon of אדוני, אתה גיבור לעולם, *Atah Gibur Le'olam Adonai* ("Yours is the greatness forever, Lord").[189]

RIDER-WAITE-SMITH SYMBOLISM

© 1971 U.S. GAMES SYSTEMS, INC.

Ace of Pentacles (*Rider-Waite-Smith Tarot*)

The Waite-Smith pentacle, round and yellow with a five-point star emblazoned in its center, is so iconic that it's easy to forget how radical it was in 1910. European tarot decks typically showed various coins in the suit; the Tarot de Marseille's coins bore a central fourfold flower. The term *pentacle* probably derives from *pantacle*, or talisman; Smith's Wheel of Fortune is based on Éliphas Lévi's "pantacle of Ezekiel." The mystical star-coin we see in this deck ties it to the world of magic and ritual, not just commerce and exchange.

Alone among the Aces, the Ace of Pentacles lets fall no droplets or *yod*s—its mysteries are hidden and self-contained. In the foreground are lilies and cropped grass before a hedge-door twined with roses. Through the arch (whose shape recalls the wreath of the World card), we glimpse what might be the mountains seen in the Ace

---

189. This may be familiar to magical practitioners as the God name intoned when facing north in the Lesser Banishing Ritual of the Pentagram.

of Swords; both "mountain" and "gate" can reference Malkuth. In a sense, the garden path breaks the fourth wall, inviting the reader "to go" (the fifth power of the sphinx).

THOTH SYMBOLISM

The Thoth disk is more than a pentacle or coin of the realm, in spite of its markings reminiscent of paper currency. It is a living emblem of creation. Crowley tells us that all Aces are associated with the pentagram. This one most of all, as it represents Spirit ruling the four elements, thus a symbol of the Triumph of Man. Earth is not an immobile, completely passive element. Every star, every planet, every atom, is not a flat disk but a whirling sphere.

Crowley has placed his personal seal on the disk, a glyph that combines the sun and moon, conjoined as a phallic motif, with his motto *to mega therion* ("The Great Beast") around the perimeter. The number of the sun, 666, is engraved upon the testicles of the motif, which is enclosed within a seven-pointed star. This is the star, or womb, of Babalon, feminine counterpart to the Beast in the Thelemic pantheon. The entirety is enclosed in a decagram to conjure the tenth sephira, Malkuth.

RELATED CARDS

The Ace of Pentacles, in a sense representing the final letter of the Divine Name, particularly refers to all the cards in the Pentacles suit—in fact, it can be said to contain them. As both "crown" and "root," the Ace is also the throne of its Page or Princess. Because Kings/Knights reside in Chokmah and represent the *yod* (whose tip is in Kether), they also relate to the Ace.

All Aces are said to revolve around the North Pole, but the "throne of the Ace" lies at the heart of the Page/Princess's domain.[190] For the Page of Pentacles, that is the heart of the Aries-Taurus-Gemini quadrant; the corresponding majors are the Emperor, the Hierophant, and the Lovers. Thus the Ace of Pentacles has a particular connection with the Hierophant, reminding us that the physical world is an expression of the divine. As the Root of the Powers of the Earth, this Ace also corresponds to the World, the trump for the element of earth.

---

190. The Page/Princess is said to rule 0° Cancer to 30° Virgo; the Ace occupies the central 45° from 22°30' Cancer to 7°30' Virgo.

2 OF PENTACLES
OR 2 OF DISKS
Lord of Change (Harmonious Change)

Dates:[191] December 21–December 30 (includes the December solstice)

Astrology: Capricorn, the sign ruled by Saturn, with Mars exalted

Element: Cardinal earth

Decan: 0°–9° Capricorn; Capricorn I, the decan ruled by Jupiter

Picatrix **Image:** A man with a reed in his right hand and a hoopoe bird in his left

Picatrix **Significations:** Happiness, joy, and bringing things to an end that are sluggish, weak, and proceeding poorly

Agrippa Image: A woman, and a man carrying full bags

Agrippa Significations: To go forth and to rejoice, to gain and to lose with weakness and baseness

Sephira/World: Chokmah in Assiah

---

191. Dates vary annually. All decanic minor dates listed in this book are based on 2019–2020 dates.

Color(s): White, flecked red, blue, and yellow, plus the colors of the associated majors

Associated Majors: The World/Universe and the Wheel of Fortune

Associated Minors: Queen of Pentacles holds the decan; relates to King/Knight as a two

Themes and Keywords: Progressive evolution. Cycles. Expansion and contraction in phases. Material prospects. Luck versus skill. Successions, divine and material. Climbing and descent are both forward motion. Opposites working in tandem through time. Exchanges across a distance.

ASTROLOGY/ELEMENT

Saturn-ruled Capricorn's first face is ruled by Jupiter, and the twos are ruled by the zodiacal circle. Jupiter is in fall in Capricorn, but the realm of the zodiac is so lofty that the naturally opposing forces of Jupiter and Saturn work concertedly, as opposites are different sides of the same coin.

The zodiac is a dimension of cyclic force, the wheel of Jupiter writ large. With the supportive boundaries of Saturn established, the wheels within wheels endlessly turn in linear time, creating change so naturally progressive that it can only be harmonious. Ups and downs, gains and losses, spiritualism and materialism, expansions and contractions, are nothing less than that which drives evolution.

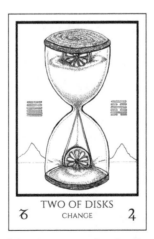

TWO OF DISKS

♑ CHANGE ♃

The hourglass of Capricorn contains the churning wheels of Jupiter: fortunes change over time. (*Tabula Mundi Tarot*)

In *Picatrix*'s image, a man holds a reed and a hoopoe bird. In Egyptian iconography reeds were of the blessed afterlife, a heavenly star realm, and the hoopoe was a symbol of patriarchal succession. The significations speak of jovial joys and saturnine necessary endings. Agrippa's couple carries full bags, with significations of going forth and both gaining and losing.

MYTHOLOGY/TIME OF YEAR

Cyclic succession is encoded in the story of Kronos (Saturn), who deposed his father Ouranos and was overthrown by his son Zeus (Jupiter). In the Titanomachy (Titan War), Zeus and the Olympians unseated Kronos and the Titans, and Zeus inherited the realm of the heavens (zodiac) as his domain.

In another story involving Capricorn Jupiter themes, monstrous Typhon, son of Gaia (Earth) and Tartarus (Hell), attempted in turn to defeat Zeus for supremacy over the cosmos. Typhon frightened the gods and Pan, in his panic, changed into a goat-fish, leaping into a river. While Zeus ultimately prevailed with his thunderbolt, in one close battle he used an adamantine sickle and was disarmed. Typhon used it to remove the tendons behind Zeus's knees. Pan, seeing him thus *lamed*, blew his reed pipes to frighten Typhon and call Hermes, who retrieved Zeus's sinews so he could win the battle.

The time of year includes Yule, and iconic Santa Claus combines elements of both Jupiter (gifts) and Saturn (consequences of behavior).

QABALAH

The 2 of Pentacles is Chokmah חכמה, "wisdom," in Assiah. Chokmah is associated with the zodiac—below the primum mobile in the celestial concentric model, but above the orbits of the seven traditional planets. It is the wellspring of the Pillar of Force; its "wisdom" is the flash of insight that appears as if from nowhere, just as Chokmah appears from the empty point of Kether.

All Pentacles correspond to the last of the four worlds, Assiah, the World of Action; here we find our familiar world of the five ordinary senses. While matter does not begin to take form until the next sephira, Binah, Chokmah in Assiah hints at its ever-shifting nature. The same initial impulse that causes form to crystallize also causes it to break down.

As the "Lord of Change," Chokmah in Assiah reminds us that in the Active World, each action corresponds to an equal and opposite reaction. In Atziluth, Briah, and Yetzirah, Chokmah similarly balances one element with another, resulting in *Dominion*, *Love*, and *Peace*.

RIDER-WAITE-SMITH SYMBOLISM

2 of Pentacles (*Rider-Waite-Smith Tarot*) (left)
What would later emerge as a lemniscate on Smith's card began as an
S-curve on Marseille-style tarots (right). It served as a convenient ribbon for
displaying the maker's mark. (*Camoin-Jodorowsky Tarot de Marseille*)

Waite describe Smith's image as "a young man in the act of dancing," bringing to mind ceaseless motion and inevitable change.[192] The hat of unusual height and nimble footwork bring to mind the whirling dervishes who wear the *sikke*, representing the tombstone of ego-death, though no one knows Smith's actual intentions.

The shape Waite describes as an "endless cord" is seen as a lemniscate, like the infinity symbols on the Magician and Strength cards. Since this is a solstice card, it

---

192. Waite, *Pictorial Key*, 278.

may allude to the analemma, which traces the sun's journey across the sky. But it also refers to the traditional woodcut designs of early tarot, where the 2 of Coins always bears a similarly S-shaped curve hugging the two rounds.

The turbulent sea with its two ships signifies both turbulent, interesting times and the act of communication over distances. It is a stage card, reminding us that this scene and the role we play in it shall soon pass.

THOTH SYMBOLISM

Crowley's *Liber LXV* is called the "Heart Girt with a Serpent." In one line he writes of a snake of emerald that encloses the universe. This is the green line that encloses the void, the bounding sense of linear time. We see the serpent as lemniscate, an ouroboros Crowley calls "of the endless band" that reminds us of the connection between earth and Spirit and the bottom and top of a cycle.[193] The serpent, ever symbolic of wisdom (Chokmah) and will, is crowned, indicative of Chokmah's direct connection to Kether. The crown has seven points, a Venusian reference, since love is the counterpart of will, and together they are driving the creative force in the material journey.

Crowley calls the serpent a glyph of the 0 = 2 equation: $(+1) + (-1) = 0$. Opposite forces are contained within the whole of the universe. The two "pantacles" spin as wheels in opposing directions. The yin-yang disks are painted in all the elemental colors, with the four dots comprising the dual centers inscribed with elemental symbols.

RELATED CARDS

The 2 of Pentacles correlates to Capricorn's first decan, ruled by Jupiter. Together the Wheel of Fortune (Jupiter) and the saturnine Devil (Capricorn) give matter momentum; indeed, as the "Lord of Change," the 2 of Pentacles is a kind of miniature Wheel. Jupiter is in the sign of its fall at the Northern Hemisphere winter solstice or shortest day; from here the light will only increase. Regardless of hemisphere, the message is the same: things are about to change.[194]

---

193. Crowley, *Book of Thoth*, 178.

194. The Southern Hemisphere equivalent is the 2 of Cups.

It is the Queen of Pentacles' middle decan (her others are the 10 of Wands/Sagittarius III and the 3 of Pentacles/Capricorn II). Her shadow decan's oppressive drive to succeed gives way to wheeling and dealing, allowing her natural productivity to flourish in her final decan.

Twos reflect conscious awareness. The 2 of Wands sees other worlds to dominate; the 2 of Cups emotionally connects another; the 2 of Swords perceives others' thoughts and opinions; the 2 of Pentacles trades with other systems of value.

Kings (RWS) and Knights (Thoth), like twos, reside in Chokmah; the King/Knight of Pentacles is the provider for the Active World.

3 OF PENTACLES
OR 3 OF DISKS
Lord of Work(s) (Material Works)

Dates:[195] December 31–January 9

Astrology: Capricorn, the sign ruled by Saturn, with Mars exalted

Element: Cardinal earth

Decan: 10°–19° Capricorn; Capricorn II, the decan ruled by Mars

***Picatrix* Image:** A man with a common ape in front of him

***Picatrix* Significations:** Seeking to do what cannot be done and to attain what cannot be

Agrippa Image: Two women, and a man looking toward a bird flying in the air

Agrippa Significations: Requiring those things which cannot be done, searching after those things which cannot be known

Sephira/World: Binah in Assiah

---

195. Dates vary annually. All decanic minor dates listed in this book are based on 2019–2020 dates.

Color(s): Gray, flecked pink, plus the colors of the associated majors

Associated Majors: The World/Universe and the Tower

Associated Minors: Queen of Pentacles

Themes and Keywords: Evolutionary striving. Building up something material. Aspiration and growth. Energy to create. Construction and production over time. Unstoppable energy awakens, building blocks of form. Cell division and multiplication. Collaboration.

ASTROLOGY/ELEMENT

Saturn's influence doubles here as it rules both Capricorn and the sphere of the threes. Mars, ruling the decan, is exalted in the sign. Combine the vigor and force of Mars with the maturing ambition of Capricorn, add Saturn's structural framework and form and the passage of time, and something will take shape. This is how organisms and empires are built: with discipline and one unit at a time. Resources are gathered and energy is applied. A blueprint is followed, and as a result, one is bound to a form.

Stinging and martial, the paper wasp works tirelessly to build its nest, here featuring alchemy's *tria prima*—mercury, sulfur, and salt. (*Rosetta Tarot*)

Picatrix gives the image of a man with a common ape in front of him, hinting at evolutionary forces. Agrippa's image has people looking toward a flying bird, suggesting upward aspiration. Both give significations about seeking what cannot be done, attained, or known. Mars strives in the sign of its exaltation, with a desire to succeed and create in spite of, or with the blessing of, Saturn's limits and boundaries. Mankind aspires and over time progresses step-by-step.

MYTHOLOGY/TIME OF YEAR

The Sumerian god Enki, identified with the goat-fish (Capricorn) and semen (Mars), was called Lord of the Earth. He was the patron and founder of Eridu, the first city ever created according to Sumerian belief. In the creation myth *Enuma Elish*, he formed the first human workers from clay and blood. They propagated until they angered the god Enlil. Their long lives and extreme fertility had to be limited (Saturn) to appease the gods.

The Mesopotamian poem *Epic of Gilgamesh* begins with the king of Uruk, called "He Who Sees the Unknown" and "He Who Saw the Abyss." King Gilgamesh meets the ape-like Enkidu, created by the gods to keep Gilgamesh in check. Enkidu becomes civilized through sexual initiation, and the two men become friends and engaged on a quest. After Enkidu is killed, Gilgamesh becomes obsessed with seeking the secret of immortality, which he ultimately learns is futile. Yet in a sense, the king achieves it through his works and building projects—and the enduring of his saga.

QABALAH

The 3 of Pentacles is Binah in Assiah. Binah בימה, the third sephira, translates as "understanding" and is associated with the slowest, outermost classical planet, Saturn. Sometimes referred to as a "palace of mirrors," Binah begins the Pillar of Form and is the Tree of Life's first experience of separateness—sea from sky, inside from outside, above from below. With Binah, reality begins to take literal form; hence Binah is also called the "Great Mother." As life gains substance, it also gains limits; in Binah's fertile seas, death too is born—reminding us that Saturn's bountiful harvests fall from the reaper's scythe.

All Pentacles correspond to the last of the four worlds, Assiah, the World of Action and the five ordinary senses. Here in Binah, the combustion-engine of matter receives

Chokmah's spark and the wheels begin to turn. As the Lord of Work(s), Binah expresses the natural drive of Pentacles to fabricate and manifest. As *Virtue*, *Abundance*, and *Sorrow*, Binah seeks to regulate, connect, and recognize.

RIDER-WAITE-SMITH SYMBOLISM

3 of Pentacles (*Rider-Waite-Smith Tarot*)

Of the three collaborators in this image, Waite chose to single out the artisan paused in his masonry work at left, suggesting that the 8 of Pentacles' "apprentice or amateur … has received his reward and is now at work in earnest." He's even standing on the 8 of Pentacles' own bench! Waite tells us the setting is a monastery, so it may be inferred that the clerical figure resides there, while the fancifully dressed figure holding the blueprint is likely a well-heeled sponsor.

In the stone arch above their heads the three pentacles are arranged like the three supernal sephiroth. At their center and in the space just below are two images of the quartered circle, symbol of earth, Malkuth, and matter. The lower one forms the center of a five-petaled rose, bringing to mind the four-and-one formula of Spirit + matter. Also, the term *sub rosa* ("under the rose") means "in secrecy"—one way to refer to the power of earth: to keep silent.

THOTH SYMBOLISM

Crowley tells us that with threes, the idea has been fertilized and the triangle formulated, creating a stability from which a child can be issued. Material creation is especially emphasized in the suit of Disks. The image in the card is of a pyramid as viewed from its apex, underscoring the idea of aspiration. At the base of the pyramid, three wheels are marked with the alchemical glyphs of mercury, sulphur, and salt and represent various types of universal building blocks: the three primal elements air, fire, and water; the gunas (tendencies) sattva, rajas, and tamas; or the three mother letters of the Hebrew alphabet: *aleph*, *mem*, and *shin*.

The wheels and pyramid are reddish for the energy of Mars. They are built upon crystallized wave forms in saturnine black and gray, representing "the Great Sea of Binah in the Night of Time." They look both like waves or sand dunes of the desert, another reference to Saturn. The frozen or solid look of the waves allude to structural integrity and form.

RELATED CARDS

The 3 of Pentacles brings us the second decan of saturnine Capricorn; this decan is ruled by Mars, which is exalted in the sign. Two fearsome major arcana, the Tower (Mars) and the Devil (Capricorn), correspond to the card—but as the Lord of the Gates of Matter, the Devil directs the Tower's fiery, stormy energy toward constructive ends, just as a piston engine puts flammable fuel to work.

THREE OF DISKS
WORK

The lightning of the Tower (Mars) sparks life into DNA and the building blocks (Capricorn) of matter. (*Tabula Mundi Tarot*)

Threes firmly shape the essence of their suit. Through tireless collaborative effort, the 3 of Pentacles converts matter into products. The 3 of Wands gives ambition a channel, the 3 of Cups supports circles of mutual affection, and the 3 of Swords harbors irreversible insights.

The 3 connects doubly to Queens: (1) it is the Queen of Pentacles' final decan, where her productivity bears fruit; and (2) Queens reside in Binah, each giving birth after her suit's nature.

Finally, three, Binah, and the World/Universe are the number, sephira, and path of Saturn—all expressing themes of closure and realization.

4 OF PENTACLES
OR 4 OF DISKS
Lord of Power (Earthly Power)

Dates:[196] January 10–January 19

Astrology: Capricorn, the sign ruled by Saturn, with Mars exalted

Element: Cardinal earth

Decan: 20°–29° Capricorn; Capricorn III, the decan ruled by the Sun

***Picatrix* Image:** A man holding a book which he opens and closes, and before him is the tail of a fish

***Picatrix* Significations:** Wealth and the accumulation of money and increase and embarking on trade and pressing on to a good end

Agrippa Image: A woman chaste in body, and wise in her work, and a banker gathering his money together on the table

Agrippa Significations: To govern in prudence, in covetousness of money, and in avarice

---

196. Dates vary annually. All decanic minor dates listed in this book are based on 2019–2020 dates.

Sephira/World: Chesed in Assiah

Color(s): Deep azure flecked yellow, plus the colors of the associated majors

Associated Majors: The World/Universe and the Sun

Associated Minors: Shadow decan of Knight/Prince of Swords

Themes and Keywords: Status and structure. Stabilizing the practical. Stagnation via solid position. The vault, the fortress, the bunker, the throne. Authority and responsibility, law and order. The CEO. Monarchs and plutocrats. Accumulating wealth. Avarice, covetousness, gluttony.

ASTROLOGY/ELEMENT

The last Capricorn decan networks the three planetary heavyweights: Saturn ruling the sign, the Sun ruling the decan, and Jupiter as sovereign of fours. Combined in the suit of Pentacles, these three icons of patriarchal supremacy confer a lot of clout: earthly power, one of Capricorn's worldly ambitions. There is great potential here for status and benevolent authority. But it is said that "absolute power corrupts absolutely." History is riddled with monarchs and moguls whose avarice know no bounds. Rulers declare themselves emperors, emperors declare themselves gods, and plutocrats pursue ever more obscene levels of wealth with single-purpose.

Power as money: a steel bank vault door, its shape suggestive of the sun glyph,
securely stows the material treasures of the 4 of Pentacles/Disks. (*Rosetta Tarot*)

Picatrix's man appears to be repeatedly consulting a book—perhaps "the books" of accountancy. Before him is a fish tail—is this a reference to the end of the zodiac and perhaps mortality? The signification mentions both financial accumulation and "pressing on to a good end." Agrippa gives a chaste and wise working woman and a banker gathering money before him with significations of both prudence and greed.

MYTHOLOGY/TIME OF YEAR

The Jupiter-Saturn-Sun combination of masculine gods is potent. The Oracle of Apollo claimed Zeus, Hades, and Helios-Dionysus (or sometimes Serapis) were "three gods in one godhead."[197] The Graeco-Egyptian solar god Serapis combined attributes of Zeus, Hades, Dionysus, and Osiris. His worship was introduced to unite the Greek and Egyptian subjects of Hellenistic times and to consolidate the power of the Ptolemaic dynasty.

Powerful gods are often hailed as the all-seeing eye, like the one seen on the US dollar. We've mentioned Capricorn as devilish Enki, Lord of the Sacred Eye. Gods of Saturn, Sun, and Jupiter are all-powerful deities in some manner, and many have been associated with or referred to as "eyes."[198] In the Orphic hymns, Sol is called Hyperion, immortal Zeus, and cosmic eye. Apollo/Helios was called the eye of Zeus.

Power combined with greed and arrogance is illustrated by stories of King Midas, follower of Pan. The king's avarice resulted in his infamous golden touch "gift" from Dionysus, and his hubris led to being cursed with the ears of an ass by Apollo.

QABALAH

The 4 of Pentacles is Chesed in Assiah. Chesed חסד, the fourth sephira, translates as "mercy" or "loving kindness" and corresponds to generous, expansive Jupiter. Chesed's counterpart is Geburah, the fifth sephira; one gives, one takes away. As the first sephira below the supernal triad and the abyss of Da'ath, Chesed is sometimes

---

197. Julian, *Hymn to King Helios*, 10.

198. Saturn: Titan Kronos and his brothers, the one-eyed Cyclopses who made Zeus's thunderbolt; Egyptian Set; Sumerian Enki. Sun: solar gods such as Ra, Horus, Sol, Hyperion, Helios, Mithras, Apollo, and Dionysus. Jupiter: Zeus, Fortuna, and the Fates, who shared an eye between them.

called the "Kether of the lower sephiroth." The loving, patriarchal provider god conceived by humans abides here, as does the first day of creation; Chesed is the ever-overflowing faucet from which our mundane reality flows.

All Pentacles correspond to the last of the four worlds, Assiah, the World of Action and the five ordinary senses. Chesed in Assiah draws together material resources, making it a storehouse or bank for all our bodies need to survive. As the Lord of Power, Chesed guarantees material security in Assiah; as *Completion*, it promotes creative visions; as *Luxury* and *Truce*, it offers points of emotional and intellectual respite before the rigors of Geburah.

RIDER-WAITE-SMITH SYMBOLISM

4 of Pentacles (*Rider-Waite-Smith Tarot*) (left)
In the image on the right, the negative space between the four coins provides the perfect space for a heraldic shield in Marseille tarots—conveying, also, the family's secure continuity. (*Camoin-Jodorowsky Tarot de Marseille*)

The Scrooge-like posture of Smith's king on the 4 of Pentacles is no accident: "He holds," Waite says, "to what he has." Coins under his feet, in his arms, and crowning his head indicate that money is literally on his mind. His "mural" crown is like Justice's—a stylization of a city's fortified walls and towers. He is clothed entirely in red, the color of embodied life, and furs (perhaps a reference to the "bestial" Devil).

What's more, if you turn the card upside down, you can imagine that the pentacles are arranged like the lowest sephiroth of the Tree of Life.

Behind him is a sizeable city, but our king is seated on a stone block (like the one in the 2 of Swords and the Devil) on a "stage" in the foreground. This suggests his acquisitiveness is self-referential and separate from the good of his people; he wears the trappings of power in the role of a king, but he is distant from the will of society.

THOTH SYMBOLISM

The image is of a mighty four-walled stronghold on a hill and plateau. In the "Rite of Saturn" Crowley describes it as the "Fortress that is upon the Frontier of the Abyss," appropriate for Chesed in the suit of earth.[199] Even the "disks" themselves are solid squares, as they are formed by the tops of the towers in each corner of the structure. Each is marked with one of the elemental symbols, fire and water above air and earth.

There is only one entrance to the citadel: the southern gate (Malkuth, the material world), which is flanked by pylons. Though the building is in a solar-colored desert, it is surrounded by a protective moat in the colors of the sephira. When the drawbridge is up, it appears there is no other way in or out, as the very small rear opening has no bridge. Each parapet is topped by crenellations, between which defensive weaponry can be aimed. There are six on each wall, the number of the Sun.

RELATED CARDS

The 4 of Pentacles brings together the Devil (Capricorn) and the Sun. Here, the Devil's adroit handling of material goods and the sun's sovereign light combine to produce not just enough, but riches to spare. With these riches comes power over the same operations that produced the wealth in the 2 and 3 and an instinct to maintain and preserve that power.

Fours gather together an abundance of their suit resources. While the 4 of Pentacles amasses treasure, the 4 of Wands publicly aligns community interests. The 4 of Cups holds a fullness of feelings; the 4 of Swords holds thoughts gathered in stillness.

---

199. Crowley, *Rites of Eleusis*.

The 4 of Pentacles is also the first or shadow decan of the Knight (RWS) or Prince (Thoth) of Swords; he knows the dark side of power and, at his best, fights idealistically to improve the rules of the game.

In planetary terms, four is Jupiter's number, and the Wheel of Fortune is Jupiter's path, for comfort and security are among the things asked of a benevolent fate.

5 OF PENTACLES
OR 5 OF DISKS
Lord of Worry (Material Trouble)

Dates:[200] April 20–April 29

Astrology: Taurus, the sign ruled by Venus

Element: Fixed earth

Decan: 0°–9° Taurus; Taurus I, the decan ruled by Mercury

Picatrix **Image:** A woman with curly hair, who has one son wearing clothing looking like flame, and she is wearing garments of the same sort

Picatrix **Significations:** Plowing, working on the land, sciences, geometry, sowing, building

Agrippa Image: A naked man, an archer, harvester or husbandman

Agrippa Significations: To sow, plough, build, people, and divide the earth, according to the rules of geometry

---

200. Dates vary annually. All decanic minor dates listed in this book are based on 2019–2020 dates.

Sephira/World: Geburah in Assiah

Color(s): Red, flecked black, plus the colors of the associated majors

Associated Majors: The Hierophant and the Magician/Magus

Associated Minors: Knight of Pentacles (RWS) or Prince of Disks (Thoth)

Themes and Keywords: Fear of losing power and stability. Poverty mentality. Nervous stress over resources and lack thereof. Planning ahead. Gears grinding and millstones turning; throttling of power. Renunciation. Severity in financial, practical, and bodily matters. Strain of inertia. Sacred doubt.

ASTROLOGY/ELEMENT

The sign of the bull is ruled by comfort-loving Venus, but decan ruler Mercury and sephira ruler Mars are not particularly comfortable with the sign. Taurus has a tendency toward inertia and deliberation, with a general dislike of being rushed. It's incompatible with Mercury's speediness of thought and contradictory to Mars's naturally impulsive drive. Taurus is an acquisitive sign, so the thought processes represented by Mercury turn to materialistic concerns. Add the irritant of Mars, and the result is fear of not having enough.

Taurus is a fertile sign, good at preparing for future harvests if one lets go of ineffective worry and applies energy productively. *Picatrix* and Agrippa only subtly hint at any poverty, through "flame-like garments"—or lack thereof. The significations both describe plowing and sowing (Mars) and using geometry (Mercury) to work and divide the land (Taurus). Will the gardens thus divided be fruitful? It is natural to fret when uncertainty potentially imperils material security. But worry leading to paralysis and inertia is fruitless.

Miniature figures enact the mercurial arts of "dividing the land," as mentioned in *Picatrix's* decan description. (*Liber T: Tarot of Stars Eternal*)

A "steampunk worry machine" captures Mercury's painstaking calculations and premonitions of disaster in a graphic representation of Murphy's Law.201 (*Rosetta Tarot*)

MYTHOLOGY/TIME OF YEAR

Sumerian goddess Inanna (Akkadian Ishtar) embodies the planetary energies, as she has the sexuality of Venus, the capriciousness and cunning of Mercury, and the war-like nature of Mars. In one particular Taurean tale, she demanded the Bull of Heaven

---

201. Meleen, *Book of Seshet*, 202.

from her father; she wanted to use it as revenge against Gilgamesh for spurning her advances. She threatened to break the gates of hell to cause the dead to eat all of the food and all of the living. After she was given the bull, it caused widespread devastation: earthquakes, spring drought, and crop destruction.

Gilgamesh and Enkidu killed the bull, and Enkidu further insulted Inanna by throwing the bull's "thigh" (genitals) at her. Enkidu is marked for death and thus becomes increasingly apprehensive, worrying about his future. He dreams of a "house of dust" whose inhabitants have only feathers to wear and only clay to eat.[202] Enkidu grows sick and dies, causing a perpetual worry in Gilgamesh, who now fears his own mortality, and pursues a quest for eternal life.

QABALAH

The 5 of Pentacles is Geburah in Assiah. Geburah גבורה, the fifth sephira, can translate as "severity," "strength," or "restraint." Corresponding to fierce Mars, Geburah acts as a corrective to the free flow of Chesed; Chesed and Geburah act as the inviting and repelling arms of divinity. Also known as *din* (judgement) and *pachad* (fear), Geburah separates individuals, giving each room to breathe; similarly, on the fifth day, the Creator divided sea from sky. It is this separating, testing, subjectively challenging nature of Geburah/Mars that gives the fives of tarot their conflictual nature.

All Pentacles correspond to the last of the four worlds, Assiah, the World of Action and the five senses. Geburah in Assiah restricts the flow of material sustenance, pushing people to acquire survival skills like planning and resourcefulness. As the Lord of Worry, Geburah forces people to face the specter of poverty and isolation. As *Strife*, *Disappointment*, and *Defeat*, it challenges people with master classes in ambition, emotional loss, and unfairness.

---

202. Dalley, *Myths from Mesopotamia*, 89.

RIDER-WAITE-SMITH SYMBOLISM

5 of Pentacles (*Rider-Waite-Smith Tarot*)

"The card foretells material trouble above all," Waite says, stating what seems fairly obvious. Two ragged figures—"mendicants," according to his *Pictorial Key*—limp past what is described as a "lighted casement" in a snowstorm.[203] Their situation is desperate, conveying both physical infirmity and poverty. The stained glass of the window signifies a church, a reminder of the card's connection to the Hierophant. Is its role to exclude, or to provide refuge? Casement windows have hinged edges, allowing them to open and shut rather than being fixed in place. Is this edifice, then, one that grants access or denies it?

Also significant is the configuration of the pentacles, which echo the arrangement of the first five sephiroth on the Tree of Life, reminding us that when we arrive at the fifth sephira, Geburah, hardship and severity is to be expected. Interestingly, Smith's way of drawing the ragged garments evokes the decan commentators' "flamelike garments," though this (like the majority of Qabalah allusions we impute to Waite-Smith cards) is surely unintentional.

---

203. Waite, *Pictorial Key*, 272.

THOTH SYMBOLISM

Crowley speaks of the word worry as a verb referring to seizing and strangling and warns that Disks can be "stolid and obstinate," some of the more negative connotations of Taurus.[204] This is shown as great wheels or gears grinding to a halt, as Mercury's motion is interrupted by the inertia of Taurus and the disruption inherent in the fives. The disks form the inverted pentagram, a disturbance of matter.

The axles of the disks are marked by the Hindu elemental *tattvas*. The red triangle of fire, the yellow square of earth, the blue circle of air, and the silver crescent of water are all weighing down on the black egg of Spirit at the lowest point. Crowley tells us that the effect is that of an earthquake and of strain due to inaction. The fire energy is lacking, as shown by the dull color of the fire symbol and the color of the sephira shown at the edges of the disks: red that has been polluted by flecks of black.

RELATED CARDS

The 5 of Pentacles juxtaposes the Magician (Mercury) and the Hierophant (Taurus)—two figures who mediate between heaven and earth. However, they do so in different ways—the lockpicking Magician seeks mercurial shortcuts and bargains with Spirit, while the key-keeping Hierophant safeguards well-worn, narrow paths to spiritual enlightenment. By using Mercury's analytic skills and the bull's stabilizing influence, the 5's *Worry* can be converted to the 6's *Success*.

As the Knight/Prince of Pentacles' central decan, the 5 of Pentacles guarantees a mind willing to sweat the details to prevent disaster. Ideally, he knows better than to rest on the 4 of Wands' (his previous decan) laurels, for his crop will not tend itself.

Fives create motion and imbalance. While the 5 of Pentacles deprives us of material resources, the 5 of Cups strips away emotional security. The 5 of Swords tests our perception of the "rules"; the 5 of Wands sets ambitions ablaze.

Finally, five is the number and Geburah is the sephira of Mars. The corresponding path is the Tower, the source of character-developing challenges we fear but also need.

---

204. Crowley, *Book of Thoth*, 181. In the body, Taurus rules the neck.

6 OF PENTACLES
OR 6 OF DISKS
Lord of Success (Material Success)

Dates:[205] April 30–May 9 (includes the cross-quarter holiday)

Astrology: Taurus, the sign ruled by Venus

Element: Fixed earth

Decan: 10°–19° Taurus; Taurus II, the decan ruled by the Moon

Picatrix **Image:** A man with a body like a camel, who has cow's hooves on his fingers, and he is completely covered by a torn linen cloth. He desires to work the land, sow, and build

Picatrix **Significations:** Nobility, power, rewarding the people

Agrippa Image: A naked man, holding in his hand a key

Agrippa Significations: Power, nobility, and dominion over people

Sephira/World: Tiphareth in Assiah

---

205. Dates vary annually. All decanic minor dates listed in this book are based on 2019–2020 dates.

Color(s): Gold amber; plus the colors of the associated majors

Associated Majors: The Hierophant and the Priestess

Associated Minors: Knight of Pentacles (RWS) or Prince of Disks (Thoth)

Themes and Keywords: Appreciation of beauty and enjoyment of the present moment. Fecundity and wealth. Harmony in practical matters. Generosity and sweetness. Philanthropy and humanitarianism. Heaven and earth. Complimentary forces joined. Body and soul, temple and spirit, priest and priestess. Eleusinian mysteries. The key to the inner sanctum. Sensuality. Fertilization. Potential realized. Kairos, the perfect moment.

ASTROLOGY/ELEMENT

The middle decan of Venusian Taurus is ruled by the Moon, exalted in the sign. The harmony is enhanced as the moon's natural consort, the sun, rules the sixes. The sun warms the earth and provides the moon's light. The sun betokens sovereignty and the moon is associated with the population. In the harmonious world of the 6, benevolent rulers and those blessed with bounty care and share with people; their altruism is a cure for the errors of the 4 and 5.

With female workers and queens, bees are Venusian (ruler of Taurus), lunar (exaltation of Taurus), and solar (representative of sixes) as daytime nectar gatherers. (*Rosetta Tarot*)

Picatrix mentions a man wishing to plant and build. His features of camel and cow denote the moon and Taurus. His linen covering could allude to the shroud of Jesus, who famously said it is "easier for a camel to go through the eye of a needle than for a rich man to get into heaven."[206] Agrippa's image is of a naked man holding a key, suggestive of the Hierophant of Taurus. The significations of both are of nobility, power, and the ruling and rewarding of the populace.

MYTHOLOGY/TIME OF YEAR

Here are holy and fertile unions: Adam and Eve in Eden; Osiris and Isis as bull and cow. The Mesopotamian trinity Nanna (moon), Utu (sun), and Inanna (the morning star, Venus), also perfectly combines the correspondences.[207]

Nanna, the moon, was son of sky and earth. He rode a winged bull and governed cattle breeding (Taurus). Some myths say he was father of Inanna (Venus) and her twin/consort Utu (sun). Like Eve, Inanna was at first virginal, but she tasted of the fruit of a tree and became "knowledgeable."

Utu took the form of a wild bull and was known for kindness, generosity, and relieving suffering. His wife Sherida was also Venusian, the goddess of beauty and sexuality.

The decan contains the Northern Hemisphere spring festival May Day, descended from Roman Floralia celebrating Flora, goddess of vegetation and fertility, and the Maiouma rites of Dionysus and Aphrodite. The Gaelic Beltane, when cattle were driven to summer pastures, encouraged growth and fecundity, and the Wiccan celebration enacts the union of Lord and Lady.

QABALAH

The 6 of Pentacles/Disks represents Tiphareth in Assiah. Tiphareth תיפארת, the sixth sephira, is the "heart" of the Tree, balanced not only between the Pillars of Mercy and Severity, but also between Kether and Yesod/Malkuth. Hermetic Qabalists translate it as "beauty"; other translations include "adornment," "splendor," and "glory." Tiphareth

---

206. Matthew 19:24 (Authorized King James Version).

207. Sumerian Nanna, Utu, Inanna equate to Akkadian deities Sin, Shamash, and Ishtar. These were divine triads corresponding to Moon, Sun, and Venus.

corresponds to the golden sun and the third day of creation (the fructifying of the land). By bringing opposing forces into proportion, Tiphareth nurtures life on earth just as our sun does. This benign creative force gives the sixes of tarot their clear sense of purpose.

Golden pentacles as eggs capture both the lunar (moon in Taurus, maternal hens) and solar (six, gold); these content domestic fowl are the picture of *Success*. (*Animal Totem Tarot*)

All Pentacles correspond to the last of the four worlds, Assiah, the World of Action and of the physical senses. Tiphareth in Assiah supplies material wherewithal; here resources find an effective channel where they can open opportunities in the real world.

As the "Lord of Success," Tiphareth brings about tangible achievements. As *Victory*, *Pleasure*, and *Science*, Tiphareth affords a sense of heroic belonging, emotional fulfillment, and solutions to tough problems.

RIDER-WAITE-SMITH SYMBOLISM

6 of Pentacles (*Rider-Waite-Smith Tarot*)

Waite and Smith viewed the central figure on this card as a model of philanthropy: "It is a testimony to his own success in life, as well as to his goodness of heart." If our true wealth is measured by what we can afford to give, it's as important to *share* what one has so it can be acquired in the first place. The almsgiver's hands convey a Kabbalistic principle key to understanding the two previous sephiroth, Chesed and Geburah: mercy is infinite, but must be meted out judiciously. It's possible that the two needy figures being helped are the mendicants of the preceding card, the 5 of Pentacles.

A close examination of the figure's apparel visually alludes to the garb of the Priestess and the Hierophant; Waite describes it as "the guise of a merchant." Given that this is a stage card, perhaps we can infer that when sharing our success, we perform a role that is pleasing to the divine—i.e., "salvation by works."

THOTH SYMBOLISM

From a distance, the image resembles the circle-and-dot motif of the sun, gold, and a fertilized ovum. The disks marked with the planetary symbols are in hexagram formation, surrounding the central rose cross representing the sun. The hexagram represents the achievement of "knowledge and conversation of the Holy Guardian Angel," or union of God and man. Those familiar with the Ritual of the Hexagram will notice the similarities in planetary placement as imposed on the Tree of Life. The rose of forty-nine petals (7 x 7, Venus) is mounted upon the cross of the sacrificial solar gods. The diagonal leaves extending diagonally behind the rose are traditionally marked with INRI alluding to Tiphareth and the Sun, and in Thelema with the IAO formula (Isis-Apophis-Osiris), a cyclic process of spiritual evolution.

The lunar (consciousness) is in balance (Tiphareth). In Disks, this rewards (Sun) the enterprising and industrious (Taurus), however transiently (Moon). Crowley, ever the realist, exhorts us to remember that all success is temporary; "how brief a halt upon the Path of Labour!"[208]

RELATED CARDS

The 6 of Pentacles brings together two guardians of the sacred: the Hierophant (Taurus) and the High Priestess (Moon). They suggest that when inner devotion aligns with external beliefs, the result is real success. In this perfect moment, our works can take root and flourish—whether they are business ventures, food crops, or creative projects.

The Knight of Pentacles knows the delights of his first decan, the 4 of Wands, cannot last; he labors in his central decan, the 5 of Pentacles/Lord of Worry, to guarantee the fruits yielded here in his final decan, the 6.

Sixes bring purpose to their suits. The 6 of Pentacles' success leads to generosity toward others. The 6 of Wands channels pride into a larger sense of identity. The 6 of Cups fosters our sense of caring and altruism; the 6 of Swords resolves conflicts.

Six is the number and Tiphareth is the sephira of the Sun, making this card a little solar as well as lunar. Each harmonizes imbalances, helping us find meaning in life and a reason for being.

---

208. Crowley, *Book of Thoth*, 182.

7 OF PENTACLES
OR 7 OF DISKS
Lord of Failure (Success Unfulfilled)

Dates:[209] May 10–May 20

Astrology: Taurus, the sign ruled by Venus

Element: Fixed earth

Decan: 20°–29° Taurus; Taurus III, the decan ruled by Saturn

Picatrix **Image:** A man of reddish complexion with large white teeth exposed outside of his mouth, and a body like an elephant with long legs, and with him one horse, one dog and one calf

Picatrix **Significations:** Sloth, poverty, misery, dread

Agrippa Image: A man in whose hand is a serpent, and a dart

Agrippa Significations: Necessity and profit, and also misery and slavery

Sephira/World: Netzach in Assiah

Color(s): Olive, flecked gold; plus the colors of the associated majors

---

209. Dates vary annually. All decanic minor dates listed in this book are based on 2019–2020 dates.

Associated Majors: The Hierophant and the World/Universe

Associated Minors: King/Knight of Swords

Themes and Keywords: Little gain for much labor. Loss of motivation. Endurance through blight. Hard work and patience. Cross and nail. Low yields, crop failures, sterility. Inertia. Loss of promising future, projects not reaching fruition. Atonement for indiscretions. Repentance. Corrections needed: back to the drawing board. Necessary patience and humility.

ASTROLOGY/ELEMENT

Given that the "lesser benefic" Venus rules both the sevens and the sign, one would expect ease, but the "greater malefic" Saturn rules the decan. Saturn chills scantily clad Venus and frosts Taurean earth. To fare well with Saturn requires discipline and endurance through hardship, unpopular with indulgent Venus. Taurus is about resources, but Saturn is about timing and proper handling, and it sometimes provides restrictions, limitations, and lessons in perseverance. "The best laid schemes o' mice an' men *gang aft agley*,"—i.e., go "oft awry" or often askew—"an' leáe us nought but grief an' pain, for promis'd joy!"[210]

The Minotaur (Taurus) is trapped in the darkness
(Saturn) of his earthen labyrinth. (*Rosetta Tarot*)

---

210. Burns, *Poems and Songs of Roburt Burns*, 62.

Seven pentacles germinate in the earth. Their value (expressed as an upside-down
Venus glyph for this Taurus decan) is hidden for now. (*Universal Wirth Tarot*)

The *Picatrix* image is of disturbing male figures and beasts of burden. Agrippa's
man holds a serpent and a dart—perhaps signifying knowledge that somehow pierces.
The significations both mention misery, poverty, and slavery, yet one mentions sloth
and the other the more proactive necessity. When success is unfulfilled, assessment is
needed to determine what went wrong and how to begin the work again, for the price
of knowledge is toil.

MYTHOLOGY/TIME OF YEAR

If the 6 was Eden, the 7 is after the fall: naked expulsion from the garden and subsequent drudgery. Destruction and pestilence are foretold: Pharaoh's dream of seven
gaunt cows and seven weak plants eating seven healthy ones. Here we tell of the dark
Aphrodite, the demons Apophis and Medusa, the seven annual sacrifices to the Minotaur, and the daughters of Atlas: the seven Pleiades and the seven weeping sisters, the
Hyades.[211]

In the Titanomachy, the Titans were defeated and imprisoned, enraging their
mother Gaia. She brought forth a race of avenging giants, her children, either with Tartarus (hell) or born, like Aphrodite, from when Kronos (Saturn) castrated Ouranos.

---

211. See the 7 of Cups.

They did not achieve success in the Gigantomachy against the Olympians. They attempted to seize the throne of heaven by piling up mountains. After their defeat they were buried under mountains, where they continue to cause subterranean mischief in the form of earthquakes and eruptions. The first seven moons of Saturn were named after Titans and Giants, Kronos's failing siblings.

QABALAH

The 7 of Pentacles is Netzach in Assiah. Netzach נצח and Hod הוד, the seventh and eighth sephiroth, work together—they are the "armies/hosts" of God and the "tactical sephiroth," channels through which we can receive divine guidance. We think of Netzach as the emotional and Hod as the intellectual sphere. Hermetic Qabalists translate *Netzach* as "victory"—more accurately, it's "eternity" or "endurance." In Venus-ruled Netzach, we find the wherewithal to follow through on what we love.

All Pentacles correspond to the last of the four worlds, Assiah (meaning "doing" or "action"); the world of the ordinary senses in which we are free to act. In Netzach in Assiah, we find within ourselves what we need to persist through our doubts on even difficult, obstacle-ridden tasks.

As the Lord of Failure (or *Success Unfulfilled*), Netzach in Assiah inspires us with the stamina to confront what has gone wrong. As *Valor*, *Debauch* (*Illusionary Success*), and *Futility* (*Unstable Effort*), Netzach fires our hearts with daring and drive, phantasmal dreams, and elaborate plans.

7 of Pentacles (*Rider-Waite-Smith Tarot*)

Of the 7 of Pentacles' brooding gardener and his pentacles, Waite remarks, "One would say that these were his treasures and that his heart was there." But he was himself unclear about the card's meaning, suggesting it could represent "business, quarrels, innocence…" The leaves resemble potato foliage, and we do know that in 1910 the great Irish potato famine was still within generational memory. Hope and concern are present, but above all, uncertainty. As with potato blight, the outcome cannot be known till the harvest.

If the 5 of Pentacles anticipated what *might* go wrong, the 7 must evaluate what *has* gone wrong. The figure's expression is inscrutable, as if he is trying to summon the mental fortitude to continue ("Nevertheless, he persisted!"). In the 8, he will do just that. The 8 can be viewed as a corrective to the stalled momentum of the 7; the 7 can be viewed as a necessary assessment tool for the hyper-focused 8.

THOTH SYMBOLISM

In what is visually the darkest card of the deck, the disks are also arranged in the direst of the geomantic forms, *Rubeus*, in which the dots take the shape of an inverted chalice, spilling all good fortune. This figure is disturbing enough that if it appears first in a geomantic reading, the reading itself must be abandoned. The disks look like they are made of lead (Crowley says, "Bad money") and are stamped with emblems of Taurus and Saturn.[212] The coins rest on ground or vegetation that is blighted and blackened, with patterns suggestive of frost.

Crowley generally mistrusted sevens as unbalanced and degenerating forms of their element. He says the 7 of Disks' extreme passivity and sloth cause lack of effort and that the weakness of the seven is exacerbated by leaden Saturn and the inertia of Taurus. He tells us that "labour has been abandoned."[213] All we can say is, this crop has failed and the field must be plowed again.

RELATED CARDS

In Taurus's final decan, the 7 of Pentacles unites solidity and confinement: the Hierophant (Taurus) and the World or Universe (Saturn); a dark and difficult inertia overtakes the bull. The majors' associated Hebrew letters—*vav* and *tav*—mean "nail" and "cross," evoking the price we pay for redemption. Only profound faith sustains us through our most uncertain moments.

Sevens are cards of seeking. The 7 of Pentacles stubbornly re-evaluates, trying to overcome previous shortfalls. The 7 of Wands defends what his ambition has secured; the 7 of Cups escapes into fevered visions; the 7 of Swords hatches schemes.

The 7 of Pentacles haunts the King/Knight of Swords' first ("shadow") decan in the form of a failure complex—motivating him, in the 8 and 9 of Swords, to process his options and arrive at ruthless decisions.

Seven, Netzach, and the Empress are the number, sephira, and path of Venus. Together they represent the unconquerable nature of the life force.

---

212. Crowley, *Book of Thoth*, 215.
213. Crowley, 183.

8 OF PENTACLES
OR 8 OF DISKS
Lord of Prudence

Dates:[214] August 23–September 1

Astrology: Virgo, the sign ruled by Mercury. Mercury exalted

Element: Mutable earth

Decan: 0°–9° Virgo; Virgo I, the decan ruled by the Sun

***Picatrix* Image:** A young girl covered with an old woolen cloth, and in her hand is a pomegranate

***Picatrix* Significations:** Sowing, plowing, the germination of plants, gathering grapes, good living

Agrippa Image: The figure of a good maid, and a man casting seeds

Agrippa Significations: Getting of wealth, ordering of diet, plowing, sowing, and peopling

---

214. Dates vary annually. All decanic minor dates listed in this book are based on 2019–2020 dates.

Sephira/World: Hod in Assiah

Color(s): Yellowish brown, flecked white; plus the colors of the associated majors

Themes and Keywords: The virtue of restraint. Self-sufficient development. Growth and refinement. Attention to detail. Craft and skill. Patiently growing, ripening. Making and perfecting. Accrual of resources. Tending, vigilance over, and care of small things. Humility and diligence.

ASTROLOGY/ELEMENT

The earth sign Virgo is ruled by Mercury, as are the eights.[215] As mutable earth, it is a sign of Earth's maturing phase. But it is the first decan of the sign, so it is the sowing before the fruition and gathering. The first decan of Virgo is ruled by the Sun. Virgo, the earth's crust, is being warmed by the sun, encouraging the growth of the secret seed. Virgo is "virginal" in the sense of self-sufficiency. Through Virgo's patient tending of the fertile soil, resources ripen in anticipation of an eventual plentiful harvest.

The care of small things (Virgo) is shown as the nest of eight eggs,
warmed by the Hermit's lantern containing the sun. (*Tabula Mundi Tarot*)

Agrippa shows us "the figure of a good maid, and a man casting seeds," suggestive of both the virtue and fertility of Virgo. The significations involve growing plants,

---

215. Mercury both rules, and is exalted in, the sign of Virgo.

wealth, and people. *Picatrix* brings in a maiden that reminds us of Persephone, robed and covered in an old woolen cloth and holding a pomegranate. The significations are also agricultural, productive, and fruitful: of sowing and plowing, germination, the gathering of grapes, and good living.

MYTHOLOGY/TIME OF YEAR

Virgo gives us maidens, goddesses of the subtle virtues: grain goddesses like Persephone, Queen of the Underworld, or Astraea, the celestial virgin. Hindu goddess Saraswati is not only pure but also mercurial, as the goddess of wisdom and healing. She was the possessor of purifying knowledge: speech, language, music, and cleansing creative work that flows and purifies the essence and self of a person.

Hermes (Mercury) also has a chthonic aspect. He is not only a child of Zeus, but a son of Maia.[216] Maia, Greek mountain nymph with lovely dark eyes, was the eldest of the Pleiades. The Roman Maia was a goddess of growth, associated with Terra (Earth), and the *Bona Dea* (Good Goddess). The Bona Dea, whose rites of both chastity and fertility were for women only, may be an aspect of nature goddess Fauna.

Maia also had ties to Vulcan, god of the forge who may have evolved from the Cretan Velchanos, god of nature and the netherworld, a youthful consort of the Great Goddess.

QABALAH

The 8 of Pentacles is Hod in Assiah. Netzach נצח and Hod הוד, the seventh and eighth sephiroth, are the "armies/hosts" of God or "tactical sephiroth." They are "spheres of prophecy" (divine guidance); Netzach in the emotional and Hod in the intellectual sphere.

Translated as "splendor" or "glory," Hod's intellect is humanity's crowning feature, but it also has overtones of piety and humility. Sphere of Mercury, Hod gives us rationality, logic, and communication skills. Hod articulates what Netzach feels.

---

216. See 8 of Wands for another double Mercury card, but with a Jupiter influence.

All Pentacles correspond to Assiah, the World of Action, where we recognize the familiar world brought to us by our senses. Hod in Assiah grounds us in a systematic approach to what is grown or fashioned. The ego is surrendered to the work itself.

If sensible Hod in Assiah helps us organize our lives, in Atziluth (*Swiftness*) it gives us the direction to hone in on our goals. As *Indolence* (*Abandoned Success*) in Briah, Hod tells us it is time to move on; in airy Yetzirah its penchant for overanalysis may lead to *Interference* (*Shortened Force*).

RIDER-WAITE-SMITH SYMBOLISM

8 of Pentacles (*Rider-Waite-Smith Tarot*) (left)
This fifteenth-century 6 of Coins (right) appears to have been an
inspiration for the Waite-Smith 8 of Pentacles. (*Sola Busca Tarot*)

Waite emphasizes this artisan's skillful work, "which he exhibits in the form of trophies." In subject matter, the 8 of Pentacles recalls the 6 of Coins of the fifteenth-century Sola Busca deck, which Smith was likely to have viewed on exhibit. In both, a mason is hard at work with his hammer, which he wields as a tool of art rather than construction. The bench he sits on is the same seen in the 3 of Pentacles (he may even be the same craftsman pictured there). In the distance and to the left is a little path leading to a town; interpreted Qabalistically, we look from Hod to Malkuth.

The apron and hammer call to mind the Masonic themes sometimes raised in this deck. (Ceremonially, the Masonic apron—albeit white rather than black—stands for purity.) Also, in the *Sefer* Yetzirah, God is said to engrave the twenty-two letters: the act of engraving is one of humility—removing a bit of oneself in order to create.

THOTH SYMBOLISM

Crowley talks of the "strength of doing nothing at all," especially in terms of material or financial matters, and the virtuous result of saving for "a rainy day": the accrual of interest.[217] As the card of husbandry, it represents the patient tending of beings and belongings. He reminds us that Virgo is associated with *Yod*, the secret seed of life, and in quintessential form, calls Virgo the "Virgin Earth awaiting the Phallic Plough."[218]

We are told the eights are a remedy for the sevens, and here the disks are also arranged as a geomantic figure: that of *Populus*, of the people. Stability and other things in the best interest of the common people reside here. The disks are presented as the flowers, eventual fruits, of a great tree with roots in the fertile land. Against a solar-colored sky are plum-colored flowers, the color of Virgo in the material world, and each has five outer petals and five inner fruiting segments—ten in all, the number of Malkuth (earth).

RELATED CARDS

The 8 of Pentacles, ruled by the Sun, is the first of three Virgo minors. Its major arcana, the Sun and the Hermit, suggest the focus one can achieve by directing the sun's lantern toward a dedicated task. Also, the Hermit safeguards the Sun's light through dark and distant places, reminding us that Hermes was a chthonic god as well as a messenger.

Eights offer system-based steps toward real-world manifestation. While the 8 of Pentacles organizes our practical lives, the 8 of Wands speeds information along at the speed of light. The 8 of Cups walks away from drowning in its own feelings, while the 8 of Swords analyzes the unanalyzable.

---

217. Crowley, *Book of Thoth*, 184–85.

218. Crowley, 216.

Central decan of the King of Pentacles (RWS) or Knight of Disks (Thoth), the 8 of Pentacles confers upon him a head for numbers and a gift for the details that make or break the job.

Finally, eight is the number and Hod is the sephira of Mercury—a comfortable placement for Mercury-ruled Virgo.

9 OF PENTACLES
OR 9 OF DISKS
Lord of Gain (Material Gain)

Dates:[219] September 2–September 11

Astrology: Virgo, the sign ruled by Mercury. Mercury exalted

Element: Mutable earth

Decan: 10°–19° Virgo; Virgo II, the decan ruled by Venus

***Picatrix* Image:** A man of beautiful color, dressed in leather, and over his garment of leather is another garment of iron

***Picatrix* Significations:** Petitions, requests, and gain, tribute and denying justice

Agrippa Image: A black man clothed with a skin, and a man having a bush of hair, holding a bag

Agrippa Significations: Gain, scraping together of wealth and covetousness

Sephira/World: Yesod in Assiah

---

219. Dates vary annually. All decanic minor dates listed in this book are based on 2019–2020 dates.

Color(s): Citrine, flecked azure; plus the colors of the associated majors

Associated Majors: The Hermit and the Empress

Associated Minors: King of Pentacles (RWS) or Knight of Disks (Thoth)

Themes and Keywords: Self-sufficiency. The ripening of the harvest. Counting one's blessings. The comfort of hearth and home. The reward of due diligence, high standards, and industrious behavior. Gracious living. Perfectionism. Solitude.

ASTROLOGY/ELEMENT

Asexual Mercury rules the sign, but Venus and the Moon rule the decan and sephira respectively, giving a decidedly feminine bent to the face. The decan also contains the exaltation of Mercury at 15°. Here Virgo gives a curious combination of virtue and fertility, combined with the virgin's self-reliance and autonomy. Though Venus is in its fall, or weakness, in Virgo, the fruitful nature of the moon enhances Venus's tendency to bestow both refinement and fecundity. But the blessings of Virgo come with effort: if they are thrice blessed, it is because they take on three times as much work with humble diligence and dedication to the pursuit of perfection. The reward for Virgo's good management here is expressed as material gain.

The abacus has long helped merchants calculate their gain; here its
beads appear in the wealth-signifying green of Venus. (*Rosetta Tarot*)

The decan images describe men with symbols of encasement: various garments and containers, perhaps indicative of Virgo's containment, self-sufficiency and desire to control the material. The significations describe a process of pursuit of gain in the form of petitions, requests, tributes, and the "scraping together of wealth."

MYTHOLOGY/TIME OF YEAR

Virgo is the largest constellation in the zodiacal band, and its alpha star is one of the brightest and most fortunate: Spica, representing the ear of grain held in the virgin's left hand. Spica's rising coincided with the Egyptian harvest season. Egypt's Dendera zodiac portrayed Virgo as Isis holding a wheat sheaf that she scattered, forming the Milky Way. The palm frond on the virgin's right arm is the star formerly known as *Vindemiatrix*, "the grape harvester."[220]

Virgo has always been associated with female goddesses who embody the tension between purity and fertility, like Ishtar, Demeter and Persephone, and Vesta, goddess of home and hearth.

The celestial virgin is also known as Astraea, last of the immortals to abandon Earth when the Golden Age degenerated to the wicked age of Iron. Astraea's maternal ancestry reflects her nature: her mother was the dawn goddess Eos, who was sister to lunar Selene and daughter to Theia the wide-shining one, whose mother was Gaia herself. Legend says Astraea's return will usher in a new Golden Age.

QABALAH

The 9 of Pentacles is Yesod in Assiah. Yesod יסוד, the ninth sephira, translates as "foundation" or "basis"—that which lies beneath the real world, Malkuth. Here the light of the previous sephiroth gathers. Yesod corresponds to the Moon, the sixth day of creation (when humans were formed), the unconscious, sex, the imagination, magic, and the first step on any spiritual journey. All nines are places of power.

All Pentacles correspond to the last of the four worlds, Assiah, the World of Action in which physical senses are used. Yesod in Assiah brings together all the wherewithal

---

220. This star has now been renamed Epsilon Virginis.

that will be required for physical life in Malkuth; beyond this threshold, limitless potential converts into reality.

As the Lord of Gain, Yesod looks ahead to what it may produce or reproduce. As *Strength*, *Happiness*, and *Cruelty*, Yesod exerts a wide range of motivations on the human character; as the moment where everything can change, it pushes us inexorably from imagined actions to concrete ones.

RIDER-WAITE-SMITH SYMBOLISM

9 of Pentacles (*Rider-Waite-Smith Tarot*)

"It is a wide domain, suggesting plenty in all things. Possibly it is her own possession."[221] As others have since, Waite saw in the 9 of Pentacles an image of feminine self-sufficiency. The floral Venus glyphs adorning her dress and her gloved hand (Hebrew letter *yod*—hand—corresponds to the Hermit) remind us this is Venus's decan of Virgo. The laden grapevines recall the robes of the King of Pentacles, for this is his final decan. Ripe and tightly trellised, they suggest control and solitude as well as abundance; even the trees are symmetrical here. The stately home glimpsed in the distance could be Malkuth, arrived at in the next card.

---

221. Waite, *Pictorial Key*, 264.

The figure turns toward the hooded bird on her hand; the falconer's art requires trust as well as control. Creeping at her feet is a tiny snail; bearing his house on his back, he is a symbol of self-sufficiency and the rewards of patient effort.

Like the Waite-Smith snail, the tortoise signifies patience, self-sufficiency, and long-term thinking. As always, the wall suggests safety, but also solitude. (*Animal Totem Tarot*)

THOTH SYMBOLISM

Crowley reports that the sacredness of 9 is the "summit of perfection," the best one can get from a practical viewpoint.[222] The 9 of Disks brings luck and material favor, though he also chides the dullness of the pursuit of materialism over true attainment. No one minds when they are counting the winnings!

The disks are placed in three groups of three. The central disks are overlapping circles, in Venus's colors of rose, sky, and emerald, forming an upright triangle extending geometric rays of light. The central circle almost looks to have a dot in it, which means the rose color could possibly represent the sun of Tiphareth that shines upon Yesod. The green and blue circles could also represent Venus and the moon. The circles are surrounded with disks forming ascending and descending triangles of coins above and below. Each coin has a bust representing one of the magical images and sigils of each planet. They are placed on concentric divisions that resemble fertile fields, laid out in the colors of Virgo.

---

222. Crowley, *Book of Thoth*, 185.

RELATED CARDS

The 9 of Pentacles, ruled by Venus, corresponds to the second of three Virgo decans. Here the Empress (Venus) and the Hermit (Virgo) negotiate the definition of perfection. While the Hermit lends his meticulous eye to the Empress's beautiful works, he also brings solitude, even loneliness; Venus is in fall here.

In nines, each suit achieves the peak of its power. While the 9 of Pentacles capitalizes on realized work, the 9 of Wands burns with determination. The 9 of Cups brims with joy; the 9 of Swords seethes with despair. The threes of each suit are the seed; the nines the fruit. Thrice abundance equals gain!

This final decan of the King of Pentacles (RWS) or Knight of Disks (Thoth) caps his efforts to provide sustenance for all through *Prudence* and *Gain*; ideally, setting to rest the specter of struggle raised in his shadow decan, the 7 of Wands.

Finally, nine is the number and Yesod is the sephira of the Moon, whose changeful nature underscores the fickle nature of profit.

10 OF PENTACLES
OR 10 OF DISKS
Lord of Wealth

Dates:[223] September 12–September 21

Astrology: Virgo, the sign ruled by Mercury. Mercury exalted

Element: Mutable earth

Decan: 20°–29° Virgo; Virgo III, the decan ruled by Mercury

Picatrix **Image:** A white man, with a great body, wrapped in white linen, and with him is a woman holding in her hand black oil

Picatrix **Significations:** Debility, age, infirmity, sloth, injury to limbs and the destruction of people

Agrippa Image: A white woman and deaf, or an old man leaning on a staff

Agrippa Significations: Weakness, infirmity, loss of members, destruction of trees, and depopulation of lands

---

223. Dates vary annually. All decanic minor dates listed in this book are based on 2019–2020 dates.

Sephira/World: Malkuth in Assiah

Color(s): Black, rayed with yellow; plus the colors of the associated majors

Associated Majors: The Hermit and the Magician/Magus

Associated Minors: Shadow decan of the Queen of Swords; relates to Page of Pentacles (RWS) or Princess of Disks (Thoth) as a ten

Themes and Keywords: Fruition, completion, finality. Accumulation. Embarrassment of riches; wealth that loses meaning without usage. Endowments and inheritances. Legacies and family dynasties. Generations. Redintigration and regeneration. The inevitable mortal progression. Old age, and its amassing of both goods and infirmities. Transitions and thresholds.

ASTROLOGY/ELEMENT

It's the last minor card, and last and thus most mutable decan of the mutable earth sign Virgo. Mercury, patron of merchants and thieves, rules the decan and rules and is exalted in Virgo. The tens are associated with both Saturn and Earth, increasing the connection with themes of aging, endings, and karmic rewards and retributions. As material life progresses toward its conclusion, there is an obligatory accumulation of goods, wealth, and the inevitable infirmities of age.

Picatrix describes a man wrapped in white linen, foreshadowing the shroud of death, and a woman holding black oil, which we associate in modern times with great wealth. The colors accentuate the polarities of life, both being associated with birth and death. Agrippa also mentions the elderly: a white woman who is deaf, and an old man leaning upon his staff like the Hermit. The significations reflect themes of infirmity and debility of people and the deforestation and depopulation of lands, perhaps a warning about what the inexhaustible pursuit of wealth could mean for the planet.

TEN OF PENTACLES

This stripped-down interpretation brings together *Picatrix's* theme of age and wealth, the faithful dogs of Waite-Smith, and the village it takes for all to thrive. (*Linestrider Tarot*)

MYTHOLOGY/TIME OF YEAR

Hestia (whose Roman equivalent is Vesta), goddess of household and hearth, was the firstborn of Kronos (Saturn) and Rhea (daughter of Earth) and the first swallowed and first regurgitated by Kronos, and thus the oldest Olympian. Her rites involved extinguishing the hearth, relighting the hearth, and ceremonies of completion and renewal. The Homeric Hymn to Hestia pairs her with Hermes (Mercury). Together they both rule transitions and liminality: Hermes as the outer traveler of boundaries, Hestia as custodian of inner thresholds.

In early Greek art Hermes was portrayed as a bearded old man, like Kronos (Saturn) or the Hermit who guides us to deeper levels of self. Hermes was a patron of merchants, a bringer of wealth, and a psychopomp. Chthonic Hermes was the only god to cross the boundary to the underworld in either direction.

In Mercury's waning, evening, or vespertine phase, it sets after the sun, descending into the earth. Astrologer Dane Rudhyar calls this the "Epimethean phase," after *Epimetheus* (hindsight) the circumspect brother of *Prometheus* (foresight) and *Atlas* (enduring).[224]

---

224. Rudhyar, *Astrological Study of Psychological Complexes.*

QABALAH

The 10 of Pentacles is Malkuth in Assiah—as the last of the sephiroth and the last of the four worlds, it is truly separate and different. Malkuth ("kingdom") hangs alone at the base of the Tree, coterminous with the fourth world, Assiah. It receives the light of the Tree, transmitting none. It corresponds to the Sabbath and the divine feminine aspect. Malkuth in Assiah is the physical world people know so well, the world perceived with the five senses. Its separateness is a blessing and a curse: fated to live apart from the divine, creation's wholeness is restored through right actions. In esoteric tarot, this is the return of the daughter to the Great Mother, Binah.

Malkuth in Assiah is the ripe fruit fallen to the ground; as its seeds burst forth, the cycle ends only to begin again: its overflow manifests here as generational connections, inheritances, and legacies. As oppression, satiety, and ruin, the extremes of Malkuth push the envelope beyond overweening ambition, emotional repleteness, and intellectual fanaticism.

RIDER-WAITE-SMITH SYMBOLISM

© 1971 U.S. GAMES SYSTEMS, INC.

10 of Pentacles (*Rider-Waite-Smith Tarot*)

Opulent and colorful, the 10 of Pentacles portrays the accumulated riches of this world, the "house and domain."[225] The built environment, previously glimpsed from afar, surrounds us completely now that we have arrived in Malkuth. Ten pentacles dominate the foreground in a Tree of Life formation, and three generations of humanity appear on the card. Separated from the lively world by a stone archway bearing symbols of his legacy, the Hermit-like ancestor nearly disappears into the tapestry of his own works. A pair of hounds (themselves psychopomp animals) recognize him, as they did Odysseus; the oldest and the youngest hands (Hermit = Hebrew letter *yod*, "hand") rest on each canine guide.

Adorning the archway we can make out some heraldic devices: a shield with a kingdom's castle and the scales of Libra (the next sign). There is also the rocky prominence from the Tower card and rippling waters, which could refer to the seas of Binah.

THOTH SYMBOLISM

As the final minor, Crowley says it's cognate to the Universe card, the sum total of all that has come before. Through the doctrine of recurrence, the bottom and top of cycles connect. He calls this the final solidification and dissipation, which is death. Here is the accumulation of wealth—but also the need to use it intelligently (Mercury) or else it becomes inert and meaningless.

The disks are arranged as the Tree of Life made of heavy coins, with the Malkuth disk largest and heaviest, pendulous as if ready to fall. All of the disks are marked with the varying symbols, sigils, glyphs, angels, and letters of Mercury—except Mercury's own sphere of Hod, which is marked with a hexagram and hexagon, six-sided figures which, when multiplied, produce Mercury's mystic number. Six-sided figures represent Tiphareth and the Sun: regeneration and the inner wisdom that facilitates it. It is worth noting that Malkuth is marked with Hermes's wand, decorated with the mother letters that generate the whole of creation.

---

225. Waite, *Pictorial Key*, 262.

TEN OF DISKS
WEALTH
♍   ☿

The card is doubly ruled by Mercury: ten disks form the image of
Mercury as Adam Kadmon and the Tree of Life. (*Tabula Mundi Tarot*)

RELATED CARDS

The 10 of Pentacles finds the Magician/Magus (Mercury) ruling and exalted in his own kingdom, Virgo (the Hermit). His gifts of communication and commerce shower riches on this card. Mercury is also a psychopomp: he carries the ancestors' messages and blessings.

Malkuth, the tenth sephira, is our world. All tens (but this one in particular) correspond to the World/Universe card in several ways.[226] The 10 of Pentacles is of this world but also shows the way out of it—death and rebirth.

Shadow decan of the Queen of Swords, the 10 of Pentacles may literally allude to the inheritance that, along with self-sufficiency and sorrow (2 and 3 of Swords), accompanies her widowhood. Her wealth is cold comfort, but at her best she clearly sees how to use it.

Tens bring endings and beginnings. The 10 of Pentacles promises resources; the 10 of Cups promises love passed between generations. The 10 of Wands ends cyclical power; the 10 of Swords ends an argument so that matters may proceed.

---

226. The World/Universe is the trump of elemental earth; the World/Universe and tens each represent the end of their sequence; the World/Universe's path leads from Malkuth (10) to Yesod (9).

COURT CARDS

Many readers find tarot's sixteen court cards particularly challenging to interpret. The images generally feature a single human figure with an inscrutable expression, perhaps accompanied by a few symbols and color clues. But the esoteric correspondences help expand upon these visible clues and draw connections with other cards within the deck. They provide a roadmap for a reader to draw out the nuances within the court cards, which ultimately may be the most complex cards of all. Here is a synopsis of some key features relating to the court cards.

GOLDEN DAWN TITLES

A number of formal epithets accompany each court card. These are primarily element-based; for example, the Wands titles refer to "fire," "flame," or "lightning"; the Cups titles refer to "water," "waves," "sea," or "flood," and so forth. The titles also include references to the four elemental beings: salamanders (fire), undines (water), sylphs (air), and gnomes (earth). These mythical beings, conceptualized by Paracelsus in the sixteenth century, are a popular feature of Western magical practice.

ELEMENTS

In addition to each suit corresponding to an element, each rank does as well. Both the four Qabalistic worlds and the four elements (the suits) correspond to the four letters of the divine name, YHVH. Kings (RWS) or Knights (Thoth) correspond to *yod* (Atziluth) and fire. Queens correspond to primal *heh* (Briah) and water. Knights (RWS) or Princes (Thoth) correspond to *vav* (Yetzirah) and air. Pages (RWS) or Princesses (Thoth) correspond to final *heh* (Assiah) and earth. As each element can therefore be expressed in four parts, there are sixteen possible sub-elements. Thus, readers often refer to the Queen of Swords as the "watery part of air"—"watery" because she is the Queen, "air" because she is a Sword court.

The elemental qualities of rank express themselves in non-physical ways: for example, the King (RWS) or Knight (Thoth) is "fiery" in that he is active, impulsive. That's why he is represented in Thoth-based decks on horseback. Water and earth are considered receptive, a quality found in the "throne" designation in both Queens (water) and Pages/Princesses (earth)—though only the Queens are depicted upon thrones, for Princesses are transmuting, as we shall see. The "chariot" of the Knight/Prince is both active like the horse and anchored like the throne, thus partaking of qualities of both parents. The Princesses are designated as embodiments of the "thrones" of the Aces—unlike the Queens who rule *from* the elemental thrones. This is because Princesses combine and materialize the forces of King, Queen, and Prince, just as the earth element is comprised of all others. As final *heh*, the Princesses are the end result and physical manifestation of the element which began at the root of the Ace. This connects them back to the first world of Atziluth (*yod* of YHVH), making them the transmuting link that restarts the cycle.[227] Thus, though they are the "passive" element of earth, their world of Assiah is one of action. This is why they are depicted as standing firmly by themselves. They don't need horses, thrones, or armor because when fully dignified, they contain all they need within themselves.

The elements and ranks also correspond to qualities and expressions. *Liber Theta* describes the elemental natures as "surging, flowing, expanding, and consolidating" and maps the four worlds to expressions of will, love, reason, and action.[228] Thus, the

---

227. See Meleen, *Book M: Liber Mundi*, 180–84 for more information on the fourfold Qabalistic court cycle.

228. Fra., *Liber Theta*, 61.

Queen of Wands as "Water of Fire" would express as love—or emotion—modifying will, while the King of Wands as "Fire of Fire" would be unmodified will.

THE PROBLEM WITH "KINGS" AND "KNIGHTS"

Anyone somewhat familiar with the Golden Dawn's naming practices will be aware that "King" and "Knight" are titles rife with confusion. The Golden Dawn's *Book T* describes the first of its male courts variously as Lord, King, or Knight and the second as Prince or King. Indeed, the Golden Dawn often seemed to use king, emperor, and prince interchangeably. This led to all manner of subsequent muddying in the nomenclature.

In the Rider-Waite-Smith deck, the court cards were King, Queen, Knight, and Page. In the Thoth deck, Crowley would use Knight, Queen, Prince, and Princess. Today, you will find many who argue that Crowley's Knight is in fact Waite's Knight, rather than Waite's King—after all, both are on horseback. And isn't the throne of Waite's King something like the chariot of Crowley's Prince? Similarly, the dispute over which one corresponds to elemental fire and which to elemental air dates even farther back.

We have settled on equating Crowley's Knight with Waite's King because we follow the order in which the deck creators presented their courts. We consider them the fiery part of their suit, and we've striven in our interpretations to provide a rationale for why. We hope the context we offer will help you come to your own conclusions about the correct correspondence, whether it's the same as ours or not.[229]

QABALISTIC CORRESPONDENCES
FOR THE COURT CARDS

We have not elaborated on the Qabalistic correspondences for the court cards in the chapters that follow, but they are fairly straightforward:

- Kings/Knights = Chokmah = sephira two of the Tree of Life

- Queens = Binah = sephira three on the Tree of Life

---

229. See Chang, *Tarot Correspondences*, 138–39 for a much longer discussion of the King/Knight conundrum.

- Knights/Princes = Tiphareth = sephira six on the Tree of Life

- Pages/Princesses = Malkuth = sephira ten on the Tree of Life

Finally, the four suits and the four ranks correspond to the four Qabalistic worlds and the four letters of the Tetragrammaton in exactly the same way they correspond to the elements, so:

- Kings/Knights = fire = Atziluth = *yod* = Wands

- Queens = water = Briah = *heh* primal = Cups

- Knights/Princes = air = Yetzirah = *vav* = Swords

- Pages/Princesses = earth = Assiah = *heh* final = Pentacles/Disks

Thus, the Knight/Prince of Wands, "Air of Fire," sometimes shows up in Hermetic Qabalah as "*vav* of *yod*" or "Tiphareth of Atziluth." You can learn more about the Qabalah of a court card by looking at its corresponding numeric minor—in the case of the Knight/Prince of Wands, that would be the 6 of Wands.

DECANS AND THE COURT CARDS

The astrology of court cards is essentially sign-based. There are twelve signs of the zodiac and there are twelve relevant court cards: the four Kings/Knights, the four Queens, and the four Knights/Princes. You can generally say that the Queen of Cups corresponds to Cancer and the King/Knight of Wands corresponds to Sagittarius.

However, it's a little more complicated than that. Each sign subdivides into three decans. Each court card corresponds to the first two decans of its sign, but also the last decan of the previous sign (also known as the "shadow decan"). So, the Queen of Cups has the first two decans of Cancer and also the last decan of Gemini. Shadow decans hold the less straightforward parts of a court card's personality—its ulterior motivations, its weaknesses, its early habits.

As for the Pages/Princesses, they correspond not to signs or decans but to whole quadrants, just as the Aces do. This is why each is known as the "throne" of its corresponding Ace. Thus, the Page of Swords spans the astrological territory all the way from the first decan of Capricorn, through all decans of Aquarius, to the final decan of Pisces.

The circular diagram in the Tables and Diagrams section at the end of this book offers a simple way to visualize how the thirty-six decans correspond to the sixteen court cards.

BALANCING THE ASTROLOGICAL QUALITIES OR QUADRUPLICITIES

The twelve zodiacal signs can be divided into three modalities of four signs each, called the qualities or quadruplicities: cardinal, fixed, and mutable. (See the section on the major arcana for more information.) These three modes relate well respectively to the alchemical trinity of sulfur, salt, and mercury, and to the "tendencies" as expressed in the gunas of Hindu philosophy: rajas, tamas, and sattva. As noted above, each court card rules three minor decans, two decans of the primary sign and one of the preceding sign. The natures of the court card ranks also correspond to the three modes, in an ingenious way that gives each one a complexly balanced nature, giving them a human quality like real personalities have.

The Kings/Knights are cardinal (sulfuric, or *rajasic*) in temperament and attribute, being active, initiating, and dynamic, yet their main decanates are mutable and their shadow decan is fixed. Queens have fixed (salty, or *tamasic*) natures, but the signs of their main two decans are cardinal, and their shadow decan is mutable. Likewise, Knights/Princes are mutable (mercurial, or sattvic) in tendency, with two fixed decans and one cardinal decan as a "shadow."

But what about the Pages/Princesses, who don't correspond to three decans but rather to an entire quadrant of the zodiac? They each span an area or full quarter of the circle of the zodiacal band, housing three signs, one of each modality: cardinal, fixed, and mutable. Just as they manifest all of the qualities of the King/Knight, Queen, and Knight/Prince within themselves, they correspond to the concept of prakriti, the primal matter of nature containing in equilibrium all the innate qualities of the three tendencies or gunas.

MYTHOLOGICAL CONSIDERATIONS

While we have eliminated the mythology section from the court card chapters, we have provided information on the "star group" for each card, listing the constellations that are in range of the three decans of the zodiac that the King/Knights, Queens, and Knights/Princes have in their domains.

For example, the King/Knight of Wands includes not only the constellation of the related sign Sagittarius, but also that of Hercules the hero and of Ophiuchus, who the Romans associated with the healer Asclepius—appropriate for the King's ownership of the middle decan of Sagittarius, the 9 of Wands, Lord of Great Strength. The King/Knight's shadow decan is the last decan of the sign Scorpio, and both Ophiuchus and Draco have serpent associations.

Exploration of the associated myths will provide interesting star lore tales relevant to the nature of these court cards for further insight. In addition, the mythology section for each of their related decans can apply.

SPACE VERSUS TIME

Once again the Pages/Princesses are different, for they are said to rule quadrants of space rather than time, and thus instead of having three zodiacal decans in their domain, they rule an entire quarter of the celestial globe—and the associated earthly continents.

- Page/Princess of Wands: Cancer-Leo-Virgo and the area of Asia

- Page/Princess of Cups: Libra-Scorpio-Sagittarius and the Pacific

- Page/Princess of Swords: Capricorn-Aquarius-Pisces and the Americas

- Page/Princess of Pentacles/Disks: Aries-Taurus-Gemini and Europe and Africa

I CHING AND GEOMANCY IN THE COURTS

Two final esoteric correspondence systems work well with court cards. As with the elements, each makes use of a four-by-four structure, which mirrors that of the courts.

I Ching figures, known as hexagrams, each comprise two "trigrams," one on top of the other. There are eight trigrams, which can generate sixty-four hexagrams. Esoteric tarot, however, uses only four of the eight trigrams, those representing thunder (*zhèn*) for fire, lake (*duì*) for water, wind (*xùn*) for air, and mountain (*gèn*) for earth. These four generate sixteen hexagrams. The shaded areas of the following diagram show the hexagrams relevant for tarot.

Geomantic divination, like I Ching, is based on a binary system. For I Ching it's broken and unbroken lines; for geomancy, it's two dots or one dot. Geomantic figures have four layers, or two "bigrams," each containing one dot or two dots: odd or even, or masculine and feminine. This generates sixteen variations, each of which corresponds to a sub-element and court card.

While there are different systems for attributing geomantic figures to the court cards, we use the one favored by the Golden Dawn. Rather than interpreting the four possible bigrams based on their shape (i.e. one dot over two dots forming the triangle of the fire element) the Golden Dawn assigned them based on Enochian workings. In this system each geomantic figure was assigned to a planetary ruler and a letter of the Enochian alphabet. Each of the seven classical planets is assigned to two geomantic figures, accounting for fourteen of the sixteen. The remaining two were assigned to the constellation Draco, symbolic of the lunar nodes known as the head and tail of the dragon (*Caput Draconis* and *Cauda Draconis*).

The sixteen geomantic figures also correspond to the twelve signs of the zodiac. How so, when there are four more geomantic figures than signs of the zodiac? Because as indicated above, the Sun and Moon have just one sign apiece (Cancer and Leo) but *two* geomantic figures apiece—*Fortuna Minor* and *Fortuna Major* for the Sun, *Via* and *Populus* for the Moon. Thus there are twelve zodiac signs and twelve geomantic figures for twelve courts: Kings/Knights, Queens, and Knights/Princes. The four Pages/Princesses correspond to the "secondary" geomantic figures of the luminaries and the lunar nodes: *Fortuna Minor*, *Via*, *Cauda Draconis*, and *Caput Draconis*.

Upper Trigram → / Lower Trigram ↓								
	1	34	5	26	11	9	14	43
	25	51	3	27	24	42	21	17
	6	40	29	4	7	59	64	47
	33	62	39	52	15	53	56	31
	12	16	8	23	2	20	35	45
	44	32	48	18	46	57	50	28
	13	55	63	22	36	37	30	49
	10	54	60	41	19	61	38	58

I Ching-tarot diagram

King/Knight of Wands	Queen of Wands	Knight/Prince of Wands	Page/Princess of Wands
Acquisitio: Gain. Jupiter/Sagittarius. Adding to, acquisition, within grasp.	*Puer*: The Boy. Mars/Aries. Youth, aggression, rash action.	*Fortuna Major*: Greater Fortune. Sun (Northern)/ Leo. Fame, wealth, success.	*Cauda Draconis*: Dragon's Tail. Malefics/South Node. Exit, leaving, ending.
King/Knight of Cups	**Queen of Cups**	**Knight/Prince of Cups**	**Page/Princess of Cups**
Laetitia: Joy. Jupiter/Pisces. Happiness, health.	*Populus*: The People. Waxing Moon/ Cancer. Public, peers, crowds.	*Rubeus*: Red. Mars/Scorpio. Temper, vice, passion.	*Via*: The Way. Waning Moon/ Cancer. Paths, journey, change.

The sixteen geomantic figures and their court card correspondences

King/Knight of Swords	Queen of Swords	Knight/Prince of Swords	Page/Princess of Swords
Albus: White. Mercury/Gemini. Wisdom, purity, planning.	*Puella*: The Girl. Venus/Libra. Innocence, peace, beauty.	*Tristitia*: Sorrow. Saturn/Aquarius. Sadness, suffering, stability.	*Fortuna Minor*: Lesser Fortune. Sun (Southern)/ Leo. Assistance, small positive.
King of Pentacles/ Knight of Disks	Queen of Pentacles/Disks	Knight of Pentacles/Prince of Disks	Page of Pentacles/ Princess of Disks
Conjunctio: Conjunction. Mercury/Virgo. Meeting, union, combining.	*Carcer*: The Prison. Saturn/Capricorn. Immobile strength, restriction, binding.	*Amissio*: Loss. Venus/Taurus. Giving away, out of grasp, sacrifice.	*Caput Draconis*: Dragon's Head. Benefics/North Node. Entrance, beginnings, profit.

The sixteen geomantic figures and their court card correspondences

KING OF WANDS
OR KNIGHT OF WANDS
Lord of the Flame and the Lightning;
King of the Spirits of Fire;
King of the Salamanders

Element: Fire of Fire

Astrology: [20°–29° Scorpio III—fixed water]; 0°–19° Sagittarius I & II—mutable fire

Star Group: Sagittarius, Ophiuchus, Hercules, Draco

Dates:[230] November 10–December 10

Associated Majors: [Death; shadow decan], Temperance/Art, Judgement/Aeon for Fire of Fire

Associated Minors: The 7 of Cups (*Debauch*/*Illusionary Success*), the 8 of Wands (*Swiftness*), the 9 of Wands (*Strength*/*Great Strength*). Also, the 2 of Wands through all Knights' association with Chokmah

---

230. Dates vary annually. All court card dates listed in this book are based on 2019–2020 dates.

Sephira/World: Chokmah in Atziluth

Tetragrammaton: *Yod* of *yod*

I Ching: Hexagram 51, *zhèn*

Geomantic Figure: *Acquisitio*

Golden Dawn Crest: Winged black horse head

Themes and Keywords: Pure will. First flash. Insight. Great force, swiftly expended. A spark. Energy expenditure, transient energy. Decisive action. Masculine power. Fired up. One explosive shot toward a goal. Impulsiveness and impetuosity. Leadership. Creating destiny. Opportunity arising. Entrepreneurial spirit.

ASTROLOGY/RELATED DECANS

The Wands' patriarch embodies the qualities of mutable fire, having ownership of the first two decans of Sagittarius. In essence he is fiery, galvanized, generous, and impulsive, charging forth with zeal. He also picks up the last decan of Scorpio as a hidden part of his nature. Scorpio's motto is "I desire," and Sagittarius says, "I aim." His desires drive him ever forward, toward a goal. On occasion he chases castles in the air. While his dreams may not always be pragmatic, they are visionary, energized, and impassioned.

Wands lizards—or lizard theriomorphs—eerily bedeck this King's throne; on the throne's back panel appears a silhouette of the Sagittarian archer. (*Mystical Tarot*)

He exemplifies the force of divine will: primal initiations and explosive creativity. The first decan of Sagittarius (Mercury-ruled) gives swiftness and inspiration.[231] Like lightning and thought itself, his power is brilliant yet transient. The lunar-ruled middle decan adds strength to his commencement, vitality arising from adaptability to the constant of change. His Scorpio decan debauch (Venus-ruled) shows a possible profligate nature when his energy wavers.[232]

ELEMENTAL

The King (RWS) or Knight (Thoth) represents the lightning flash, the "fiery part of fire."[233] Fire being the first of the four elements, he lights the way for the other court cards. All Wands concern the life force, the will, human drives; he in particular has the fiery qualities of swiftness and flammability or contagiousness. His brilliance can be an inspiring source of guidance, but his heat is quickly spent. Like fuel, he bears immense potential energy, rapidly consumed. Like flames on tinder, he leaps impulsively from one thing to the next; his charisma challenges all to follow or be left behind.

This King/Knight rides among fire elementals carrying the
blazing torch of the Ace of Wands. (*Rosetta Tarot*)

---

231. Mercury is in detriment in Sagittarius, yet in rulership of the eights.

232. Venus is also in detriment in Scorpio, yet in rulership of the sevens.

233. Crowley, *Book of Thoth*, 151.

GEOMANTIC FIGURE/I CHING HEXAGRAM

He is assigned the geomantic figure *Acquisitio* (gain), associated with diurnal Jupiter and Sagittarius. It represents two upright bowls holding bounty, for in essence it denotes acquiring things: resources, benefits, desires, honors, and knowledge. It's considered generally positive in almost all situations—except where loss is desired.

His I Ching hexagram is 51, *zhèn*, "thunder," where the trigram of thunder or fire is twice repeated. It's also called the "arousing," the "shocking," the "thunderclap," and—especially appropriate for the primal *yod*—the beginning of movement. The motion may be startling, but it leads to success. One goes forward resolutely with both apprehension and confidence.

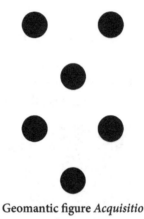

Geomantic figure *Acquisitio*

Hexagram 51, *zhèn*

RIDER-WAITE-SMITH SYMBOLISM

King of Wands (*Rider-Waite-Smith Tarot*)

Salamanders, creatures born and dwelling in flame, are the wand court's emblems. Along with lion silhouettes (an allusion to fiery Leo), they appear on the King's throne and in the robes of all except the Queen.[234] The King's crown bears flame-like points. The only king viewed in profile, he holds his wand like a walking stick, as if his eager and enterprising spirit is prompting him to rise. As in other wand courts, the land glimpsed beyond appears dry and brightly lit.

THOTH SYMBOLISM

True to the Golden Dawn's *Book T* description, the Knight wears a black horse-head helm and rides a black steed with flaming mane and tail. The black horse is a symbol of strength and swiftness and symbolically combines his decans: Scorpio (Death; black) and Sagittarius (horses). He epitomizes volatility as his horse rears and leaps, erupting upward as if about to blast off with meteoric velocity. The Knight carries an oversized, phallic, flaming club (like Hercules, whose constellation is part of this

---

234. The King's sign is Sagittarius, though, not Leo. Courts in this deck tend to emphasize their shared element—in this case, fire—rather than their associated sign.

card's star group). His flaming club looks remarkably like the Ace of Wands, a reference to his initiatory force.

RELATED CARDS

The King/Knight of Wands corresponds to three decans and their associated minor cards: the 7 of Cups (Scorpio III), the 8 of Wands (Sagittarius I), and the 9 of Wands (Sagittarius II). While the Sagittarius decans highlight his role as an adventurous leader, the Scorpio decan suggests not all his visions are based in reality. Through these three minors, he also connects to Death (Scorpio) and Temperance/Art (Sagittarius)—two cards which emphasize how transformation and aspiration shape great enterprises.

On the Tree of Life, all Kings/Knights correspond to the second sephira, Chokmah, and therefore all twos, as well as the Ace of Wands because the tip of the *yod* is said to be in Kether.[235] He has a relationship to the other King/Knights (also the fiery part of their suits) and to the other Wand court cards. Finally, his fiery nature connects him to the Judgement/Aeon card—the card of elemental fire.

---

235. See Ace of Wands.

QUEEN OF WANDS
Queen of the Thrones of Flame;
Queen of the Salamanders

Element: Water of Fire

Astrology: [20°–29° Pisces III—mutable water]; 0°–19° Aries I & II—cardinal fire

Star Group: Pisces, Aries, Andromeda, Cassiopeia

Dates:[236] March 10–April 9 (includes March equinox)

Associated Majors: [The Moon; shadow decan], The Emperor, The Hanged Man and Judgement/Aeon for Water of Fire

Associated Minors: The 10 of Cups (*Satiety/Perfected Success*), the 2 of Wands (*Dominion*), the 3 of Wands (*Virtue/Established Strength*)

Sephira/World: Binah in Atziluth

Tetragrammaton: Primal *heh* of *yod*

I Ching: Hexagram 17, *suí*

Geomantic Figure: *Puer*

---

236. Dates vary annually. All court card dates listed in this book are based on 2019–2020 dates.

Golden Dawn Crest: Winged leopard head

Themes and Keywords: Steady force. Will established: will, modified by love. Will, directed by emotional maturity, is subconsciously prepared. Shakti. Feminine power. Sensuality, sexuality, and magnetism. Transformative processes. Control versus surrender to ecstasy. Meditative inner fire. Courage, nobility, and fierceness. Persistent energy. Social networking. Extroverted emotional intelligence.

ASTROLOGY/RELATED DECANS

The Queen of Wands has command over both the end and beginning of the zodiacal cycle. She has the first two Aries decans and degree 0, marking the March equinox. She also holds the last degree and decan in Pisces. Cardinal fire sign Aries, the most cardinal of signs, declares "I am." Her hidden nature reflects mutable water and the most mutable of all, malleable Pisces, whose motto is "I believe." Her star group includes Andromeda, meaning "ruler of men"; Andromeda's story has both Aries and Pisces themes.

She's undeniably feminine, yet connected thrice to Mars which typifies masculine drive. Mars rules Aries and has specific rulership over the first decan of Aries and the last decan of Pisces. Her other Aries decan is ruled by the Sun, exalted in Aries. Aries takes the lead, conquers and establishes *Dominion*, and then governs with *Virtue (Established Strength)*. But her Pisces decan reveals a potential unraveling: a secret longing for the surrender and dissolution of satiety.

ELEMENTAL

The Queen of Wands is the "watery part of fire."[237] Although that sounds like a contradiction in terms, we can think of "watery" as a synonym for "connecting" or "adaptable." Thus while all Wands concern the life force, will, and drives, the Queen specializes in connecting and magnifying these forces—in the way that fire may catch from one fuel source to another, or the way fire may be reflected and amplified on the water's surface. She is a social connector, bringing people into each other's spheres on

---

237. Crowley, *Book of Thoth*, 152.

a flowing current of enthusiasm. Her inverse is the King/Knight of Cups, who inspires by compassionate example.

GEOMANTIC FIGURE/I CHING HEXAGRAM

Her geomantic figure is *Puer*, which is associated with Mars and Aries. *Puer* is Latin for "the boy," and the figure looks like an erect phallus and testes. It's not contradictory at all for this feminine Queen when one considers her forceful martial nature and the youthful energy of the sign. *Puer* is only considered positive in two things: love and war.

The I Ching hexagram is 17, *suí*, meaning "following," which combines the trigrams for thunder and lake: reflection upon impulse. One serves before ruling. It's indicative of the virtue through which she leads by example, ruling steadily, adapting to change, and encouraging others to follow.

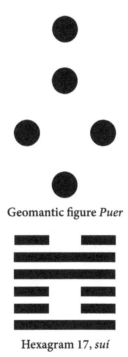

Geomantic figure *Puer*

Hexagram 17, *suí*

© 1971 U.S. GAMES SYSTEMS, INC.

Queen of Wands (*Rider-Waite-Smith Tarot*) (left)
The image on the right borrows and foregrounds both the feline theme and solar sunflowers
from Pamela Colman Smith's Queen of Wands. (*Animal Totem Tarot*)

Historically, the bold and sexually charismatic Queen of Wands has been a frank, friendly "country woman"—more "magnetic," Waite says, than her King.[238] Her playing-card counterpart, Queen of Diamonds, has been described as Amazonian queen Penthesilea and biblical matriarch Rachel.

Feline imagery abounds: a cat brooch; the lions of Leo (triplicity counterpart to the Queen's Aries and the King's Sagittarius); a black-furred familiar thought to be the cat Snuffles, belonging to Smith's friend Ellen Terry.[239] Sunflowers allude both to the solar decan (the 3 of Wands) and to solar Leo. Her crown bears the Wands' living foliage. Her at-ease stance, facing forward and outward, reminds us that she is comfortable with her own sexuality.

238. Waite, *Pictorial Key*, 172.

239. Katz and Goodwin, *Secrets of the Waite-Smith Tarot*, 231.

THOTH SYMBOLISM

**She has the leopard as crest and companion, and bears
the thyrsus wand of the Maenads.** (*Rosetta Tarot*)

An archetypal scarlet woman on a throne of flame towers over us. Her seated familiar (and her helm crest) is a leopard, and she carries an immense thyrsus wand topped with a phallic pine cone. Her face, per the *Book T* description, is "beautiful and resolute."[240] Crowley says it expresses the ecstasy of mind "well in-drawn to the mystery" within.[241] Her character is described as calmly authoritative, prideful, generous—though on her own initiative—and occasionally savage. Her crown has twelve solar looking rays, representing the band of the zodiac around the sun. She rests her hand on the leopard, shepherding the animal soul that drives primal urges.

RELATED CARDS

The Queen of Wands' three decan cards are: the 10 of Cups (*Satiety*/Pisces III), the 2 of Wands (*Dominion*/Aries I), and the 3 of Wands (*Virtue*/Aries II). The first two, marking the watery end of the old zodiacal year and the fiery beginning of the new, are the only consecutive decans ruled by the same planet: Mars. Where water and fire meet, a numinous rainbow forms—a fleeting bridge from "I believe" to "I am." In her

---

240. Fra., *Liber Theta*, 65.

241. Crowley, *Book of Thoth*, 152.

third decan, the sun's exaltation in Aries signals a society rightly led. The associated majors, the Moon and the Emperor, follow the same path from reactive dissolution and surrender to the decisive, new construction of society.

On the Tree of Life, Queens correspond to the third sephira, Binah; so do the minor threes. Womb-like, they form what is unmanifest and inchoate into the real. She shares the dynamic will of other Wand courts and the refining elemental fire of the Judgement/Aeon card.

KNIGHT OF WANDS
OR PRINCE OF WANDS
The Prince of the Chariot of Fire;
Prince and Emperor of the Salamanders

Element: Air of Fire

Astrology: [20°–29° Cancer III—cardinal water]; 0°–19° Leo I & II—fixed fire

Star Group: Leo, Leo Minor, Ursa Minor, Southern Dog. Includes Regulus, Royal Watcher of the North

Dates:[242] July 12–August 12 (includes cross-quarter holiday)

Associated Majors: [The Chariot; shadow decan], Strength/Lust, Fool and Judgement/Aeon for Air of Fire

Associated Minors: The 4 of Cups (*Luxury/Blended Pleasure*), the 5 of Wands (*Strife*), the 6 of Wands (*Victory*)

Sephira/World: Tiphareth in Atziluth

---

242. Dates vary annually. All court card dates listed in this book are based on 2019–2020 dates.

Tetragrammaton: *Vav* of *yod*

I Ching: Hexagram 42, *yí* (see footnote to I Ching section)

Geomantic Figure: *Fortuna Major*

Golden Dawn Crest: Winged lion head

Themes and Keywords: Reason directs the will after feelings. Product of fire's force and form. Dramatic entrances. Royal and regal. Wins in the long run. Fame and fortune, quests for glory. Pride and kingship, generosity and ego. Striving for victory, luxury, and achievement. Heart and backbone. Love of the spotlight. Performative charisma.

ASTROLOGY/RELATED DECANS

The fire son represents the full-strength, fixed version of fire. Leo's motto is "I will." The Prince-Knight's two decans of Leo straddle two related concepts: the tension of *Strife* in Leo I representing striving, and the honors of harmony and *Victory* in Leo II. Leo I is Saturn ruled, lending pressure to his endeavors, already stressed by the martial influence of the five. In Leo II, his happy place, the sign and sixes are ruled by the Sun, and the decan was ruled by fortunate Jupiter.

Only the solar and lunar "planets" rule over just one sign and the fire son has them both, for his hidden decan is the last decan of cardinal water sign Cancer, doubly ruled by the Moon. Cancer's motto is "I feel"—it's this that gives him craving for emotional highs and drama.

The Leo constellation includes Regulus, Royal Watcher of the North, the "little King" and heart of the Lion, bringing potential for glory with honorable behavior.

PRINCE OF WANDS
AIR OF FIRE

The Prince has motifs of his three decans: the volcano (5 of Wands/Leo I) the laurel-crowned lion (6 of Wands/Leo II), and the scallop shell with pearl (his shadow decan 4 of Cups/Cancer III). (*Tabula Mundi Tarot*)

ELEMENTAL

The Knight/Prince of Wands represents the "airy part of fire."[243] Airy qualities are freedom and communicability—the intellect's power to transmit and receive. While all Wands concern the life force, will, and drives, the Knight/Prince of Wands is a powerful and visible conductor of those energies. Hot air feeds his flames; he enthusiastically savors the spotlight. Neither self-conscious nor self-aware, he enjoys his mother's social staying power and his father's inspired charisma. His brilliance draws the eye, making him equally compelling as a performer and a messenger. His inverse is the King/Knight of Swords, who commands the rules of intellectual engagement.

GEOMANTIC FIGURE/I CHING HEXAGRAM

The Knight/Prince of Wands is assigned the geomantic figure *Fortuna Major*, which is as good as it sounds. It is associated with Leo and represents a flowering or fruiting stalk open at the top to receive the blessings of fame, fortune, and divine assistance, and it is beneficial in all situations, especially the start of new ventures and contests.

---

243. Crowley, *Book of Thoth*, 153.

The hexagram is 42, *yí*, "augmenting," or the idea of increase, the combination of thunder and wind.[244] To advance, the fire son must seize the day. With sincere heart he avoids peril and emerges victorious. An increase in opportunity leads to enhanced prosperity.

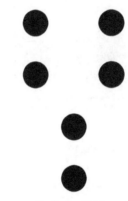

Geomantic figure *Fortuna Major*

Hexagram 42, *yí*

---

244. Hexagram 42 and 27 (Princess of Wands, his consort) have the same phoneme and accent but are different words.

RIDER-WAITE-SMITH SYMBOLISM

Knight of Wands (*Rider-Waite-Smith Tarot*) (left)
In the image on the right, the normal equine steed of Knights has been
replaced with a giant, surreal, fiery, golden Wands lizard! (*Mystical Tarot*)

The impetuous but rarely hostile Knight of Wands lightly holds the reins as his spirited steed rears. As Waite points out, he "is not on a warlike errand." The sky is clear and sunny, reminding us of this knight's connection with solar Leo as well as the solar sephira Tiphareth. On the Knight's surcoat appears the salamander emblem (worn also by the King and Page). Extravagant plumage on his helm and armbraces imitates flames, and three-leaved shamrocks adorn his horse's tack. The mountains seen in the other wand courts appear to be squared off here, like pyramids—symbols of human ambition and achievement rather than natural phenomena.

THOTH SYMBOLISM

Crowley's ascendant is in Leo I; thus, like his sun sign court card, it's one of the only with pupils in the eyes.[245] It's also marked with his personal sigil. Like the Queen, the Prince wears a solar-rayed crown; his has eleven rays, referencing Leo's Lust card. His crest is the winged lion's head, per *Book T*. He bears the phoenix wand of power

---

245. See the Queen of Swords.

and energy. Though *Book T* specifies flames both "waved and salient" (fire's force and form—the parents), his chariot travels only upon the salient flames of his mother. Crowley describes him as emphatic, vigorous in opinion, essentially just, noble, romantic, boastful, proud, and generous.

RELATED CARDS

In moving from the 4 to the 5 to the 6, all Princes (or RWS Knights) move from stasis to disruption to balance. For this Prince, it's the 4 of Cups (*Luxury*/Cancer III), the 5 of Wands (*Strife*/Leo I), and the 6 of Wands (*Victory*/Leo II). If he can set aside coddled comfort for risk and push himself to achieve, he will prevail publicly; in the starring role, he wins the attention he so enjoys. The strictures of decan-ruler Saturn, in the 5, lead to the rewards of decan ruler Jupiter, in the 6. His associated major arcana, the Chariot and Strength/Lust, portray a similar passage from lunar saturation to solar radiance.

On the Tree of Life, this Knight/Prince corresponds other Knights/Princes, as well as all minor sixes—each embodying power and purpose in life. As with all members of his family, his will drives all his actions; the refining fire of the Judgement/Aeon card continually tests their mettle.

PAGE OF WANDS
OR PRINCESS OF WANDS
Princess of the Shining Flame;
Rose of the Palace of Fire;
Princess and Empress of the Salamanders;
Throne of the Ace of Wands

Element: Earth of Fire

Astrology: Cancer-Leo-Virgo; centered on Kerubic fire sign Leo

Dates: N/A; Pages rule quadrants of space rather than time

Geographical Quadrant: Continent of Asia

Associated Majors: The World/Universe and Judgement/Aeon for Earth of Fire

Associated Minors: Ace of Wands as Throne; the 10 of Wands as Malkuth. All Wands as progression from root to rose

Sephira/World: Malkuth of Atziluth

Tetragrammaton: Final *heh* of *yod*

I Ching: Hexagram 27, *yí* (see footnote to I Ching section)

Geomantic Figure: *Cauda Draconis*

Golden Dawn Crest: Winged tiger head

Themes and Keywords: Both initiation and flowering of creative processes. Volatility and transition. Strength in beauty, creating beauty. Vitality and passion. Action, rightly taken. Sudden love or anger. Brilliance, courage, and daring. Messages and news. The flame of incarnation.

ASTROLOGY/RELATED DECANS

The Page/Princess of Wands rules over the quadrant spanning the signs Cancer, Leo, and Virgo. As she is part of the fire court, her primary expression is around the central sign, Leo.[246] The strength inherent in fire is revealed in fixed fire. It is undeniably evident; she is a force of nature.[247] Like the sun, she blazes and lesser objects fall into her orbit; like fire itself, she absorbs all of the air in a room. All eyes fall upon her and cannot look away. She is not necessarily reliable, but she is courageous, brilliant, enthusiastic, combustive, theatrical, all-consuming, and implacable.

In the Northern Hemisphere, the progression from Cancer, through Leo, and into Virgo takes place in the summer quarter of the year, aligning with her fiery nature. But Pages/Princesses in tarot don't rule over quadrants of time. Instead, they rule space. Her spatial sector contains the Eastern continent of Asia.

ELEMENTAL

The Page/Princess of Wands is the "earthy part of fire": the fuel—whether wood, charcoal, or flint—that feeds the fire.[248] While the previous elemental parts express fiery qualities, it is earth that they produce and which ultimately sustains them all. As the earthy part of fire, she presages the phoenix-like renewal of the life cycle from earth to

---

246. Leo also represents her sibling and consort, the Prince of Wands.

247. Although Waite refers to Pages as "he," we use "she," both to balance the court in terms of archetypal masculine and feminine and also to recognize the Page's identity as a Princess. In actual interpretation, all courts can represent all genders.

248. Crowley, *Book of Thoth*, 155.

fire, from pentacles to wands. We think of her as expressing "news" or "newness," for she represents reincarnation itself—the flame of life forever rekindled in new vehicles. Her counterpart is the King/Knight of Pentacles, who commands the world of matter sustaining her.

GEOMANTIC FIGURE/I CHING HEXAGRAM

Cauda Draconis is the "tail of the dragon," corresponding to the south node of the moon.[249] It's only considered good for bringing releases and completions; it has absorbed all and is letting go. It's contradictory for it brings evil to good, yet good to evil. Generally speaking, it is a challenge, for it heralds disruptions.

Hexagram 27 at first glance involves the other end of the dragon (its head), but it's ultimately related. It's called *yí*, or "nourishment, jaws."[250] The trigrams of thunder and mountain combined indicate a need to reflect upon what fuel (inner visions) we are taking in and how we are using them to direct our actions toward what matters.

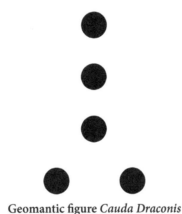

Geomantic figure *Cauda Draconis*

---

249. Interestingly, the south node is exalted in fire sign Sagittarius (Temperance/Art; and the Knight/Prince of Wands, whose "eld" she awakens).

250. Hexagram 27 and 42 (Knight/Prince of Wands, her consort) have the same phoneme and accent but are different words.

Hexagram 27, *yí*

RIDER-WAITE-SMITH SYMBOLISM

PAGE of WANDS.

Page of Wands (*Rider-Waite-Smith Tarot*) (left)
The salamander totem animal glimpsed on Waite-Smith Wands courts takes center stage
in the image on the right, along with a rippling, flame-bright ribbon. (*Animal Totem Tarot*)

The Page of Wands is ever a stranger bearing the news, standing "in the act of proclamation." She wears the same salamander raiment as her brother and father. Unlike others in the family, she gazes intently at her staff; perhaps toward the future. She recognizes the power of the tidings the staff represents. Like her sister Pages of Cups and Pentacles, she wears a soft hat rather than a crown or helmet; it bears the flame (or *yod*) of the Wands suit. The background is the same dry and sandy dunescape glimpsed in other Wand courts.

THOTH SYMBOLISM

In *Book T*, Princesses are described as being contradictory: "permanent yet volatile" and "stable, yet erratic." It fits especially well for Miss Earth of Fire. Like all Princesses, she is complete and contains all the potential inherent in the King, Queen, and Prince. She needs no armor and no horse, throne, or chariot. Within a *yod*-shaped flame, she is appropriately unclothed except for a plumed crown. She holds a solar wand with thirty rays (reference to the path of *resh*/Sun) and is literally grasping the tiger (her crest) by the tail. Her altar is adorned with rams (Aries/solar spring) and five roses for the earthly senses.

PRINCESS OF WANDS
EARTH OF FIRE

The Princess has the flaming tree of her counterpart, the Ace of Wands, and the passionate crest of the tiger. (*Tabula Mundi Tarot*)

RELATED CARDS

All the force of the Wands suit comes to rest here, in the "throne of the Ace of Wands," this Page/Princess; she represents its self-sufficient power to act in the earthly realm. She wields the Ace's potential. Her minor cards may trace the arc from *Dominion* to *Oppression* (the 2 to 10 of Wands). Or they may correspond to the "summer quadrant"—Cancer, Leo, Virgo (the 2, 3, 4 of Cups; the 5, 6, 7 of Wands; the 8, 9, 10 of Pentacles)—a journey which begins in *Love*, climaxes in *Success*, and ends in *Wealth*. Her major arcana are the Chariot, Strength/Lust, and the Hermit: the armored warrior surrenders to the naked goddess, who then sends her light underground.

This Princess corresponds to all other Princesses, as well as all the tens. Qabalistically, tens are the "fruit of the Tree," creation's way of renewing itself. The will expressed by all Wands courts becomes concrete here; the Spirit forged by Judgement/ Aeon's refining fire now sets events in motion.

KING OF CUPS
OR KNIGHT OF CUPS
Lord of the Waves and the Waters;
King of the Hosts of the Sea;
King of the Undines and Nymphs

Element: Fire of Water

Astrology: [20°–29° Aquarius III—fixed air]; 0°–19° Pisces I & II—mutable water

Star Group: Pegasus. The Square, Cepheus

Dates:[251] February 9–March 9

Associated Majors: [The Star; shadow decan], The Moon, Judgement/Aeon and the Hanged Man for Fire of Water

Associated Minors: The 7 of Swords (*Futility/Unstable Effort*), the 8 of Cups (*Indolence*), the 9 of Cups (*Happiness*), Also, the 2 of Cups through all Knights' association with Chokmah

Sephira/World: Chokmah in Briah

---

251. Dates vary annually. All court card dates listed in this book are based on 2019–2020 dates.

Tetragrammaton: *Yod* of primal *heh*

I Ching: Hexagram 54, *guī mèi*

Geomantic Figure: *Laetitia*

Golden Dawn Crest: Peacock with open wings

Themes and Keywords: Will directs the emotions. Romantic, imaginative, sensitive, dilettante. To love and to dare. Passive/indolent but ardent if roused to passion. Transcendental. Chivalry. Spiritual questing, the Holy Grail. Chasing dreams. Poetry and the arts. Dissolving boundaries. Soul transmutation. Spiritual teaching.

ASTROLOGY/RELATED DECANS

The King/Knight of Cups is mainly mutable water sign Pisces, ruled by Jupiter and Neptune. Pisces is a true believer and goes forth with faith in something higher. The intent is to transcend. The first decan of Pisces, however, is ruled by Saturn, a dragging anchor. *Indolence* (*Abandoned Success*) represents the King's potential for listless passivity as he loses heart in the creative process. In Pisces II, *Happiness*, decan of his sign's ruler Jupiter, his faith is rewarded and his heart's desire is achieved. His shadow decan, or the hidden part of his nature, is Aquarius III, *Futility* or *Unstable Effort*. Aquarius is a sign of visionary thoughts and hope, but the third decan is ruled by the inconstant Moon. Thus on his spiritual quests, the Knight must find the perfect balance, seeking fulfillment and true joy, while avoiding the pitfalls of stagnation and idleness on one side and vacillation and diffusion on the other.

KNIGHT OF CUPS
FIRE OF WATER

The Knight bears motifs of his decans on his shield: the figurehead of the lunar barge (8 of Cups/Pisces I), the wishbone (9 of Cups/Pisces II), and the overladen camel (his shadow, 7 of Swords/Aquarius III). (*Tabula Mundi Tarot*)

ELEMENTAL

The King/Knight of Cups represents the "fiery part of water."[252] Like all Kings/Knights, he has the ability to inspire. Cups and water concern the emotional world, making him a philosopher of the human heart. His gift is to move the masses through compassionate example rather than individual encounters. He may be an inspirational speaker, a guru, a pontiff, a preacher, and a patron of art and humanistic ideals. Like sunlight on water, his visions are ephemeral; his message of love must be absorbed into our own emotional worlds to spread. His inverse is the Queen of Wands, who connects and ignites kindred spirits rather than proselytizing.

GEOMANTIC FIGURE/I CHING HEXAGRAM

Laetitia means "joy" and is associated with Pisces and Jupiter. The figure is shaped like an archway or rainbow and points upward to something higher. It is a literally buoyant figure that brings happiness, delight, and the ability to rise above sorrows.

The I Ching hexagram 54, *guì mèi*, is "marrying maiden," comprised of the trigrams for thunder and marsh/lake. It is about acceptance of what cannot be changed

252. Crowley, *Book of Thoth*, 156.

and following propriety. One adapts to circumstances and transforms. There are possible pitfalls: mistakes made at the beginning of a situation will have to be lived with. One must use discrimination when setting forth on a path.

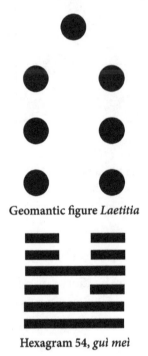

Geomantic figure *Laetitia*

Hexagram 54, *gui mei*

RIDER-WAITE-SMITH SYMBOLISM

King of Cups (*Rider-Waite-Smith Tarot*) (left)
On the right, the fish King's scaly greaves and sabots rest on the usual platform-in-the-sea throne.
Waite-Smith's three-masted vessel appears here too, slightly enlarged. (*Pre-Raphaelite Tarot*)

Water, water everywhere: waves adorn his crown; his throne is literally surrounded by them. A fish leaps to his left, another dangles from his chain of office; even his feet are scaly! Fish appear in the Queen and Page too; here, they may specifically allude to Pisces. His short scepter (its form echoed in throne) is cuplike; he has a diplomat's calm and soft power. The ship to his right suggests his message may travel far, if carried by the conviction of people of faith. Cartomantically, he corresponds to Charlemagne the lawgiver, as well as to the King of Hearts (or "Suicide King").

THOTH SYMBOLISM

He rides a white horse leaping over the waves, appropriate since the Pegasus constellation is in his star group. It gives him the air of Galahad, the Knight of the Grail known for gallantry and purity. True to the *Book T* description, he holds a grail from which a crab issues. While the crab is a symbol of Cancer, it's also often seen on the moon cards (Pisces) as an emblem of the waters of the subconscious rising.

The peacock on the card is his traditional crest, signifying a stage of alchemical transformation wherein matter becomes spiritualized. The Knight is winged; he too has been cleansed and transformed.

RELATED CARDS

The King/Knight of Cups corresponds to the 7 of Swords (*Futility*/Aquarius III), the 8 of Cups (*Indolence*/Pisces I), and the 9 of Cups (*Happiness*/Pisces II). In the Aquarius decan, he learns the pointless emptiness of self-serving action; in the Pisces decans, he journeys through the soul's dark night into joy. The corresponding majors, the Star and the Moon, capture both his idealism and his need to disseminate the spiritual lessons he has learned at a collective level.

On the Tree of Life, all Kings/Knights correspond to the second sephira, Chokmah, and therefore all twos. Like the other King/Knights (also the fiery part of their suits), his mission is to light the way for the suit. Alongside his family, the court cards of the Cups, he rules over the heart's acts of daring: to feel, to desire, to believe. The Hanged Man represents the sacrificial impulse which animates his quest.

QUEEN OF CUPS
Queen of the Thrones of the Waters;
Queen of the Nymphs and Undines

Element: Water of Water

Astrology: [20°–29° Gemini III—mutable air]; 0°–19° Cancer I & II—cardinal water

Star Group: Castor/Pollux for Gemini decan. Praesepe, the Manger. Canis Minor, Argo Navis, Ursa Minor

Dates:[253] June 11–July 11 (includes June solstice)

Associated Majors: [The Lovers; shadow decan], The Chariot, The Hanged Man for Water of Water

Associated Minors: The 10 of Swords (*Ruin*), the 2 of Cups (*Love*), the 3 of Cups (*Abundance*)

Sephira/World: Binah in Briah

Tetragrammaton: Primal *heh* of primal *heh*

I Ching: Hexagram 58, *dui*

---

253. Dates vary annually. All court card dates listed in this book are based on 2019–2020 dates.

Geomantic Figure: *Populus*

Golden Dawn Crest: Ibis with open wings

Themes and Keywords: Pure emotions, feelings. Dreams and the astral. Memories and visions. To love. Nurturing. Feminine qualities. Reflective properties. Blurring of self and other. Lunar forces. The anima. Extrasensory perception and clairvoyance. Receptivity. Dissolution of boundaries between reality and illusion. Empathy. Counseling.

ASTROLOGY/RELATED DECANS

Cardinal water, Cancer, is maternal, nurturing, and protective. Cancer is ruled by the Moon. The sky's great reflector has long been an emblem of the Great Mother goddesses. This lunar quality also gives her psychic ability, popular favor, fruitfulness, and the ability to reflect the nature of those who behold her just as the moon mirrors the light of the sun. Cancer feels deeply, and wants to support and nourish those she cares about. These traits increase her popularity, for who does not want to be loved, comforted, and mirrored?

Cancer I is Venus ruled, increasing her feminine capacity for unconditional *Love*. Cancer II is ruled by Mercury, expanding her ability to plumb deep and cross subconscious barriers, bringing forth *Abundance* willingly shared with those in her inner circle. Her latent decan, Gemini III, interjects the possibly of disharmony and internal division disturbing her placidity. Like a stone thrown into a clear pond, the Lord of Ruin creates ripples disrupting her reflective nature.

Two lotuses float in the rippling water for the 2 of Cups,
her Cancer I decan. (*Rosetta Tarot*)

ELEMENTAL

The Queen of Cups is the "watery part of water," the most archetypally feminine of queens.[254] Thus she embodies both of water's properties—"reflecting" and "connecting"—and its metaphorical domain as the "feeling realm." As an empath, she reflects emotions; as a psychic, she connects with them. Because she also magnifies feeling, her moods may be a force to reckon with. Just as rain becomes one with the sea it falls on, she dissolves the boundary between self and other. She waxes and wanes, rises and falls with the tide; while she herself may be unknowable, nothing can be hidden from her intuition.

254. Crowley, *Book of Thoth*, 157.

The wavelike overhang of the throne appears in early Queen of Cups images, as does the closed cup, symbol of depths sounded through intuition only. (*Camoin-Jodorowsky Tarot de Marseille*)

GEOMANTIC FIGURE/I CHING HEXAGRAM

The geomantic figure associated with the (waxing) moon and Cancer is *Populus*, Latin for "the people."[255] All of the possible places are filled, as if one is looking down upon a crowd. The assembly of people affects the outcome of the situation: the figure reflects what it is paired with, bringing favor to the favorable and disfavor to the unfavorable.

Hexagram 58, lake over lake, is *duì* or "joyousness." It indicates delight, good cheer, conversation, and entertainments with friends. Shared pleasures, encouragement, commonality, and shared experiences are bonding and create loyalty among people, as long as the shallow waters of mere self-indulgence are avoided.

---

255. The waning moon's geomantic figure is *Via*, which is assigned to the Queen's daughter, the Page/ Princess of Cups.

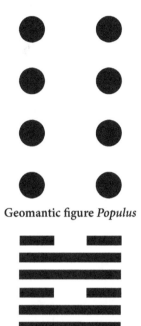

Geomantic figure *Populus*

Hexagram 58, *duì*

RIDER-WAITE-SMITH SYMBOLISM

Queen of Cups (*Rider-Waite-Smith Tarot*)

© 1971 U.S. GAMES SYSTEMS, INC.

Traditionally blond, associated with self-sacrificing heroines like the warrior Judith and the Trojan princess Polyxena, the Queen of Cups inclines her head toward an ornate reliquary, her eyes downcast. Like the crab whose sign she represents, the cup is completely encased, but it need not be open for her to divine its contents. Her watery robes merge with tides. Her throne bears shell motifs and, like all Queen's thrones except the Queen of Wands', sculpted cherub forms. Behind, sheer cliffs give way suddenly to the sea's edge; where certainty ends, the waters of intuition and belief begin.

THOTH SYMBOLISM

There is much visual similarity between this Queen and the Priestess, card of the moon. The moon rises and its fluctuating rays veil her, representing the astral light reflected in the waters below. She gazes into the mirrorlike surface as she cradles a cup formed from a shell. A crayfish issues from the cup, symbolizing Cancer, the moon, and the source of subconscious emotion. This, like the lotus of the suit she holds, is per her *Book T* description, as is the Ibis of Thoth that she rests her hand upon.[256] Her lotus has nine petals: the number of Yesod and the moon.

RELATED CARDS

The Queen of Cups' associated minor arcana are the 10 of Swords (*Ruin*/Gemini III), the 2 of Cups (*Love*/Cancer I), and the 3 of Cups (*Abundance*/Cancer II). All too acquainted with the devastation resulting from black-and-white thinking from her Gemini shadow decan, she embarks on the heart's work of forgiveness and redemption in the ensuing decans: in the Venus- and Mercury-ruled 2 and 3 of Cups, affections are easily transmitted and received. In her associated majors, the Lovers and the Chariot, we see a similar shift from a mind burdened by choice to a soul aligned with its own mission, from "I think" to "I feel."

---

256. Thoth is associated with both the Moon, Cancer's ruler, and Mercury, the ruler of her decan, Cancer II. It's also a fitting example of the transition from Gemini (the intellect, Mercury) to Cancer (the emotions, Moon).

On the Tree of Life, Queens correspond to the third sephira, Binah ("understanding"); so do the minor threes. Womb-like, they give shape to formless water and manifest what is inchoate into the real. The Queen inhabits the collective unconscious with the other Cups courts and partakes of the Hanged Man's sacrificial quest for understanding.

KNIGHT OF CUPS
OR PRINCE OF CUPS
Prince of the Chariot of the Waters;
Prince and Emperor of Nymphs and Undines

Element: Air of Water

Astrology: [20°–29° Libra III—cardinal air]; 0°–19° Scorpio I & II—fixed water

Star Group: Scorpion, Serpens, Lupus. Includes Antares, Royal Watcher of the West

Dates:[257] October 12–November 10 (includes cross-quarter holiday)

Associated Majors: [Justice/Adjustment; shadow decan], Death, The Fool and the Hanged Man for Air of Water

Associated Minors: The 4 of Swords (*Truce/Rest from Strife*), the 5 of Cups (*Disappointment/Loss in Pleasure*), the 6 of Cups (*Pleasure*)

Sephira/World: Tiphareth in Briah

Tetragrammaton: *Vav* of primal *heh*

---

257. Dates vary annually. All court card dates listed in this book are based on 2019–2020 dates.

I Ching: Hexagram 61, *zhōng fú*

Geomantic Figure: *Rubeus*

Golden Dawn Crest: Eagle

Themes and Keywords: Intellect applied to emotional realms. Intense, secretive, ruthless, duplicitous, mysterious, subtle. Passions underlying a serene exterior. Extremes of pleasure and suffering, satisfaction and hunger. Violent emotions and attraction to dark wisdom. Passive aggression and jealousy. Hidden inner tensions between mind and emotions. Expression of deep feelings and desires. Personal magnetism. Fiction as the artist's truth.

ASTROLOGY/RELATED DECANS

The magnetism of fixed water sign Scorpio underlies his calm visage. Scorpios have passions and desires veiled in mystery. The sign has all the potency of sex and death, as Scorpio is ruled by Mars and Pluto. Both sexuality and mortality are agents of transformation that allow new forms to develop from hidden depths. Life and death are two sides of the same coin, and like all Princes, the water son experiences extremes; here, those of sensual pleasure and the loss thereof. Scorpio I is thrice ruled by Mars; here Mars's burning desires can never be quenched, which leads to *Disappointment*. Scorpio II expresses the opposite idea of *Pleasure*, as the sun's rulership of both decan and sephira warms the waters rather than burning them completely away. His shadow decan is Libra III. He prefers the climax, both height and depth, and only enters into rest and the balance of *Truce* when completely burned out.

This Knight of Water rides a seahorse, an appropriate emblem for the
sign of Pisces (the fish) ruled by Jupiter (the centaur). (*Mystical Tarot*)

ELEMENTAL

The Knight/Prince of Cups represents the "airy part of water."[258] Airy court cards
move freely, and easily transmit and receive. While all Cups concern feeling states and
unconscious forces, the Knight/Prince of Cups communicates them with particular
power. He is potent wielder of story as both medicine and weapon. Like the air in a
fermented beverage, truth bubbles up through his fictions, transforming those who
hear it. It pays to heed his tales, but be wary of his relationship with fact. He is the
inverse of the Queen of Swords, whose love of the truth cuts through his fabrications.

GEOMANTIC FIGURE/I CHING HEXAGRAM

The geomantic figure of Scorpio and Mars is *Rubeus*, meaning "red": an extremely bad
glyph of passion and anger. It represents an upended glass from which all is lost; its
inverted nature indicates good in the evil and evil within good. This has some resonance that this Knight/Prince has great powers for extremes, both good and bad, but
is sometimes more attracted to the supremacy that evil wisdom promises.

---

258. Crowley, *Book of Thoth*, 157.

Paradoxically, we also have hexagram 61, *zhōng fú*, wind over lake, meaning "inner truth" or "return to center," the other extreme of a very beneficial glyph of good fortune, where opposites coming together lead to positive transformation.

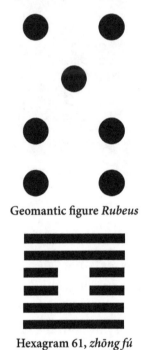

Geomantic figure *Rubeus*

Hexagram 61, *zhōng fú*

RIDER-WAITE-SMITH SYMBOLISM

Knight of Cups (*Rider-Waite-Smith Tarot*) (left)
The sorcerous "Natanabo" (Nectanebo), deceitful seducer,
appears in early Knight of Cups renditions (right). (*Sola Busca Tarot*)

The Knight of Cups bears "the higher graces of the imagination," says Waite. He rides at ease, his cup borne before him as though waiting for a pour, certain of his welcome. Cartomancy connects him to the sorcerer Nectanebo, who in serpent form fathered Alexander the Great. His surcoat bears waves and the fish seen in the Page and King of Cups, albeit in a distinctive red (letter *nun*—"fish"—corresponds to the path of Scorpio/Death). His winged helm and sabatons perhaps refer to Scorpio's highest form, the eagle. The water found in all Cups court backgrounds manifests here as a river, as in the 5 of Cups.[259]

THOTH SYMBOLISM

His wings are steam: air of water. His chariot is drawn by the black eagle of his crest. Black is a color of death, and the eagle is the highest or "airiest" part of the tripartite water sign Scorpio. He holds the lotus common to the emotional suit, inverted. He prefers that emotion be channeled by intellect (air), so instead he gazes at the cup,

---

259. A river flowing in one direction can be thought of as "fixed water," the mode and element of Scorpio.

from which a serpent peers. The serpent is another manifestation of Scorpio and a glyph of wisdom and intellect as well as life and transformation. The third aspect, the scorpion, is hidden, appropriate for the secretive nature of this Prince.

RELATED CARDS

All Knights/Princes share a dramatic journey: from stasis (4) to disruption (5) to balance (6). For this one, it's the 4 of Swords (*Truce*/Libra III), the 5 of Cups (*Disappointment*/Scorpio I), and the 6 of Cups (*Pleasure*/Scorpio II). If he can refrain from temporizing, he will experience the heights and depths of human experience. His passion has a magnetic effect on others, attracting and compelling their fascination. His associated majors, Justice/Adjustment and Death, signal that the rational must always give way to what is felt, just as balance gives way to desire. Patron of metaphor, he transforms facts into story and story into truth.

This Prince corresponds to all other Princes on the Tree of Life, as well as all minor sixes—each embodying power and purpose in life. As is true of other members of his family, his instrument is the human heart; the Hanged Man's sacrifice informs all their acts of daring.

PAGE OF CUPS
OR PRINCESS OF CUPS
Princess of the Waters;
Lotus of the Palace of Floods;
Princess and Empress of
the Nymphs and Undines;
Throne of the Ace of Cups

Element: Earth of Water

Astrology: Libra-Scorpio-Sagittarius; centered on Kerubic water sign Scorpio

Dates: N/A; Pages rule quadrants of space rather than time

Geographical Quadrant: Pacific Ocean

Associated Majors: The World/Universe and Hanged Man for Earth of Water

Associated Minors: Ace of Cups as Throne; the 10 of Cups as Malkuth. All Cups as progression from root to lotus

Sephira/World: Malkuth of Briah

Tetragrammaton: Final *heh* of primal *heh*

I Ching: Hexagram 41, *sŭn*

Geomantic Figure: *Via*

Golden Dawn Crest: Swan with open wings

Themes and Keywords: The muse and oracle, feminine and elusive. Visioning and manifesting dreams into reality. Acting upon emotions, responding to intuition. Flowering of the power to love. Rapture and romance. Dreamy and imaginative, artistic. Helpful companion. Higher soul connection and divine union. Acting with love. Depths of the dream world. Active imagination.

ASTROLOGY/RELATED DECANS

The Page/Princess of Cups rules over a quarter of the zodiac: the signs of Libra, Scorpio, and Sagittarius. It's centered around the fixed water sign Scorpio, the sign of dissolution into the west: symbolic death. The transition flows from Libra's harmony and balance, ruled by Venus and the emotion of love, the power of the suit. The impulse centers itself in Scorpio's deep desires and then transmutes in the Great Work, the aim of Sagittarius's "Art." It's a transformative process involving Libra's love of connection, Scorpio's merging and healing, and Sagittarius's higher inspiration. Altogether, it makes the water daughter a creative, intuitive, imaginative, and romantic figure.

The signs correlate to autumn in the Northern Hemisphere, the time of transitions and conclusions. While this resonates with Scorpio's connection with transformative processes, Pages/Princesses relate to quadrants of space rather than time. Along with her Ace, she occupies the quadrant centered over the Pacific Ocean.

ELEMENTAL

The Princess/Page of Cups is the "earthy part of water," in which the term "earthy" conveys stasis, receptivity, silence, fertility.[260] All cups concern feeling states and the realm of the unconscious, but the daughter of the family incubates that emotional content. Through dream and psychic connection, she provides the fertile ground

---

260. Crowley, *Book of Thoth*, 158.

where potent forces like longing, pain, and desire can take root. She is the irrigated, crystalline garden of the unconscious imagination, where divine love may incarnate as a human soul. Her inverse is the Queen of Pentacles/Disks, gardener of material wealth and canny steward of resources.

On Marseille "Valet de Coupes" cards, the Page's wavelike drapery crests over the cup; this version features a tiny seashell in the corner. (*Camoin-Jodorowsky Tarot de Marseille*)

GEOMANTIC FIGURE/I CHING HEXAGRAM

The Page/Princess of Cups has one of the two lunar associated geomantic figures: *Via*, the complement to that of her mother, the Queen (*Populus*). *Via* means "the way," and the figure of four single dots in a line represents a path taken. More than any other figure it indicates change, an action, or a transformation. It's a benign figure unless change is undesirable.

Hexagram 41, *sŭn*, means "decreasing." It's a becalming or decline that is natural after a period of flowering. It doesn't necessarily mean loss but rather a surrender, diminishing the passions of the lower self in order to increase the higher instinct, a sacrifice that is beneficial if sincere.

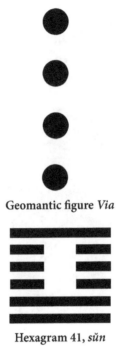

Geomantic figure *Via*

Hexagram 41, *sŭn*

RIDER-WAITE-SMITH SYMBOLISM

© 1971 U.S. GAMES SYSTEMS, INC.

Page of Cups (*Rider-Waite-Smith Tarot*) (left)
On the right, a fantastical reinterpretation: the usual "fish in a cup" is now a seahorse
in a cup; the fish itself, a giant Moorish idol used as a shield. (*Mystical Tarot*)

While fish adorn three out of four Cups courts, this one is no ordinary fish: it's "pictures of the mind taking form," says Waite.[261] The Page is not only regarding but *listening* to the fish, recognizing it as an oracular phenomenon. Hers is the only court styled as a "stage card"—her imagination is the theatre of the heart. Unlike her family, she is separate from the waters of the suit. Like other pages, she wears on her head an elemental signifier: here, a turban whose plume froths like a wave. Her blossom-bedecked tunic reminds us she is the Lotus of the Palace of Floods.

THOTH SYMBOLISM

Her face is rapturous as she holds out a large shell-like cup. Its shape and the scalloped edges of her dress visually recall the design of the scalloped web of light on the Ace, root to her flower. Eleven (number of magic, divinity, and inspiration) salt crystals (earth of water) decorate the hem. Her skin is the green of earth (earth of water) and Venus (love). The tortoise in her cup indicates Cancer. The "dolphin" beside her is associated with Pisces.[262] These are the two other water signs and the signs of her mother and father, respectively. Her crest is the swan, also associated with Venus and love.

RELATED CARDS

The power of the Cups suit comes to rest in this Page/Princess, the "earthy part of water" and the "throne of the Ace of Cups"; she represents its self-sufficient power to act in the earthly realm.[263] Vessel of the Ace's potential, her minor cards journey from *Love* to *Satiety* (the 2 to 10 of Cups). Alternately, she rules the cards of the "autumn quadrant"—Libra, Scorpio, Sagittarius (the 2, 3, 4 of Swords; the 5, 6, 7 of Cups; the 8, 9, 10 of Wands): an arc which travels from *Peace* to *Pleasure* to *Oppression*. In this quadrant her majors are Justice/Adjustment, Death, and Temperance/Art: her search

---

261. Waite, *Pictorial Key*, 204.

262. The dolphin is also associated with Venus, exalted in Pisces. The dolphin also appears on the 2 of Cups, *Love*, one of the decans of her mother, the Queen of Cups, and indicative of the power of the suit, "to love."

263. Crowley, *Book of Thoth*, 159; Regardie and Greer, *Golden Dawn*, 392.

for cosmic symmetry takes her through surrender and transformation, and finally to the Great Work.

All Princesses and all tens are Qabalistically related; they are the fruit of the Tree of Life, through which creation renews itself. She embodies the daring work of the human heart cultivated by her family; she is the secret wisdom bought by the Hanged Man's sacrifice.

KING OF SWORDS
OR KNIGHT OF SWORDS
Lord of the Winds and the Breezes;
King of the Spirits of Air;
King of the Sylphs and Sylphides

Element: Fire of Air

Astrology: [20°–29° Taurus III—fixed earth]; 0°–19° Gemini I & II—mutable air

Star Group: Castor and Pollux. Auriga. Canis Major and Minor

Dates:[264] May 10–June 10

Associated Majors: [The Hierophant; shadow decan], The Lovers, Judgement/Aeon and the Fool for Fire of Air

Associated Minors: The 7 of Pentacles/Disks (*Failure/Success Unfulfilled*), the 8 of Swords (*Interference/Shortened Force*), the 9 of Swords (*Cruelty* and *Despair*), Also, the 2 of Swords through all Knights' association with Chokmah

Sephira/World: Chokmah in Yetzirah

---

264. Dates vary annually. All court card dates listed in this book are based on 2019–2020 dates.

Tetragrammaton: *Yod* of *vav*

I Ching: Hexagram 32, *héng*

Geomantic Figure: *Albus*

Golden Dawn Crest: Winged six-pointed star

Themes and Keywords: Will over the intellect. Clever and skillful, but domineering. Intellectual brilliance. Decision making. Military intelligence. Active, fierce, discriminating, analytical. Overly forceful in small matters. Possibly pitiless, cold, deceitful, or lacking in reflection. Storm and activity. Strategy. Versatility. Inconstancy. The scientific methods. Judicious or judgmental.

ASTROLOGY/RELATED DECANS

His main attributes are that of mutable air, the mercurial sign of Gemini. Gemini's motto is "I think," for it is a sign of the rational mind and the mind's tendency to divide, thinking things through and breaking them down in order to make a selection between an ever-widening variety of choices. The sign is versatile, intellectually mobile, clever, clear, and objective. But though brilliant, the scientific mind can be insensitive, noncommittal, and indifferent to anything but cold logic. Gemini I, called *Interference* or *Shortened Force*, combines expansive Jupiter with Mercury's minutiae, revealing a tendency to apply excessive force to trivial things. Gemini II, under the influence of Mars, is ruthless and domineering, prone to *Cruelty*. At best, it is mentally disciplined and precise; at worst, it is a source of anxiety to self and others. His hidden influence, Taurus III, *Failure*, shows Saturn's inertia and patience, concepts foreign to him that he secretly fears.

KNIGHT OF SWORDS

FIRE OF AIR

The Knight bears the emblems of his decans: the poniards (8 of Swords/Gemini I and the Dioscuri star of his crest), the pierced boar head (9 of Swords/Gemini II), and the bull horns for his shadow decan (7 of Pentacles/Taurus III). (*Tabula Mundi Tarot*)

ELEMENTAL

The King/Knight of Swords is the "fiery part of air."[265] Metaphysically, fire is quick to initiate and easily caught; thus it falls to him to lead other minds. All swords patrol the realm of intellect and conflict; as their sovereign, the King/Knight of Swords sets rules and policies that all must follow. His judgment can be as incisive and brilliant as lightning—but also as unforgiving and destructive. He is as piercing as the sun dispelling clouds and as remote as a star in a clear sky. His inverse is the Knight/Prince of Wands, hot air enthusiast and promoter extraordinaire.

---

265. Crowley, *Book of Thoth*, 159.

Air is the vast kingdom of the eagle, king of birds. As in Waite-Smith and Thoth, he occupies the heights; his sharp vision discerns all. (*Animal Totem Tarot*)

GEOMANTIC FIGURE/I CHING HEXAGRAM

The geomantic figure associated with Gemini and Mercury is *Albus*, meaning "white," as in the brightness of clarity and intelligence. It represents an upright glass, standing for wisdom and purity. It's beneficial for profitable ventures and new starts and good for most things involving planning and mental discipline.

Hexagram 32, *héng*, has the trigrams of thunder above wind, meaning "enduring" or "duration." It's something that would benefit Gemini to work on: commitment and consistency, a message repeated by the King/Knight's shadow decan Taurus III. By maintaining constancy in the face of change and perseverance in what is right, good fortune follows.

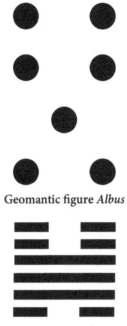

Geomantic figure *Albus*

Hexagram 32, *héng*

RIDER-WAITE-SMITH SYMBOLISM

King of Swords (*Rider-Waite-Smith Tarot*)

Waite points out the King's resemblance to Justice, saying he wields "the power of life and death." As in all sword courts, we see bare heights, windblown trees, pale blue skies, and robes, their sharp red color contrasting accessories. Creatures of air appear, too: carved butterflies on the throne and two birds for Gemini (though they also resemble the Aquarius glyph). His crown, alone among Kings, bears a winged cherub head, perhaps signifying the supreme power of the human mind. Despite the apparent symmetry of the card, he and his weapon are a bit off-center, suggesting that his judgment is only human, after all.

THOTH SYMBOLISM

On his helm he wears a "revolving wing" with blades marked with the four directions. He travels between south and east (fire and air). At the center is the six-pointed star, described as his crest in *Book T*; this and the swallows at his side are associated with travel and the *Dioscuri*.[266]

Crowley describes his steed as "maddened" and says the Knight represents the "Spirit of the Tempest" and the idea of attack. In one hand he holds a sword with a guard that looks like butterfly wings (air), and in the other, a poniard, a short dagger in line with the idea of "shortened force."

RELATED CARDS

The King/Knight of Swords corresponds to the 7 of Pentacles (*Failure*/Taurus III), the 8 of Swords (*Interference*/Gemini I), and the 9 of Swords (*Cruelty*/Gemini II). From his shadow Taurus decan, he knows the inertia that results when effort flags. In his Gemini decans, he makes hard choices and rules dispassionately; his impartiality can seem ruthless. His corresponding majors, the Hierophant and the Lovers, signal a shift from material motives to principled ones: what I *have* may be lost, but what I *know* is certain.

On the Tree of Life, Kings/Knights correspond to the second sephira, Chokmah, and twos—matters of balance and opposition. As the fiery part of their suits, these rulers light the way for the minors and other courts. Like all Swords courts, the King of Swords negotiates the battlefield of the mind with the weapons of balance, communication, and knowledge. All swords share this elemental-air journey toward wisdom with the Fool.

---

266. Castor and Pollux, twins of Gemini.

QUEEN OF SWORDS
Queen of the Thrones of Air;
Queen of Sylphs and Sylphides

Element: Water of Air

Astrology: [20°–29° Virgo III—mutable earth]; 0°–19° Libra I & II—cardinal air

Star Group: The Scales. Hydra. Bootes. Corona. Crux

Dates:[267] September 12–October 11 (includes September equinox)

Associated Majors: [The Hermit; shadow decan], Justice/Adjustment, The Hanged Man and the Fool for Water of Air

Associated Minors: The 10 of Pentacles/Disks (*Wealth*), the 2 of Swords (*Peace/ Peace Restored*), the 3 of Swords (*Sorrow*)

Sephira/World: Binah in Yetzirah

Tetragrammaton: Primal *heh* of *vav*

I Ching: Hexagram 28, *dà guò*

Geomantic Figure: *Puella*

---

267. Dates vary annually. All court card dates listed in this book are based on 2019–2020 dates.

Golden Dawn Crest: Winged child head

Themes and Keywords: Accurate, perceptive, mature, confident, particular, keen, just. Emotional intelligence. Perception of patterns and insights. Old maids, widows, divorcées, teachers. Standing firm alone. Liberating the mind from the lower nature. Skills of precision. Concerned with accuracy in trivial things. Attractive and graceful. Impartial. Sometimes sorrowful or severe, autocratic and intimidating. Does not suffer fools gladly.

ASTROLOGY/RELATED DECANS

It's ironic that the Queen associated with separation (the action of the suit of Swords) mainly rules over the sign of partnership, Libra. This cardinal air sign is ruled by Venus, who bestows grace, charm, good manners, and powers of attraction. But she is a woman of the sword as well and it is good to remember that it is Saturn that is exalted in the sign. Libra is interested in fairness and justice, for its motto is "I balance."

Moon-ruled Libra I, *Peace Restored*, involves equilibrating polarities and divisions, achieving balance between intellect and emotion. Libra II is ruled by Saturn, the sign's exaltation. It teaches a profound lesson, but the *Sorrow* of division is all the more painful in the sign of union and in the sephira of motherhood, which is unconditional love. Her shadow decan Virgo III, *Wealth*, associated with harvests, old age, and endings, is a place of discomfort for her.

QUEEN OF SWORDS
WATER OF AIR

Her throne is made from the scales (2 of Swords/Libra I) and the tripod
(3 of Swords/Libra II); from the scales, serpentine coins are suspended
(her shadow decan, 10 of Pentacles/Virgo III). (*Tabula Mundi Tarot*)

ELEMENTAL

The Queen of Swords is the "watery part of air."[268] Like water, she connects, reflects, and adapts, but—like all Swords courts—in the realm of mind and intellect. An astute critic and lover of the truth, she connects the dots, recognizing patterns in ideas, language, aesthetics, relationships. Because she glosses over nothing, her view of humanity can be severe, like a biting wind blowing out a candle. She expertly navigates misty gray areas; she floats thought bubbles only to puncture them with realism. Her inverse is the Knight/Prince of Cups, whose compelling fictions uncomfortably question the clarity of her views.

---

268. Crowley, *Book of Thoth*, 161.

Birds and an air glyph illustrate the Queen's element; the severed mask or head traditional to her image appears here as a cloud formation. (*Mystical Tarot*)

GEOMANTIC FIGURE/I CHING HEXAGRAM

The geomantic figure is *Puella*, meaning "girl," which is appropriate for Venus (Libra), in spite of this Queen's noted maturity. The glyph is supposed to suggest either the vulva or a woman with breasts, and it relates to beauty and both innocence and sexuality. It's indicative of peace and passive response, and usually it is positive, especially in relation to situations involving women.

The I Ching hexagram 28, *dà guò*, is lake over wind. It resembles a beam weakened by pressure and has meanings of "exceeding," "critical mass," and interestingly, in light of Saturn's exaltation in Libra, "law of karma." It involves standing firm even though alone.

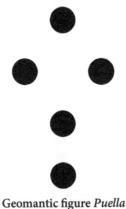

Geomantic figure *Puella*

Hexagram 28, *dà guò*.

RIDER-WAITE-SMITH SYMBOLISM

Queen of Swords (*Rider-Waite-Smith Tarot*)

"Her countenance," says Waite, "suggests familiarity with sorrow."[269] A breeze animates the treetops and mounting cumulus clouds; a single bird takes the air. Butterflies, her suit emblem, adorn her crown and throne. She sits in profile, one side completely invisible; the sword which divides right from wrong leaves only one side showing. Her left hand is raised as if holding invisible scales; what might be a rosary (the physical representing words) rests on her wrist. Severed heads are traditionally associated with her counterpart in Thoth and the infamous Queen of Spades in playing cards, lending a shadowy undertone to the cherubic carving found on all Queens' thrones.

---

269. Waite, *Pictorial Key*, 228. No surprise, since the 3 of Swords, Lord of Sorrow, is part of her realm.

THOTH SYMBOLISM

This Queen holds the decan of Crowley's sun sign, Libra II.[270] She is an awe-inspiring figure, high upon a throne of clouds. She stabs a sword point downward and holds in her other hand a severed, bearded head of what looks like an older man; perhaps indicative of the Hermit's end in Virgo III. Her crest also involves a head: a winged head of a child, like the cherubs (Venus) who guard temples and tombs (Saturn). It's a strange combination of youth and beauty (Venus) and old age (Saturn). The old head has been removed. Old thoughts are excised by the sword of reason, separating the mind from lower influences.

RELATED CARDS

The Queen of Swords' associated minors and decans are: the 10 of Pentacles (Virgo III), the 2 of Swords (Libra I), and the 3 of Swords (Libra II). As *Wealth, Peace,* and *Sorrow,* they contribute to her image as the well-off widow. She knows all too well that money can't buy everything, and she relies on the power of reason to redress life's inequalities. In her associated majors, the Hermit and Justice/Adjustment, we see a similar effort to right the scales of the material world: through analysis, balance.

On the Tree of Life, Queens correspond to the third sephira, Binah ("understanding"), as do the minor threes; these cards bring what is inchoate into the real. With other Swords courts, she explores and negotiates the bounds of the intellect; along with all others in the suit, she shares the Fool's restless questing after what can be known.

---

270. The Thoth Queen of Swords is one of the only two court cards with pupils, like his Ascendant court, the Prince of Wands. He writes much less of her, though makes the interesting concluding observation that "such people acquire intense love and devotion from the most unexpected quarters."

KNIGHT OF SWORDS
OR PRINCE OF SWORDS
Prince of the Chariot of the Winds;
Prince and Emperor of Sylphs and Sylphides

Element: Air of Air

Astrology: [20°–29° Capricorn III—cardinal earth]; 0°–19° Aquarius I & II—fixed air

Star Group: Aquarius. Southern fish, dolphin, swan. Includes Fomalhaut, Royal Watcher of the South

Dates:[271] January 10–February 8 (includes cross-quarter holiday)

Associated Majors: [The Devil; shadow decan], The Star, The Fool for Air of Air

Associated Minors: The 4 of Pentacles/Disks (*Power/Earthly Power*), the 5 of Swords (*Defeat*), the 6 of Swords (*Science/Earned Success*)

Sephira/World: Tiphareth in Yetzirah

Tetragrammaton: *Vav* of *vav*

---

271. Dates vary annually. All court card dates listed in this book are based on 2019–2020 dates.

I Ching: Hexagram 57, *xùn*

Geomantic Figure: *Tristitia*

Golden Dawn Crest: Winged angelic head with a pentagram on its brow

Themes and Keywords: Pure intellect. Intelligence and reasoning. Progressive thinking. Competing thoughts, overthinking, monkey mind, mind pulled in multiple directions. Search for innovative solutions. Technical progress and theoretical solutions. Revolution versus dogma. Mind that creates and destroys. Smart talker, intelligent conversation. Humanitarianism. Bold advocacy.

ASTROLOGY/RELATED DECANS

Aquarius and Capricorn, the signs spanned by his decans, are both ruled classically by Saturn, giving a cool exterior and a mindset geared toward steady progress. But fixed air sign Aquarius is co-ruled by modern planet Uranus, associated with more radical means of development. Whether working for evolution or revolution, the Aquarian is a humanitarian. His mind is a tool for benefiting a cause, pursuing social justice, or seeking an ideal. He goes his own way, with a fixity of purpose, allowing others as much freedom as he requires personally.

The clever rook, bird of Saturn (who rules Aquarius), perches on a rook, the "knight" of the chessboard. (*Animal Totem Tarot*)

In Venus-ruled Aquarius I, altruism and pacifism make a humane lover of intellectual pursuits. Yet an unfortunate tendency toward passivity leads to *Defeat* when attacked by more aggressive forces. Tellingly, he finds earned success in Aquarius II, also known as *Science*. Mercury's rulership here gives innovation and brilliance. In weak times, his shadow, Capricorn III (*Power*), traps him in patterns of rigidity and dominance.

ELEMENTAL

The Knight of Air rides the wind courtesy of the eagle, a bird sometimes associated with the Ganymede/Aquarius myth. The similarly airy scales appear below. (*Mystical Tarot*)

The Knight/Prince of Swords is the "airy part of air."[272] Metaphysically, airiness is freedom of movement, while Swords is the realm of the intellect. Thus this Knight/Prince represents mental agility—the freedom of mind to conjecture, opine, posit, and wander. Due to this flexibility, he is the most changeable and wide-ranging of characters. But because his modal quality is fixed (Aquarius = fixed air), he is reliably idealistic. Like a traveler heading unwaveringly toward a guiding star, or a steady wind driving a boat across an ocean, his individualism has purpose. Gusts and flurries aside, his course maintains its vector.

---

272. Crowley, *Book of Thoth*, 161.

GEOMANTIC FIGURE/I CHING HEXAGRAM

The geomantic figure for Saturn and Aquarius is *Tristitia*, with the very saturnine meaning of "sorrow." It resembles a stake being driven into the ground. It's usually unwelcome due to its association with mourning, but it can be beneficial for things dealing with Saturn's themes of stability and structure.

Hexagram 57 is made of two trigrams of wind (Air of Air). It is called *xùn*, or "wind, gently penetrating." Through service and complaisance, one has a gradual lasting influence on others. Just as gentle winds over time (Saturn's domain) can erode a mountain, constancy of ideals can wear down any obstacle.

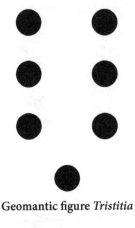

Geomantic figure *Tristitia*

Hexagram 57, *xùn*

RIDER-WAITE-SMITH SYMBOLISM

Knight of Swords (*Rider-Waite-Smith Tarot*)

Waite compares this Knight to Galahad, "whose sword is swift and sure because his is clean of heart." Smith's image emphasizes fixed rather than changeable aspects—there is no turning aside this lethal warrior from his righteous cause. A strong wind shreds the clouds and treetops; five birds struggle in the overhead currents (perhaps referring to the 5 of Swords). The warrior and his maddened steed charge leftward furiously, their attire ornamented with the bird and butterfly suit emblems and the red feather (seen also on Death). The sword, partly cut off by the frame, suggests impetuous action. He shows one bare hand for dexterity. The other is gloved for protection.

THOTH SYMBOLISM

He holds both a sword (air, reason) and a sickle (Saturn). He uses the former to create ideas and the latter to simultaneously kill them, for "any one idea is as good as another." Per *Book T*, his chariot is drawn by "Arch-Fays" who pull him hither and yon in ever conflicting directions, just as the mind flits from thought to thought. His crest is an angelic head symbolizing the Angel as Kerub of Aquarius. The eight (Mercury, mind) bubbles of air extend dually from the heads of the figures. The whole is conspicuously yellow (air) and green—which is a color of the Fool (air) in Yetzirah (air).

RELATED CARDS

All Knights/Princes traverse the narrative arc from stasis (4) to disruption (5) to balance (6). The Knight of Swords corresponds to the 4 of Pentacles (*Power*/Capricorn III), the 5 of Swords (*Defeat*/Aquarius I), and the 6 of Swords (*Success*/Aquarius II). His shadow decan acquaints him with the establishment's rigidity; in his Aquarian decans, he upends the regime and sets a course toward utopia. He is a tireless rethinker of the rules. His associated majors, the Devil and the Star—both saturnine—signal a shift in norms: from conventional usage to newly acquired knowledge; from the constructed to the imagined.

This Knight/Prince corresponds to all other Knights/Princes and the sephira Tiphareth ("beauty") on the Tree of Life, as well as all minor sixes—each balancing agency with purpose in life. Like other Swords courts, he reshapes reality through the intellect; the Fool epitomizes their restless search for knowledge.

PAGE OF SWORDS OR
PRINCESS OF SWORDS
Princess of the Rushing Winds;
Lotus of the Palace of Air;
Princess and Empress of Sylphs and Sylphides;
Throne of the Ace of Swords

Element: Earth of Air

Astrology: Capricorn-Aquarius-Pisces; centered on Kerubic air sign Aquarius

Dates: N/A; Pages rule quadrants of space rather than time

Geographical Quadrant: The Americas

Associated Majors: The World/Universe and the Fool for Earth of Air

Associated Minors: Ace of Swords as Throne; the 10 of Swords as Malkuth. All Swords as progression from root to lotus

Sephira/World: Malkuth of Yetzirah

Tetragrammaton: Final *heh* of *vav*

I Ching: Hexagram 18, *gū*

Geomantic Figure: *Fortuna Minor*

Golden Dawn Crest: Head of Medusa

Themes and Keywords: Mind-body connection. Acting on thoughts or in response to ideas. Manifesting ideas. Battling for wisdom. The power "to know." Freedom through science and truth. Affecting the material through the astral—magic and sorcery. Vigilance over thought. Defense and offense. Alertness and dexterity. Fixation of the volatile. Clearing the air and settling conflict. Avenging wrongs. Liberty. Perpetual trying.

ASTROLOGY/RELATED DECANS

Her quadrant spans the signs Capricorn, Aquarius, and Pisces. As the final flowering of the Swords suit, her form is centered around the fixed air sign Aquarius. She combines the mighty powers of the three preceding courts of the suit. Here in Swords, she gives the most truth to the motto of all Pages/Princesses: "Woe to whosoever shall make war upon her when thus established!"[273] She wields intellect like a weapon.

Light on her feet like Minerva, she stands before a smoking altar with
the quartered cross marking her sector of the globe. (*Rosetta Tarot*)

---

273. Fra., *Liber Theta*, 63.

In Capricorn the eye (Hebrew letter *ayin*) of knowledge opens in the world of matter. In Aquarius it is turned toward heavenly ideals. In Pisces she enters the realm of the astral and manipulates reality, becoming causation. She straddles the worlds between the mundane and celestial, her goal to manifest heaven upon earth.

In the Northern Hemisphere this is a season of cold, bitter, cleansing winds. But Pages/Princesses rule space, not time. Her quadrant encompasses the Americas, the New World of innovation and ideals.

ELEMENTAL

The Page/Princess of Swords is the "earthy part of air."[274] Earthy qualities concern the physical, static, and receptive; the realm of air is the mind with all its conflicting thoughts. The Page/Princess's restless senses see beneath the surfaces of things. Like Medusa's, her piercing gaze travels beyond that which is apparent and crystallizes that which is in motion. She tunnels invisibly beneath the structures of matter, aerating reality. She floats between airy magical cause and terrestrial result. Her inverse is the steadfast Knight of Pentacles (RWS) or Prince of Disks (Thoth), bending his mind only to the tangible work before him.

His sash tossed by gusts of wind, the calculating knave of air plots his next
move on the vast floating chessboard of life. (*Universal Wirth Tarot*)

---

274. Crowley, *Book of Thoth*, 163.

GEOMANTIC FIGURE/I CHING HEXAGRAM

Though she relates mainly to the sign of Aquarius, her geomantic figure is *Fortuna Minor* which has to do with the opposite sign on the axis, Leo, and the sun in southern declinations. The glyph is supposed to represent beams of light. This is the "lesser fortune": aid that comes from outside help. It is positive in situations that can be quickly resolved.

Hexagram 18, *gū*, is mountain over wind. The meanings involve remedying and renovation, repairing what has been corrupted and destroying degeneration. It is useful to concern oneself with universal development and beneficial to not recoil from work or danger.

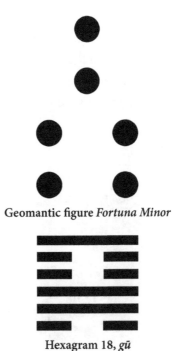

Geomantic figure *Fortuna Minor*

Hexagram 18, *gū*

RIDER-WAITE-SMITH SYMBOLISM

Page of Swords (*Rider-Waite-Smith Tarot*)

Waite describes this page's bearing as "alert and lithe ... as if an expected enemy might appear at any moment."[275] As previously noted, she seeks truth within the codes of matter; traditionally, this card may refer to espionage. Above her head, birds circle in a configuration which might be an analemma. Unlike the other Pages, she is bareheaded, her head exposed to her family's element, air. A brisk breeze—not as violent as the gale shown in her brother's image—lifts her hair and chases the mounting cumulus across the sky. Her sword is truncated by the frame, for her action is not completed.

THOTH SYMBOLISM

An Amazon whirls a sword through smoke and dust (earth of air). *Book T* describes her as a mixture of Minerva (Athena, goddess of wisdom, strategy, and warfare) and Diana (lunar goddess of the hunt). Her crest is the head of Medusa, the Gorgon whose visage graced Athena's aegis and whose image indeed "fixed the volatile," turning the viewer to stone. She stands by angry clouds and a smoking, barren altar, "as if to avenge its profanation." She wears the talaria (winged sandals) of Mercury, planet of

---

275. Waite, *Pictorial Key*, 232.

the mind, exalted in Aquarius. The talaria were loaned by Hermes to Perseus, so that he could fight Medusa from the air.

RELATED CARDS

The formidable powers of the mind find the means to act in the earthly realm with this Page/Princess, the "throne of the Ace of Swords."[276] As the Swords' final avatar, she may embody the stark journey from *Peace* to *Ruin* (the 2 through 10 of Swords). Traditionally, she corresponds to the "winter quadrant"—Capricorn, Aquarius, Pisces (the 2, 3, 4 of Pentacles; the 5, 6, 7 of Swords; the 8, 9, 10 of Cups), a domain which extends from *Change* through *Science* to *Satiety*. Her majors are the Devil, the Star, and the Moon: rooted in the body, her imagination encompasses the firmament; her rituals shape the world's dreaming.

All other Pages/Princesses and all tens are akin to each other. Qabalistically, they are the fruit of the Tree of Life, through which creation renews itself. All Swords courts concern themselves with obtaining, disseminating, and weaponizing the knowledge whose invisible workings she studies. In this tireless quest they are represented by the Fool.

---

276. Regardie and Greer, *Golden Dawn*, 694.

KING OF PENTACLES
OR KNIGHT OF DISKS
Lord of the Wide and Fertile Lands;
King of the Spirits of Earth;
King of Gnomes

Element: Fire of Earth

Astrology: [20°–29° Leo III—fixed fire]; 0°–19° Virgo I & II—mutable earth

Star Group: Virgin/Astraea. Spica. Hunting dogs, Crater, Corvus

Dates:[277] August 13–September 11

Associated Majors: [Strength/Lust; shadow decan], The Hermit, Judgement/Aeon and the World/Universe for Fire of Eart

Associated Minors: The 7 of Wands (*Valor*), the 8 of Pentacles/Disks (*Prudence*), the 9 of Pentacles/Disks (*Gain/Material Gain*), Also, the 2 of Pentacles/Disks through all Knights' association with Chokma

Sephira/World: Chokmah in Assiah

---

277. Dates vary annually. All court card dates listed in this book are based on 2019–2020 dates.

Tetragrammaton: *Yod* of final *heh*

I Ching: Hexagram 62, *xiǎo guò*

Geomantic Figure: *Conjunctio*

Golden Dawn Crest: Winged stag head

Themes and Keywords: Will applied to bodily needs and actions. The King as one with the land. Generative quality of earth. Agricultural production. Attention to detail. Cultivating resources. Hardworking and patient. Reliable but preoccupied with the material. Provisions and harvests. Love of the good life.

ASTROLOGY/RELATED DECANS

The decans tell a story of sun-warmed earth and cultivation. His major qualities are of mutable earth sign Virgo, ruled by Mercury, closest to the sun. The Hermit is the bearer of the hidden solar flame. Virgo is practical and hardworking, paying attention to small things and patiently cultivating material products. It's ripe with agricultural and husbandry metaphors, seeding the earth and overseeing procreative generation. Here the fire force, will, is applied to worldly endeavors.

The inner side of the King/Knight's shield is marked with the hexagram and rays, symbols of the solar energy necessary for successful harvest. (*Rosetta Tarot*)

Sun-ruled Virgo I nurtures the earth and its creatures. Growth patiently unfolds with *Prudence*. The Venus-ruled Virgo II is *Gain*, offering the sweetness of life to the virgin's self-sufficient domain. With Venus's help, goods and fortunes are increased; blessings are tallied with Virgo's precision. In Leo III, *Valor*, the solar sign, combines with Mars's rulership. As his shadow, it indicates his skill is best applied to the care of things with humility rather than heroism, no matter his longings for glory.

ELEMENTAL

The King of Pentacles (RWS) or Knight of Disks (Thoth) is the "fiery part of earth."[278] Like all Kings/Knights, he bears the responsibility of leadership. All Pentacles/Disks concern our material resources, and as their sovereign, he must act as the ultimate provider. He is the warm sun whose attention persuades the sprouts to germinate and the crops to mature; he is the oven that produces abundant and delicious food for all to enjoy. He also embodies the harvest—the god-king whose Dionysian sacrifice assures thriving crops. His inverse is the Page/Princess of Wands, whose springlike powers of renewal depend on this bounty.

Richly garbed and crowned with golden sheaves or leaves, this King nearly merges with his land.
As in the Waite-Smith image, his kingdom appears in the background. (*Mystical Tarot*)

---

278. Crowley, *Book of Thoth*, 164.

GEOMANTIC FIGURE/I CHING HEXAGRAM

The geomantic figure for Mercury/Virgo is *Conjunctio*, meaning "conjunction" or union. It looks like a crossroads—an appropriate meeting place for travel god Mercury. Just as Mercury is hermaphoditic, the sign is neutral in influence, though beneficial for connection. Good remains good and evil negative; it conjoins with whatever surrounds it.

Hexagram 62, thunder over mountain, *xiǎo guò*, is "small powers." It's about attempting the small and avoiding the great. Small powers get by, just as a small bird succeeds if it does not attempt to rise too high. It also means an excess of small things, such as the overattention to detail commonly attributed to Virgo.

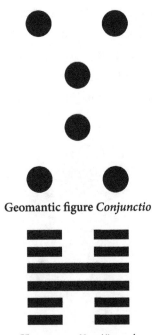

Geomantic figure *Conjunctio*

Hexagram 62, *xiǎo guò*

RIDER-WAITE-SMITH SYMBOLISM

King of Pentacles (*Rider-Waite-Smith Tarot*)

Waite particularly points out the King's "realizing intelligence," suggesting he may have an acute business sense and mathematical aptitude.[279] Four bulls' heads adorn his throne; as is often the case in courts, they refer not to his own sign but an elementally related one, Taurus. His garments are so lavishly embroidered with grapes (seen also in his final decan card, the 9 of Pentacles) that he nearly disappears into the surrounding vineyard, emphasizing his identification with the land. A castle—no other court card features human architecture—signifies civilization. Like all the members of his family, he looks at his pentacle, well aware of its worth. Even his sky is gold.

THOTH SYMBOLISM

This Knight rides the most inactive steed. The horse of the earth realm is content to crop the grasses and grains of Virgo with all four feet solidly planted. The Knight is short and, though armored, his visor is raised, for he is more concerned with his farm than with warfare. Illustratively, Crowley and Harris have turned his traditional scepter into a harvester's flail. His shield radiates golden concentric rays of solar light and

---

279. Waite, *Pictorial Key*, 254.

looks to be embossed with solar and earth motifs. His crest of the stag brings themes of the horned god and the king's ability to regenerate the land.

RELATED CARDS

The King of Pentacles/Knight of Disks corresponds to the 7 of Wands (*Valor*/Leo III), the 8 of Pentacles (*Prudence*/Virgo I) and the 9 of Pentacles (*Gain*/Virgo II). His shadow decan teaches him that heroics only go so far; at some point, one must turn to the painstaking labor of production. In his Virgo decans, he gives himself over to the task completely, and the fertile land generously rewards his efforts. Strength/Lust and the Hermit, his associated majors, similarly show a shift from radiant solar expression to solar husbandry—safeguarding the secret seed of the light.

On the Tree of Life, all Kings/Knights correspond to the second sephira, Chokmah, and therefore all twos. As the fiery portion of the court cards, Kings/Knights light the way. All Pentacles/Disks are devoted to the silent tasks of matter: to use, to have, to analyze. The World/Universe, the card's elemental major, reveals the King's ultimate purpose: incarnation itself.

QUEEN OF PENTACLES OR QUEEN OF DISKS

Queen of the Thrones of Earth;
Queen of Gnomes

Element: Water of Earth

Astrology: [20°–29° Sagittarius III—mutable fire]; 0°–19° Capricorn I & II—cardinal earth

Star Group: Capricorn. Lyra. Aquila. Sagitta

Dates:[280] December 11–January 9 (includes December solstice)

Associated Majors: [Temperance/Art; shadow decan], The Devil, The Hanged Man and the World/Universe for Water of Earth

Associated Minors: The 10 of Wands (*Oppression*), the 2 of Pentacles/Disks (*Change/Harmonious Change*), the 3 of Pentacles/Disks (*Work/Works*)

Sephira/World: Binah in Assiah

---

280. Dates vary annually. All court card dates listed in this book are based on 2019–2020 dates.

Tetragrammaton: Primal *heh* of final *heh*

I Ching: Hexagram 31, *xián*

Geomantic Figure: *Carcer*

Golden Dawn Crest: Winged goat head

Themes and Keywords: Emotions lead to fertile action. Steadiness applied to material ends. Constriction leading to expansion and building. From darkness light ascends. Rising high, competence. Climbing and descent. Carrying the load through change and works. Intuition brings fruition. Endings and beginnings, height and depth, light and darkness. Mature, ambitious, lusty. Acumen in business and things of growth. Time and necessity. Plans hatched in silence. Worldly practicality.

ASTROLOGY/RELATED DECANS

Zodiacal moguls Saturn and Jupiter form a functional pair, providing this Queen's interesting polarities. She primarily has traits of cardinal earth: practical, hardworking Capricorn ruled by Saturn. Capricorn is the zenith and the sun's rebirth from darkness.[281] The archer shoots upward, and from there the goat strives to climb to the top. Capricorn uses resources in a constructive and conservative manner. It's a builder of stable structures, though sometimes afflicted with Saturn's melancholy or dour nature.

Capricorn I's decan ruler is buoyant Jupiter, bringing expansion and cyclic movement to offset Saturn's contraction and inertia, leading to *Harmonious Change*. In doubly Saturn-influenced Capricorn II, decan ruler Mars provides the drive and spark necessary for building great *Works*. Her shadow decan is Sagittarius III, the sign under the sovereignty of Jupiter but oppressed by Saturn's decan and sephira association. Falling into a controlling role and the autocratic behaviors of *Oppression* will undermine her gift for gestation.

---

281. Capricorn as the tenth sign appears at the Midheaven or top of the natural horoscope wheel, yet in the Northern Hemisphere the start of Capricorn season at December solstice signifies the Sun's lowest point and the darkest day of the year. From here light increases until the June solstice.

QUEEN OF DISKS
WATER OF EARTH

She holds the alchemical building blocks (3 of Pentacles/Disks), while
her other decans are shown by Saturn's hourglass (2 of Pentacles/Disks)
and hammer and pick (10 of Wands). (*Tabula Mundi Tarot*)

ELEMENTAL

The Queen of Pentacles (RWS) or Disks (Thoth) is the "watery part of earth."[282] Water
connects and flows, joining parts that were previously separate; the realm of earth is
organic matter. She is the force that coaxes growing life to take up and convert nutrients into new forms; she is the designer who expresses our genes as physical features.
Like fertile loam, she encourages new endeavors to take root; like a mountain, she has
the perspective to plan now for long-term benefits. Her inverse is the Page/Princess of
Cups, in whose imagination dreams take root and become reality.

---

282. Crowley, *Book of Thoth*, 166.

What do you get when you combine water and earth? Mud! This Queen of Pentacles is literally in her element. (*Animal Totem Tarot*)

GEOMANTIC FIGURE/I CHING HEXAGRAM

The geomantic figure for Capricorn and Saturn is *Carcer*, Latin for "the prison." Its confining nature is symbolic of Saturn's boundaries, restrictions, and bindings. Indeed, for in shape it looks like an enclosure or cell. While this figure is generally unfavorable, it provides the strength of immobility for saturnine themes of structure, security, and willpower.

Hexagram 31, lake over mountain, is *xián*, meaning "influence." It has significations of wooing, inviting, attraction, and the coming together of opposites. Persistence, perseverance, and being willing to receive others with openness and humility brings fulfillment. One should go forward methodically and consistently to obtain influence.

Geomantic figure *Carcer*

Hexagram 31, *xián*

RIDER-WAITE-SMITH SYMBOLISM

© 1971 U.S. GAMES SYSTEMS, INC.

Queen of Pentacles (*Rider-Waite-Smith Tarot*)

The traditionally wealthy and generous Queen of Pentacles "contemplates her symbol and may see worlds therein." There is no limit to what she can conceive! This introspective sovereign occupies a lush, rose-framed bower. Though there is no single animal symbol for the pentacles court, a rabbit, symbol of fertility, crouches at one corner. Ripe pear carvings and the usual infant's head adorn the throne, signifying her maternal inclinations. She wears white sleeves (purity of intention) and red robes (passionate life) similar to those on the Hierophant and Magician cards. In the distance appears a golden sky and what might be the hills of Malkuth.

THOTH SYMBOLISM

Book T describes her as best represented in profile, having one side of her face in light and one in darkness, highlighting her position at solstice. She looks toward a desert oasis (water of earth) from her desert plant throne. Her companion (and crest) is the climbing goat of Capricorn; she wears the oversized horns of the mountain markhor goat. Their spiral force signifies fecundity. Crowley reminds us that the Great Work is fertility and that she represents "the ambition of matter to take part in the Great Work of Creation."[283] She holds a golden orb (sun) with thirteen rings (moon) and a wand with hexagram (sun) and cube (earth).

RELATED CARDS

Minors associated with the Queen of Pentacles/Disks are the 10 of Wands (*Oppression*/Sagittarius III), the 2 of Pentacles (*Change*/Capricorn I), and the 3 of Pentacles (*Work*/Capricorn II). She is a warden of the solstice, and at her best, her understanding of cyclical growth permits her to launch new enterprises and dedicate herself to their productive well-being. Excessive control, the bane of her shadow decan, is a danger which stalks her. Her associated majors, Temperance/Art and the Devil, trace her constant passage from aspiration to practical application.

---

283. Crowley, *Book of Thoth*, 166.

On the Tree of Life, Queens correspond to the third sephira, Binah ("understanding"); so do the minor threes. They amplify and give form to ideas and manifest what is inchoate into the real. With other courts of her suit, the Queen focuses on a world of the senses: what she can use, obtain, and dissect. The World/Universe is the work-in-progress shared by all Pentacles/Disks.

KNIGHT OF PENTACLES
OR PRINCE OF DISKS
Prince of the Chariot of Earth;
Prince and Emperor of Gnomes

Element: Air of Earth

Astrology: [20°–29° Aries III—cardinal fire]; 0°–19° Taurus I & II—fixed earth

Star Group: Taurus. Perseus. Throne of Cassiopeia. Eridanus. Includes Aldebaran, Royal Watcher of the East

Dates:[284] April 10–May 9 (includes cross-quarter holiday)

Associated Majors: [The Emperor; shadow decan], The Hierophant, The Fool and the World/Universe for Air of Earth

Associated Minors: The 4 of Wands (*Completion/Perfected Work*), 5 of Pentacles/ Disks (*Worry/Material Worry*), the 6 of Pentacles/Disks (*Success/Material Success*)

Sephira/World: Tiphareth in Assiah

---

284. Dates vary annually. All court card dates listed in this book are based on 2019–2020 dates.

Tetragrammaton: *Vav* of final *heh*

I Ching: Hexagram 53, *jiàn*

Geomantic Figure: *Amissio*

Golden Dawn Crest: Winged bull head

Themes and Keywords: Reason applied to matter. Accounting and bookkeeping. Mind and energy applied to practical things. Business intelligence, responsibility. Consistent course of action. Bull in the harness: predictable, hardworking, fertile, and somewhat stubborn and dull. Balance between material worry and success. Conscientious, enduring, imperturbable, sensual. Slow to anger but furious when roused. Increase of resources. Maintenance to conserve value. Daily attention and routines.

ASTROLOGY/RELATED DECANS

Fixed earth sign Taurus is as strong and predictable as a bull in the harness. It's the earthy side of Venus that is concerned with material resources, unabashedly interested in financial returns. Taurus likes the finer things and is willing to work for them. The earth son inclines his mind to practical matters with a strong sense of purpose. He isn't fast, but he is consistent and enduring; he's not exciting, but he is sensual. His decans span Aries and Taurus. The bull plows and settles the land the ram discovers, increasing production and yield.

In Mercury-ruled Taurus I, he contemplates potential material hardship. Taurus has *Worry* about having enough! In Taurus II the Moon is exalted in the sign and placed in the solar sephira, a sensual and fertile pairing generating dividends. His shadow decan, Aries III, is *Completion*. Relying on faith that his works will be perfected impedes his strength: obsessive, tangible progress.

ELEMENTAL

The Knight of Pentacles (RWS) or Prince of Disks (Thoth) is the "airy part of earth."[285] Air represents the mind's freedom to transmit and receive; this figure applies his intelligence to matters of the tangible earth. His mind is a cleared worktable, a ploughed field; he is a consummate workman, attentive to what may yet go wrong and what still can be fixed. As fixed earth, his goal is the smooth running of all mechanisms. He works to optimize whatever there is to work with; his inverse, the Page (RWS) or Princess (Thoth) of Swords, seeks to rewrite the blueprint altogether.

This bull-drawn chariot is scattering windblown seeds (Air of Earth). (*Rosetta Tarot*)

---

285. Crowley, *Book of Thoth*, 167.

A prairie dog, diligent tunneler of dirt, pokes his head up into
the air to get the lay of the land. (*Animal Totem Tarot*)

GEOMANTIC FIGURE/I CHING HEXAGRAM

The geomantic figure *Amissio* applies to Taurus and Venus. The figure is comprised of two overturned bowls symbolizing loss. This reflects Taurus's fear of not having enough, as seen in his first Taurus decan of material worry. It's considered negative, of things being out of reach, but it can be sometimes positive for giving your heart away, something under Venus's domain.

The hexagram for wind over mountain is 53, *jiàn*, "developing gradually." Gradual progress is made as one perseveres, working slowly and with stability. An acorn eventually grows into a mighty oak, and the slower it grows, the stronger it becomes.

Geomantic figure *Amissio*

Hexagram 53, *jiàn*

RIDER-WAITE-SMITH SYMBOLISM

Knight of Pentacles (*Rider-Waite-Smith Tarot*)

Waite, rather disparagingly, compares the Knight of Pentacles to his own "slow, enduring, heavy horse." In place of plumes, both horse and rider sport tufts of greenery on their heads. While the other knights' steeds race, trot, or prance, this placid, black Shire horse has all four hooves solidly planted on the ground. Traditionally, knights are the "thoughts" of their rulers enacted; thus he is the agent executing the material plans and designs of his King and Queen; he has cultivated the well-tended field in the background, set amidst the usual green hills, blue mountains, and golden sky of the suit.

THOTH SYMBOLISM

His crest is the bull of Taurus that pulls his chariot, a symbol of steadfast productivity. Both he and the bull are the red earth color of man and Taurus. His chariot is packed with swelling seeds or the root nodules of nitrogen-fixing plants (air of earth). The background shows various pods, vegetation, and fruit. His scepter is topped with the orb and cross, symbol of world dominion and the Emperor. He cradles an orb of solar gold like his mother the Queen, but his has a cube and cross (earth) within three gyroscopic circles, perhaps a rearrangement of those carried by the Hierophant (Taurus).

RELATED CARDS

Knights/Princes correspond to 4, 5, and 6 in the minors: from stasis to disruption to balance. The Knight/Prince's domain is the 4 of Wands (*Completion*/Aries I), the 5 of Pentacles (*Worry*/Taurus I), and the 6 of Pentacles (*Success*/Taurus II). With Venus ruling his shadow decan and the sign of his two main decans, beauty is never far from his mind. He holds in mind an image of perfection—although perfection is fleeting by nature, he works tirelessly to make it permanent. The Emperor and the Hierophant are his corresponding majors, as to be responsible for something means dedicating yourself to preserving it.

All Knights/Princes and all minor sixes are related Qabalistically—each portraying power and agency in life. Like all his family, he is silently devoted to matter and all its works, and to the great project of continual incarnation represented by the World/ Universe.

PAGE OF PENTACLES
OR PRINCESS OF DISKS
Princess of the Echoing Hills;
Rose of the Palace of Earth;
Princess and Empress of Gnomes

Element: Earth of Earth

Astrology: Aries-Taurus-Gemini; centered on Kerubic earth sign Taurus

Dates: N/A; Pages rule quadrants of space rather than time

Geographical Quadrant: Europe and Africa

Associated Majors: The World/Universe for Earth of Earth

Associated Minors: Ace of Pentacles/Disks as Throne; the 10 of Pentacles/Disks as Malkuth. All Pentacles/Disks as progression from root to rose

Sephira/World: Malkuth of Assiah

Tetragrammaton: Final *heh* of final *heh*

I Ching: Hexagram 52, *gèn*

Geomantic Figure: *Caput Draconis*

Golden Dawn Crest: Golden Dawn court crest

Themes and Keywords: Material action. Fully realized manifestation. Potential fulfilled. Completion and succession. The Great Work. Human between heaven and earth. Sleep versus awakening as self-awareness. Individuation and transfiguration. To keep silent, and to go forth and do the work of will. Ripening and perfecting of the will force. Pregnant with possibility. The 10,000 joys and sorrows of life in all fullness. Sacred womanhood, mothers and daughters, earth goddesses. Fertile ground: the time is ripe. Introspection. The thing in itself.

ASTROLOGY/RELATED DECANS

The daughter of earth is the last court card, just as the World/Universe is the final trump and the 10 of Pentacles/Disks is the last minor. As such she represents both fruition and regeneration of the entire cycle. This is reflected by her quadrant, which spans Aries, Taurus, and Gemini, the first three signs. Her powers are centered around the earthy Kerubic sign Taurus, ruled by Venus. She embodies the fertility of earth and the Great Mother. As Aries she offers potential, renewal, and sovereignty of self. In Gemini, the sacred marriage alchemically changes her. In her main attribution of Taurus, she stands still as a mountain yet is filled with life itself in all its fruitful complexity.

The signs encompass spring in the Northern Hemisphere, which is a time of the earth's awakening. But Pages/Princesses rule space, not time. Her spatial quadrant contains the Old World of Europe and the source of life in Africa.

ELEMENTAL

The Page of Pentacles (RWS) or Princess of Disks (Thoth) is the "earthy part of earth."[286] Earth is the ultimate receptive and fruitful incubator, the moldable clay. The realm of earth is all material substance. Thus this Page/Princess is matter pregnant with itself: a body within a body, a gem within raw ore. If the Page of Wands is a reincarnate soul in a new vessel, the Page of Pentacles shapes and produces that vessel. All her silent attention

---

286. Crowley, *Book of Thoth*, 169.

focuses inward on what is taking form. Like the 10 of Pentacles or the World/Universe, she represents not only the destination of the entire journey, but its capacity to begin again.

In Tarot de Marseille decks, only Pages of coins feature two of their suit emblems rather than one. One coin remains buried in earth, hidden—or planted and renewed.
(*Camoin-Jodorowsky Tarot de Marseille*)

GEOMANTIC FIGURE/I CHING HEXAGRAM

Her geomantic figure is *Caput Draconis*. This is the "head of the dragon" or north node of the moon. The appendage is the head upon the serpentine body or a door at the end of a path. It represents journeys and taking in, and so it is good for beginnings and new experiences. It has to do with the coming of fortune upon earth and is a stable, long-lasting influence.

Hexagram 52, mountain over mountain, is *gèn*, "keeping still." It has connotations of silence, calm, and rest after a long journey, achieving tranquility in relation to the entirety of life.

Geomantic figure *Caput Draconis*

Hexagram 52, *gèn*

RIDER-WAITE-SMITH SYMBOLISM

Page of Pentacles (*Rider-Waite-Smith Tarot*)

Perhaps the most important thing to notice about this Page's pentacle is that it is hovering rather than held: this is a magic pentacle that has taken on a life of its own. Beholding this miracle, the Page is "insensible of that which is about him."[287] Interestingly, Waite observes that the Page "moves slowly," whereas the other Pages are standing.[288] While earth may be the most steadfast of elements, its nature is to change. The Page is clad in earth tones; we also see the Knight's cultivated field, a grove of trees, yellow sky, blue-shaded mountains—blending, as in other Pentacles courts, human and natural endeavor.

THOTH SYMBOLISM

Symbolically, she is at the brink of transfiguration, shown by her advanced pregnancy, her oxen-horned headdress (*aleph*, ox), the ouroboros on her disk, and her staff, which has a diamond crystal (Kether) penetrating Earth. (*Rosetta Tarot*)

The Princess stands firm, pregnant and glowing with inner light. Crowley says she is "on the brink of transfiguration." She is in a grove of bare branches, dressed in fur or ram's fleece, yet surrounded by solar brilliance. It gives the impression of the bridge between winter and spring. Her crest is the ram of Aries, the first sign in her quadrant. She holds a scepter pointed downward into the earth. The crystal on the end emits

---

287. Waite, *Pictorial Key*, 260.

288. This recalls the fifth power of the sphinx. The first four are to will (Wands), to dare (Cups), to know (Swords), and to keep silent (Pentacles). But once brought together, they have the power to go.

light; its diamond shape represents first sephira Kether, the godhead that is in Malkuth "after another manner" (according to Qabalistic doctrine). She holds a pentacle with thirty-six petals, representing the completed thirty-six decans of the zodiac.

RELATED CARDS

The ultimate reset button, the Page/Princess touches every card—especially the above-mentioned endpoints and the starting points (Fool, Ace of Wands, King/Knight of Wands). She is the "throne of the Ace of Pentacles," setting in motion the earthly cycle—the Pentacles' trajectory from *Change* to *Wealth*.[289] In the life-renewing "spring quadrant," Aries, Taurus, Gemini (the 2, 3, 4 of Wands; the 5, 6, 7 of Pentacles; the 8, 9, 10 of Swords), she journeys from *Dominion* to *Success* to *Ruin*. Her majors are the Emperor, the Hierophant, and the Lovers; her focus unfolds from being to having to choosing.

This Page corresponds to all other Pages as well as the tens, each a symbol of regeneration on the Tree of Life. All Pentacles/Disks devote themselves to the silent work of nature; her preservation and reproduction through destructive and creative acts. The fruit and seed of these efforts can be seen in the World/Universe card.

---

289. Regardie and Greer, *Golden Dawn*, 753.

CONCLUSION

A FEW WORDS FROM THE WHEELHOUSE

On a Wednesday in 2017, a day of Mercury, the *Fortune's Wheelhouse* podcast officially released its first show: "Episode 0: The Fool." Our initial intention was simply to share a somewhat-orderly conversation between two friends who were equally obsessive about esoteric tarot. We would have a good look at the symbols in the major arcana of the Rider-Waite-Smith and Thoth decks and we'd see where that took us. But no sooner had we completed "Episode 21: The World/Universe" than we realized our mission had only just begun, for we were powerless to resist the call of the minor arcana. So we forged onward, eventually completing a full treatment of the entire seventy-eight-card tarot.

Three years, over one hundred episodes, and three hundred thousand downloads later, *Fortune's Wheelhouse* has become a community. Listeners meet one other at the Fortune's Wheelhouse Academy Facebook group, patrons support new episodes, and every week new tarot readers discover our original seventy-eight episodes and use them as a resource for developing their own practices.

Averaging at about one hour per card, the individual episodes offer material that is both systematic and freewheeling. The early-twentieth-century creators of the Rider-Waite-Smith and Thoth decks encoded vast quantities of esoteric information into their images: astrology, numerology, Qabalah, elements, mythology, and more. It's tarot's genetic corpus of occult knowledge and the study of a lifetime, and in the podcast we took it upon ourselves to unpack the coding as comprehensively as possible. But we also dove down many wormholes, added our personal interpretations, and occasionally shared some very off-color jokes.

Tarot Deciphered, while originating in the podcast, is a separate entity. In it we've laid out the basic correspondence structures introduced in the show in the most accessible way possible. Here, we hope, you'll have found everything you need to start making sense of modern tarot's secrets. And if you'd like much, much more speculative commentary, wormhole excavation, and phallic humor, be sure to listen to the episodes.

For those of us called to tarot, it is an intensely personal practice, a living language, even a way of looking at the world. Tarot opens doors to further adventures in innumerable disciplines: history, philosophy, linguistics, geometry, religion, art, literature. Yet there is no post-doctorate degree in tarot, no tarot bar exam, no accredited certifying board. What we learn, we learn on our own or with the help of fellow travelers.

We divided the work of writing this book equally: Mel wrote the card sections on astrology, mythology, I Ching/geomancy and the Thoth deck, and compiled a few suggestions for further exploration. Susie wrote the card sections on Qabalah, the elements, relationships between the cards, and the Rider-Waite-Smith deck. The opening explanatory paragraphs for the majors, minors, and courts evolved organically, with each of us contributing parts as we added and responded to what the other included. In the course of our research for book and podcast, we've sought out hundreds of primary and secondary sources (see the Bibliography and Suggested Reading sections), and we've drawn from the thousands of readings we've logged over our combined fifty-plus years in divination. We regularly fact-check and consult with each other.

That said, we don't claim any particular authority in the fields represented here. And we certainly don't claim that our way of looking at the cards is the only way. Do not expect us to answer to the titles of "expert" or "guru" or "maven." You *can* call us wanderers of the fringe, explorers of hidden realms, or even—as we say on *Fortune's*

Wheelhouse—heroes of the astral plane! And we invite you to continue journeying with us with your eyes and ears, your hearts and minds—whether you wish to simply come along for the ride or whether you choose to use our work as a launchpad for wormhole expeditions we have yet to imagine ourselves.

TABLES AND DIAGRAMS

TREE OF LIFE DIAGRAM

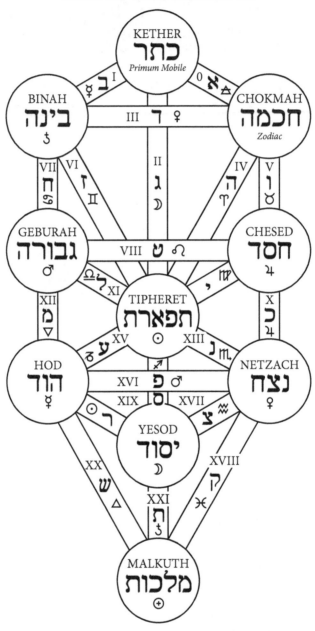

Golden Dawn correspondences between the major arcana, the ten sephiroth, and the twenty-two paths, as understood in Hermetic Qabalah. It's based on the Tree of Life layout devised by seventeenth-century scholar Athanasius Kircher.

TABLE OF DECANS

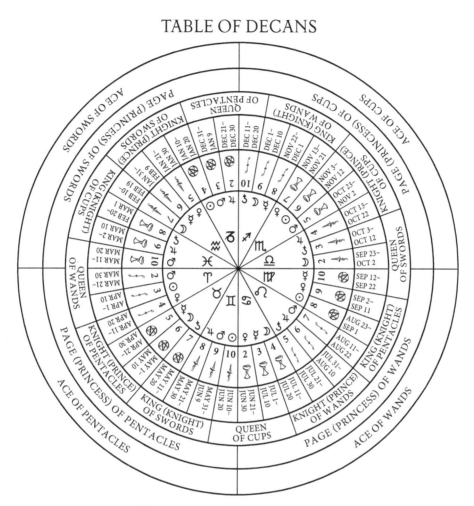

All the astrological correspondences for the
minor arcana—both courts and numeric minors

MINOR ARCANA DECAN INFORMATION

Zodiac	Suit	Planet ruling decan*	Decan image from the *Picatrix*
0°–9° Aries	2 of Wands	Mars	A black man, with a large and restless body, having red eyes and with an axe in his hand, girded in white cloth
10°–19° Aries	3 of Wands	Sun	A woman dressed in green clothes, lacking one leg
20°–29° Aries	4 of Wands	Venus	A restless man, holding in his hands a gold bracelet, wearing red clothing, who wishes to do good, but is not able to do it
0°–9° Taurus	5 of Pentacles/Disks	Mercury	A woman with curly hair, who has one son wearing clothing looking like flame, and she is wearing garments of the same sort

Correspondences between the thirty-six astrological decans
and the thirty-six 2-through-10 minors of the tarot.

MINOR ARCANA DECAN INFORMATION

Zodiac	Decan signification from the *Picatrix*	Decan image from Agrippa's 3 Books of Occult Philosophy	Decan signification from Agrippa
0°–9° Aries	Strength, high rank, wealth without shame	A black man, standing and clothed in a white garment, girdled about, of a great body, with reddish eyes, and great strength, and like one that is angry	Boldness, fortitude, loftiness and shame-lessness
10°–19° Aries	High rank, nobility, wealth, rulership	A woman, outwardly clothed with a red garment, and under it a white, spreading abroad over her feet	Nobleness, height of a Kingdom, and great-ness of dominion
20°–29° Aries	Subtlety, subtle mastery, new things, instruments and simi-lar things	A white man, pale, with reddish hair, and clothed with a red gar-ment, who carrying on the one hand a golden bracelet, and holding forth a wooden staff, is restless, and like one in wrath, because he cannot perform that good he would	Wit, meekness, joy and beauty
0°–9° Taurus	Plowing, working on the land, sciences, geometry, sowing, building	A naked man, an archer, harvester or husbandman	To sow, plough, build, people, and divide the earth, according to the rules of geometry

Correspondences between the thirty-six astrological decans
and the thirty-six 2-through-10 minors of the tarot.

MINOR ARCANA DECAN INFORMATION

Zodiac	Suit	Planet ruling decan*	Decan image from the *Picatrix*
10°–19° Taurus	6 of Pentacles/Disks	Moon	A man with a body like a camel, who has cow's hooves on his fingers, and he is completely covered by a torn linen cloth. He desires to work the land, sow, and build
20°–29° Taurus	7 of Pentacles/Disks	Saturn	A man of reddish complexion with large white teeth exposed outside of his mouth, and a body like an elephant with long legs, and with him one horse, one dog and one calf
0°–9° Gemini	8 of Swords	Jupiter	A beautiful woman, a mistress of stitching, two calves and two horses
10°–19° Gemini	9 of Swords	Mars	A man whose face is like an eagle and his head is covered by linen cloth; clothed and protected by a coat of leaden mail, and on his head is an iron helmet above which is a silk crown, and in his hand he has a bow and arrows

Correspondences between the thirty-six astrological decans and the thirty-six 2-through-10 minors of the tarot.

MINOR ARCANA DECAN INFORMATION

Zodiac	Decan signification from the *Picatrix*	Decan image from Agrippa's 3 Books of Occult Philosophy	Decan signification from Agrippa
10°–19° Taurus	Nobility, power, rewarding the people	A naked man, holding in his hand a key	Power, nobility, and dominion over people
20°–29° Taurus	Sloth, poverty, misery, dread	A man in whose hand is a serpent, and a dart	Necessity and profit, and also misery and slavery
0°–9° Gemini	Writing, computation and number, giving and taking, the sciences	A man in whose hand is a rod, and he is, as it were, serving another	Wisdom, and the knowledge of numbers and arts in which there is no profit
10°–19° Gemini	Oppression, evils, and subtlety	A man in whose hand is a pipe, and another being bowed down, digging the earth	Infamous and dishonest agility, as that of jesters and jugglers; labors and painful searching

Correspondences between the thirty-six astrological decans
and the thirty-six 2-through-10 minors of the tarot.

MINOR ARCANA DECAN INFORMATION

Zodiac	Suit	Planet ruling decan*	Decan image from the *Picatrix*
20°–29° Gemini	10 of Swords	Sun	A man clothed in mail, with a bow, arrows, and quiver
0°–9° Cancer	2 of Cups	Venus	A man whose fingers and head are distorted and slanted, and his body is similar to a horse's body; his feet are white, and he has fig leaves on his body
10°–19° Cancer	3 of Cups	Mercury	A woman with a beautiful face, and on her head she has a crown of green myrtle, and in her hand is a stem of the water lily, and she is singing songs of love and joy
20°–29° Cancer	4 of Cups	Moon	A celhafe [turtle] with a snake in his hand, who has golden chains before him

Correspondences between the thirty-six astrological decans and the thirty-six 2-through-10 minors of the tarot.

MINOR ARCANA DECAN INFORMATION

Zodiac	Decan signification from the *Picatrix*	Decan image from Agrippa's 3 Books of Occult Philosophy	Decan signification from Agrippa
20°–29° Gemini	Audacity, honesty, division of labor, and consolation	A man seeking for arms, and a fool holding in the right hand a Bird, and in his left a pipe	Forgetfulness, wrath, boldness, jests , scurrilities, and unprofitable words
0°–9° Cancer	Instruction, knowledge, love, subtlety and mastery	A young virgin, adorned with fine clothes, and having a crown on her head	Acuteness of senses, subtlety of wit, and the love of men
10°–19° Cancer	Games, wealth, joy, and abundance	A man clothed in comely apparel, or a man and woman sitting at the table and playing	Riches, mirth, gladness, and the love of women
20°–29° Cancer	Running, riding, and acquisition by means of war, lawsuits, and conflict	A man, a hunter with his lance and horn, bringing out dogs for to hunt	The contention of men, the pursuing of those who fly, the hunting and possessing of things by arms and brawlings

Correspondences between the thirty-six astrological decans and the thirty-six 2-through-10 minors of the tarot.

MINOR ARCANA DECAN INFORMATION

Zodiac	Suit	Planet ruling decan*	Decan image from the *Picatrix*
0°–9° Leo	5 of Wands	Saturn	A man wearing dirty clothes, and the image of a rider looking to the north, and his body looks like the body of a bear and the body of a dog
10°–19° Leo	6 of Wands	Jupiter	A man who wears a crown of white myrtle on his head, and he has a bow in his hand
20°–29° Leo	7 of Wands	Mars	A man who is old and black and ugly, with fruit and meat in his mouth and holding a copper jug in his hand
0°–9° Virgo	8 of Pentacles/Disks	Sun	A young girl covered with an old woolen cloth, and in her hand is a pomegranate

Correspondences between the thirty-six astrological decans
and the thirty-six 2-through-10 minors of the tarot.

MINOR ARCANA DECAN INFORMATION

Zodiac	Decan signification from the *Picatrix*	Decan image from Agrippa's 3 Books of Occult Philosophy	Decan signification from Agrippa
0°–9° Leo	Strength, generosity, and victory	A man riding on a lion	Boldness, violence, cruelty, wickedness, lust and labors to be sustained
10°–19° Leo	Beauty, riding, the ascension of a man who is ignorant and base, war and naked swords	An image with hands lifted up, and a man on whose head is a crown; he hath the appearance of an angry man, and one that threateneth, having in his right hand a sword drawn out of the scabbard, and in his left a buckler	Hidden contentions, and unknown victories, and upon base men, and upon the occasions of quarrels and battles
20°–29° Leo	Love and delight and food trays and health	A young man in whose hand is a whip, and a man very sad, and of an ill aspect	Love and society, and the loss of one's right for avoiding strife
0°–9° Virgo	Sowing, plowing, the germination of plants, gathering grapes, good living	The figure of a good maid, and a man casting seeds	Getting of wealth, ordering of diet, plowing, sowing, and peopling

**Correspondences between the thirty-six astrological decans
and the thirty-six 2-through-10 minors of the tarot.**

MINOR ARCANA DECAN INFORMATION

Zodiac	Suit	Planet ruling decan*	Decan image from the *Picatrix*
10°–19° Virgo	9 of Pentacles/Disks	Venus	A man of beautiful color, dressed in leather, and over his garment of leather is another garment of iron
20°–29° Virgo	10 of Pentacles/Disks	Mercury	A white man, with a great body, wrapped in white linen, and with him is a woman holding in her hand black oil
0°–9° Libra	2 of Swords	Moon	A man with a lance in his right hand, and in his left hand he holds a bird hanging by its feet
10°–19° Libra	3 of Swords	Saturn	A black man, a bridegroom having a joyous journey
20°–29° Libra	4 of Swords	Jupiter	A man riding a donkey with a wolf in front of him

Correspondences between the thirty-six astrological decans
and the thirty-six 2-through-10 minors of the tarot.

MINOR ARCANA DECAN INFORMATION

Zodiac	Decan signification from the *Picatrix*	Decan image from Agrippa's 3 Books of Occult Philosophy	Decan signification from Agrippa
10°–19° Virgo	Petitions, requests, and gain, tribute and denying justice	A black man clothed with a skin, and a man having a bush of hair, holding a bag	Gain, scraping together of wealth and covetousness
20°–29° Virgo	Debility, age, infirmity, sloth, injury to limbs and the destruction of people	A white woman and deaf, or an old man leaning on a staff	Weakness, infirmity, loss of members, destruction of trees, and depopulation of lands
0°–9° Libra	Justice, truth, good judgment, complete justice for the people and weak persons, and doing good for beggars	An angry man, in whose hand is a pipe, and the form of a man reading in a book	Justifying and helping the miserable and weak against the powerful and wicked
10°–19° Libra	Tranquility, joy, abundance and good living	Two men furious and wrathful and a man in a comely garment, sitting in a chair	Indignation against the evil, and quietness and security of life with plenty of good things
20°–29° Libra	Evil works, sodomy, adultery, singing, joy and flavors	A violent man holding a bow, and before him a naked man, and also another man holding bread in one hand, and a cup of wine in the other	Wicked lusts, singings, sports and gluttony

Correspondences between the thirty-six astrological decans
and the thirty-six 2-through-10 minors of the tarot.

MINOR ARCANA DECAN INFORMATION

Zodiac	Suit	Planet ruling decan*	Decan image from the *Picatrix*
0°–9° Scorpio	5 of Cups	Mars	A man with a lance in his right hand and in his left hand he holds the head of a man
10°–19° Scorpio	6 of Cups	Sun	A man riding a camel, holding a scorpion in his hand
20°–29° Scorpio	7 of Cups	Venus	A horse and a rabbit
0°–9° Sagittarius	8 of Wands	Mercury	The bodies of three men and one body is yellow, another white and the third is red
10°–19° Sagittarius	9 of Wands	Moon	A man leading cows and in front of him he has an ape and a bear
20°–29° Sagittarius	10 of Wands	Saturn	A man with a cap on his head, who is murdering another man

Correspondences between the thirty-six astrological decans
and the thirty-six 2-through-10 minors of the tarot.

MINOR ARCANA DECAN INFORMATION

Zodiac	Decan signification from the *Picatrix*	Decan image from Agrippa's 3 Books of Occult Philosophy	Decan signification from Agrippa
0°–9° Scorpio	Settlement, sadness, ill will and hatred	A woman of good face and habit, and two men striking her	Comeliness, beauty, and strifes, treacheries, deceits, detractions, and perditions
10°–19° Scorpio	Knowledge, modesty, settlement, and of speaking evil of one another	A man naked, and a woman naked, and a man sitting on the earth, and before him two dogs biting one another	Impudence, deceit, and false dealing, and for to send mischief and strife amongst men
20°–29° Scorpio	Evil works and flavors, and forcing sex upon unwilling women	A man bowed downward upon his knees, and a woman striking him with a staff	Drunkenness, fornication, wrath, violence, and strife
0°–9° Sagittarius	Heat, heaviness, growth in plains and fields, sustenance and division	A man armed with a coat of mail, and holding a naked sword in his hand	Boldness, malice, and liberty
10°–19° Sagittarius	Fear, lamentations, grief, sadness, misery and troubles	A woman weeping, and covered with clothes	Sadness and fear of his own body
20°–29° Sagittarius	Evil desires, adverse and evil effects, and fickleness in these and evil wishes, hatred, dispersion, and evil conduct	A man like in color to gold, or an idle man playing with a staff	Following our own wills, and obstinacy in them, and activeness for evil things, contentions, and horrible matters

Correspondences between the thirty-six astrological decans
and the thirty-six 2-through-10 minors of the tarot.

MINOR ARCANA DECAN INFORMATION

Zodiac	Suit	Planet ruling decan*	Decan image from the *Picatrix*
0°–9° Capricorn	2 of Pentacles/Disks	Jupiter	A man with a reed in his right hand and a hoopoe bird in his left
10°–19° Capricorn	3 of Pentacles/Disks	Mars	A man with a common ape in front of him
20°–29° Capricorn	4 of Pentacles/Disks	Sun	A man holding a book which he opens and closes, and before him is the tail of a fish
0°–9° Aquarius	5 of Swords	Venus	A man whose head is mutilated and he holds a peacock in his hand
10°–19° Aquarius	6 of Swords	Mercury	A man who looks like a king, who permits much to himself and abhors what he sees
20°–29° Aquarius	7 of Swords	Moon	A man having a mutilated head, and an old woman is with him

Correspondences between the thirty-six astrological decans
and the thirty-six 2-through-10 minors of the tarot.

MINOR ARCANA DECAN INFORMATION

Zodiac	Decan signification from the *Picatrix*	Decan image from Agrippa's 3 Books of Occult Philosophy	Decan signification from Agrippa
0°–9° Capricorn	Happiness, joy, and bringing things to an end that are sluggish, weak, and proceeding poorly	A woman, and a man carrying full bags	To go forth and to rejoice, to gain and to lose with weakness and baseness
10°–19° Capricorn	Seeking to do what cannot be done and to attain what cannot be	Two women, and a man looking towards a bird flying in the air	Requiring those things which cannot be done, searching after those things which cannot be known
20°–29° Capricorn	Wealth and the accumulation of money and increase and embarking on trade and pressing on to a good end	A woman chaste in body, and wise in her work, and a banker gathering his money together on the table	To govern in prudence, in covetousness of money, and in avarice
0°–9° Aquarius	Misery, poverty, and slavery	A prudent man, and of a woman spinning	The thought and labor for gain, in poverty and baseness
10°–19° Aquarius	Beauty and position, having what is desired, completion, detriment and debility	A man with a long beard	Understanding, meekness, modesty, liberty and good manners
20°–29° Aquarius	Abundance, accomplishing of will, giving offense	A black and angry man	Insolence and impudence

Correspondences between the thirty-six astrological decans
and the thirty-six 2-through-10 minors of the tarot.

MINOR ARCANA DECAN INFORMATION

Zodiac	Suit	Planet ruling decan*	Decan image from the *Picatrix*
0°–9° Pisces	8 of Cups	Saturn	A man with two bodies, who looks as though he is giving a gesture of greeting with his hands
10°–19° Pisces	9 of Cups	Jupiter	A man upside down with his head below and his feet raised up, and in his hand is a tray from which the food has been eaten
20°–29° Pisces	10 of Cups	Mars	A sad man full of evil thoughts, thinking of deception and treachery, and before him is a woman with a donkey climbing atop her, and in her hand is a bird

Correspondences between the thirty-six astrological decans
and the thirty-six 2-through-10 minors of the tarot.

MINOR ARCANA DECAN INFORMATION

Zodiac	Decan signification from the *Picatrix*	Decan image from Agrippa's 3 Books of Occult Philosophy	Decan signification from Agrippa
0°–9° Pisces	Peace and humility, debility, many journeys, misery, seeking wealth, miserable life	A man carrying burdens on his shoulder, and well clothed	Journeys, change of place, and in carefulness of getting wealth and clothes
10°–19° Pisces	Great reward, and strong will in things that are high, serious and thoughtful	A woman of a good countenance, and well adorned	To desire and put oneself on or about high and great matters
20°–29° Pisces	Advancement and lying with women with a great appetite, and of quiet and seeking rest	A man naked, or a youth, and nigh him a beautiful maid, whose head is adorned with flowers	Rest, idleness, delight, fornication, and embracings of women

Correspondences between the thirty-six astrological decans
and the thirty-six 2-through-10 minors of the tarot.

When you see planet and sign designations on minor arcana in the Golden Dawn tradition, that refers to which planet rules, or governs, the decan associated with that card. For example, U and A on the 2 of Wands means that the planet Mars rules the first decan, or ten degrees, of Aries. For insights into interpretation, you can then look at the associated majors, the Tower (Mars) and the Emperor (Aries).

The *Picatrix* is an eleventh-century Arabic text on magic and astrology, later translated into Spanish and then Latin. The text used here is drawn from John Michael Greer's and Christopher Warnock's translation from the Latin (*The Complete Picatrix: The Occult Classic of Astrological Magic Liber Atratus Edition*, n.p.: Adocentyn Press, 2010–2011). Agrippa's decan images and signification from some three centuries later are based on *Picatrix* as well. The text used here is the one compiled by Donald Tyson (*Three Books of Occult Philosophy*, St. Paul, MN: Llewellyn Publications, 1993). These are just two of the many decan commentaries that can be found in all astrological traditions, whether Indian, Arabic, or European. Each set of thirty-six images differs in small or large ways from the others.

The Golden Dawn did not explicitly associate its imagery for the numeric minor arcana with any of the traditional images associated with the decans. But when you compare the images and meanings provided in ancient astrological texts with the images and meanings presented on the cards, some very compelling parallels arise. For a thorough comparison of tarot and decanic imagery, Austin Coppock's *36 Faces: The History, Astrology, and Magic of the Decans* is a good source.

PLANETARY DIGNITIES

This chart shows "essential dignity" for the seven traditional planets. Each rules two signs, except the two luminaries (Sun and Moon), which each rule one. Conversely, each except the luminaries is in detriment in two signs. Each has an "exaltation degree" where it is treated as an "honored guest," and each has an opposing "fall degree."

In tarot, the thirty-six numeric minor cards each correspond to one of thirty-six decans, 10° divisions of the zodiac. Each decan is ruled by a different planet, and there are three decans per sign. At times, a planet that rules a particular decan will also be in rulership or detriment based on its sign. These special cases are indicated in parentheses, and they are worth extra consideration if you use astrological correspondences in your tarot practice.

*Decan rulers may also find themselves in exaltation or in fall. The Sun is the only decan ruler which is also in exaltation by exact degree, at 19° Aries/3 of Wands. However, in some astrological traditions, exaltation and fall are considered to extend throughout the sign. If we use this looser, sign-based definition, then:

- Saturn is exalted by sign in Libra while ruling the decan of the 3 of Swords.

- Mars is exalted by sign in Capricorn while ruling the decan of the 3 of Pentacles/Disks.

- Mercury is exalted by sign in Virgo while ruling the decan of the 10 of Pentacles/Disks.

- Moon is exalted by sign in Taurus while ruling the decan of the 6 of Pentacles/Disks.

- Jupiter is fallen by sign in Capricorn and while ruling the decan of the 2 of Pentacles/Disks.

- Venus is fallen by sign in Virgo while ruling the decan of the 9 of Pentacles/Disks.

PLANETARY DIGNITIES

Planet	Rulership	Rulership	Detriment
Saturn	Capricorn	Aquarius	Cancer
Jupiter	Sagittarius	Pisces (9 of Cups)	Gemini (8 of Swords)
Mars	Aries (2 of Wands)	Scorpio (5 of Cups)	Libra
Sun	Leo	—	Aquarius
Venus	Taurus	Libra	Scorpio (7 of Cups)
Mercury	Gemini	Virgo (10 of Pentacles/Disks)	Sagittarius (8 of Wands)
Moon	Cancer (4 of Cups)	—	Capricorn

Essential dignities for the seven traditional planets

PLANETARY DIGNITIES

Planet	Detriment	Exaltation	Fall
Saturn	Leo (5 of Wands)	21° Libra	21° Aries
Jupiter	Virgo	15° Cancer	15° Capricorn
Mars	Taurus	28° Capricorn (3 of Pentacles)*	28° Cancer
Sun	—	19° Aries (3 of Wands)	19° Libra
Venus	Aries (4 of Wands)	27° Pisces	27° Virgo (9 of Pentacles/Disks)*
Mercury	Pisces	15° Virgo (10 of Pentacles/Disks)*	15° Pisces
Moon	—	3° Taurus (6 of Pentacles/Disks)*	3° Scorpio

Essential dignities for the seven traditional planets

GOLDEN DAWN COLOR SCALES
TABLE: MAJOR ARCANA

Arabic number	Roman numeral		Atziluth "King Scale" "Knight Scale" in Thoth	Briah "Queen Scale"	Yetzirah "Emperor Scale" "Prince Scale" in Thoth	Assiah "Empress Scale" "Princess Scale"
0	0	The Fool	Bright pale yellow	Sky blue	Blue emerald green	Emerald, flecked gold
01	I	The Magician	Yellow	Purple	Grey	Indigo, rayed violet
02	II	The High Priestess	Blue	Silver	Cold pale blue	Silver, rayed sky blue
03	III	The Empress	Emerald green	Sky blue	Early spring green	Bright rose or cerise, rayed pale green
04	IV	The Emperor	Scarlet	Red	Brilliant flame	Glowing red
05	V	The Hierophant	Red orange	Deep indigo	Deep warm olive	Rich brown
06	VI	The Lovers	Orange	Pale mauve	New yellow leather	Reddish grey, inclined to mauve

Color scales for the major arcana

Arabic number	Roman numeral		Atziluth "King Scale" "Knight Scale" in Thoth	Briah "Queen Scale"	Yetzirah "Emperor Scale" "Prince Scale" in Thoth	Assiah "Empress Scale" "Princess Scale"
07	VII	The Chariot	Amber	Maroon	Rich bright russet	Dark greenish brown
08/11	VIII/IX	Strength	Yellow (greenish)	Deep purple	Grey	Reddish amber
09	IX	The Hermit	Green (yellowish)	Slate grey	Green grey	Plum color
10	X	The Wheel of Fortune	Violet	Blue	Rich purple	Bright blue, rayed yellow
11/08	XI/VIII	Justice	Emerald green	Blue	Deep blue-green	Plum color
12	XII	The Hanged Man	Deep blue	Sea-green	Deep olive-green	White, flecked purple
13	XIII	Death	Green blue	Dull brown	Very dark brown	Livid indigo brown
14	XIV	Temperance	Blue	Yellow	Green grey	Dark vivid blue

Color scales for the major arcana

Arabic number	Roman numeral		Atziluth "King Scale" "Knight Scale" in Thoth	Briah "Queen Scale"	Yetzirah "Emperor Scale" "Prince Scale" in Thoth	Assiah "Empress Scale" "Princess Scale"
15	XV	The Devil	Indigo	Black	Blue-black	Cold dark grey nearing black
16	XVI	The Tower	Scarlet	Red	Venetian red	Bright red, rayed azure or emerald
17	XVII	The Star	Violet	Sky blue	Bluish mauve	White, tinged purple
18	XVIII	The Moon	Crimson (ultra violet)	Buff, flecked silver white	Light translucent pinkish brown	Stone color
19	XIX	The Sun	Orange	Gold yellow	Rich amber	Amber, rayed red
20	XX	Judgement	Glowing orange scarlet	Vermilion	Scarlet, flecked gold	Vermilion, flecked crimson and emerald
21	XXI	The World	Indigo	Black	Blue-black	Black, rayed blue

Color scales for the major arcana

According to the Golden Dawn, each major arcana path corresponds to a different color in each of the four worlds of the Tree of Life: Atziluth, the Archetypal World; Briah, the Creative World; Yetzirah, the Formative World; and Assiah, the Active World. In most colored representations of the Tree of Life, the paths of the Tree are given the Atziluthic color of their corresponding trump. The ten sephiroth also have four colors apiece for the four worlds, but they are usually represented with their Briatic colors.

GOLDEN DAWN COLOR SCALES
TABLE: MINOR ARCANA

Number	Sephira	Planetary association	Atziluth "King Scale" "Knight Scale" in Thoth	Briah "Queen Scale"	Yetzirah "Emperor Scale" "Prince Scale" in Thoth	Assiah "Empress Scale" "Princess Scale"
			Yod (Fire) N	Heh (Water) P	Vav (Air) M	Heh (Earth) O
			Wands	Cups	Swords	Pentacles
1	Kether	The "Primum Mobile"	Brilliance	White brilliance	White brilliance	White flecked gold
2	Chokmah	The Zodiac	Soft Blue	Grey	Bluish mother of pearl	White flecked red, blue, yellow
3	Binah	Saturn	Crimson	Black	Dark brown	Grey flecked pink
4	Chesed	Jupiter	Deep Violet	Blue	Deep purple	Deep azure flecked yellow
5	Geburah	Mars	Orange	Scarlet-Red	Bright scarlet	Red flecked black
6	Tiphereth	Sun	Clear Pink Rose	Yellow (Gold)	Rich salmon	Gold amber
7	Netzach	Venus	Amber	Green	Orange	Olive flecked gold
8	Hod	Mercury	Violet-Purple	Orange	Red Russet	Yellow-brown flecked white

Color scales for the minor arcana

Number	Sephira	Planetary association	Atziluth "King Scale" "Knight Scale" in Thoth	Briah "Queen Scale"	Yetzirah "Emperor Scale" "Prince Scale" in Thoth	Assiah "Empress Scale" "Princess Scale"
9	Yesod	Moon	Indigo	Purple	Very dark purple	Citrine flecked azure
10	Malkuth	Earth	Yellow	Russet-Olive-Citrine-Black	4 colors flecked gold	Black rayed yellow

Color scales for the minor arcana

You'll note that colors run thematically in rows—all fives have a reddish hue, which is characteristic of Geburah, the sephira of severity, which is associated with Mars. To find the color associated with a numeric minor, check the suit column against the numeric row. For example, the color of the 2 of Swords is "bluish mother of pearl."

The planetary associations come from Kircher's model of the Tree of Life, as used by the Golden Dawn.

SUGGESTED READING

The topics of esoteric tarot include tarot itself and tarot origins, but also works on specific iconic esoteric decks by their creators (and subsequent scholars), symbol decoding, correspondences, magic, mythology, astrology, and Qabalah. Each of these topics alone is broad and layered, worthy of a lifetime of study. Studying all of Crowley's "technical Libers" and magical visions referenced in his *Book of Thoth* would keep one busy for years, and likewise, interpreting Waite's often-veiled references in the *Pictorial Key* requires dissection. We have divided our recommendations by subject below, listing just some of the many works of varying densities that we have referenced in the *Fortune's Wheelhouse* podcast.

TAROT

If you're just getting started on your tarot journey with a Rider-Waite-Smith deck, Rachel Pollack's and Mary Greer's books, plus Waite's *Pictorial Key*, are a great place to start. If you're just getting started with a Thoth deck, Crowley's *Book of Thoth* and Lon Milo DuQuette's *Understanding Aleister Crowley's Thoth Tarot* are essential. For the roots of Golden Dawn tarot, turn to Mathers's *Book T* and the Thelemic updated version, *Liber Theta*. If you're following along with the *Fortune's Wheelhouse* podcast, you'll find it helpful to turn to Susie's *Tarot Correspondences* and Mel's *Book M: Liber Mundi* as references.

Amberstone, Wald, and Ruth Ann Amberstone. *The Secret Language of Tarot*. San Francisco: Red Wheel/Weiser, 2008.

Chang, T. Susan. *Tarot Correspondences: Ancient Secrets for Everyday Readers.* Woodbury, MN: Llewellyn Publications, 2018.

———. *36 Secrets: A Decanic Journey through the Minor Arcana of the Tarot.* Self-published, Anima Mundi Press, 2021.

Crowley, Aleister. *The Book of Thoth: A Short Essay on the Tarot of the Egyptians.* York Beach, ME: Weiser Books, 2017.

David, Jean-Michel. *Reading the Marseille Tarot.* Victoria, Australia: Association for Tarot Studies, 2011.

Decker, Ronald. *The Esoteric Tarot: Ancient Sources Rediscovered in Hermeticism and Cabalah.* Wheaton, IL: Quest Books, 2013.

DuQuette, Lon Milo. *Understanding Aleister Crowley's Thoth Tarot.* York Beach, ME: Weiser Books, 2003.

Fra., G∴H∴, ed. *Liber Theta: Tarot Symbolism and Divination.* Los Angeles: College of Thelema, 2012.

Greer, Mary K. *Tarot for Your Self: A Workbook for Personal Transformation.* York Beach, ME: Weiser Books, 2002.

Huson, Paul. *Mystical Origins of the Tarot: From Ancient Roots to Modern Usage.* Rochester, VT: Destiny Books, 2004.

Katz, Marcus, and Tali Goodwin. *Secrets of the Waite-Smith Tarot: The True Story of the World's Most Popular Tarot.* Woodbury, MN: Llewellyn Publications, 2015.

Kenner, Corrine. *Tarot and Astrology: Enhance Your Readings with the Wisdom of the Zodiac.* Woodbury, MN: Llewellyn Publications, 2011.

Louis, Anthony. *Tarot Beyond the Basics: Gain a Deeper Understanding of the Meanings Behind the Cards.* Woodbury, MN: Llewellyn Publications, 2014.

Mathers, MacGregor and Harriet Felkin. *Book T—The Tarot: Comprising Manuscripts N, O, P, Q, R, and an Unlettered Theoricus Adeptus Minor Instruction.* London: Hermetic Order of the Golden Dawn, 1888.

Meleen, M. M. *Book M: Liber Mundi.* Barre, MA: Atu House, 2015.

———. *The Book of Seshet: Guide to the Rosetta Tarot*. Barre, MA: Atu House, 2011.

Place, Robert M. *The Tarot, Magic, Alchemy, Hermeticism, and Neoplatonism*. New York: Hermes Publications, 2017.

Pollack, Rachel. *Seventy-Eight Degrees of Wisdom: A Book of Tarot*. York Beach, ME: Weiser Books, 2007.

Powell, Robert, trans. *Meditations on the Tarot: A Journey into Christian Hermeticism*. New York: Jeremy P. Tarcher / Putnam, 2002.

Seckler, Phyllis. *The Kabbalah, Magick, and Thelema*. Edited by David Shoemaker. Los Angeles: College of Thelema of Northern California, 2012.

———. *The Thoth Tarot, Astrology, and Other Selected Writings*. Edited by David Shoemaker. Los Angeles: College of Thelema of Northern California, 2010.

Snuffin, Michael Osiris. *The Thoth Companion: The Key to the True Symbolic Meaning of the Thoth Tarot*. Woodbury, MN: Llewellyn Publications, 2007.

Thomson, Sandra A. *Pictures from the Heart: A Tarot Dictionary*. New York: St. Martin's Press, 2003.

Waite, Arthur Edward. *The Pictorial Key to the Tarot*. Stamford, CT: US Games Systems, 1971.

Wang, Robert. *The Qabalistic Tarot: A Textbook of Mystical Philosophy*. N.p.: Marcus Aurelius Press, 2004.

ASTROLOGY

For a quick start exploring the links between astrology and tarot, have a look at Anthony Louis's and Corrine Kenner's books in the previous list as well as Mel's *Book of Seshet*, which has a basic 101 for how the planets and zodiac signs work in relation to their corresponding cards in tarot. In the astrology list, Austin Coppock's *36 Faces* is a comprehensive guide to the decanic material we relate to the minor arcana. Alan Oken's book is thorough on the astrological basics, and Linda Goodman's book, though socially dated, is a classic for a reason, as it is a consummate resource for all things related to the mundane expression of the zodiacal signs as personalities.

Brady, Bernadette. *Predictive Astrology: The Eagle and the Lark*. York Beach, ME: Weiser Books, 1999.

———. *Brady's Book of Fixed Stars*. York Beach, ME: Weiser Books, 1999.

Brennan, Chris. *Hellenistic Astrology: The Study of Fate and Fortune*. Denver, CO: Amor Fati Publications, 2017.

Coppock, Austin. *36 Faces: The History, Astrology and Magic of the Decans*. Contra Costa County, CA: Three Hands Press, 2014.

———, and Daniel A. Schulke, eds. *The Celestial Art: Essays on Astrological Magic*. Contra Costa County, CA: Three Hands Press, 2018.

Cornelius, Geoffrey, and Emma Harding. *The Starlore Handbook: The Starwatcher's Essential Guide to the 88 Constellations, Their Myths and Symbols*. London: Duncan Baird Publishing, 2000.

Goodman, Linda. *Linda Goodman's Sun Signs*. London: Bluebird, 2019.

March, Marion D., and Joan McEvers. *The Only Way to Learn Astrology: Basic Principles*. ACS Publications, 1980.

Oken, Alan. *Alan Oken's Complete Astrology: The Classic Guide to Modern Astrology*. Lake Worth, FL: Ibis Press, 2006.

Parker, Julia, and Derek Parker. *Parkers' Astrology: New Edition*. London: Dorling Kindersley, 2009.

MAGIC AND SYMBOLISM

When discussing symbolic meanings in esoteric tarot, the text we probably turn to most often is *The Penguin Dictionary of Symbols*, while for magical correspondence the standards are Crowley's *777* and Agrippa's *Three Books of Occult Philosophy*.

Agrippa, Henry Cornelius. *Three Books of Occult Philosophy*. Edited by Donald Tyson. Translated by James Freake. St. Paul, MN: Llewellyn Publications, 1993.

Athanassakis, Apostolos N. *The Orphic Hymns*. Translated by Benjamin M. Wolkow. Baltimore, MD: Johns Hopkins University Press, 2013.

Chevalier, Jean, and Alain Gheerbrant. *The Penguin Dictionary of Symbols*. Translated by John Buchanan-Brown. London: Penguin Books, 2008.

Crowley, Aleister. *777 And Other Qabalistic Writings of Aleister Crowley: Including Gematria & Sepher Sephiroth*. Edited by Israel Regardie. York Beach, ME: Weiser Books, 1996.

———. *Magick: Book 4, Parts I–IV*. York Beach, ME: Weiser Books, 1994.

Greer, John Michael, and Christopher Warnock. *Picatrix: The Classic Medieval Handbook of Astrological Magic*. Iowa City, IA: Adocentyn Press, 2011.

Hall, Manly P. *The Secret Teachings of All Ages*. Radford, VA: A & D Publishing, 2007.

Hulse, David Allen. *The Eastern Mysteries: An Encyclopedic Guide to the Sacred Languages & Magickal Systems of the World*. Woodbury, MN: Llewellyn Publications, 2000.

———. *The Western Mysteries: An Encyclopedic Guide to the Sacred Languages & Magickal Systems of the World*. Woodbury, MN: Llewellyn Publications, 2000.

al-Majriti, Maslama ibn Aḥmad. *Picatrix: A Medieval Treatise on Astral Magic*. University Park, PA: Pennsylvania State University Press, 2019.

Moore, Alan, and J. H. Williams III. *Promethea*. London: Titan, 2003.

Regardie, Israel, and John Michael Greer. *The Golden Dawn: The Original Account of the Teachings, Rites, and Ceremonies of the Hermetic Order*. Woodbury, MN: Llewellyn Publications, 2015.

Roob, Alexander. *Alchemy & Mysticism: The Hermetic Museum*. Translated by Shaun Whiteside. Cologne, Germany: Taschen, 2019.

Skinner, Stephen. *The Complete Magician's Tables*. Singapore: Golden Hoard Press, 2005.

Whitcomb, Bill. *The Magician's Companion: A Practical & Encyclopedic Guide to Magical & Religious Symbolism*. Woodbury, MN: Llewellyn Publications, 2007.

QABALAH AND THE TREE OF LIFE

It's particularly difficult to know where to begin when it comes to Qabalistic material, but Lon Milo DuQuette's and Rachel Pollack's works in this list are particularly accessible. Regardie, Case, and Fortune all offer insights into the way the Golden Dawn interpreted the Tree of Life. If you continue to delve deeper into the larger Kabbalistic (as opposed to Qabalistic) historic tradition, a copy of the *Sefer* Yetzirah is a must. John Bonner's magical primer is recommended for a Thelemic take on Qabalah, and Godwin's encyclopedia has proved a useful resource that provides food for thought in our Qabalistic explorations.

Bonner, John. *Qabalah: A Magical Primer*. York Beach, ME: Weiser Books, 2002.

Case, Paul Foster. *The Book of Tokens: 22 Meditations on the Ageless Wisdom*. Los Angeles: Builders of the Adytum, 1989.

Crowley, Aleister. *The Book of Lies*. York Beach, ME: Weiser Books, 2000.

Dunn, Patrick. *The Orphic Hymns: A New Translation for the Occult Practitioner*. Woodbury, MN: Llewellyn Publications, 2018.

DuQuette, Lon Milo. *The Chicken Qabalah of Rabbi Lamed Ben Clifford*. York Beach, ME: Weiser Books, 2010.

Fortune, Dion. *The Mystical Qabalah*. London: Aziloth Books, 2011.

Godwin, David. *Godwin's Cabalistic Encyclopedia*. Woodbury, MN: Llewellyn Publications, 2004.

Kaplan, Aryeh. *Sefer* Yetzirah: *The Book of Creation*. San Francisco: Red Wheel/ Weiser, 2004.

Kliegman, Isabel Radow. *Tarot and the Tree of Life: Finding Everyday Wisdom in the Minor Arcana*. Wheaton, IL: Quest Books, 2013.

Knight, Gareth. *A Practical Guide to Qabalistic Symbolism*. London: Kahn and Averill, 1998.

Matt, Daniel Chanan, trans. *Zohar: The Book of Enlightenment*. Mahwah, NJ: Paulist Press, 1983.

Pollack, Rachel. *The Kabbalah Tree: A Journey of Balance & Growth*. Woodbury, MN: Llewellyn Publications, 2004.

Regardie, Israel. *A Garden of Pomegranates: Skrying on the Tree of Life*. St. Paul, MN: Llewellyn Publications, 1995.

Sturzaker, Doreen, and James Sturzaker. *Colour and the Kabbalah*. London: Thorsons, 1975.

Sturzaker, James. *Kabbalistic Aphorisms*. Wheaton, IL: Theosophical Publishing House, 1971.

MYTHOLOGY

We focus mainly on myths from the Greek, Roman, Egyptian, and Mesopotamian traditions. While tarot itself can form connections to any story lineage, these are the legends which most closely inform the Rider-Waite-Smith and Thoth decks, which in turn influenced much of modern tarot.

Athanassakis, Apostolos N. *The Orphic Hymns*. Translated by Benjamin M. Wolkow. Baltimore, MD: Johns Hopkins University Press, 2013.

Bulfinch, Thomas. *Bulfinch's Mythology: The Classic Introduction to Myth and Legend*. New York: Jeremy P. Tarcher / Penguin, 1913.

Dalley, Stephanie, trans. *Myths from Mesopotamia: Creation, the Flood, Gilgamesh, and Others*. Oxford: Oxford University Press, 2008.

Flaum, Eric, and David Pandy. *The Encyclopedia of Mythology: Gods, Heroes, and Legends of the Greeks and Romans*. Philadelphia, PA: Courage Books, 1993.

Frazer, James George. *The Golden Bough*. London: Macmillan, 1966.

Gayley, Charles Mills. *The Classic Myths in English Literature and in Art*. Boston: Athenaeum Press, 1911.

Graves, Robert. *The Greek Myths: The Complete and Definitive Edition*. London: Penguin Books, 2017.

Pinch, Geraldine. *Egyptian Mythology: A Guide to the Gods, Goddesses, and Traditions of Ancient Egypt*. Oxford: Oxford University Press, 2002.

Shelmerdine, Susan C., trans. *The Homeric Hymns*. Newburyport, MA: Focus Publishing, 1995.

Staal, Julius D. W. *The New Patterns in the Sky: Myths and Legends of the Stars*. Granville, OH: McDonald and Woodward, 1988.

Wilkinson, Richard H. *The Complete Gods and Goddesses of Ancient Egypt*. London: Thames & Hudson, 2017.

Willis, Roy, ed. *World Mythology*. New York: Henry Holt, 1996.

BIBLIOGRAPHY

Agrippa, Henry Cornelius. *Three Books of Occult Philosophy*. Edited by Donald Tyson. Translated by James Freake. St. Paul, MN: Llewellyn Publications, 1993.

Alliette, Jean-Baptiste. *Manière de Tirer Le Grand Etteilla: Ou Tarots Égyptiens*. Paris: B. P. Grimaud, 1935.

Amberstone, Wald, and Ruth Ann Amberstone. *The Secret Language of Tarot*. San Francisco: Red Wheel/Weiser, 2008.

Budge, E. A. Wallis. *The Egyptian Book of the Dead*. New York: Dover Publicatoins, 1967.

Bulfinch, Thomas. *Bulfinch's Mythology: The Classic Introduction to Myth and Legend*. New York: Jeremy P. Tarcher / Penguin, 1913.

Burns, Robert. *The Complete Poems and Songs of Robert Burns*. N.p.: Pantianos Classics, 2017.

Case, Paul Foster. *The Tarot: A Key to the Wisdom of the Ages*. New York: Jeremy P. Tarcher / Penguin, 2006.

Chang, T. Susan. *Tarot Correspondences: Ancient Secrets for Everyday Readers*. Woodbury, MN: Llewellyn Publications, 2018.

———. *36 Secrets: A Decanic Journey through the Minor Arcana of the Tarot*. Self-published, Anima Mundi Press, 2021.

Chevalier, Jean, and Alain Gheerbrant. *The Penguin Dictionary of Symbols*. Translated by John Buchanan-Brown. London: Penguin Books, 2008.

Crowley, Aleister. *The Book of Lies*. York Beach, ME: Weiser Books, 2000.

———. *The Book of the Law: Liber Al Vel Legis Sub Figura CCXX*. San Francisco: Weiser Books, 1976.

———. *The Book of Lies*. San Francisco: Weiser Books, 1981.

———. *The Book of Thoth: A Short Essay on the Tarot of the Egyptians*. York Beach, ME: Weiser Books, 2017.

———. *Gems from the Equinox: Instructions by Aleister Crowley for His Own Magical Order*. Edited by Israel Regardie. St. Paul, MN: Llewellyn Publications, 1974.

———. *The I Ching: A New Translation of the Book of Changes by the Master Therion*. San Francisco: Level Press, 1974.

———. *Konx Om Pax*. London: Walter Scott Publishing, 1907.

———. *Magick: Liber ABA. Book 4, Parts I-IV*. San Francisco: Weiser Books, 1994.

———. *Rites of Eleusis*. Sequim, WA: Holmes Publishing Group, 1993.

———. *777 And Other Qabalistic Writings of Aleister Crowley: Including Gematria & Sepher Sephiroth*. Edited by Israel Regardie. York Beach, ME: Weiser Books, 1996.

Dalley, Stephanie, trans. *Myths from Mesopotamia: Creation, the Flood, Gilgamesh, and Others*. Oxford: Oxford University Press, 2008.

Dee, Jonathan. *Fortune Telling with Playing Cards*. Charlottesville, VA: Hampton Roads Publishing, 2018.

Dunn, Patrick. *The Orphic Hymns: A New Translation for the Occult Practitioner*. Woodbury, MN: Llewellyn Publications, 2018.

Flaum, Eric, and David Pandy. *The Encyclopedia of Mythology: Gods, Heroes, and Legends of the Greeks and Romans*. Philadelphia, PA: Courage Books, 1993.

Fra., G∴H∴, ed. *Liber Theta: Tarot Symbolism and Divination*. Los Angeles: College of Thelema, 2012.

Frazer, James George. *The Golden Bough*. London: Macmillan, 1966.

George, Andrew, trans. *The Epic of Gilgamesh: The Babylonian Epic Poem and Other Texts in Akkadian and Sumerian*. London: Penguin Books, 2003.

Greer, John Michael. *Earth Divination, Earth Magic: A Practical Guide to Geomancy*. St. Paul, MN: Llewellyn Publications, 1999.

———, and Christopher Warnock. *Picatrix: The Classic Medieval Handbook of Astrological Magic*. Iowa City, IA: Adocentyn Press, 2011.

Hall, Manly P. *The Secret Teachings of All Ages*. Radford, VA: A & D Publishing, 2007.

———. *The Hermetic Marriage: Being a Study in the Philosophy of the Thrice Greatest Hermes*. Mansfield Centre, CT: Martino Publishing, 2013.

Homer. *The Odyssey*. Translated by Emily Wilson. New York: W. W. Norton, 2018.

Huang, Alfred. *The Complete I Ching: The Definitive Translation*. Rochester, VT: Inner Traditions, 2004.

Huson, Paul. *Mystical Origins of the Tarot: From Ancient Roots to Modern Usage*. Rochester, VT: Destiny Books, 2004.

Julian. *Hymn to King Helios*. N.p.: Rise of Douai, 2015.

Kaplan, Aryeh. *Sefer* Yetzirah: *The Book of Creation*. San Francisco: Red Wheel/Weiser, 2004.

Kaplan, Stuart R., Mary K. Greer, Elizabeth Foley O'Connor, and Melinda Boyd Parsons. *Pamela Colman Smith: The Untold Story*. Stamford, CT: US Games Systems, 2018.

Katz, Marcus, and Tali Goodwin. *Secrets of the Waite-Smith Tarot: The True Story of the World's Most Popular Tarot*. Woodbury, MN: Llewellyn Publications, 2015.

Kramer, Samuel Noah, and John Maier. *Myths of Enki, the Crafty God*. Oxford: Oxford University Press, 1989.

Lévi, Éliphas. *Transcendental Magic: Its Doctrine and Ritual*. Translated by Arthur Edward Waite. Mansfield Centre, CT: Martino Publishing, 2011.

Malory, Thomas. *Le Morte Darthur*. Edited by Stephen H. A. Shepherd. New York: W. W. Norton, 2004.

Meleen, M. M. *Book M: Liber Mundi*. Barre, MA: Atu House, 2015.

———. *The Book of Seshet: Guide to the Rosetta Tarot*. Barre, MA: Atu House, 2011.

Morris, William. *The Well at the World's End*. London: Ballantine, 1973.

Orpheus. *The Orphic Hymns*. Translated by Apostolos N. Athanassakis. Atlanta, GA: Scholars Press, 1988.

Place, Robert M. *The Tarot, Magic, Alchemy, Hermeticism, and Neoplatonism*. New York: Hermes Publications, 2017.

Regardie, Israel, and John Michael Greer. *The Golden Dawn: The Original Account of the Teachings, Rites, and Ceremonies of the Hermetic Order*. Woodbury, MN: Llewellyn Publications, 2015.

Rudhyar, Dane. *An Astrological Mandala: The Cycle of Transformations and Its 360 Symbolic Phases*. New York: Vintage Books, 1974.

———. *An Astrological Study of Psychological Complexes*. Boulder, CO: Shambhala, 1976.

Shakespeare, William. *Henry IV*. Edited by Barbara A. Mowat and Paul Werstine. New York: Simon & Schuster, 2009.

———. *The Taming of the Shrew*. Edited by Barbara A. Mowat and Paul Werstine. New York: Simon & Schuster, 2014.

Sophocles. *The Oedipus Cycle: An English Version*. Translated by Dudley Fitts and Robert Fitzgerald. New York: Harcourt Brace, 1977.

Tennyson, Lord Alfred. *Idylls of the King*. N.p.: Pantianos Classics, 1959.

Tolkien, J. R. R. *The Lord of the Rings*. Boston: Houghton Mifflin, 1986.

Virgil. *The Aeneid*. Translated by Robert Fagles. New York: Penguin Books, 2010.

———. *The Eclogues of Virgil (Bilingual Edition)*. Translated by David Ferry. New York: Farrar, Straus, and Giroux, 2000.

Waite, Arthur Edward. *The Pictorial Key to the Tarot*. Stamford, CT: US Games Systems, 1971.

Wang, Robert. *The Qabalistic Tarot: A Textbook of Mystical Philosophy*. N.p.: Marcus Aurelius Press, 2004.

Whitcomb, Bill. *The Magician's Companion: A Practical & Encyclopedic Guide to Magical & Religious Symbolism*. Woodbury, MN: Llewellyn Publications, 2007.

ART CREDIT LIST

1. Four elements (created by the authors and Llewellyn art department), page 7

2. The seven traditional planets (created by the authors and Llewellyn art department), page 8

3. The classical domiciles of the seven planets (created by the authors and Llewellyn art department), page 9

4. Astrological rulerships diagram (created by the authors and Llewellyn art department), page 10

5. Zodiacal correspondences and the major arcana (created by the authors and Llewellyn art department), pages 10–11

6. The Fool corresponds to elemental air. This image captures a grasshopper in aerial midflight, while also picking up on the traditional sun and hobo-bag iconography. (*Animal Totem Tarot*), page 16

7. 0. The Fool. Tree of Life. (Created by the authors and Llewellyn art department), page 18

8. This Fool is about to step into a wormhole in the fabric of space-time that is in the center of three concentric ouroboros serpents representing the negative veils before Kether: *Ain*, *Ain Soph*, and *Ain Soph Aur*. (*Tabula Mundi Tarot*), page 19

9. The Fool (*Rider-Waite-Smith Tarot*), page 19

10. The "ape of Thoth" trope on the Thoth deck's Magus is a Mercurial reference; here is the ape-as-Magician, complete with the usual wand and analemma. (*Linestrider Tarot*), page 25

11. I (1). The Magician/The Magus. Tree of Life. (Created by the authors and Llewellyn art department), page 26

12. The Magus in this card is a cosmic DJ, a mix-master bringing down the "house" (*beth*, his letter). (*Tabula Mundi Tarot*), page 27

13. The Magician (*Rider-Waite-Smith Tarot*), page 28

14. The moon, associated with the Priestess since the earliest esoteric tarot correspondences, dominates this modern-day reworking of the image. (*Animal Totem Tarot*), page 34

15. II (2). The High Priestess/The Priestess. Tree of Life. (Created by the authors and Llewellyn art department), page 35

16. The High Priestess (*Rider-Waite-Smith Tarot*), page 37

17. The Priestess's veil and book, inherited from the early woodcut images, would go on to appear in all Priestess cards up to the present day. (*Ancient Italian Tarot*), page 38

18. A Demeter figure wears the zodiacal crown (Chokmah) next to a door (*daleth*) opening seven (Venus) visible levels over the sea of Binah. (*Pharos Tarot*), page 43

19. III (3). The Empress. Tree of Life. (Created by the authors and Llewellyn art department), page 44

20. This Empress's shield opens like a door (*daleth*), showing a magnified diagram of her heart chambers as a beehive full of honey: the bees of Venus fly out in a golden spiral ratio. (*Tabula Mundi Tarot*), page 45

21. The Empress (*Rider-Waite-Smith Tarot*), page 45

22. Before a wall of bricks in the Fibonacci sequence, the Emperor con-templates a bee skep and the structure of the hive, as opposed to the

wildness of the bees and nature seen in the Empress. (*Tabula Mundi Tarot*), page 50

23. The number four appears as a square surmounting the throne and in its quadrangular pedestal base. The shield is a holdover from the early Marseille decks, where matching shields typically appear on the Emperor and Empress cards. (*Mystical Tarot*), page 52

24. IV (4). The Emperor. Tree of Life. Golden Dawn path attribution. (Created by the authors and Llewellyn art department), page 52

25. IV (4). The Emperor. Tree of Life. Thoth path attribution. (Created by the authors and Llewellyn art department), page 53

26. The Emperor (*Rider-Waite-Smith Tarot*), page 54

27. V (5). The Hierophant. Tree of Life. (Created by the authors and Llewellyn art department), page 61

28. This Priest-Prince holds a nail scepter (*vav*) between pillars that have combined with the Kerubic beasts as lamassu sphinxes. (*Pharos Tarot*), page 62

29. The Hierophant (*Rider-Waite-Smith Tarot*), page 63

30. In this stripped-down Hierophant, the crossed keys and iconic hand gesture (borrowed from the Waite-Smith deck) subtly suggest the human-divine conjunction. (*Linestrider Tarot*), page 64

31. Within lunar and solar mirrors that together form the glyph of Gemini, mythological stories of choice appear: Perseus rescuing Andromeda on the left, and on the right, either the serpent offering Eve the apple—or Paris, offering the apple to Aphrodite, choosing her as the fairest. (*Rosetta Tarot*), page 68

32. VI (6). The Lovers. Tree of Life. (Created by the authors and Llewellyn art department), page 70

33. The Lovers (*Rider-Waite-Smith Tarot*), page 71

34. This updated Tarot de Marseille imagery adopts the Eros figure as its angel; the lover appears to choose between "respectable" and "common" consorts. (*Universal Wirth Tarot*), page 72

35. In this Marseille-based image, we see many precursors later expressed as Cancer tropes: starry canopy, moonlike epaulets, armored warrior. (*Camoin-Jodorowsky Tarot de Marseille*), page 76

36. VII (7). The Chariot. Tree of Life. (Created by the authors and Llewellyn art department), page 78

37. The enclosing fence of letter *cheth* becomes a wall of cardinal water as the charioteer rides the pipeline in perfect balance. (*Tabula Mundi Tarot*), page 79

38. The Chariot (*Rider-Waite-Smith Tarot*), page 79

39. Babalon as the Scarlet Woman rides an ecstatic spiral in the form of the lion-serpent (Leo and *teth*) showing Crowley's "joy of strength exercised." (*Pharos Tarot*), page 85

40. VIII (8). Strength / XI (11). Lust. Tree of Life. (Created by the authors and Llewellyn art department), page 86

41. Strength (*Rider-Waite-Smith Tarot*), page 87

42. Ideas of physical and moral force blend in this Soprafino-based design. The elaborate headpiece foreshadows the infinity sign that would appear in Waite-Smith. (*Ancient Italian Tarot*), page 88

43. The Hermit in this image walks the labyrinth, a journey of introspection and solitude, symbolic of the process of going within. (*Rosetta Tarot*), page 95

44. IX (9). The Hermit. Tree of Life. (Created by the authors and Llewellyn art department), page 96

45. Here the Hermit is shown as the *yod*-shaped flame within the lantern usually held in the hand of the Hermit. (*Pharos Tarot*), page 97

46. The Hermit (*Rider-Waite-Smith Tarot*), page 97

47. A spinning wheel spins the blue thread that is woven into life's fabric using a vajra (weapon of Jupiter) as a shuttle. (*Tabula Mundi Tarot*), page 102

48. X (10). The Wheel of Fortune/Fortune. Tree of Life. (Created by the authors and Llewellyn art department), page 104

49. The Wheel of Fortune (*Rider-Waite-Smith Tarot*), page 105

50. Even in this minimalist image, we see traces of Waite-Smith's Kerubic beasts as astrological glyphs. The iconic Wheel inscriptions also remain. (*Linestrider Tarot*), page 107

51. While Justice's sword and scales are still clearly evident, this version has a particularly Venusian (for Libra) character. (*Pre-Raphaelite Tarot*), page 112

52. Sword, scales, crown, wings—this is Justice as the cardinal virtue, expressed in goddess-like form. (*Ancient Italian Tarot*), page 114

53. XI/VIII (11/8). Justice/Adjustment. Tree of Life. (Created by the authors and Llewellyn art department), page 114

54. Justice (*Rider-Waite-Smith Tarot*), page 116

55. This honey pot ant, a living reservoir of nectar and water for its community, reinterprets the Hanged Man's realm of service, sacrifice, and elemental water. (*Animal Totem Tarot*), page 122

56. The Hanged Man is shown as Odin, who hung upon Yggdrasil and gave up his eye to Mimir for a taste of elemental water from the Well of Wisdom. (*Tabula Mundi Tarot*), page 124

57. XII (12). The Hanged Man. Tree of Life. (Created by the authors and Llewellyn art department), page 124

58. The Hanged Man (*Rider-Waite-Smith Tarot*), page 125

59. This skeleton wears the atef crown of Osiris and rides a composite beast comprised of the three forms of Scorpio: the eagle, serpent, and scorpion. (*Tabula Mundi Tarot*), page 131

60. The skeleton wearing the serpent represents the widow Isis: her husband Osiris was dismembered and thrown into the sea, and only thirteen of the fourteen parts were found. (*Pharos Tarot*), page 132

61. XIII (13). Death. Tree of Life. (Created by the authors and Llewellyn art department), page 133

62. Death (*Rider-Waite-Smith Tarot*), page 134

63. Within the egg-shaped vessel of the crucible, nocturnal Artemis holds the lunar bow and arrow and diurnal Apollo holds the solar lyre and horn; they combine as a green-robed hermaphrodite. (*Pharos Tarot*), page 141

64. XIV (14). Temperance/Art. Tree of Life. (Created by the authors and Llewellyn art department), page 142

65. While far removed from esoteric tarot in many ways, this image retains one core symbol: the rainbow, symbol of reconciliation between opposites. (*Animal Totem Tarot*), page 143

66. Temperance (*Rider-Waite-Smith Tarot*), page 144

67. The goat-horned satyr of Capricorn holds the hourglass of Saturn in one hand; in the other he holds a mirror shaped like an eye (*ayin*). (*Rosetta Tarot*), page 151

68. XV (15). The Devil. Tree of Life. (Created by the authors and Llewellyn art department), page 152

69. A giant eye for Hebrew letter *ayin*, a Saturnine hourglass, and the double helix architecture of DNA accompany the Lord of the Gates of Matter. (*Tabula Mundi Tarot*), page 153

70. The Devil (*Rider-Waite-Smith Tarot*), page 154

71. XVI (16). The Tower. Tree of Life. (Created by the authors and Llewellyn art department), page 161

72. In the Tarot de Marseille's "La Maison de Dieu," the divine message appears as a multicolored plume, its corrective effect more startling than disastrous. (*Camoin-Jodorowsky Tarot de Marseille*), page 163

73. By the nineteenth century, the plume had morphed into the catastrophic lightning flash familiar from today's Tower cards. (*Ancient Italian Tarot*), page 163

74. The Tower (*Rider-Waite-Smith Tarot*), page 164

75. Here the traditional golden cup pours the setting sun, while her silver cup is the crescent moon pouring the celestial waters of Aquarius. (*Tabula Mundi Tarot*), page 170

76. Many themes remain consistent across all Star cards: the naked water bearer, the starry night sky, even the bird (here an owl) on its tree. (*Ancient Italian Tarot*), page 171

77. XVII (17). The Star. Tree of Life. Golden Dawn path attribution. (Created by the authors and Llewellyn art department), page 172

78. XVII (17). The Star. Tree of Life. Thoth path attribution (Created by the authors and Llewellyn art department), page 173

79. The Star (*Rider-Waite-Smith Tarot*), page 174

80. Perilous subconscious crossings are illustrated by Greek mythological beings: Scylla, who is shown here as a sea monster with the heads of a dog, wolf, and crayfish-handed woman, and Charybdis, the whirlpool stairway leading into the depths of the subconscious (the sea). (*Rosetta Tarot*), page 180

81. XVIII (18). The Moon. Tree of Life. (Created by the authors and Llewellyn art department), page 182

82. The barge of the moon travels the waters of sleep through the gates of horn (hand of witchcraft, Neptune) and ivory (phrenology head, *qoph*), which tell true dreams from false. (*Tabula Mundi Tarot*), page 183

83. The Moon (*Rider-Waite-Smith Tarot*), page 183

84. At the juncture point of a solar analemma, two fingers inspired by Michelangelo's Sistine Chapel meet: the hand of God breathing life into his twin, Adam. (*Rosetta Tarot*), page 190

85. The sun is shown as a lamp emblazoned with solar icons: the four stations of *Liber Resh*: Ra at dawn in the east, Hathor at noon on the zenith, Atum at sunset in the west, and Khepra at midnight below. (*Pharos Tarot*), page 192

86. XIX (19). The Sun. Tree of Life. (Created by the authors and Llewellyn art department), page 192

87. The Sun (*Rider-Waite-Smith Tarot*), page 192

88. This angel could be Gabriel with his horn or Michael with his sword, flying above a prophet who climbs out from under the rubble on Judgment Day. (*Tarot Egyptiens*), page 201

89. XX (20). Judgement/Aeon. Tree of Life. (Created by the authors and Llewellyn art department), page 202

90. Judgement (*Rider-Waite-Smith Tarot*), page 203

91. Themes of major cyclic change abound: solar analemma, lunar Aubrey holes, Omphalos/Orphic egg, sprouting seed, comet, flaming keyhole tomb opening, Stonehenge sunrise, ouroboros, and the glyphs of the signs at the end and beginning of the zodiac. (*Tabula Mundi Tarot*), page 205

92. The maiden of the Universe twirls spiral galaxies, manipulating "*dextro* and *laevo* rotary" cyclic forces, and, like Eurynome, stands poised above the head of the serpent Ophion of creative force. (*Rosetta Tarot*), page 211

93. XXI (21). The World/The Universe. Tree of Life. (Created by the authors and Llewellyn art department), page 212

94. The World (*Rider-Waite-Smith Tarot*), page 213

95. Even this nineteenth-century design shows the four Kerubic beasts. The ribboned ovoid of the wreath prefigures Waite-Smith, though the nude dancer bears no wands. (*Ancient Italian Tarot*), page 214

96. This naturalistic Ace clearly shows its tree-borne origins, but the living leaves and nuts can also remind us of the Wands' eternal life force. (*Ancient Italian Tarot*), page 229

97. The hints of form coalescing in the bark are the "first swirlings" of manifestation, while the ancient bearded face evokes the many titles of Kether like the Most High, the Head That Is Not, and the Vast Countenance. (*Tabula Mundi Tarot*), page 230

98. Ace of Wands (*Rider-Waite-Smith Tarot*), page 230

99. A fiery ram's head and wands shaped like Mars glyphs underscore the Mars-in-Aries decan rulership of this card. (*Rosetta Tarot*), page 234

100. In modern tarot, a globe has come to signify the concept of "Dominion" and the idea that a new year and new world begin together. (*Linestrider Tarot*), page 235

101. 2 of Wands (*Rider-Waite-Smith Tarot*), page 236

102. The woman in green stands with one leg visible, as described in the decan image of *Picatrix*, but her head is that of a heron, associated with the Bennu bird. (*Liber T: Tarot of Stars Eternal*), page 240

103. The wands topped with pine cones are symbols of the pineal gland that receives light at the center of the head: a reference to *resh*, the letter of the Sun card that rules the decan. (*Tabula Mundi Tarot*), page 241

104. 3 of Wands (*Rider-Waite-Smith Tarot*), page 242

105. Structure (the measuring tools of the Emperor-Aries) and nature (the honey and bees of the Empress-Venus) complete each other. (*Tabula Mundi Tarot*), page 247

106. In the background is a castle compound (fours, Chesed) and a tower (Mars, ruler of Aries) with five (Mars) circular rings, seven (Venus)

levels in all, and topped by a flag decorated with the salamander, a symbol of the element fire. (*Mystical Tarot*), page 248

107. 4 of Wands (*Rider-Waite-Smith Tarot*), page 249

108. The wands have the red ribbons of elemental fire, while the badger is black (Saturn) and known for its aggression (fire). (*Animal Totem Tarot*), page 252

109. Mesopotamian deity Zurvān is shown carrying the *tau* cross and flanked by scythes; his form combines the lion of Leo with parts of the other Kerubic beasts (Saturn). (*Tabula Mundi Tarot*), page 253

110. 5 of Wands (*Rider-Waite-Smith Tarot*), page 254

111. In this heraldic image the "lion sejant" of Leo wears the laurel wreath and poses in shared victory with the crowned owl "in its vigilance" from the top of Fortune's wheel (Jupiter) in this deck. (*Tabula Mundi Tarot*), page 259

112. This monumental figure, bearing the usual laurels of Jupiter, shows one facet of *Victory*: fame. The falling leaves and spectral sidekick ask: Will it last? (*Linestrider Tarot*), page 260

113. 6 of Wands (*Rider-Waite-Smith Tarot*), page 261

114. The foreground's flaming torch evokes the classic theme of "one against many"; in the background, a martial homage to the Waite-Smith Tower looms. (*Tabula Mundi Tarot*), page 264

115. The central wand is a blunt object of martial force, while the inner-most flanking pairs of wands are ceremonial daggers shaped like the glyph of Mars and decorated with the lions of Sekhmet (Venus and Leo). (*Rosetta Tarot*), page 265

116. 7 of Wands (*Rider-Waite-Smith Tarot*), page 266

117. The doubling of mercurial influence is shown by the caduceus and taleria (winged sandals) of Hermes (Mercury), while the rainbow of

Temperance/Art references the sign of Sagittarius and the idea of heavenly messages and ephemeral fire. (*Tabula Mundi Tarot*), page 271

118. Here the Lord of Swiftness is a horse, apt representative for Sagittarius, the half-equine centaur figure of mythology. (*Animal Totem Tarot*), page 272

119. 8 of Wands (*Rider-Waite-Smith Tarot*), page 273

120. Bow imagery is a constant in esoteric tarot cards related to fiery Sagittarius; the Priestess's scroll symbolizes the inner knowledge or certainty underlying *Strength*. (*Tabula Mundi Tarot*), page 277

121. While the moon rules this card's decan, the sun also appears—a reference to Temperance/Art (Sagittarius)'s path between Sun and Moon on the Tree of Life. (*Rosetta Tarot*), page 278

122. 9 of Wands (*Rider-Waite-Smith Tarot*), page 278

123. The card is doubly saturnine, shown by the hammer and pick of the oppressed working classes and the heavy anvil weighing down the alchemical vessel from Sagittarius's Temperance/Art card. (*Tabula Mundi Tarot*), page 283

124. 10 of Wands (*Rider-Waite-Smith Tarot*) (left), page 284

125. On the right is the 10 of Swords, not Wands, from the *Sola Busca Tarot*. Nevertheless, its influence on the Waite-Smith 10 of Wands is self-evident. (*Sola Busca Tarot*), page 284

126. The Ace as the Holy Grail and cup of Babalon: the waters form the symbol of *heh* primal. (*Tabula Mundi Tarot*), page 289

127. Ace of Cups (*Rider-Waite-Smith Tarot*), page 290

128. Echoes of Waite-Smith's Ace of Cups: the inverted "M" (or upright "W") and the quartered circle symbol. (*Linestrider Tarot*), page 291

129. Dolphins are associated with Venus and the womb (Cancer); here they are paired as *argent* (silver) and *or* (gold). (*Rosetta Tarot*), page 295

130. Silver (lunar) and gold (solar) cups, red and white roses: symbols of the alchemical marriage or union of opposites traditionally associated with the card. (*Universal Wirth Tarot*), page 296

131. 2 of Cups (*Rider-Waite-Smith Tarot*), page 297

132. Along with the three light phases of the moon, symbols of abundance (golden apple, pomegranate, wheat) are held up from hands within cups (from the Magician card, Mercury). (*Tabula Mundi Tarot*), page 300

133. 3 of Cups (*Rider-Waite-Smith Tarot*), page 302

134. Marseille versions of the 3 of Cups traditionally bear pomegranates in their arabesques. Did this influence Lady Frieda Harris's Thoth painting? (*Camoin-Jodorowsky Tarot de Marseille*), page 303

135. A rare sighting: the central figure as a turtle warrior, the "celhafe" (Arabic: *salihafa*, سلحفاة) described in *Picatrix*. (*Liber T: Tarot of Stars Eternal*), page 307

136. The fence of *cheth* (Cancer) is a wave of cardinal water surrounding the four phases of the moon and the pearl in its enclosure. (*Tabula Mundi Tarot*), page 308

137. 4 of Cups (*Rider-Waite-Smith Tarot*), page 309

138. The lotus plant has roots tracing the glyphs of Mars and Scorpio; the seabed is dry and there are no flowers. (*Rosetta Tarot*), page 313

139. The parched setting and fish skeleton (Hebrew letter *nun*, corresponding to Death/Scorpio) emphasize the dry, destructive tendencies of Geburah as a five. (*Tabula Mundi Tarot*), page 314

140. 5 of Cups (*Rider-Waite-Smith Tarot*), page 315

141. A solar *yantra* glows in the center of six golden cups filled by gold lotuses, whose roots form the glyph of Scorpio. (*Rosetta Tarot*), page 319

142. The twelve-pointed symbol of the Sun rises as the eagle of Scorpio glides. (*Tabula Mundi Tarot*), page 319

143. 6 of Cups (*Rider-Waite-Smith Tarot*), page 321

144. 7 of Cups (*Rider-Waite-Smith Tarot*) (left), page 326

145. On the right, the Venusian illusions suggested by the Waite-Smith 7 of Cups take on nuances from another mythic archetype: Pandora's box. (*Pre-Raphaelite Tarot*), page 326

146. The impure tiger lilies of the Thoth card here become putrefying corpse (Scorpio) lilies (Venus). (*Rosetta Tarot*), page 327

147. A silver salmon for Pisces swims upstream beneath a luminous moon; the Moon major arcanum corresponds to Pisces. (*Animal Totem Tarot*), page 331

148. The barge of the Moon card (Pisces) has run aground (Saturn) on the shores, bordering the ocean of the brain waves of sleep (Pisces) (*Tabula Mundi Tarot*), page 331

149. 8 of Cups (*Rider-Waite-Smith Tarot*), page 333

150. The three creatures from *Tabula Mundi*'s Fortune card (Jupiter) get the bigger half of the wishbone and celebrate among the nine lucky fish of Pisces. (*Tabula Mundi Tarot*), page 336

151. 9 of Cups (*Rider-Waite-Smith Tarot*) (left), page 338

152. Many readers describe the smug Waite-Smith 9 of Cups as the cat eating the canary. In the image on the right, that phrase has been made literal. (*Linestrider Tarot*), page 338

153. Poppy pods evoke the narcotic mists of the Moon (the major governing the Pisces decans). A martial griffin presides over the year's dissolute end. (*Tabula Mundi Tarot*), page 342

154. The cups are shaped like rams' heads (Mars as ruler of Aries) and all are satiated, as they each are biting (Mars) the fish of Pisces. (*Rosetta Tarot*), page 343

155. 10 of Cups (*Rider-Waite-Smith Tarot*), page 345

156. The upraised sword points at the crown of Kether (Fool, air) marked with the letters: *aleph* is hidden and *lamed* is central; these are *AL* (God) and *LA* (not or naught). (*Tabula Mundi Tarot*), page 349

157. What we now call the "crown of Kether" has long been part of the Ace of Swords; here, oak and laurel replace palm and olive. (*Ancient Italian Tarot*), page 349

158. Ace of Swords (*Rider-Waite-Smith Tarot*), page 350

159. The light man holds a bird and pipe and the dark man holds a lance and book, interchanging the decan imagery from *Picatrix* and Agrippa. (*Liber T: Tarot of Stars Eternal*), page 355

160. Below the dark and light moon, the two swords become scales of Justice/Adjustment (Libra), between the pillars and above the scroll—emblems of the Priestess (moon). (*Tabula Mundi Tarot*), page 356

161. 2 of Swords (*Rider-Waite-Smith Tarot*), page 357

162. Amongst various Saturn symbols, the cracked heart jar of Ma'at (Libra) is upon the tripod of the Delphic oracle, whose motto is "Know thyself." (*Tabula Mundi Tarot*), page 360

163. 3 of Swords (*Rider-Waite-Smith Tarot*) (left), page 362

164. The card that launched a billion tattoos! The image on the right is likely the inspiration for Pamela Colman Smith's iconic 3 of Swords design. (*Sola Busca Tarot*), page 362

165. Leaves from Jupiter's oak float within the safe space described by the swords—almost certainly an astrological coincidence. (*Ancient Italian Tarot*), page 366

166. 4 of Swords (*Rider-Waite-Smith Tarot*), page 368

167. The vajra, Jupiter's weapon, weaves between the swords while the feathers of Justice/Adjustment (Libra) write the alpha and omega. (*Tabula Mundi Tarot*), page 369

168. The "beheaded man with a peacock" image from *Picatrix*, signifying tough times and an arduous path for all. (*Liber T: Tarot of Stars Eternal*), page 372

169. The dove of Venus is attacked by the raptor of Aquarius and the red sword of Mars. (*Tabula Mundi Tarot*), page 373

170. 5 of Swords (*Rider-Waite-Smith Tarot*), page 374

171. These scientific tools are mercurial: the orrery is also solar (six) and the sextant navigates the stars (Aquarius). (*Tabula Mundi Tarot*), page 378

172. 6 of Swords (*Rider-Waite-Smith Tarot*) (left), page 380

173. Over the years, the Waite-Smith deck's influence has made the 6 of Swords' iconic "journey in a boat" the defining feature on modern versions of the card. (*Linestrider Tarot*) (right), page 380

174. The moon's ascendancy and the sun's closed eyes suggest subterfuge under cover of night. (*Universal Wirth Tarot*), page 385

175. 7 of Swords (*Rider-Waite-Smith Tarot*) (left), page 386

176. The dramatically furtive body language of the figure in the right image may well have inspired Smith's own thieving protagonist. (*Sola Busca Tarot*), page 386

177. The twins of Gemini are represented by the alchemical lion and eagle from a medieval illustration called the *Battle of Sol and Luna*, and the decan rulership of Jupiter is shown by the thread of the spinning wheel and the four-pronged vajra (Jupiter). (*Tabula Mundi Tarot*), page 391

178. 8 of Swords (*Rider-Waite-Smith Tarot*) (left), page 393

179. On the right, a mole takes the place of the traditional blindfolded victim. He feels his way through darkness and uncertainty without the benefit of sight. (*Animal Totem Tarot*), page 393

180. The swords' hilts have glyphs of Gemini and Mars and form the teeth of a gaping mouth (*peh*, Mars). (*Rosetta Tarot*), page 396

181. 9 of Swords (*Rider-Waite-Smith Tarot*) (left), page 398

182. In the rendition on the right, the nocturnal whip-poor-will, bane of insomniacs, gives form to the cruel, sleep-depriving voices implied in the Waite-Smith 9 of Swords. (*Animal Totem Tarot*), page 398

183. The sword-in-the-stone motif references Gemini (*zayin*); the swords pierce the twin serpents (Gemini and solar twins). (*Tabula Mundi Tarot*), page 402

184. Only in the 10 of Swords do straight swords cross in Tarot de Marseille–derived decks. This is a duel to the death, and the enmeshed swords in the background admit no mediation. (*Ancient Italian Tarot*), page 403

185. 10 of Swords (*Rider-Waite-Smith Tarot*), page 404

186. The "Root of the Powers of Earth," represented as the complete cosmos and reposing among literal roots. (*Universal Wirth Tarot*), page 408

187. A cross section of a tree, interlocking Trees of Life, eyes, and maple keys all echo themes of sun, earth, growth, and becoming. (*Rosetta Tarot*), page 409

188. Ace of Pentacles (*Rider-Waite-Smith Tarot*), page 410

189. The hourglass of Capricorn contains the churning wheels of Jupiter: fortunes change over time. (*Tabula Mundi Tarot*), page 414

190. 2 of Pentacles (*Rider-Waite-Smith Tarot*) (left), page 416

191. What would later emerge as a lemniscate on Smith's card began as an S-curve on Marseille-style tarots (right). It served as a convenient ribbon for displaying the maker's mark. (*Camoin-Jodorowsky Tarot de Marseille*), page 416

192. Stinging and martial, the paper wasp works tirelessly to build its nest, here featuring alchemy's *tria prima*—mercury, sulfur, and salt. (*Rosetta Tarot*), page 420

193. 3 of Pentacles (*Rider-Waite-Smith Tarot*), page 422

194. The lightning of the Tower (Mars) sparks life into DNA and the building blocks (Capricorn) of matter. (*Tabula Mundi Tarot*), page 424

195. Power as money: a steel bank vault door, its shape suggestive of the sun glyph, securely stows the material treasures of the 4 of Pentacles/Disks. (*Rosetta Tarot*), page 426

196. 4 of Pentacles (*Rider-Waite-Smith Tarot*) (left), page 428

197. In the image on the right, the negative space between the four coins provides the perfect space for a heraldic shield in Marseille tarots—conveying, also, the family's secure continuity. (*Camoin-Jodorowsky Tarot de Marseille*), page 428

198. Miniature figures enact the mercurial arts of "dividing the land," as mentioned in *Picatrix*'s decan description. (*Liber T: Tarot of Stars Eternal*), page 433

199. A "steampunk worry machine" captures Mercury's painstaking calculations and premonitions of disaster in a graphic representation of Murphy's Law. (*Rosetta Tarot*), page 433

200. 5 of Pentacles (*Rider-Waite-Smith Tarot*), page 435

201. With female workers and queens, bees are Venusian (ruler of Taurus), lunar (exaltation of Taurus), and solar (representative of sixes) as daytime nectar gatherers. (*Rosetta Tarot*), page 438

202. Golden pentacles as eggs capture both the lunar (moon in Taurus, maternal hens) and solar (six, gold); these content domestic fowl are the picture of *Success*. (*Animal Totem Tarot*), page 440

203. 6 of Pentacles (*Rider-Waite-Smith Tarot*), page 441

204. The Minotaur (Taurus) is trapped in the darkness (Saturn) of his earthen labyrinth. (*Rosetta Tarot*), page 444

205. Seven pentacles germinate in the earth. Their value (expressed as an upside-down Venus glyph for this Taurus decan) is hidden for now. (*Universal Wirth Tarot*), page 445

206. 7 of Pentacles (*Rider-Waite-Smith Tarot*), page 447

207. The care of small things (Virgo) is shown as the nest of eight eggs, warmed by the Hermit's lantern containing the sun. (*Tabula Mundi Tarot*), page 450

208. 8 of Pentacles (*Rider-Waite-Smith Tarot*) (left), page 452

209. This fifteenth-century 6 of Coins (right) appears to have been an inspiration for the Waite-Smith 8 of Pentacles. (*Sola Busca Tarot*), page 452

210. The abacus has long helped merchants calculate their gain; here its beads appear in the wealth-signifying green of Venus. (*Rosetta Tarot*), page 456

211. 9 of Pentacles (*Rider-Waite-Smith Tarot*), page 458

212. Like the Waite-Smith snail, the tortoise signifies patience, self-sufficiency, and long-term thinking. As always, the wall suggests safety, but also solitude. (*Animal Totem Tarot*), page 459

213. This stripped-down interpretation brings together *Picatrix*'s theme of age and wealth, the faithful dogs of Waite-Smith, and the village it takes for all to thrive. (*Linestrider Tarot*), page 463

214. 10 of Pentacles (*Rider-Waite-Smith Tarot*), page 464

215. The card is doubly ruled by Mercury: ten disks form the image of Mercury as Adam Kadmon and the Tree of Life. (*Tabula Mundi Tarot*), page 466

216. I Ching-tarot diagram (created by the authors and Llewellyn art department), page 474

217. The sixteen geomantic figures and their court card correspondences (created by the authors and Llewellyn art department), pages 475–76

218. Wands lizards—or lizard theriomorphs—eerily bedeck this King's throne; on the throne's back panel appears a silhouette of the Sagittarian archer. (*Mystical Tarot*), page 478

219. This King/Knight rides among fire elementals carrying the blazing torch of the Ace of Wands. (*Rosetta Tarot*), page 479

220. Geomantic figure *Acquisitio* (created by the authors and Llewellyn art department), page 480

221. Hexagram 51, *zhèn* (created by the authors and Llewellyn art department), page 480

222. King of Wands (*Rider-Waite-Smith Tarot*), page 481

223. Geomantic figure *Puer* (created by the authors and Llewellyn art department), page 485

224. Hexagram 17, *suí* (created by the authors and Llewellyn art department), page 485

225. Queen of Wands (*Rider-Waite-Smith Tarot*) (left), page 486

226. The image on the right borrows and foregrounds both the feline theme and solar sunflowers from Pamela Colman Smith's Queen of Wands (*Animal Totem Tarot*), page 486

227. She has the leopard as crest and companion, and bears the thyrsus wand of the Maenads. (*Rosetta Tarot*), page 487

228. The Prince has motifs of his three decans: the volcano (5 of Wands/ Leo I) the laurel-crowned lion (6 of Wands/Leo II), and the scallop shell with pearl (his shadow decan, 4 of Cups/Cancer III). (*Tabula Mundi Tarot*), page 491

229. Geomantic figure *Fortuna Major* (created by the authors and Llewellyn art department), page 492

230. Hexagram 42, *yí* (created by the authors and Llewellyn art department), page 492

231. Knight of Wands (*Rider-Waite-Smith Tarot*) (left), page 493

232. In the image on the right, the normal equine steed of Knights has been replaced with a giant, surreal, fiery, golden Wands lizard! (*Mystical Tarot*), page 493

233. Geomantic figure *Cauda Draconis* (created by the authors and Llewellyn art department), page 497

234. Hexagram 27, *yí* (created by the authors and Llewellyn art department), page 498

235. Page of Wands (*Rider-Waite-Smith Tarot*), page 498

236. The salamander totem animal glimpsed on Waite-Smith Wands courts takes center stage in the image on the right, along with a rippling, flame-bright ribbon. (*Animal Totem Tarot*), page 498

237. The Princess has the flaming tree of her counterpart, the Ace of Wands, and the passionate crest of the tiger. (*Tabula Mundi Tarot*), page 499

238. The Knight bears motifs of his decans on his shield: the figurehead of the lunar barge (8 of Cups/Pisces I), the wishbone (9 of Cups/Pisces II), and the overladen camel (his shadow, 7 of Swords/Aquarius III). (*Tabula Mundi Tarot*), page 503

239. Geomantic figure *Laetitia* (created by the authors and Llewellyn art department), page 504

240. Hexagram 54, *gui mei* (created by the authors and Llewellyn art department), page 504

241. King of Cups (*Rider-Waite-Smith Tarot*) (left), page 505

242. On the right, the fish King's scaly greaves and sabots rest on the usual platform-in-the-sea throne. Waite-Smith's three-masted vessel appears here too, slightly enlarged. (*Pre-Raphaelite Tarot*), page 505

243. Two lotuses float in the rippling water for the 2 of Cups, her Cancer I decan. (*Rosetta Tarot*), page 509

244. The wavelike overhang of the throne appears in early Queen of Cups images, as does the closed cup, symbol of depths sounded through intuition only. (*Camoin-Jodorowsky Tarot de Marseille*), page 510

245. Geomantic figure *Populus* (created by the authors and Llewellyn art department), page 511

246. Hexagram 58, *duì* (created by the authors and Llewellyn art department), page 511

247. Queen of Cups (*Rider-Waite-Smith Tarot*), page 511

248. This Knight of Water rides a seahorse, an appropriate emblem for the sign of Pisces (the fish) ruled by Jupiter (the centaur). (*Mystical Tarot*), page 517

249. Geomantic figure *Rubeus* (created by the authors and Llewellyn art department), page 518

250. Hexagram 61, *zhōng fú* (created by the authors and Llewellyn art department), page 518

251. Knight of Cups (*Rider-Waite-Smith Tarot*) (left), page 519

252. The sorcerous "Natanabo" (Nectanebo), deceitful seducer, appears in early Knight of Cups renditions (right). (*Sola Busca Tarot*), page 519

253. On Marseille "Valet de Coupes" cards, the Page's wavelike drapery crests over the cup; this version features a tiny seashell in the corner. (*Camoin-Jodorowsky Tarot de Marseille*), page 523

254. Geomantic figure *Via* (created by the authors and Llewellyn art department), page 524

255. Hexagram 41, *sŭn* (created by the authors and Llewellyn art department), page 524

256. Page of Cups (*Rider-Waite-Smith Tarot*) (left), page 524

257. On the right, a fantastical reinterpretation: the usual "fish in a cup" is now a seahorse in a cup; the fish itself, a giant Moorish idol used as a shield. (*Mystical Tarot*), page 524

258. The Knight bears the emblems of his decans: the poniards (8 of Swords/Gemini I, and the Dioscuri star of his crest), the pierced boar head (9 of Swords/Gemini II), and the bull horns for his shadow decan (7 of Pentacles/Taurus III). (*Tabula Mundi Tarot*), page 529

259. Air is the vast kingdom of the eagle, king of birds. As in Waite-Smith and Thoth, he occupies the heights; his sharp vision discerns all. (*Animal Totem Tarot*), page 530

260. Geomantic figure *Albus* (created by the authors and Llewellyn art department), page 531

261. Hexagram 32, *héng* (created by the authors and Llewellyn art department), page 531

262. King of Swords (*Rider-Waite-Smith Tarot*), page 531

263. Her throne is made from the scales (2 of Swords/Libra I) and the tripod (3 of Swords/Libra II); from the scales the serpentine coins are suspended (her shadow decan, 10 of Pentacles/Virgo III). (*Tabula Mundi Tarot*), page 535

264. Birds and an air glyph illustrate the Queen's element; the severed mask or head traditional to her image appears here as a cloud formation. (*Mystical Tarot*), page 536

265. Geomantic figure *Puella* (created by the authors and Llewellyn art department), page 536

266. Hexagram 28, *dà guò* (created by the authors and Llewellyn art department), page 537

267. Queen of Swords (*Rider-Waite-Smith Tarot*), page 537

268. The clever rook, bird of Saturn (who rules Aquarius), perches on a rook, the "knight" of the chessboard. (*Animal Totem Tarot*), page 540

269. The Knight of Air rides the wind courtesy of the eagle, a bird sometimes associated with the Ganymede/Aquarius myth. The similarly airy scales appear below. (*Mystical Tarot*), page 541

270. Geomantic figure *Tristitia* (created by the authors and Llewellyn art department), page 542

271. Hexagram 57, *xùn* (created by the authors and Llewellyn art department), page 542

272. Knight of Swords (*Rider-Waite-Smith Tarot*), page 543

273. Light on her feet like Minerva, she stands before a smoking altar with the quartered cross marking her sector of the globe. (*Rosetta Tarot*), page 546

274. His sash tossed by gusts of wind, the calculating knave of air plots his next move on the vast floating chessboard of life. (*Universal Wirth Tarot*), page 547

275. Geomantic figure *Fortuna Minor* (created by the authors and Llewellyn art department), page 548

276. Hexagram 18, *gŭ* (created by the authors and Llewellyn art department), page 548

277. Page of Swords (*Rider-Waite-Smith Tarot*), page 549

278. The inner side of the King/Knight's shield is marked with the hexagram and rays, symbols of the solar energy necessary for successful harvest. (*Rosetta Tarot*), page 552

279. Richly garbed and crowned with golden sheaves or leaves, this King nearly merges with his land. As in the Waite-Smith image, his kingdom appears in the background. (*Mystical Tarot*), page 553

280. Geomantic figure *Conjunctio* (created by the authors and Llewellyn art department), page 554

281. Hexagram 62, *xiǎo guò* (created by the authors and Llewellyn art department), page 554

282. King of Pentacles (*Rider-Waite-Smith Tarot*), page 555

283. She holds the alchemical building blocks (3 of Pentacles/Disks), while her other decans are shown by Saturn's hourglass (2 of Pentacles/Disks) and hammer and pick (10 of Wands). (*Tabula Mundi Tarot*), page 559

284. What do you get when you combine water and earth? Mud! This Queen of Pentacles is literally in her element. (*Animal Totem Tarot*), page 560

285. Geomantic figure *Carcer* (created by the authors and Llewellyn art department), page 561

286. Hexagram 31, *xián* (created by the authors and Llewellyn art department), page 561

287. Queen of Pentacles (*Rider-Waite-Smith Tarot*), page 561

288. This bull-drawn chariot is scattering windblown seeds (Air of Earth). (*Rosetta Tarot*), page 567

289. A prairie dog, diligent tunneler of dirt, pokes his head up into the air to get the lay of the land. (*Animal Totem Tarot*), page 568

290. Geomantic figure *Amissio* (created by the authors and Llewellyn art department), page 568

291. Hexagram 53, *jiàn* (created by the authors and Llewellyn art department), page 569

292. Knight of Pentacles (*Rider-Waite-Smith Tarot*), page 569

293. In Marseille decks, only Pages of coins feature two of their suit emblems rather than one. One coin remains buried in earth, hidden—or planted and renewed. (*Camoin-Jodorowsky Tarot de Marseille*), page 573

294. Geomantic figure *Caput Draconis* (created by the authors and Llewellyn art department), page 574

295. Hexagram 52, *gèn* (created by the authors and Llewellyn art department), page 574

296. Page of Pentacles (*Rider-Waite-Smith Tarot*), page 574

297. Symbolically, she is at the brink of transfiguration, shown by her advanced pregnancy, her oxen-horned headdress (*aleph*, ox), the

ouroboros on her disk, and her staff, which has a diamond crystal (Kether) penetrating Earth. (*Rosetta Tarot*), page 575

298. Golden Dawn correspondences between the major arcana, the ten sephiroth, and the twenty-two paths, as understood in Hermetic Qabalah. It's based on the Tree of Life layout devised by seventeenth-century scholar Athanasius Kircher. (Created by the authors and Llewellyn art department), page 582

299. All the astrological correspondences for the minor arcana—both courts and numeric minors (created by the authors and Llewellyn art department), page 583

300. Correspondences between the thirty-six astrological decans and the thirty-six 2-through-10 minors of the tarot. (Created by the authors and Llewellyn art department), pages 584–99

301. Essential dignities for the seven traditional planets (created by the authors and Llewellyn art department), pages 602–3

302. Color scales for the major arcana (created by the authors and Llewellyn art department), pages 604–6

303. Color scales for the minor arcana (created by the authors and Llewellyn art department), pages 608–9

TO WRITE TO THE AUTHORS

If you wish to contact the authors or would like more information about this book, please write to the authors in care of Llewellyn Worldwide Ltd. and we will forward your request. The authors and publisher appreciate hearing from you and learning of your enjoyment of this book and how it has helped you. Llewellyn Worldwide Ltd. cannot guarantee that every letter written to the authors can be answered, but all will be forwarded. Please write to:

T. Susan Chang

M. M. Meleen

℅ Llewellyn Worldwide

2143 Wooddale Drive

Woodbury, MN 55125-2989

Please enclose a self-addressed stamped envelope for reply,
or $1.00 to cover costs. If outside the U.S.A., enclose
an international postal reply coupon.

Many of Llewellyn's authors have websites with additional information and resources. For more information, please visit our website at http://www.llewellyn.com.